Evidence-Based Approaches to Peace and Conflict Studies

Volume 1

This series aims to publish books on peace and conflict with evidence-based approaches, befitting an era best characterized by uncertainty and complexity. Even if occurrence of major wars among sovereign states has dramatically decreased, from 5 million soldiers killed between 1938 and 1945 per annum; through 100,000 soldiers killed between 1945 and 1989 per annum; to 10,000 soldiers killed between 1989 and 2019 per annum; many kinds of peace and conflict keep arising in the world, with extraordinary technological progress and unprecedented spatial coverage. All parts of the world now are so well connected and interdependent. At the same time, they easily and suddenly become sources of immense vulnerability and fragility, bringing one or another of them to the verge of collapse and destruction. The causes are diverse: climate change, migration, pandemic and epidemic disease, civil strife, religious dissonance, economic competition, arms races, terrorism, corruption—a virtual plethora of sources. Kofi Annan, former UN Secretary General, calls these and many others "problems without passports."

The basic methodological orientation sought in this series is broadly that of modern social and behavioral science. Of importance is that verifiable evidence (quantitative and qualitative, graphs and photos) be solidly attached to whatever arguments are advanced. Overseen by a panel of renowned scholars led by Editor-in-Chief Takashi Inoguchi, this book series employs a single-blind review process in which the Editor-in-Chief, the series editors, editorial board members, and specialized scholars designated by the Editor-in-Chief or series editors rigorously review each proposal and manuscript to ensure that every submission makes a valuable contribution that will appeal to a global scholarly readership.

More information about this series at http://www.springer.com/series/16598

Takashi Inoguchi · Lien Thi Quynh Le

Digitized Statecraft in Multilateral Treaty Participation

Global Quasi-Legislative Behavior of 193 Sovereign States

Springer

Takashi Inoguchi
J. F. Oberlin University
Tokyo, Japan

Lien Thi Quynh Le
College of Economics
Hue University
Hue, Vietnam

ISSN 2730-5651 ISSN 2730-566X (electronic)
Evidence-Based Approaches to Peace and Conflict Studies
ISBN 978-981-33-4484-6 ISBN 978-981-33-4485-3 (eBook)
https://doi.org/10.1007/978-981-33-4485-3

This Springer imprint is published by the registered company Springer Nature Singapore Pte Ltd.
The registered company address is: 152 Beach Road, #21-01/04 Gateway East, Singapore 189721, Singapore

Preface

This volume attempts to show that multilateral treaties represent a bundle of quasi-social contracts among nations. Multilateral treaties deal with "problems without passports" (Annan 2002). They are joined by a number of sovereign states whose preference is broadly in sync both with their respective national citizens' preference and their global citizens' preferences. It is important to stress that sovereign states are free to choose to join, or not to join, multilateral treaties. Sovereign states are not like legislators in a national parliamentary setting. First of all, there is no fixed institutionalized legislative body which claims to be representative of and responsible to global citizens. Second, sovereign states are neither elected nor selected bodies by their global citizens. Each time multilateral problems are perceived as needing a global solution, as contrasted to a national solution, multilateral treaties are called upon. For this task the United Nations plays a big role: UN specialized agencies and bureaucratic agencies of many national governments play the role of orchestrating research and drafting along with global scientists, academics, specialists, non-governmental organizations, and expert volunteers (Inoguchi and Marsh 2008; Weiss and Wilkinson 2018). Yet multilateral treaties touch all the problems without passports such as human rights, the environment, trade, commerce, and communications, intellectual property rights, health and labor, peace and disarmament. In the mid- and late nineteenth century and the early twentieth-century health, migration, and disarmament were considered as such areas, where the searches for global solutions were apt and feasible. In the mid-twentieth century, with the birth and development of the United Nations Organization, multilateral treaties in such areas as trade, commerce, and communications, and peace and disarmament rose in number while more traditional areas such as health, labor, standards, and rules showed the steady increase. In the late twentieth century such areas as human rights, the environment, and intellectual property rights, rose in number. By the dawn of the new millennium digitized globalization had permeated the entire globe. Every part of the globe has been connected ubiquitously and densely. One ironical consequence of digitized globalization is that the degree of vulnerability along with the ubiquitous and dense connectivity has increased dangerously (Inoguchi and Le 2019, p. 128). One solid evidence of the increased level of vulnerability is the number of multilateral treaties becoming into effect has been stalled in the early twenty-first century (Hale,

Held, and Young 2013). As of this writing, Coronavirus has reigned supreme on the earth, "Waving goodbye to the greatest era of globalization." (Friedman 2020).

In this volume we attempt to describe and explain the rise and stagnation of multilateral treaties in the latter half of the twentieth and the early quarter of the twenty-first century. In doing so, we argue that the vehicle and at the same time the agent of the liberal world order after World War II are multilateral treaties. To review the literature around the subject and debate, there have been two major lines of explanations: (1) theory of hegemonic change (Gilpin 1983) and (2) theory of shared norms by governing elites (Putnam and Bayne 1988; Acharya 2009; Suzuki 2009; and Ikenberry 2020). The former tries to explain the advent and diffusion of the liberal world order by hegemonic change. A hegemon tries to envision, diffuse, and permeate the order of its own making, that is, the Anglo-American tradition (Ikenberry 2020). The level of explanation is that of the national level. The sources of power are its major focus. They are a combination of might, wealth, ideology, and soft power (Nye 2004; Inoguchi and Le 2019). Thus, the evidence used most frequently is power sources of some kinds (for example, Lowy Institute's Asia Power Index 2019). The second line tries to explain the rise of the liberal world order by transmitting norms held by the governing elites of sovereign states, especially of the G7 (Putnam and Bayne 1988), ASEAN (Acharya 2009), and Japan (Suzuki 2009). The explanatory focus is the transmission of those norms held by governing elites of sovereign states. Stressed are those governing elites who accommodate hegemon's norms. The level of explanation is that of the national elite level. Thus, the evidence used most frequently are those utterances of such national elites expressing their political bent and policy predilection.

In this volume we argue that the key vehicle and at the same time the key agency is the transformative nature of multilateral treaties themselves. Sovereign states have to harmonize two preferences: that is, national citizens' preference and global citizens' preference along with global environmental preferences, in their own action, such as joining or not joining multilateral treaties. The focus of explanation is sovereign states' calculi or global statecraft facing the choice of joining or not joining. The level of explanation encompasses the following six instrumental variables at the national and global levels. The menu of checking point areas is: (a) the degree of willingness of states in joining treaties measured by the elapsed number of years between promulgation and ratification, (b) the number of current members of treaties, (c) the year of ratification, (d) the year of treaties deposited to the relevant body (the United Nations Depository, the International Labor Organization [ILO]'s or the World Intellectual Property Organization [WIPO]'s sub-depositories), (e) policy domains of treaties, and (f) broadly similarly disposed groups of states in geographical, historical and cultural terms. Why are multilateral treaties transformative? Sovereign states have to meet head-on two broad requirements: namely, national citizens' preferences on the one hand and global citizens' preferences and environmental harmony on the other.

For example, domestic laws and dominant practices pertaining to gender equality, say, as well as those laws and practices in domestic societies on parental authority over children and on family inheritance, may not be in sync with a treaty or its draft. Also, intellectual property rights in domestic law and dominant practices pertaining to it may not be in sync with a treaty or its draft to a certain number of sovereign states. Another case would be those companies that try to absorb advanced technology when foreign capital tries to invest in them. In that way they try to minimize the research and development costs of advanced technology innovation in order to catch up quickly with the innovating companies. Revising domestic laws often poses difficult tasks for sovereign states. It may also collide with dominant national citizens' preference or strong national opposition parties or a certain number of sectors. Another example is the tenacity of sovereign states' geo-historico-cultural traditions and their barriers to prevent them from taking distance from a group. For example, the Treaty on the Prohibition of Nuclear Weapons has seen more states promulgating and more recently ratifying it. As of August, 8, 2020, the signatories number 82, whereas of that number, 43 are ratifiers (Mainichi Shimbun 2020). Those states allied with the United States tend to go with the United States registering abstention for their vote. The Netherlands is one notable exception. It is one of the North Atlantic Treaty Organization members registering opposition but participating in the group's discussion thereafter as well. With 50 ratifiers the treaty will go effective.

This line of explanation is that of global politics, taking into account those backgrounds at national and global levels simultaneously. The aforementioned two lines of explanation tend to focus on one of the two levels. Befitting the era of global politics, our argument makes use of the two levels simultaneously. Hence it is all the more powerful and comprehensive. Furthermore, our line of explanation makes the best and deft use of solid statistical figures. They are sovereign states' physical actions and movements and attributes such as their regional identity as well as multilateral treaties' attributes such as their membership size. All the abovementioned variables are either specific year of ratification, group membership of a certain geo-historico-cultural group or some specific figures like the number of elapsed years after promulgation till ratification. All these are derived from the UN Depository and UN specialized agencies' sub-depositories with open access. Hence the approach is all the more evidence-based. It is *sine qua non* for a good explanation (Pinker 2018). On this, the first and second lines of explanation take more ambiguous data specifications. For the first line of explanation such data as GNP, weapons, communist ideology, and soft power are sometimes messy and their translation to power may often be too context-dependent and confusing. The second line of explanation is messier and often less convincing due to post-truth era expressions. Words often bespeak persons well. More recently, as in the G7 2019 meeting in southwestern France, the Macron-led joint communiqué was too short and avoid differences among the seven.

This volume's examination is based on the 600 substantive and substantial multilateral treaties between 1945 and 2019, barring those excessively procedural and/or more regional than global (see Appendix A: The list of 600 multilateral treaties examined in this book).

Tied in with this line of explanation, three concepts need to be clarified.

1) "Social contract writ global" is the hunch whereby our work started and the subtitle of our 2019 book. It is the concept that captures the systemic level of our project.
2) "Global legislative behavior" is the concept at the national actor level. It captures two kinds of behavior, internal and external, sovereign states manifest with regard to multilateral treaty participation. Sovereign states have to harmonize two kinds of preferences, namely, national citizens' preference and global citizens' preference along with global environmental preferences. Why bother both preferences and their environments, national and global? Because sovereign states are semi-sovereign (Keohane 2002) not only at the national level but also at the systemic level. At the national level domestic contenders often reject states to act as sovereign despite its name and claim. At the systemic level sovereign states have never been sovereign despite the name and assumption in the United Nations. The force of globalization compromises sovereign states' pretention of being sovereign relentlessly (Badie 2019). Hence the adjective attached to the characterization of contemporary sovereign states, semi-sovereign states in a partially globalizing era (cf. Keohane 2002).
3) "Digitalized statecraft" is the third concept and also the main title of this book (Inoguchi and Le 2021) whereas "global legislative behavior" is the subtitle of this book.

This volume is a sequel to *The Development of Global Legislative Politics: Rousseau and Locke Writ Global* (Inoguchi and Le 2019). Our key concept in the 2019 volume is the social contract writ global. In other words, Jean-Jacques Rousseau and John Locke envisaged social contract between the ruler and the ruled, between government and society as if they could be agreed upon by both. Rousseau's thinking is communitarian whereas Locke's thinking is utilitarian in reaching the goal of democracy. Our 2019 book argued by way of showing the reasonably high correlations found between global citizens' preferences for values and norms (Welzel 2013) and those preferences expressed in sovereign states' participation modes in terms of values and norms that both are positively related (Inoguchi and Le 2019). In other words, as long as the set of values and norms expressed by global citizens in public polls the world over and by sovereign states expressed in multilateral treaty participation modes, global democracy of a sort can be envisaged. In this sequel, our key concept is "global quasi-legislative behavior." In other words, sovereign states' participation modes are focused in terms of speed, angle, and strategy. In the previous volume, emphasis was on globalizing social contract between states and citizens whereas in this volume, emphasis is on highlighting sovereign states' global quasi-legislative behavior. They are confronted by the choice between fast and slow in making their decision to join multilateral treaties, by the choice between weighing global commons and individual interests, and by the choice between these sovereign states prioritizing broad aspirations with similarly hearted and those sovereign states emphasizing strict abiding spirit with similarly minded. Along these three dimensions of states' participation modes, eight types of 193 sovereign states are yielded by factor analysis with varimax rotation. By "global quasi-legislative behavior," we mean how each sovereign state joins multilateral treaties (or not). Their behavior patterns are shown as their quasi-legislative behavior by way of hexagonal profiles with each of six policy domains given relative prioritizations in global comparative terms (i.e., provided that global means and standard deviations taken into account). Their quasi-legislative records are shown as if they were their global statecraft in a broad sense of the word.

This volume is entitled: *Digitized Statecraft in Multilateral Treaty Participation: Global Quasi-Legislative Behavior of 193 Sovereign States*. Whereas the key concept deployed in our earlier volume is "social contract writ global," the key concept deployed in the present volume is "global quasi-legislative behavior." Both volumes systematically and extensively use the United Nations-deposited multilateral treaties data: The earlier book adopts the systemic approach to global politics whereas this title uses the sovereign state approach to sovereign states' actions, "global quasi-legislative behavior." Whereas the first book's sample size of multilateral treaties is 120, the sample size of multilateral treaties here is 600. The former sample of 120 has been dictated by the criteria of minimum-necessary selection of being primarily universal rather than regional in scope and primarily substantive rather than procedural in content. The latter sample of multilateral treaties has been enlarged to see more deeply into each sovereign state's action from the bottom-up approach to multilateral treaties. While the two criteria remain the same as the former book, the scope of selection has been primarily based on those deposited in the Secretary-General of the United Nations (roughly 500 treaties) and some others (more than 100 treaties) deposited in the specialized agencies of the United Nations (such as the World Intellectual Property Organization [WIPO] and the International Labor Organization [ILO]).

Writing the latter volume has been prompted by our further reading of Jean-Jacques Rousseau (1968) and John Locke (1993), active during the period of European-wide Reformation and post-Reformation, and further back to Niccolò Machiavelli (Skinner 2000), who was active in the European-wide Renaissance. What differences have we noticed between the two periods, Reformation and Renaissance? One is theology, in pondering the nature of God. The other is teleology in imagining state and society. The debates on God's existence in Christianity in the early Renaissance produced nominalism in theology spearheaded by William of Ockam in England. Nominalism led further to the birth of science in the Renaissance—vide Galileo Galilei and Leonardo da Vinci. The debates on God's place and function in relation to the Vatican prompted the consolidation of power by kings during the Reformation and the taming of power of kings in the Post-Reformation—vide Jean Bodin and Thomas Hobbes first in justifying absolutism and then Locke and Rousseau in promoting democracy.

What has prompted us to contrast Machiavelli in the Renaissance and Locke and Rousseau in the post-Reformation? It is the basic differences toward their stance about social reality (Berlin 1953). Machiavelli focused on empirical observation and description whereas Locke and Rousseau endeavored to imagine their respective social ideals while engaging with a bit of engineering with social contract. Thus, for instance, Rousseau at one time called Machiavelli's *The Prince* a satire, with basic sympathy with Machiavelli's republican idea.

To make a long story short, this book delves each sovereign state's calculus of statecraft. How is statecraft defined? It is defined as policymaker's scheme, skill, and judgment. Or to use Machiavelli's own words, virtue, and fortune. By virtue, he means whatever is necessary for the prince to execute his political ambition. By fortune he uses it in combination with prudence to mean that ambition is never too high when prudence tames and controls high ambition. Conventionally, statecraft is used to mean that a decision-maker's perception and judgment are apt and right without too much being specific about scheme, skill, and judgment. Here in this book we use the following formula (Cf. Baldwin 2019; Blackwill and Harris 2016).

The calculi of sovereign states are formulated as the combination of the following six variables:

1) *Year of ratification to become a member of a multilateral treaty*
   Multilateral treaty participation tends to take time. To reach the stage of ratification overcoming some parliamentary paths is often quite a barrier. The hypothesis is that the faster, the more willing to join.
2) *Year for a multilateral treaty to be deposited in a relevant UN organization*
   A multilateral treaty becomes effective only when a certain percentage of states ratify. This takes time. The hypothesis is that the more recent the year a treaty becomes effective, the less popular a treaty is.
3) *Number of current members of a multilateral treaty as of 2019*
   The number of current members of a multilateral treaty is indicative of its popularity among 193 states. The hypothesis is that having more current members equates to greater popularity.
4) *Policy domain*
   In the Secretary-General of the United Nations Treaty Collection (UNTC), treaties are categorized into 29 subdomains. Because of the two reasons—first, too many categories and second, the comparability lost with our previous 2019 volume definitions of policy domain categories—in our current volume, treaties are categorized in six domains with corresponding subdomains of UNTC based on their main target of solving a given issue of global governance: human rights, peace and disarmament, trade, commerce and communication, the environment, intellectual property, and labor and health.
   Some domains, such as trade, commerce, and communications, see participation by a very large number of states. Such domains as labor and health, and peace and disarmament are represented by a medium number of states, and domains such as human rights, the environment, and intellectual property have attracted more participants since the Cold War. The hypothesis is that some domains are more popular whereas some other domains are less popular.
5) *Treaty Participation Index (TPI)*
   The year of ratification minus the year of promulgation is a key component. Its inverse (to be more precise, its inverse minus one) is indicative of how fast

or slow in treaty participation. The hypothesis is that the higher TPI, the more willing states are.

6) *Geo-historico-cultural regions in the world*
Christian Welzel (2013) categorizes world regions as ten such groups. They are: (1) Old West, (2) New West, (3) Reformed West, (4) Returned West, (5) Orthodox East, (6) Indic East, (7) Sinic East, (8) Islamic East, (9) Sub-Saharan Africa, and (10) Latin America. We have modified the Welzel scheme with more member affiliation. The hypothesis is that some regional groups are more willing and that some other regional groups are less willing to participate in a multilateral treaty.

These variables are instrumental variables of sorts.

It is very important to note that these instrumental variables are used in the sense of relation, not in the sense of causal direction. What we need is to show the basic validity of global social contract is relational.

These six variables are factor-analyzed with varimax rotation, which yields the three-dimensional profiles of 193 sovereign states. The three dimensions are: speed, angle, and strategy, meaning that (1) states are agile vs. cautious in multilateral treaty participation, (2) states are inclined to prioritize global commons vs. individual interests, and (3) states lean more to aspirational bonding vs. mutual binding. We describe these three-dimensional profiles of sovereign states as digitized statecraft. On these three-dimensional graphs each of the 193 sovereign states is located visually with each of the ten geo-historico-cultural groups.

Each dimension produces two types of states, high value vs. low value on each dimension. Thus, with three dimensions we get eight types of multilateral treaty participation in terms of eight combinations of high or low three-dimensional values. Accordingly, we interpret and discuss the calculi of statecraft for 193 sovereign states.

Having notified that the rebalancing of East and West (Milanovic 2019) has been recently taking place in the new millennium and that the Sinic East has spearheaded this rebalancing, we closely examine how the Sinic East has adapted to multilateral treaties. The People's Republic of China, Japan, the Republic of Korea, the Democratic People's Republic of Korea, and the Socialist Republic of Vietnam are here examined.

Comparing types of Sinic East multilateral treaty participation in an era of digitized globalization, we come up with what may be called global comparative politics of Sinic East. We portray each one of Sinic East as adaptive in extraordinary givens as of 1945, the end of World War II and the beginning of Pax Americana through 2020 (Bacevich 2020; Kimmage 2020; Ikenberry 2020; Nye 2020).

In each case of Sinic East there have been tumultuous ups and downs during which some pathways for leaping upward has been well navigated more or less, creating conditions of rebalancing East and West.

Tokyo, Japan — Takashi Inoguchi
Hue, Vietnam — Lien Thi Quynh Le

References

Acharya, Amitav. 2009. *Whose Ideas Matter?: Agency and Power in Asian Regionalism*. Ithaca, NY: Cornell University Press.
Annan, Kofi. 2002. Problems Without Passports. *Foreign Policy* 132: 30–31.
Bacevich, Andrew J. 2020. *The Age of Illusions: How America Squandered Its Cold War Victory*. New York: Metropolitan Books.
Badie, Bertland. 2019. *New Perspectives on the International Order: No Longer Alone in This World*. London: Palgrave Macmillan.
Baldwin, David A. 2019. *Economic Statecraft*. Princeton: Princeton University Press.
Berlin, Isaiah. 1953. *The Originality of Machiavelli*, renewed in May 2019.
Blackwill, Robert, D., and Jennifer M. Harris. 2016. *War by Other Means: Geoeconomics and Statecraft*. Cambridge, MA: Harvard University Press.
Friedman, Thomas L. 2020. How We Broke the World. *New York Times International Edition*, 9 and 11.
Gilpin, Robert. 1983. *War and Change in World Politics*. Princeton: Princeton University Press.
Hale, Thomas, David Held, and Kevin Young. 2013. *Gridlock: Why Global Cooperation Is Failing When We Need It Most*. Cambridge: Polity Press.
Ikenberry, G. John. 2020. *A World Safe for Democracy: Liberal Internationalism and the Crises of Global Order*. New Haven, Conn.: Yale University Press.
Inoguchi, Takashi, and Ian Marsh. Eds. 2008. *Globalization, Public Opinion and the State*. London: Routledge.
Inoguchi, Takashi, and Lien Thi Quynh Le. 2019. *The Development of Global Legislative Politics: Rousseau and Locke Writ Global*. Singapore: Springer Nature.
Inoguchi, Takashi and Lien Thi Quynh Le. 2021. *Digitized Statecraft in Multilateral Treaty Participation: Global Quasi-Legislative Behavior of 193 Sovereign States*. Singapore: Springer Nature.
Keohane, Robert O. 2002. *Power and Governance in a Partially Globalizing World*. London: Routledge.
Kimmage, Michael. 2020. *The Abandonment of the West: The History of an Idea in American Foreign Policy*. New York: Basic Books.
Locke, John. 1993. *Two Treaties of Government*. New York: Everyman Paperback.
Lowy Institute. 2019. *Asia Power Index 2019*. Sydney: Lowy Institute.
Mainichi Shimbun. 2020. *Kakukin joyaku hijun, aratani san ka koku* (The Treaty on the Prohibition of Nuclear Weapons Newly Ratified by Three States), August 8, 8.
Milanovic, Branko. 2019. *Capitalism, Alone: The Future of the System That Rules the World*. Cambridge, MA: Harvard University Press.
Nye, Joseph S. 2004. *Soft Power: The Means to Success in World Politics*. New York: Perseus Books Shop.
Nye, Joseph S. 2020. *Do Morals Matter? Principles and Foreign Policy from FDR to Trump*. Oxford: Oxford University Press.
Pinker, Steven. 2018. *Enlightenment Now: The Case for Reason, Science, Humanism and Progress*. New York: Penguin Books.
Putnam, Robert, and Nicholas Bayne. 1988. *Hanging Together: Cooperation and Conflict in the Seven-Power Summits, Revised and Enlarged Edition*. Cambridge, MA: Harvard University Press.
Rousseau, Jean-Jacques, and Cranston, M. 1968. *The Social Contract*. London: Penguin Classics.
Skinner, Quentin. 2000. *Machiavelli: A Very Short Introduction*. Oxford: Oxford University Press.
Suzuki, Shogo. 2009. *Civilization and Empire: China and Japan's Encounter with Western International Society*. London: Routledge.
Weiss, Thomas G., and Rorden Wilkinson. 2018. *International Organization and Global Governance*. London: Routledge.
Welzel, Christian. 2013. *Freedom Rising: Human Empowerment and the Quest for Emancipation*. New York: Cambridge University Press.

Acknowledgments

When we started in 2014 the project of an evidence-based analysis of multilateral treaties participation since 1945, we naturally did not know when we would be writing acknowledgments for our publications, as we are doing now. Two books have been published since 2014: One revolves around the concept of global quasi-social contract, suggested by Jean-Jacques Rousseau and John Locke while the other around the concept of global calculus of statecraft, suggested by Chanakya Kautilya and Niccolò Machiavelli. Our thanks go first of all to these philosophers and pundits. Our first volume is entitled *The Development of Global Legislative Politics: Rousseau and Locke Writ Global* and our second volume is entitled *Digitized Statecraft in Multilateral Treaty Participation: Global Quasi-Legislative Behavior of 193 Sovereign States*. Secondly, we express our heartfelt gratitude to those who encouraged our endeavor most vigorously, especially on our first volume: Anne-Marie Slaughter (Princeton University), William R. Thompson (Indiana University), Andrew J. Nathan (Columbia University), Doh Chull Shin (University of California, Irvine), Miguel Basanez (Tufts University), Peter J. Katzenstein (Cornell University), and the late David Held (Durham University). Those who have given us endorsements on or an introduction to this volume, i.e., Ezra F. Vogel (Harvard University), William R. Thompson (Indiana University), Anne-Marie Slaughter (Princeton University), Bruce M. Russett (Yale University), and Richard J. Estes (University of Pennsylvania), are gratefully acknowledged. Most sadly, Professor Ezra Vogel suddenly passed away a few days before the galleys of this Acknowledgments reached me. Those who gave critically constructive comments on our presentations at the Federation of Japanese Statiscians annual meeting (September 2018, Chuo University, Tokyo), the Japanese Behaviormetric Society annual meeting (September 2018, Keio University), and the Japanese Association of International Relations annual meeting (November 2019, Niigata City Conference Hall), and the Japanese Behaviormetric Society annual meeting (September 2020, Waseda University) are gratefully acknowledged. At J.F. Oberlin University, Tokyo, I express my heartfelt gratitude to Chancellor and President Toyoshi Sato for providing me an ideal environment. Most sadly, the late Toyoshi Sato suddenly passed away before this volume came out. My deepest condolence. At Oberlin University in Tokyo, Masae Toyoizumi and Yi Cai most professionally helped me with grace and efficiency. Also, Mr. Yamagishi and

Mr. Fukuhara have helped me with my office work to be carried out with speed. At Springer in Tokyo, Juno Kawakami, editor in economics, business, law, political science, has been most professional in guiding me to go through myriad steps with relative ease. Her boss in Singapore, William Auschauer, has been most helpful in moving on to finish this volume. Finally, we acknowledge all their encouragement and advice in our partners' no less busy schedules, Kuniko Inoguchi, an academic turned parliamentarian, and Dzung Quoc Ho, a fellow engineering academic. Our heartfelt gratitude to them both. The Japan Society for the Promotion of Science has given Takashi Inoguchi the grant to work on Asia–Europe democracy survey, on Asia quality of life survey, on multiple democracy, and on multilateral treaties with its grants [JSPS KAKENHI Grant Numbers: JP11102001, JP17002002, JP26285029, and JP19H00583.] The National Foundation for Science and Technology Development of Vietnam has enabled Lien Thi Quynh Le to work on Asian states' foreign policies through their participation in multilateral treaties with its grant [NAFOSTED Grant Number: 506.01-2019.301.]

Praise for *Digitized Statecraft in Multilateral Treaty Participation*

"Inoguchi and Le have written a highly original book. Building on their 2019 volume on Digitized Globalization, they analyze the world's 193 states in terms of their 'quasi-legislative behavior' of signing and ratifying some 600 multilateral treaties. By analyzing the variables of speed, angle, and strategy, they are able to build a three-dimensional profile of each state's characteristic preferences and proclivities to engage in statecraft under conditions of digitized globalization. They aim to use artificial intelligence methods to use these profiles to predict state behavior in connection with specific treaties. The most interesting part of their analysis arises from the regional differences they identify in terms of the number and density of treaties, particularly their description of the 'Sinic East.' Notwithstanding the emphasis on treaties, Inoguchi and Le push well beyond formal legal variables, examining a wide range of social characteristics and life satisfaction in profiling different societies. Their multi-volume project, drawing on sources from Machiavelli to machine learning, pushes the boundaries of traditional international relations by drawing on the techniques and technologies available in a Digital Age."

—Anne-Marie Slaughter, *CEO, New America, Bert G. Kerstetter '66 University Professor Emerita of Politics and International Affairs, Princeton University*

"This is a terrific book. Imaginative yet fully solid in research on the differences between the year of promulgation and the year of ratification in multilateral treaty participation of sovereign states along with such a treaty's policy domain and participating states geo-historical-cultural groups. Truly a most original and solidly researched work!"

—Bruce Russett, *Dean Acheson Research Professor of International Politics and Professor of International and Area Studies in the MacMillan Center, Yale University*

"Relatively few books can be identified as 'rare', 'innovative', or 'groundbreaking'. This new volume by two of the field's most prolific researchers warrants such an attribution. Professors Inoguchi and Le have performed a great service to scholars and public policy makers everywhere in analyzing the origins, nature, and political processes that contributed to the development of more than 600 major multilateral treaties entered into by the 193 of the world's most socially and economically influential nations. Their analysis of some 600 such treaties deposited in the archives of the United Nations in digital format truly provides scholars with a unique approach to analyzing and understanding complex multilateral agreements that otherwise would elude many from being able to work within the constraints of a print document alone environment. This volume belongs on the shelf of all social scientists engaged in research on international relations as well as those of leading public policy makers engaged in strengthening the capacity of nations to provide more fully the needs of their citizens through effective statecraft. This book should be regarded as 'must reading' by policy makers and policy researchers the world over."

—Richard J. Estes, *Professor, School of Social Policy & Practice, University of Pennsylvania*

"In Hollywood, sequels are dangerous. Is it possible for them to do as well as the first production in the sequence? Inoguchi and Le's second book on 'quasi-legislative behavior,' the sequel to their The Development of Global Legislative Politics takes some of the questions raised in the first book to a higher level. We are all familiar with local and national politics. Less familiar are the realms of regional and global (not to be equated with international) politics. These are the two levels of analysis examined in this sequel. Their primary focus is again placed on multilateral treaties, which they have expanded to 600 cases (from 120 in the first book) encompassing the 1945-2019 period, that they view as a globalization vector. States choose to join multilateral treaties in issue areas (human rights, environment, trade and communications, intellectual property rights, health and labor, peace and disarmament) that appeal to their interests and preferences. They join quickly or slowly, with mixed motives, and for aspirational or binding intentions. Geo-historical-cultural regions also make some difference in which policy domains states choose to participate. In this book, they give special emphasis to the behavior of the Sinic East region as an instance of East-West rebalancing. Yet, overall, the outcome is greater, if uneven, connectivity at a planetary level. Hegemons make some difference to how this plays out but they do not dictate the outcome which is seen as driven by interactions among individual (state), regional, and global preferences. Moreover, the trend line of this behavior is non-linear. Its progress has stalled in the early twenty-first century. Why is that the case? The empirically-based answers to these questions are not carved in stone, but they do carve out new questions to which scholars of world politics need to pay attention."

—William R. Thompson, *Distinguished Professor and Rogers Chair in Political Science Emeritus, Indiana University*

"In this book, Takashi Inoguchi and Lien Thi Quynh Le consider the nature of international treaties and what international treaties tell us about the linkages between the individual nation and the broader relations between nations. Since treaties are now done by digital communication they refer to the formation of international treaties as 'digitized statecraft.'

Inoguchi was for many years a professor of political science at the University of Tokyo and since his retirement from the University of Tokyo he has taken on the presidency of Niigata Prefectural University, the province where Inoguchi grew up. Inoguchi has had a broad perspective on political issues. Having grown up in Niigata, he followed closely the career of Tanaka Kakuei, of Niigata, who became Japan's master politician. He studied at the University of Tokyo under Sato Seizaburo, who was not only a brilliant political scientist but also a close confidant and advisor to Prime Minister Nakasone. He was for a while an official at UN University in Tokyo. His wife Kuniko is also a political scientist, one of the small number of female Diet members. Lien Thi Quynh Le is a lecturer at Hue University, Vietnam. Lien Thi Quynh Le and Inoguchi had previously collaborated on the book *The Development of Global Legislative Politics.*

In this new volume on Digitized Statecraft, Inoguchi Takashi and Lien Thi Quynh Le examine some 600 international treaties which are deposited at the United Nations. They analyze these treaties to provide perspective on how nations use treaties to deal with global issues. They look at different countries and examine the variety of ways in which some 193 countries, large and small, make use of treaties."

—Ezra F Vogel, *Henry Ford II Professor of the Social Sciences, Harvard University*

Contents

Part I Calculus of Statecraft

1 Aphorism by Pundits: Chanakya and Machiavelli 3
1.1 How Does the United Nations Secretary-General Categorize Its Problems Without Passports? 4
1.2 Chanakya Kautilya's *Arthashastra* and Niccolò Machiavelli's *the Prince* on Statecraft 5
References 7

2 Data-Driven Empirical Modeling: The Advent of Globalization and Multilateral Treaties 9
2.1 Policy Domains and Subdomains of Multilateral Treaties 9
2.2 The Number of Multilateral Treaties Participation by Sovereign States: Rankings 14
2.3 Data Driven Empirical Modeling 25
References 30

Part II One Hundred Ninety-Three Calculi of Statecraft

3 The Development of Multilateral Treaty Participation 35
3.1 The Scope of Multilateral Treaties Examined 35
3.2 Who Joins Multilateral Treaties Most Actively and Least Actively over the Years Between 1945 and 2019? 38
3.3 Global Quasi-Legislative Behavior: Eight Types 41
References 43

4 Three Dimensions of Global Legislative Politics: Ten Regional Groups 45
4.1 How Can Three-Dimensional Locations Reveal and Illuminate Sovereign States' Global Quasi-Legislative Behavior? 45
4.2 Location of Sinic East Members 45
4.3 Location of Indic East Members 48
4.4 Location of Islamic East Members 50

4.5 Location of Orthodox East Members ... 51
4.6 Location of Sub-Saharan Africa Members ... 53
4.7 Location of Latin America Members ... 54
4.8 Location of Old West Members ... 57
4.9 Location of New West Members ... 58
4.10 Location of Reformed West Members ... 60
4.11 Location of Returned West Members ... 61
References ... 63

5 Global Quasi-Legislative Behavior: Eight Types ... 65
References ... 71

Part III Sinic Calculi of Statecraft

6 Adaptation to Multilateral Treaties ... 75
6.1 The East Learn from the West in Multilateral Treaties ... 75
6.2 History of Sinic East's Adaptation to Multilateral Treaties ... 77
6.2.1 People's Republic of China ... 77
6.2.2 Japan ... 79
6.2.3 Republic of Korea ... 80
6.2.4 Democratic People's Republic of Korea ... 82
6.2.5 Socialist Republic of Vietnam ... 83
6.3 Daily Life Satisfaction 2019 in Sinic East Countries ... 84
6.4 Preference for Global or National Solutions ... 89
References ... 93

7 Comparative Statecraft in Sinic East ... 97
Reference ... 100

8 Multilateral Treaty Participation Triggers Upward Leap in Sinic East ... 101
8.1 Multilateral Treaty Participation Are in Sync with Economic Development ... 102
8.2 Japan ... 102
8.3 China ... 104
8.4 South Korea ... 105
8.5 North Korea ... 107
8.6 Vietnam ... 108
8.7 Throughout Sinic East ... 109
8.8 Regional Dynamics of Sinic East ... 110
8.9 Japan ... 112
8.10 South Korea ... 115
8.11 China ... 120
8.12 North Korea ... 124
8.13 Vietnam ... 127
References ... 131

9 Typology of Global Quasi-Legislative Behavior and Typology of Societies Focusing on Sinic East 133
References 142

Conclusion 145

Appendix A: List of 600 Multilateral Treaties by Domain 149

Appendix B: Categorization of 193 UN Member States in Ten Groups of Geo-Historico-Cultural Regions 213

Appendix C: Hexagonal Profiles of 193 UN Member States 219

Appendix D: Typology of Global Quasi-Legislative Behavior of 193 UN Member States 253

Appendix E: Methodological Notes of Social Surveys Used for the Book: The AsiaBarometer Quality of Life Survey; The Asia-Europe Democracy Survey; The Sinic East Survey (The Asia Poll) 259

Index 263

About the Authors

Takashi Inoguchi Ph.D. from MIT, is Emeritus Professor, University of Tokyo, former UN Assistant Secretary General, former President, the University of Niigata Prefecture, currently Eminent Scholar-Professor at J.F. Oberlin University (Tokyo). He writes prolifically on Japan, Asia's quality of life and international affairs. Among his publications are: *The Development of Global Legislative Politics: Rousseau and Locke Writ Global* (Springer, 2019), *The SAGE Handbook of Asian Foreign Policy*, 2 vols., (SAGE Publications, 2019), *American Democracy Promotion* (Oxford University Press, 2000), *The Political Economy of Japan* Vol. 2 (Stanford University Press, 1988), *The Quality of Life in Asia* (Springer, 2013), *Exit, Voice and Loyalty in Asia* (Springer, 2017). He is founding editor of *Japanese Journal of Political Science* (Cambridge University Press, 2000–2018), *International Relations of the Asia-Pacific* (Oxford University Press, 2000–2005), and *Asian Journal of Comparative Politics* (SAGE, 2016–); In Japanese, *Political Theory* (Minerva shobo, 2015); *Happiness in Asia* (Iwanami shoten, 2014); *Governance* (University of Tokyo Press, 2012), *Constructing the Empirical Political Science* (Minerva shobo, 2011), *The Genealogy of International Relations* (University of Tokyo Press, 2011). He is Director of the AsiaBarometer Survey focusing on quality of life in 32 Asian societies. He is a Co-Director of the Multilateral Treaties Survey with Lien T. Q. Le.

Lien Thi Quynh Le is Lecturer of College of Economics, Hue University, Vietnam. She received her Master's Degree and Doctor's degree from Nagaoka University of Technology, Japan. She has published mainly on international regimes and global governance. Her most recent book is *The Development of Global Legislative Politics: Rousseau and Locke Writ Global* (co-author, 2019). Her current research interests include the quantitative methods for analysis and understanding of the structure and the effectiveness of the global governance regimes. Among these, the social network analysis perspective for the understanding of structure and relations between sovereign states, multilateral institutions, or international organizations is the angle of her expertise.

List of Figures

Fig. 2.1 Number of treaties by period and by domain (1) 14
Fig. 2.2 Number of treaties by period and by domain (2) 15
Fig. 2.3 The growth of UN treaties and UN membership coverage (All domains) 18
Fig. 2.4 The growth of UN treaties and UN membership coverage (Labor and Health domain) 19
Fig. 2.5 The growth of UN treaties and UN membership coverage (Human Rights domain) 19
Fig. 2.6 The growth of UN treaties and UN membership coverage (Environment domain) 20
Fig. 2.7 The growth of UN treaties and UN membership coverage (Peace and Disarmament domain) 20
Fig. 2.8 The growth of UN treaties and UN membership coverage (Intellectual Property domain) 21
Fig. 2.9 The growth of UN treaties and UN membership coverage (Trade, Commerce, and Communication domain) 21
Fig. 2.10 How fast have the groups of countries joined the UN multilateral treaties in Labor and Health domain 22
Fig. 2.11 How fast have the groups of countries joined the UN multilateral treaties in Intellectual Property domain 23
Fig. 2.12 How fast have the groups of countries joined the UN multilateral treaties in Peace and Disarmament domain 23
Fig. 2.13 How fast have the groups of countries joined the UN multilateral treaties in Environment domain 24
Fig. 2.14 How fast have the groups of countries joined the UN multilateral treaties in Human Rights domain 24
Fig. 2.15 How fast have the groups of countries joined the UN multilateral treaties in Trade, Commerce, and Communication domain 25
Fig. 4.1 Locations of Sinic East countries on SPEED and ANGLE dimensions 46

Fig. 4.2 Locations of Sinic East countries on SPEED and STRATEGY dimensions 47
Fig. 4.3 Locations of Indic East countries on SPEED and ANGLE dimensions 48
Fig. 4.4 Locations of Indic East countries on SPEED and STRATEGY dimensions 49
Fig. 4.5 Locations of Islamic East countries on SPEED and ANGLE dimensions 50
Fig. 4.6 Locations of Islamic East countries on SPEED and STRATEGY dimensions 51
Fig. 4.7 Locations of Orthodox East countries on SPEED and ANGLE dimensions 52
Fig. 4.8 Locations of Orthodox East countries on SPEED and STRATEGY dimensions 52
Fig. 4.9 Locations of Sub-Saharan Africa countries on SPEED and ANGLE dimensions 53
Fig. 4.10 Locations of Sub-Saharan Africa countries on SPEED and STRATEGY dimensions 54
Fig. 4.11 Locations of Latin America countries on SPEED and ANGLE dimensions 55
Fig. 4.12 Locations of Latin America countries on SPEED and STRATEGY dimensions 56
Fig. 4.13 Locations of Old West countries on SPEED and ANGLE dimensions 57
Fig. 4.14 Locations of Old West countries on SPEED and STRATEGY dimensions 58
Fig. 4.15 Locations of New West countries on SPEED and ANGLE dimensions 59
Fig. 4.16 Locations of New West countries on SPEED and STRATEGY dimensions 59
Fig. 4.17 Locations of Reformed West countries on SPEED and ANGLE dimensions 60
Fig. 4.18 Locations of Reformed West countries on SPEED and STRATEGY dimensions 61
Fig. 4.19 Locations of Returned West countries on SPEED and ANGLE dimensions 62
Fig. 4.20 Locations of Returned West countries on SPEED and STRATEGY dimensions 62
Fig. 8.1 The participation in UN multilateral treaties of Japan 104
Fig. 8.2 The participation in UN multilateral treaties of China 104
Fig. 8.3 The participation in UN multilateral treaties of South Korea 106
Fig. 8.4 The participation in UN multilateral treaties of North Korea 107
Fig. 8.5 The participation in UN multilateral treaties of Vietnam 109
Fig. 8.6 Japan's participation in human rights multilateral treaties 113

Fig. 8.7 Japan's participation in trade, commerce, and communication multilateral treaties 113
Fig. 8.8 Japan's participation in intellectual property rights multilateral treaties 114
Fig. 8.9 Japan's participation in environment multilateral treaties 114
Fig. 8.10 Japan's participation in labor and health multilateral treaties ... 115
Fig. 8.11 Japan's participation in peace and disarmament multilateral treaties 115
Fig. 8.12 South Korea's participation in peace and disarmament multilateral treaties 117
Fig. 8.13 South Korea's participation in human rights multilateral treaties 117
Fig. 8.14 South Korea's participation in trade, commerce, and communication multilateral treaties 118
Fig. 8.15 South Korea's participation in intellectual property multilateral treaties 118
Fig. 8.16 South Korea's participation in environment multilateral treaties 119
Fig. 8.17 South Korea's participation in labor and health multilateral treaties 119
Fig. 8.18 China's participation in peace and disarmament multilateral treaties 121
Fig. 8.19 China's participation in human rights multilateral treaties 122
Fig. 8.20 China's participation in trade, commerce, and communication multilateral treaties 122
Fig. 8.21 China's participation in intellectual property multilateral treaties 123
Fig. 8.22 China's participation in environment multilateral treaties 123
Fig. 8.23 China's participation in labor and health multilateral treaties ... 124
Fig. 8.24 North Korea's participation in peace and disarmament multilateral treaties 125
Fig. 8.25 North Korea's participation in human rights multilateral treaties 125
Fig. 8.26 North Korea's participation in trade, commerce, and communication multilateral treaties 126
Fig. 8.27 North Korea's participation in intellectual property multilateral treaties 126
Fig. 8.28 North Korea's participation in environment multilateral treaties 127
Fig. 8.29 North Korea's participation in labor and health multilateral treaties 127
Fig. 8.30 Vietnam's participation in peace and disarmament multilateral treaties 128
Fig. 8.31 Vietnam's participation in human rights multilateral treaties 129

Fig. 8.32 Vietnam's participation in trade, commerce, and communication multilateral treaties 129
Fig. 8.33 Vietnam's participation in intellectual property multilateral treaties 130
Fig. 8.34 Vietnam's participation in environment multilateral treaties 130
Fig. 8.35 Vietnam's participation in labor and health multilateral treaties 131

List of Tables

Table 2.1 List of multilateral treaties covered in the dataset 16
Table 3.1 Factor analysis of six variables on 600 multilateral treaty dataset 43
Table 5.1 Six variables of the factor analysis on multilateral treaties data 66
Table 5.2 Factor analysis using principal component analysis with varimax rotation and Kaiser normalization: Rotated component matrix 67
Table 7.1 Typology of global quasi-legislative behavior of Sinic East countries 98
Table 9.1 Domestic societal types and global quasi-legislative behavior types 135
Table 9.2 Eight typologies of global quasi-legislative behavior 139
Table 9.3 Types of societies 139
Table 9.4 Some representative Asian states based on typologies of global quasi-legislative behavior 140
Table 9.5 Some representative Asian states based on daily life satisfaction 140
Table 9.6 Subregional Asian Member States 140
Table 9.7 Daily life satisfaction and multilateral treaty participation across Asia 141

Part I
Calculus of Statecraft

Abstract

Statecraft is often used to denote varieties of things in running the state. It is sometimes focused on the combination of scheme, skill, and judgment. It is other times defined as the effective use of policy means to actualize policy goals and ambitions. In Part I we attempt to digitize statecraft. In chapter 1 statecraft is taken as aphorisms by pundits serving autocrats, taking examples of Chanakya Kautilya (Chanaka Kautilya and R. M. Shamasastry 1915) serving Chandragupta Maurya and Niccolò Machiavelli (Skinner 2000) serving Piero de' Medici. In Chapter 2 aphorisms are digitized to find out what are key elements of statecraft. The approach adopted is data-driven empirical modeling. First, we take multilateral treaty participation modes as our gauging focus. Multilateral treaty participation modes are the key to understand what kind of statecraft for 193 sovereign states is used in joining or not joining multilateral treaties. The most important mode is the elapsed years between promulgation and ratification. Associated importance is given to sovereign states group attribute and multilateral treaty's policy domain attribute. One may also quickly notice that a multilateral treaty's content is not taken but a sovereign state's action (the difference between promulgation and ratification) is taken seriously. We follow Antoine de Saint Exupéry's (Saint Exupéry 2011) *Le Petit Prince*, saying: "One only sees clearly with the heart. What is essential is invisible to the eye." The difference between promulgation and ratification can be called hesitation, procrastination, or inability to move on toward ratification, all of which you cannot see with your eyes.

References

Kautilya, Chanakya, and R. M. Shamashastry. 1915. *Arthashastra*, translated by R. M. Shamashastra, India.

Saint Exupéry, Antoine de. 2011. *Le Petit Prince*. Oakham: Omillia Languages, 79.

Skinner, Quentin. 2000. *Machiavelli: A Very Short Introduction*. Oxford: Oxford University Press.

Chapter 1
Aphorism by Pundits: Chanakya and Machiavelli

Abstract Statecraft is often used to mean the skill and flair of running the state. What it means is often taken as aphorism provided by pundits. This chapter shows two examples of Chanakya Kautilya (Kautilya and Shamashastry 1915) and Niccolò Machiavelli (Skinner 2000) serving their respective king and prince at an ancient Indian context and at a Renaissance Florentine context respectively. This chapter is to prepare readers to what we call digitized statecraft to be explained in Chapter 2: Data-Driven Empirical Modeling.

This chapter takes up a concept of statecraft as used by a man of the Renaissance era, Niccolò Machiavelli (Skinner 2000). *Virtu* (virtue) and *fortuna* (fortune) are two key words used by him in advising to the prince. *Virtu* is more broadly used by Machiavelli than virtue as used in a man of virtue in the modern era. A man of *virtu* is more a man of might, who is feared and admired simultaneously by many. *Fortuna* does not come to a man if he is passive. *Fortuna* comes to a proactive man who observes empirical reality and describes it, inspires masses and mortifies his possible assassins. Niccolò Machiavelli was not well received by his contemporaries and more modern men of literature. Jean-Jacques Rousseau thought Machiavelli's *The Prince* is a satire, not serious advice to the monarch. In the era of the Renaissance, statecraft is used without too much streak of Christianity and morality. Chapter 1: Aphorism by Pundits: Chanakya, Machiavelli, Bodin and Hobbes describes how the word statecraft is used for aphorism by pundits to the monarch and the emerging absolutist king.

Moving into the early modern period of the absolute monarch, Bodin (Franklin 1973) and Hobbes (2014) began the theorization of modern states. These philosophers displayed real imagination in so doing, contributing to the enrichment and consolidation of the modern political philosophy. John Locke (1993) and Jean-Jacque Rousseau (1968), for instance, are regarded widely as founders of democracy. In *the Development of Global Legislative Politics: Rousseau and Locke Writ Global* (Inoguchi and Le 2019), we deployed their social contract theories. The task of making the social contract global has been carried out initially by showing that global citizens' values

T. Inoguchi and L. T. Q. Le, *Digitized Statecraft in Multilateral Treaty Participation*, Evidence-Based Approaches to Peace and Conflict Studies 1,
https://doi.org/10.1007/978-981-33-4485-3_1

and norms expressed in opinion polls worldwide are broadly in sync with those sovereign states' modes of participation in multilateral treaties, focusing on values and norms. More operationally, using Welzel's (2013) factor analysis results (two-dimensional representations of global citizens' values and norms) are correlated with three-dimensional representations of 193 multilateral treaties participation modes, showing that they are convergent more or less. In other words, global public opinion and multilateral treaties participation modes exhibit convergent patterns of preferred values and norms (Inoguchi and Le 2019). Hence *Social Contract Writ Global* stands as the subtitle of the book (Inoguchi and Le 2019).

Having resolved the issue of social contract writ global if only at first and in a small way, we move on to sovereign states' *global legislative behavior*. For that purpose, digitized statecraft is deployed as the key concept of this book. The Renaissance version of digitized statecraft is best represented by Niccolò Machiavelli. In a nutshell, Machiavelli's advice to the prince is: Try to build *virtu* and induce *fortuna*. Machiavelli was a man of the Renaissance, not a man of the Reformation. Thus, he is painting the observed human world during the era of the Renaissance as he sees it, with neither religious tone nor moralistic flavor. The Renaissance is in harmony with the fledgling empirical positivistic approach adopted in this book. The extraordinary range of works of Machiavelli's contemporary Leonardo da Vinci exemplifies the Renaissance's open and critical spirit of his empirical methods, which were unorthodox in his times. At the same time, *virtu* and *fortuna* sound like aphorisms by pundits. It may be an attractive subject to ponder what exactly Machiavelli had in mind in terms of his political philosophy. But for our purpose of empirically constructing indicators of external legislative behavior by 193 sovereign states, we have to move on to the digital era.

1.1 How Does the United Nations Secretary-General Categorize Its Problems Without Passports?

When the United Nations tries to seek global solutions to 'problems without passports' (Annan 2002), what do problems without passports mean? How does the United Nations categorize problems without passports? Problems without passports mean that to tackle them, national solutions are not enough. Global solutions are called for. Because problems are similar across nations more or less, some collaborative solutions would be likely to be more efficient and effective. Then the question is: How can one come up with ways of finding global solutions? One possibility is multilateral treaties, whereby sovereign states agree multilaterally helped by solidarity-derived passion and cost-sharing reasoning to carry out tasks concerned. Multilateral treaties have been on the steady increase in number since the end of World War II but somewhat stalled in the first quarter of the twenty-first century with some 600-odd multilateral treaties entering the United Nations Secretary-General's Depository. The precise number of multilateral treaties depends on how to count treaties. Sovereign states participate in multilateral treaties sometimes with reservations attached. Problems can also evolve as time goes by and auxiliary treaties or agreements are added. In addition, procedural matters need additional detailed agreements, etc. Then how does the United Nations categorize the kinds of problems without passports? The multilateral treaties deposited with the Secretary-General are divided into 28 segments called "chapters" (the Charter of the United Nations is excluded), with each chapter relating to a given subject-matter. To simplify the categories of treaties for our analysis, the multilateral treaties of relevant subject-matters are grouped in six domains based on their main target of solving a given issue of global governance:

1. Human rights
2. Peace and disarmament
3. Trade, commerce, and communications
4. The environment
5. Intellectual property
6. Labor and health

This list is a simple enough but reasonably comprehensive list of problems without passports. It represents the kind of problems and associated multilateral treaties this book is set out to analyze. Before moving on to that task, we need to take a quick glance at the kinds of tasks and the ways and means of solving problems without passports when neither sovereign states nor multilateral treaties existed: ancient Indian Chanakya Kautilya, an ancient Indian strategist and advisor serving the first Mauryan emperor, Chandragupta Maurya (370–283 BC) and Niccolò Machiavelli, a Renaissance Florentine serving the Florentine Prince, Piero de' Medici (1492–1494 AD).

1.2 Chanakya Kautilya's *Arthashastra* and Niccolò Machiavelli's *the Prince* on Statecraft

Arthashastra is like an advanced graduate course on statecraft or political science in ancient India before Christ. R. M. Shamasastry's, *Kautilya's Arthashastra*, is a book translated from Sanskrit to English published from an Indian publisher in 1915. It consists of 15 books, entitled:

1. Concerning Discipline
2. Duties of Superintendents
3. Concerning Law
4. The Removal of Thorns
5. The Conduct of Courtiers
6. The Sources of Sovereign States
7. The End of Six-Fold Policy
8. Concerning Vices and Calamities

9. The Work of an Invader
10. Relating to War
11. The Conduct of Corporations
12. Concerning a Powerful Enemy
13. Strategic Means to Capture a Fortress
14. Secret Means
15. The Plan of Treaties

The scope of *Arthashastra* looks very comprehensive about statecraft in the ancient Indian context. It explains the statecraft of a state to protect itself from threats from within and without. To carry out the task of governance, i.e., protecting people's religion (*dharma*) and sustaining power upon people, knowledge is the basis of power: (1) philosophy, (2) four classes and four orders, (3) economics (especially agriculture, cattle breeding, and the trade to strengthen national power), (4) *dadaniti* (the science of governance and politics). With power and knowledge, those to be protected are: (1) the sovereign king, (2) the ministers, (3) the people and the land of people, (4) fort or the defense system to protect its people, (5) national reservoir or treasury, (6) army of a state, (7) allies.

Arthashastra is a guidebook for a ruler of a state to attain the ultimate goal of these sutras, i.e., to aim at the conquest of the world. The statecraft detailed in the book includes manipulation, deception, monopoly, justice for the indigenous population, better administration, and rules of a successful kingship. The book describes qualities ideal rulers should attain: practical politicism, administrative ethics and moral order in society, and local level espionage to sabotage conspiracies, rebellions, and dissent. In Kautilya's words: "A wise king though only ruling over a small territory will surely conquer the world if he gathers around him the best as the other constituent elements" (Kautilya and Shamsastry 1915).

Turning to Niccolò Machiavelli's *The Prince* on statecraft, one immediately notices that throughout all the advice Macchiavelli gives to the prince in Florence, two key concepts stand out: *virtu* (virtue) and *fortuna* (fortune). *Virtu* is more broadly used by Machiavelli than virtue as used in the expression of a man of virtue in the modern era. A man of *virtu* is more a man of might, who is feared and admired simultaneously by many. *Fortuna* does not come to a man if he is passive. *Fortuna* comes to a proactive man who observes empirical reality and correctly describes it, inspires masses and mortifies his latent assassins. Niccolò Machiaveli was not well received by his contemporaries and more modern men of literature. Jean-Jacques Rousseau for one, more than two centuries later, thought Machiavelli's *The Prince* is a satire. In the era of the Renaissance, statecraft is used without too strong a streak of Christianity and morality. A century later, Max Weber (quoted in Keohane 2009) notes:

> Truly radical Machiavellianism is classically expressed in the Indian literature, *Arthashastra* of Kautilya, written before the birth of the Christ, ostensibly in the time of Chandragupta Maurya. Compared to it Machiavelli's *The Prince* is harmless.

The Renaissance version of statecraft is best represented by Machiavelli: It has neither religious flavor nor moralizing tone. The Renaissance is in harmony with empirical positivistic approach adopted in this book. The extraordinary range of works of Machiavelli's contemporary, Leonardo da Vinci, exemplify the Renaissance's emergently open and critical spirit of his empirical methods which were unorthodox even in his times. Machiavelli's *The Prince* or Chanakya's *Arthashastra* in their times may not have been sound received as Rousseau or Weber felt respectively. After the Reformation era, whether it is the period of the French Revolution or the interwar period between World Wars I and II, both Chanakya and Machiavelli offered the pundit's advice to the Mauryan emperor, Changupta Maurya and the monarch in Florentine respectively. Both Chanakya and Machiavelli had well-articulated thoughts about how to govern. In the next chapter onward, we will attempt to construct what calculi of statecraft each of 193 sovereign states draws in the background of digitized globalization, going beyond the aphorism by pundits.

References

Annan, Kofi. 2002. "Problems without Passports." *Foreign Policy.* 132: 30–31.

Franklin, Julian. 1973. *Jean Bodin and the Rise of Absolutist Theory*. Cambridge: Cambridge University Press.

Hobbes, Thomas. 2014. *Thomas Hobbes: Leviathan.* Oxford: Oxford University Press.

Inoguchi, Takashi, and Lien Thi Quynh Le. 2019. *The Development of Global Legislative Politics: Rousseau and Locke Writ Global*. Singapore: Springer.

Kautilya, Chanakya, and R. M. Shamashastry. 1915. *Arthashastra*, trans. R. M. Shamashastry. India.

Keohane, Robert. 2009. "Political Science as a Vocation." *PS: Political Science and Politics* 42 (2): 359–363.

Locke, John. 1993. *Two Treaties of Government.* New York: Everyman Paperback.

Rousseau, Jean-Jacques and Cranston, M. 1968. *The Social Contract.* London: Penguin Classics.

Skinner, Quentin. 2000. *Machiavelli: A Very Short Introduction.* Oxford: Oxford University Press.

Welzel, Christian. 2013. *Freedom Rising: Human Empowerment and the Quest for Emancipation.* New York: Cambridge University Press.

Chapter 2
Data-Driven Empirical Modeling: The Advent of Globalization and Multilateral Treaties

Abstract By statecraft one often means the skill and flair of running the state. Instead of uttering aphorisms to approach this subject, we attempt to create digitized statecraft since we know that we are not pundits. In order to hone skill and nurture flair in deciding whether or not to join a multilateral treaty, one must grasp what are keys in joining or not joining multilateral treaty. Multilateral treaties are a form of communication with messages and modes to allure sovereign states to join. Here we focus on communication modes rather than communication messages. In other words, we take a close look at sovereign states' physical action (i.e., promulgation and ratification) rather than their words. As Antoine de Saint Exupéry (2011) in his *Le Petit Prince* says, "One only sees clearly with the heart. What is essential is invisible to the eye."

2.1 Policy Domains and Subdomains of Multilateral Treaties

For this book, the collection of United Nations multilateral treaties is the dataset of 600 treaties which are mainly the treaties deposited in the Secretary-General of the United Nations (roughly 500 treaties) and some others (more than 100 treaties) deposited in UN special agencies (the World Intellectual Property Organization and the International Labor Organization). For the treaties deposited in the Secretary-General of the United Nations, we have accessed the data of "UN Treaty Collection" at its website at https://treaties.un.org. The Treaty Section of the Office of Legal Affairs of the United Nations who makes every effort to provide the most up-to-date information of multilateral treaties deposited with the Secretary-General available to it in electronic format (United Nations 2020). These are the multilateral treaties that cover a broad range of subject matters such as human rights, peace and disarmament, protection of the environment, labor and health, trade, commerce, and communications, and intellectual property. These treaties are categorized in domains and corresponding subdomains based on their main target of solving a given issue of global governance. The burst of these new categories of policy domains has been caused by

T. Inoguchi and L. T. Q. Le, *Digitized Statecraft in Multilateral Treaty Participation*, Evidence-Based Approaches to Peace and Conflict Studies 1,
https://doi.org/10.1007/978-981-33-4485-3_2

the accelerated digitized globalization in the 1990s through 2010s (Baldwin 2016, 2019). The advent and diffusion of information and communications technology has been the key enabler of the burst of multilateral treaties on the supply side of the explosion of multilateral treaties (Hidalgo 2016). Underlying this explosion on the demand side are the accelerated connectivity and vulnerability of states and societies: Companies and communities the world over have been driving those forces to make criteria, rules, and regulations on the basis of harmonization of norms and values manifested on the elite level such as the UN, the G7, G20, and the World Economic Forum as well as the nongovernmental level such as opinion polls, nongovernmental organizations, and transnational movements. To meet these demands, the endeavors on the supply side has been insufficient and weak. The Vienna Convention on the Law of Treaties concluded in Vienna in 1980 recognized the need publicly. But the insufficient and weak ability of international organizations and multilateral treaties make it harder to cope with and counteract major tasks expected of the world of dense connectivity and high vulnerability (Hale and Held 2017, Hale, Held and Young 2012). It has been laid bare a number of times after 1989: the Asian monetary crisis of 1997–1998, the Lehman-triggered global recession of 2008, the SARS, MERS, and Covid crises of 2003, 2013, and 2020 virus contagion. The explosion of the categorization of multilateral treaties is part of the supply-side phenomena. But for this book we have kept the six-policy domain categorization system intact and the consistency from 1945 intact.

Environment: The environment domains register 52 treaties. This policy domain jumped upward steadily after 1989, when the major anxiety of the major security confrontation between the Soviet-led and the US-led confrontation more or less dissipated. Although climate warming has been recognized widely and seriously in the new millennium especially since the late 2010s, and although the Paris climate change accord was agreed in 2018, its implementation has not been moving forward:

1. because the United States, the second largest CO_2 emitter, withdrew from the accord and registered a great setback; and
2. because China and many developing countries have been given extraordinary privilege for CO_2 emission payments to the accord to be widely agreed on (Cf. Teske 2019).
3. Furthermore, the visibly laxed endeavor toward CO_2 emission among developed countries and emerging-economy countries has exacerbated global warming to an increasingly intolerable degree: For example, Arctic melting has caused the upward shift of sea level, threatening many countries such as the Maldives in the Indian Ocean and Kiribati in the Pacific, as well as major coastal cities such as Jakarta, Boston, New York, and Amsterdam.
4. *Pari passu* with increasingly intolerable global warming, the voices of environmentalists have joined those of business elites as well. In Germany, for instance, this kind of coalition is glimpsed at in the rise of the Green Party (and the decline of the SPD) on the one hand and on the other hand in the rise of the Alternative for Germany at the expense of The Christian Democratic Union (CDU) and the Christian Social Union (CSU). It must be noted that the combined force of the

CDU and the CSU since the Covid-19 global assault has moved up from 27% in December 2019 to 37% in April 2020 at the expense of the Alternative for Germany, which dropped from 15% in December 2019 to 11% in April 2020 (YouGov Opinion Poll cited by Mainichi Shimbun 2020).

Human rights: Human rights treaties amount to 53, the number rising since newly independent states after World War II joined the United Nations. Many of those in Asia joined in the 1950s through 1970s and many in Sub-Saharan Africa joined in the 1970s through 1990s. Many of those in the Middle East and North Africa did so in the 1960s through 1980s, while many in the Pacific and in the Caribbean joined in the 1970s through 2000s. The treaties focusing most on human rights are the UN Declaration of Human Rights and the United Nations Educational, Cultural, and Scientific Organization. Other than human rights, such subdomains as freedom of information, slavery, obscene publications, refugees and stateless persons, status of women, and traffic in persons exist. The UN Special Commissioner's Office for Refugees is a distinct organization for raising the cause of helping refugees. Many of those developing states define human rights as not only the rights and measures of respect for persons but also social, racial, and cultural rights. In contrast, developed states tend to focus on the rights and respects for persons and gender equality. However, those analyzing domestic politics of human rights pay attention to social and economic rights in random (Simmons 2009). Thus, developing states tend to rally around the latter flag of human rights in the latter sense when they demonstrate their force around the UN General Assembly, UNESCO, and on other related occasions (Alston and Goodman 2012). On the perennial issue of two different difficulties of human rights, Alston (2017) called for a reframing of "economic and social rights as human rights rather than as welfare of developing objectives." The Under-Secretary-Generals of the UN specialized agencies such as the World Trade Organization, the International Meteorological Organization, the UN Food and Agriculture Organization, the UN Industrial Development Organization, and the Intellectual Property Organization have recently been from those developing states. Alarmed by the increasingly influence in the United Nations of the developing South and by China shaping human rights agendas "from within", Foot (2020a) underlines that "the argument that economic development is unlikely to be sustained without accountable political institutions and independent national human rights institutions still carries weight" (see also Foot 2020b).

Intellectual Property: Intellectual property-related multilateral treaties amount to 36. They are deposited at the World Intellectual Property Organization, not at the UN Secretary-General. The domain of intellectual property has steadily become noteworthy since 1968 and especially after 1989. The view that intellectual property should be protected is most pronounced among developed states in which those inventors and innovators of new ideas, scientific new discovery, technological innovations, literary and artistic creativity tend to be appreciated with awards and rewards. Conversely, the views that intellectual property should be shared by those users often comes from the developing states. The tariff and technology war between the United

States and China has been partially and independently but deeply related to the different definitions of intellectual property (Vaidhyanathan 2017).

Labor and Health: Labor and health is the oldest domain of multilateral treaties, contemporary with those concerned with peace and disarmament. The products are is the International Labor Organization (ILO) and the World Health Organization. Nineteenth-century ideas of taking care of labor and health in factories gave birth to the ILO in 1919. Its Philadelphia Declaration, propounded in 1944, calls for "universal and sustainable peace can be brought about only with social justice." In contrast to conditions in factories, ideas of taking care of captured and injured soldiers and sailors produced the international law of war, the Red Cross, and Red Crescent, further developing to the World Health Organization (WHO). The policy domain of labor and health register 110 multilateral treaties. ILO administers 78 multilateral treaties out of 110 multilateral treaties under the category of Labor and Health. The rest, 32 multilateral treaties under our category of Labor and health deposited at UN Secretary-General, relate to narcotic drug and psychotropic substance management. Since the domain of labor and health is fundamental to human lives, it has produced one of the oldest of multilateral treaties and international organizations. It is of utmost importance to developing states where hygiene and nutrition are not sufficiently of high level to prevent diseases and malnourishment from causing a huge number of infantile deaths. It is the voice heard most recently in 2020 in the global diffusion of pandemic to many developing countries where washing hands as carefully and frequently as possible cannot be practiced where fresh water is not readily available (Cf. Gilani 2020).

Peace and Disarmament: The domain of peace and disarmament register 84 multilateral treaties. This domain is one of the oldest domains along with that of labor and health. Those subdomains are as follows: disarmament, law of the sea, outer space, pacific settlement of international disputes penal matters, privileges and immunities, diplomatic and consular relations. The last subdomain is one of the oldest in keeping peace in diplomacy. It amounts to 37 multilateral treaties. Outer space, one of the newest, is expanding, deepening and sharpening its scope with the utilization of outer space becoming the frontier of science, technology and humanity. The last of which means that given the increasing number of humans on earth, the idea of exploring and using outer space has arrived. It means not only exploiting outer space for humans to live but also before that possibility, the ways and means of testing living bodies to extremes of temperature, air pressure, moisture, and physical exercise in terms of well-functioning of all organs, nerves, blood tubes, etc., while of exploiting material resources and energy resources to alleviate the excessive utilization of water, land, air, and sunlight resources on the Earth (Galloway 1960). Its race among powers has become relentless.

Trade, Commerce, and Communications: This is one of the oldest domains although use of multilateral treaties has been a relatively recent phenomenon. The shift from pigeon to steamships took place in early nineteenth century. Pigeon transmitted the English victory in the battle at Waterloo across the Dover Strait to London. The shift from oared and sailing ships to steamships was quite recent, in the early nineteenth century. In 1793 English King George III sent his emissary to Qing Emperor

Qianlong by wind-driven ships. In 1849 English steamships attacked Hong Kong and ports and further, deep into the Canton delta plain against Qing China. Wars and trade were governed by military force and by geographical discovery of ports and their hinterland. This domain of trade, commerce, and communications is numerically most important domain of 600 multilateral treaties analyzed in this book. It amounts to 265. Of that total, more than two thirds (197) are in the subdomains of transport and communications. This is extraordinary, indicating the deep penetration of globalization in terms of physical transport and communications of correspondence. Deciding the kind of norms and rules that govern this subdomain with multilateral treaties has become one of the central tasks of multilateral treaties in this sense (Baldwin 2016, 2019; Blackwill and Harris 2016). If transport and communications are one of the most important tasks of multilateral treaties' missions, the other hidden task is the harmony between multilateral treaties and domestic laws governing each of 193 sovereign states. The Vienna Convention on the Law of Treaties, concluded in 1980, presented the UN pronouncement of its hope that international law, or multilateral treaties, should be above domestic laws governing each member state. Yet hope is hope and hope does not necessarily mean each sovereign state follows this international law, which places multilateral laws are above domestic laws. In order to promote harmonization, one of the tasks is the translation of all the domestic laws of member states into English and deposit them in the UN. This translation task has been fast or slow depending on domestic preferences and English proficiency level. In Japan the task has been slow in part because of manpower insufficiency and in part because the large portions of living domestic laws were legislated between the late nineteenth century and mid-twentieth century. Although many civil laws, penal laws, and commercial laws have been subsequently revised to meet the times, the consistency of domestic laws over years have been deliberately kept basically solid. These factors have kept the translation of the living domestic laws slower. As of 2018 the translated laws amount to 10% in Japan. In comparison, South Korea's translated laws amount to 60% (Nihonkeizai Shimbun 2018). South Korea was Japan's colony until 1945 and their laws were legislated de novo since 1948 when it declared its independence. Also, only in 1991 it was admitted into the United Nations. Japan's entry into the United Nations took place in 1956.

For this book, the collection of United Nations multilateral treaties is the dataset of 600 treaties which are mainly the treaties deposited in the Secretary-General of the United Nations (roughly 500 treaties) and some others (more than 100 treaties) deposited in the specialized agencies of the UN (such as WIPO and ILO). These are the multilateral treaties that cover a broad range of subject matters such as human rights, peace and disarmament, and protection of the environment. The treaties are categorized in domains and corresponding subdomain based on their main target of solving a given issue of global governance (Figs. 2.1–2.15 and Table 2.1).

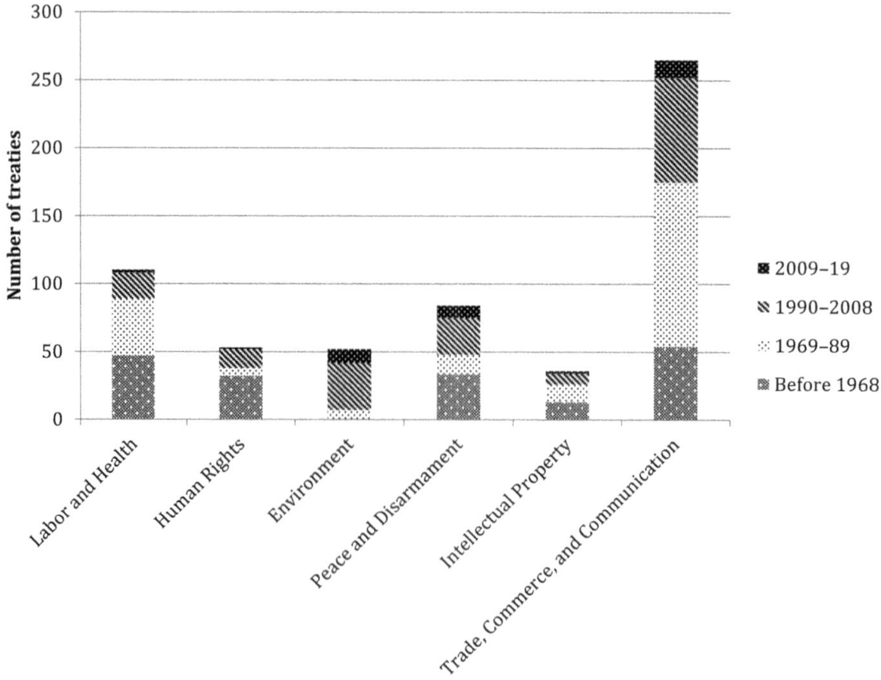

Fig. 2.1 Number of treaties by period and by domain (1)

2.2 The Number of Multilateral Treaties Participation by Sovereign States: Rankings

The number of multilateral treaties participation is ranked by sovereign states, by regional groups, and by policy domains. Let us take a look at the top ten states. It is not surprising to find that West European states monopolize the top ten in multilateral treaty participation. Out of 600 multilateral treaties, the Netherlands participates in 436 treaties as number one. Belgium, Finland, Slovakia, Czech Republic, Luxembourg, Norway, Germany, France, and Sweden follow the Netherlands. All of them are members of the European Union. The European Union has the peculiar characteristic of being ideationally universalist but territorially regionalist. In other words, in terms of the norms and values that members uphold they are universalist and globalist. But in terms of geographical locationality, they are European, starting with the Schengen Five (France, Belgium, the Netherlands, Germany, and Italy) which are the core of the first European Community institutions, that is, the Coal and Steel community and the community without passports among them. With the fall of the Berlin Wall, Eastern Europe has partially joined the European Union. In other words, those "Returned West" include the Baltic states, Central European states such as the part of Germany that formed East Germany, Poland, Hungary, Czech Republic, Slovakia, and some Balkan states such as Slovenia, Croatia, Northern Macedonia, Montenegro,

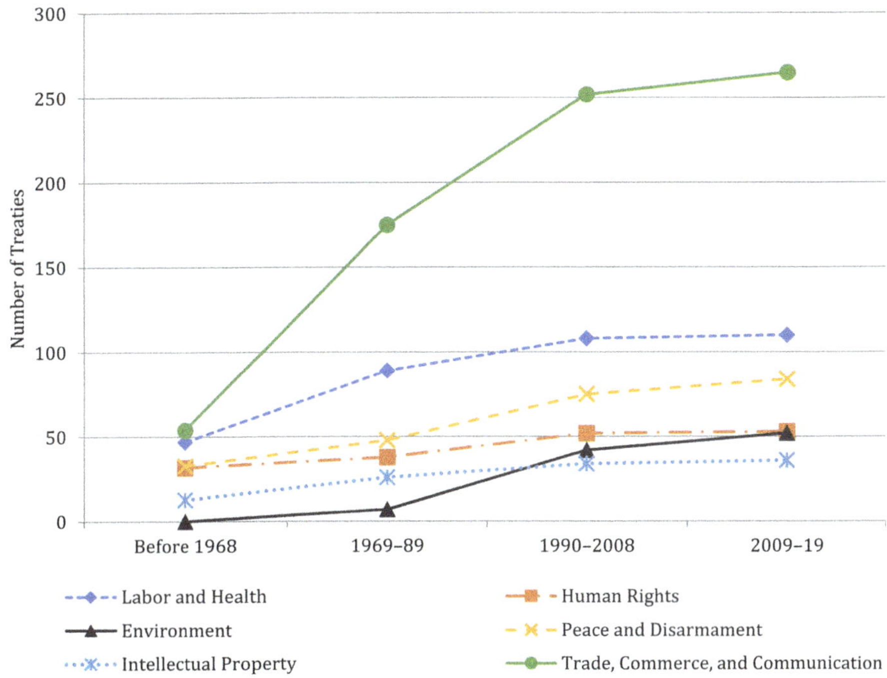

Fig. 2.2 Number of treaties by period and by domain (2)

and Kosovo. Turkey, a member of the North Atlantic Treaty Organization, had wanted to join the European Union was discouraged from joining it. Serbia has been branded and punished for having carried out war crimes of aggressively persecuting Kosovo Albanians. Ukraine, Belarus, and Georgia have been indicating some signs of joining it but have not seriously been considered. Russia, Azerbaijan, and Kazakhstan are members of the Eurasian Economic Union, thus hinting the possibility of linking Europe and Asia (Central Asia and the Caucasus for the start) in a nebulous future. Most recently, the United Kingdom has withdrawn its membership from the EU in 2019–2020. The core regional group is called by Welzel (2013) the Reformed West, that is, those West European states that built foundations of sovereign states during the Reformation period. The basic tenets are based on reformist Christianity pronounced during the Reformation period, which are characterized as being secular in daily life and being fond of rule-drafting and rule-abiding in politics. The EU exemplifies this practice. Many of EU members make it a rule in their respective national parliament to semi-automatically ratify those promulgated treaties by their national representatives in the EU to be ratified. For instance, Denmark's parliament automatically ratifies EU-related laws, which occupy some 30 to 40% of those laws nationally legislated.

Those states ranked from the 11th to the 50th are still European dominant. Of 40 states thus ranked, only 11 are from outside Europe. They are: Turkey (29th), Egypt

Table 2.1 List of multilateral treaties covered in the dataset

Domain	Subdomain	Number of treaties	Source of data
Environment (52 treaties)	Environment	52	United Nations Treaty Collection (UNTC)
Human Rights (53 treaties)	Freedom of Information	1	UNTC
	Human Rights	27	
	Slavery	3	
	Obscene Publications	5	
	Refugees and Stateless Persons	4	
	Status of Women	3	
	Traffic in Persons	10	
Intellectual Property (36 treaties)	WIPO-Administered	26	WIPO
	Other IP-related	10	WIPO
Labor and Health (110 treaties)	Health	13	UNTC
	ILO-Administered	78	ILO
	Narcotic Drugs and Psychotropic Substances	19	UNTC
Peace ad Disarmament (84 treaties)	Disarmament	13	UNTC
	Law of the Sea	10	
	Outer Space	2	
	Pacific Settlement of International Disputes	1	
	Penal Matters	21	
	Privileges and Immunities, Diplomatic and Consular Relations	37	
Trade, Commerce, and Communication (265 treaties)	Commercial Arbitration	3	UNTC
	Commodities	13	
	Economic Statistics	2	
	Educational and Cultural Matters	5	
	International Trade and Development	24	
	Navigation	13	
	Telecommunications	8	
	Transport and Communications	197	
Total		600	

(30th), Nigeria (38th), Armenia (39th), Malaysia (40th), Japan (42th), Australia (44th), New Zealand (46th), Brazil (47th), South Africa (48th), and Mexico (50th). About 40-odd states are members of the Organization of Economic Cooperation and Development (OECD), a club of developed states. They have been members of the United Nations for a long time, and many are founding members. Out of 193 sovereign states in the United Nations, the number of developing states is 144. Because they are late in joining the UN and because many of them are reluctant to join those multilateral treaties, they are not ranked the highest 10 or highest 50 so much. Developing states have been encouraged to participate in multilateral treaties because the United Nations, as is clear from the Declaration of the United Nations pronounced in 1945, has aspired to be universal, inclusive, and egalitarian. Many multilateral treaties do not have clauses of punishing those violators or saboteurs. They are privileged in that sense. Yet the exception of privilege from those duties met the purposes of the shapers and managers of the United Nations. In particular the key shaper, the United States, has adopted both Wilsonian and Monrovian principles. Wilsonianism means national self-determination, electoral democracy, and free-market capitalism. The first principle is very important to newly independent states, joining the UN. It is the first principle of the United States. Some European colonial powers resisted and wanted to delay the date of national independence. Yet they both were eager to expand world markets on free market capitalism after the unprecedented devastations in World War II. Furthermore, they both wanted to block Soviet-led communist influences from expanding at their home and abroad, that is, in developing states. The Monrovian principle is one of the old principles of the United States not to let others interfere in Latin American affairs as if it were the US's sphere of influence.

During the Cold War period (1945–1989) the key members of the developed states were eager to encourage newly independent states to combine electoral democracy and free-market capitalism. They were successful on the whole despite often rampant authoritarianism and protectionism. But their success was modest in the sense that the Atlantic angle of building democracy and capitalism (Lipset and Rokkan 1967; Ikenberry 2020) had the limit. A series of US-led trade and economic liberalization rounds (especially the last one) were not very successful in expanding world markets. In order to expand world markets on the free-market capitalist principle, the General Agreements on Tariffs and Trade (GATT) needed to be revised. The World Trade Organization was established to help make consultations and adjustments among parties concerned more efficient and effective. The results are half success, half failure. Frustrated, the United States President, Donald Trump has changed the course. UK Prime Minister Boris Johnson changed the course. During those post-Cold War years, the position of developing states in the United Nations and its specialized agencies has evolved. They have consolidated their self-assertion while the developed states have continued their principle of preserving the statues of those developing states by exempting them from tight application of liberalization (Fig. 2.3).

Let us take a look at multilateral treaties by domains. Taking all domains, we find that, on average 30% of UN members joined the multilateral treaties deposited with

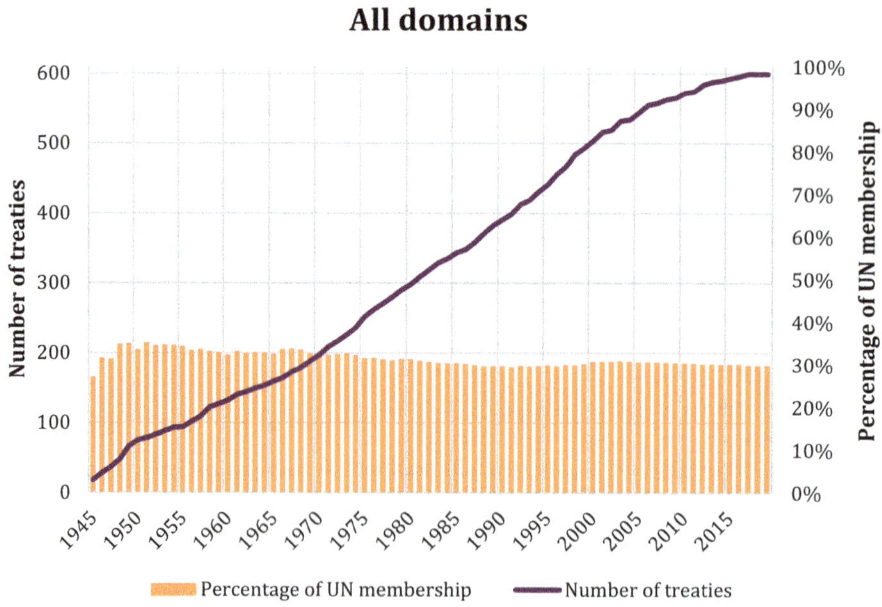

Fig. 2.3 The growth of UN treaties and UN membership coverage (All domains)

UN Secretary-General in each of the 75 years (1945–2019). In other words, there are many multilateral treaties in which some 70% of UN members do not join. There are two domains in which the percentage of participation is less than the average of 30%, i.e., labor and health, and trade, commerce and communications. The former registers some 30% while the latter registers barely 20%. On labor and health, some standards and criteria are set to be eligible to a member. In a similar vein, on trade, commerce, and communications, certain standards and criteria are set to be eligible to a member. Other domains register some 40% of UN members participation. Peace and disarmament contains multilateral treaties whose membership is conditional on clauses of punishment in case of non-abiding. Intellectual property registers some 40% of UN members' participation. The trend of participation in UN member is reducing as the treatment of developing states has become less generous. Human rights registers some 45%. With developing states' self-assertion on the rise on social aspects of human rights definition, UN members' participation has gradually risen. The environment registers the rise in the 1980s and 1990s. Since then the trend registers the reduction in UN members' participation. As the stringent criteria of paying costs of emitting CO_2 are set even to developing states, the participation reduces. When stringent criteria are moderated, the 2018 Paris accord has been agreed by a majority. The result is that the United States withdrew and that the effectiveness of the treaty in curbing global warming and other negative aspects of climate change has visibly reduced (Figs. 2.4, 2.5, 2.6, 2.7, 2.8, and 2.9).

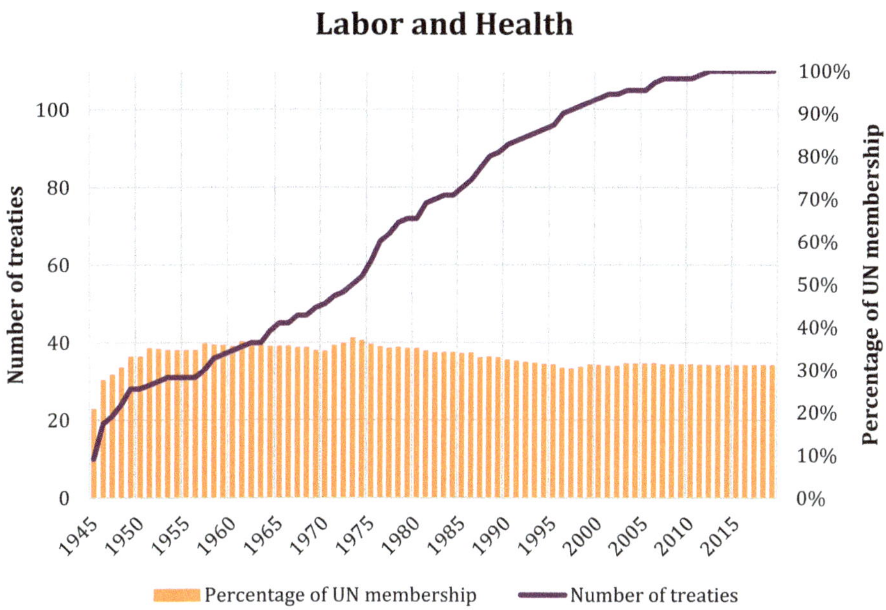

Fig. 2.4 The growth of UN treaties and UN membership coverage (Labor and Health domain)

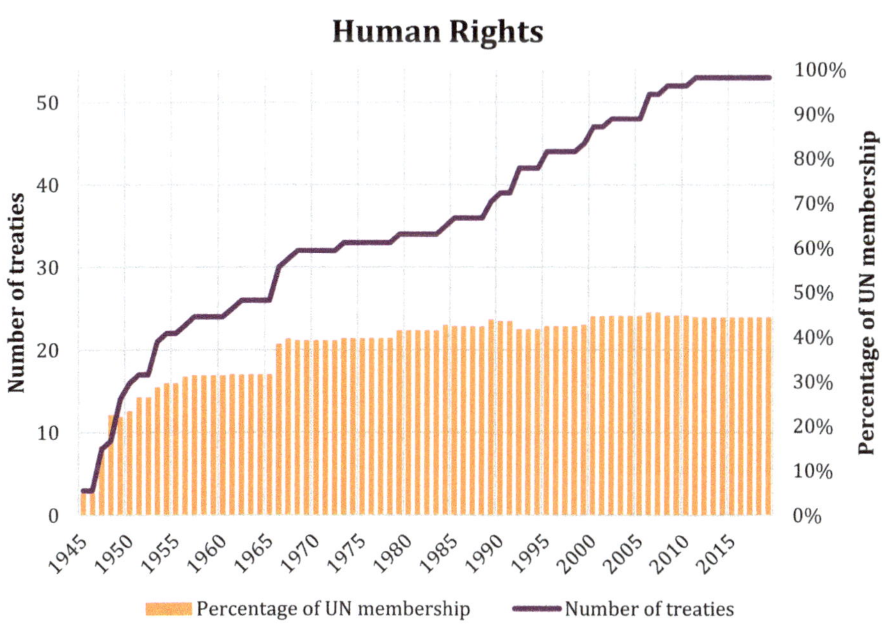

Fig. 2.5 The growth of UN treaties and UN membership coverage (Human Rights domain)

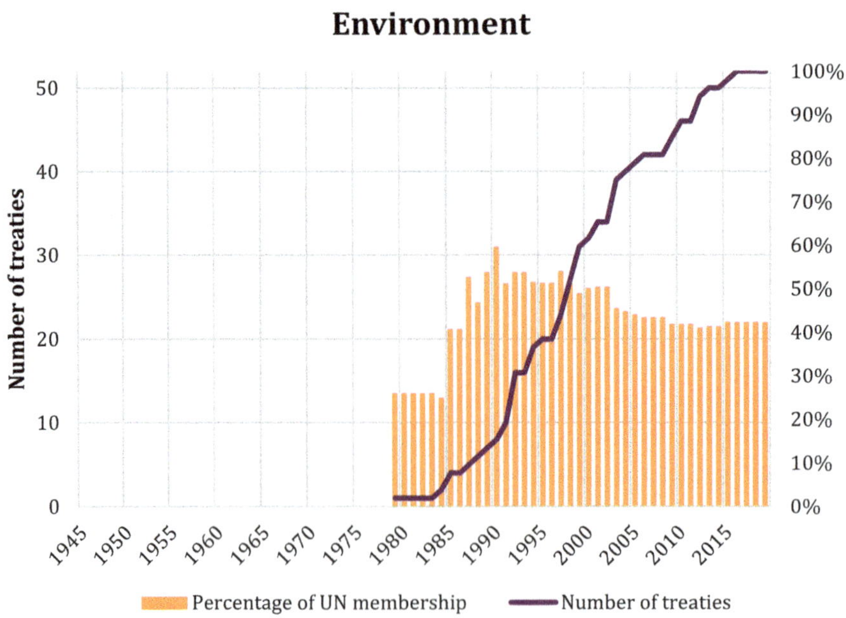

Fig. 2.6 The growth of UN treaties and UN membership coverage (Environment domain)

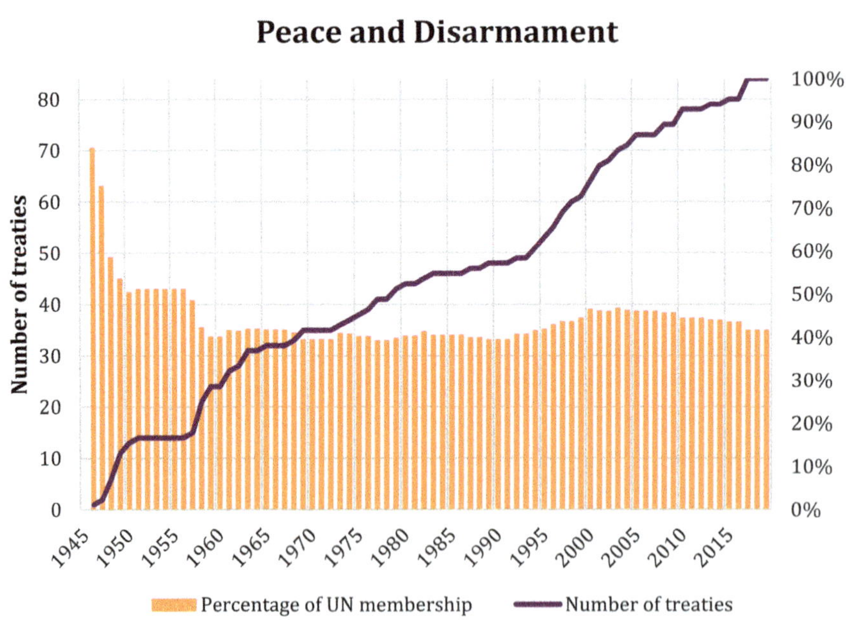

Fig. 2.7 The growth of UN treaties and UN membership coverage (Peace and Disarmament domain)

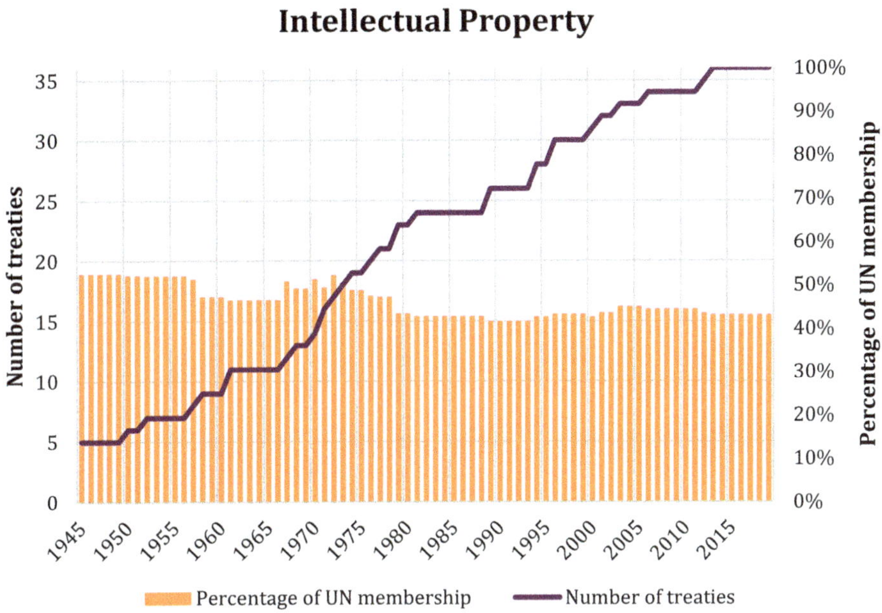

Fig. 2.8 The growth of UN treaties and UN membership coverage (Intellectual Property domain)

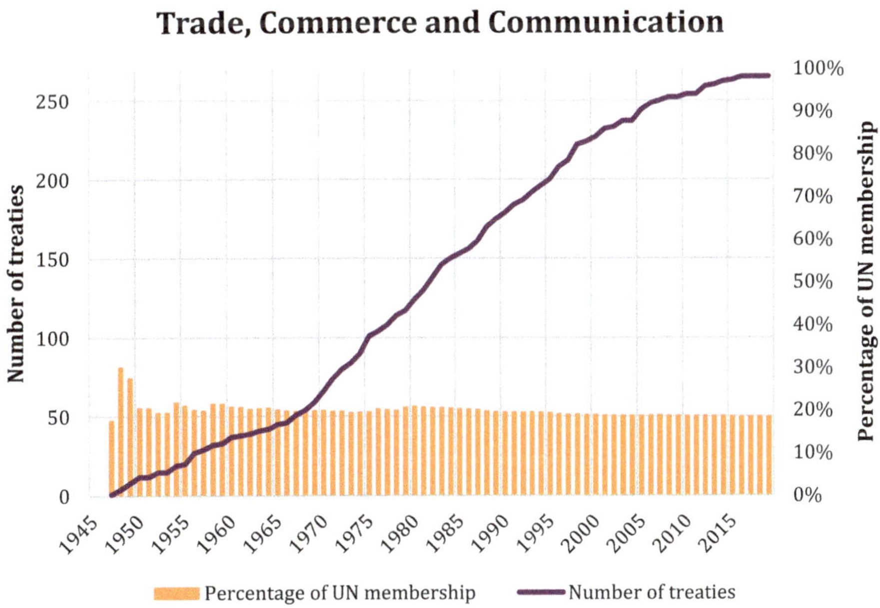

Fig. 2.9 The growth of UN treaties and UN membership coverage (Trade, Commerce, and Communication domain)

Let us take a look at how fast the countries joined UN multilateral treaties by the Treaty Participation Index (TPI) or the metric derived from the inverse in the number of elapsed years after promulgation of treaty until a state's ratification. The state that ratified the treaty immediately without any delay is rewarded the highest value of treaty participation score of 1; while the country that has not yet joined this given treaty is scored 0. The starting point of 1945–1968 registers the high percentage of joining in the domains of peace and disarmament, human rights, labor and health and intellectual property. This makes sense after World War II those multilateral treaties in peace and disarmament were joined as World War II, civil wars and wars of independence ended; those multilateral treaties in human rights were joined as human rights and dignity were respected as wars ended; those multilateral treaties in labor and health were joined fast and continuously joined as working life continued; those multilateral treaties in intellectual property were joined after wars when people ascertained their own intellectual property. Those multilateral treaties in human rights went up during the 1968–1989 period which ended with the fall of the Berlin Wall and the disintegration of the Soviet Union (Figs. 2.10, 2.11, 2.12, 2.13, 2.14, and 2.15).

Also significantly pronounced is the upward trend of the number of those multilateral treaties joined during the 1990–2008 in such domains as labor and health, peace and disarmament, intellectual property, human rights and trade, commerce, and communications. To explain this, we have to bring readers to a bit earlier days. Henry Kissinger warned against the Soviet introduction of Intermediate Nuclear Weapons targeted at Western Europe in 1984, saying that the Soviet Union has to

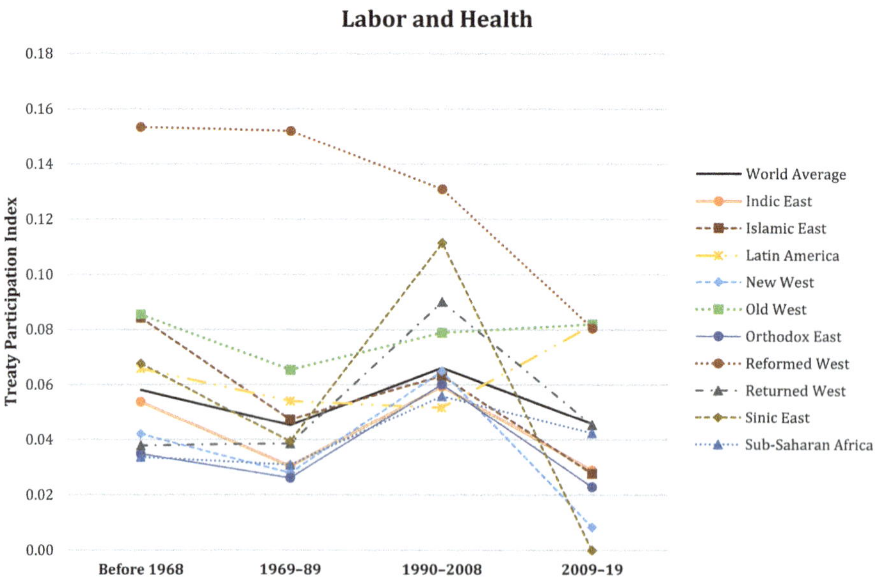

Fig. 2.10 How fast have the groups of countries joined the UN multilateral treaties in Labor and Health domain

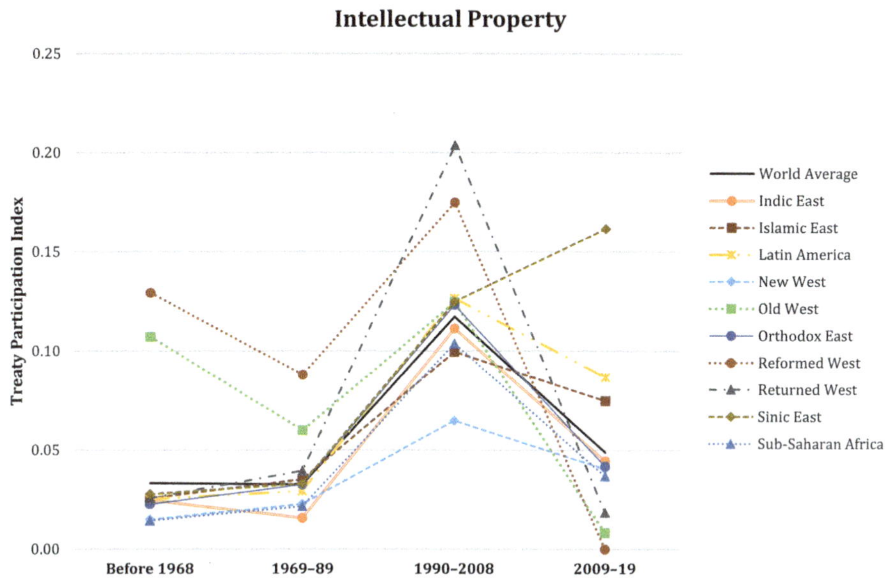

Fig. 2.11 How fast have the groups of countries joined the UN multilateral treaties in Intellectual Property domain

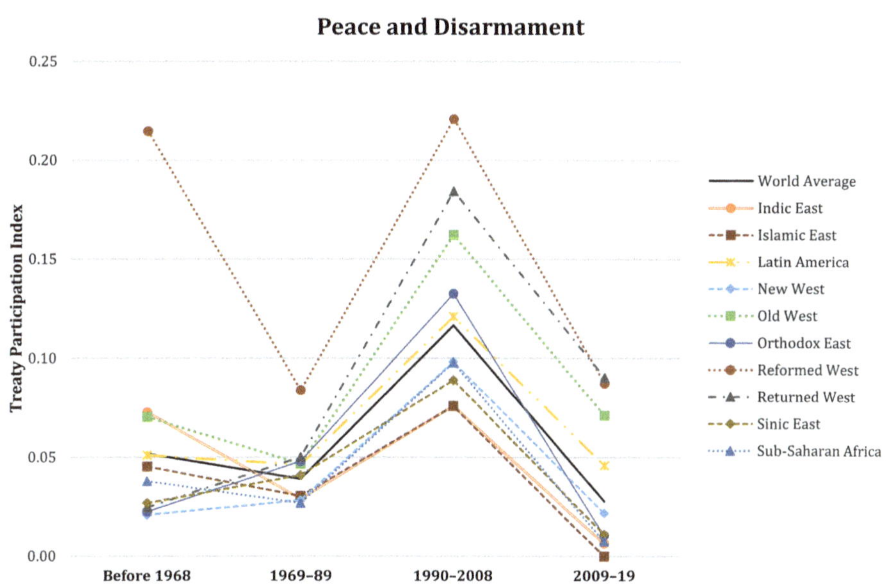

Fig. 2.12 How fast have the groups of countries joined the UN multilateral treaties in Peace and Disarmament domain

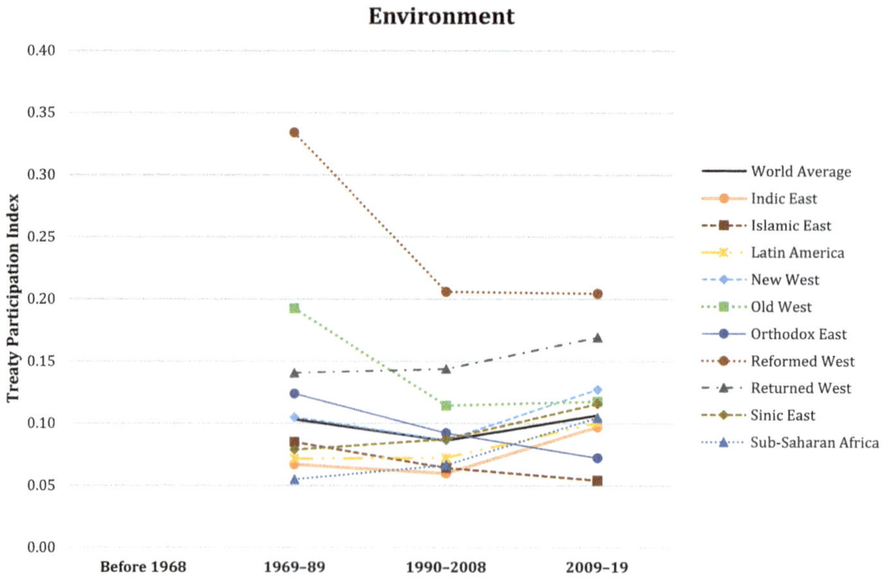

Fig. 2.13 How fast have the groups of countries joined the UN multilateral treaties in Environment domain

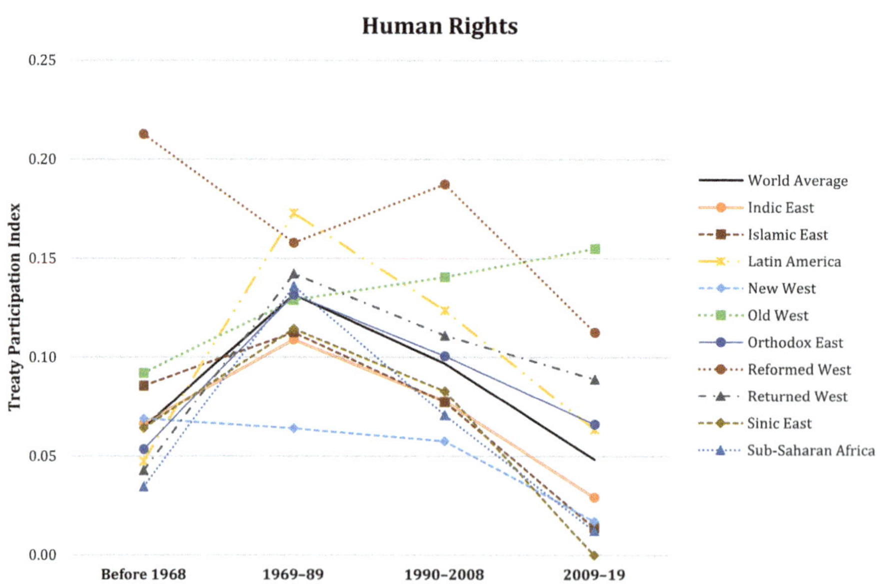

Fig. 2.14 How fast have the groups of countries joined the UN multilateral treaties in Human Rights domain

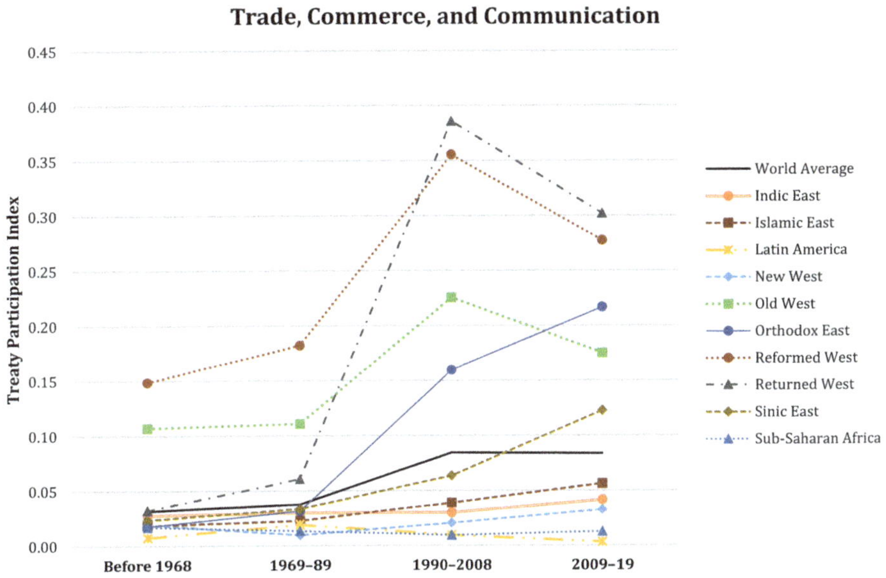

Fig. 2.15 How fast have the groups of countries joined the UN multilateral treaties in Trade, Commerce, and Communication domain

choose either the cause or the country, meaning that they have to choose the option of keeping the Soviet Union and the Soviet bloc or the option of keeping the Russian state and that otherwise you would lose both (Kissinger 1985, cited by Roberts 2010). In response Georgy Arbatov counterattacked in the *New York Times*, saying that if the United States loses the Enemy (that is, the Soviet Union), the United States will go astray, meaning that the United States would lose its course (Fettweis 2018). The results are that the United States chose the course of waging wars of many kinds without peace settlements (Iraq, Afghanistan, Iran, North Korea [nuclear power stations and nuclear weapons and missiles], and China [tariff wars]). All these ended up with the Lehman-triggered global recession of 2008 and furthermore with the Corona-triggered global recession of 2020.

2.3 Data Driven Empirical Modeling

This chapter describes how statecraft is used in the digital era when the Earth's singularity is characterized as Information because of the outburst of data when compared to the star (whose singularity is Matter) and to the blackhole (whose singularity is Energy) (Hidalgo 2016). The Earth's singularity has been made possible by the invention of World Wide Web in 1990 by Tim Berners-Lee working at the Centre European de Recherche Nucleaire (CERN). As the amount of data flows on the Earth steadily increased in the 1990s and 2000s in tandem with the extraordinary diffusion worldwide of personal computers and smart phones, vehicles of information. No less critical to the outburst of data on the Earth is the incredible fast improvement of computers' capacity to process the astronomically massive and complex operations almost instantaneously. The era of digitized globalization steadily deepened and sharpened around the dawn of the new millennium.

An important development is artificial intelligence (AI), a research domain linked to all kinds of human intellectual behavior. It articulates logic and prepares algorithms, collects data on backgrounds and known information, operates mechanically as workable artificial intelligence, and most importantly tests it against real human behavioral data. The concept of artificial intelligence was popularized by the sensation it generated through AI's victory over human game players of *go* or *weichi* and poker. The idea that artificial intelligence might soon supersede the human brain has fascinated theoreticians of philosophy, history, mathematics, biology, physics, and computer science. Yuval Noah Harari (2018) has prophesied that likelihood in his magnum opus of human history. We are interested in the way in which academics in the domain of artificial intelligence organize their schemes, which seem to be isomorphic with what we have been doing (Inoguchi and Le 2019, 2021).

First, our aim is to validate the hunch-cum-hypothesis of the liberal world order generated through the institutional vehicle called multilateral treaties, which has been blossomed after World War II (Ikenberry 2020). Inoguchi and Le (2019) have shown the hunch-cum-hypothesis has been *grosso modo* validated as a first attempt of empirical testing on the basis of features of multilateral treaties. The intellectual debate has thus been going on between the institutional vehicle school (like multilateral treaties) and the socialization school (like elite socialization through sharing of culture).

The latter school has been predominant among scholars of international relations and political science. It contains two major sub-schools: the hegemony and power transition school and cultural sharing on the basis of adaptation. The hegemony school is predominant after World War II among American academics: Gilpin (1983) stands out by highlighting hegemonic power's role in power transition. After all, the predominant military power of the United States has been kept for years despite all declinists' voice. Nye (2004) has been consistent on this point with his concept of soft power adding further additional strength to the United States. The clash of civilization thesis of Huntington (1997) is a metamorphosis of the hegemony school in that after the Cold War and demise of the USSR new ideological challengers such as Islam and China are on the rise. The culture sharing sub-school is no less predominant among American academics: Lipset and Rokkan (1967) highlight the vehicle of democracy in electoral politics among Atlantic states in northwestern Europe and North America. Putnam and Bayne (1988) highlight how the Group of Seven shared the same elite culture after the earth-shaking oil crisis of 1973. The reputation ranking of powers (Pouliot 2016) belongs to this school in that reputation combines physical sources of power and cultural harmony.

The former school, the institutional vehicles school, is new and old. It is new in that Inoguchi and Le (2019) have only recently empirically and statistically tested the hypothesis and shown positive results. It is old in that Fairbank and Teng (1941) and Fairbank (1968) advance the hypothesis that the tributary system as practiced in the Sinocentric world (as contrasted to the international treaty system as practiced in the Eurocentric world) are qualitatively different or—to put it simply–incompatible. Fairbank (1968) is similar to Huntington (1997) in that cultural differences loom very large. Suzuki (2009) argues on the basis of modern Japanese adaptation and Chinese non-adaptation to the international treaty system that modern Japanese and Chinese elite socialization in their respective cultural schemes made differences. Suzuki (2009) is akin to the elite socialization sub-school in the hegemony school. Inoguchi and Le (2019) can be categorized as the institutionalist school but cannot be categorized as the institutionalist of neoliberal persuasion. More directly referring to the dawn of the new millennium and the liberal world order, Ikenberry (2011, 2020) advances the kind of the institutional vehicles school in that the liberal world order might not demise even if the position of military predominant of the United States might be lost in the future.

Second, Inoguchi and Le (2019) adopt the strategy of using instrumental variables if it is solidly empirical in light of the need to use empirical data to explain whether sovereign states decide to join or not to join multilateral treaties.

One of the key indicators of such decisions is naturally the number of years between the year of promulgation and of ratification. The slower the decision of ratification, the less willing governments are to join the multilateral treaties concerned. Reasons for tardiness can be anything:

1. A government decides to join it but parliament and public opinion reject it;
2. A government decides to join because public opinion literally forces it to sign it or because of a paramount instinct to stay in power, but the government tries to see to it that somewhere in executive agencies, judiciary branches are bound to block, or international organizations work against ratification;
3. A government decides to join it, but given the large gap between the treaty's stringent clause about heavy duties such as criteria of offering official development assistance to the developing South and government inability to implement for the immediate future, the government keeps working hard to qualify as a member of such treaties without being able to ratify it when they will decide to join;
4. A government decides to join it, but procrastinates about ratifying it because some promulgator-states keep themselves exempt from duties, i.e., keep benefiting from the status of the developing South after government signing it;
5. A government decides to join it, but having been notified thereafter about the change from those states which are densely connected with the country in terms of the economy and technology.

At any rate, "the swifter the decision on ratification, the more willing to join multilateral treaties concerned" is one of the key hypotheses using instrumental variables. This is represented by the Treaty Participation Index.

In addition to the willingness to join the multilateral treaty after promulgation, the treaty's popularity is vital in deciding to join it. Popularity in this sense means that the treaty is composed of many member states rather than a small number of member states. Ceteris paribus, the larger the number of member states the better. You cannot be too late in getting on a bus. Thus, the number of treaty members cannot be underestimated. The more members of the treaty, the stronger it becomes. Furthermore, the year of ratification is important. The distinction among being the founding member of the treaty, the early joiner, or the latecomer, is important in being a good standing in the multilateral treaty concerned. Needless to say, the year of ratification is important. That is the year that membership is deposited.

We have two important instrumental variables: policy domain and civilization. Policy domain refers to the six areas of policy dealing with multilateral treaties: human rights, peace and disarmament, trade, commerce and communications, the environment, intellectual property, and labor and health. Each deals with certain aspects of our daily life. In the sense that multilateral treaties deal with all the "problems without passports" (Annan 2002), how sovereign states place priorities to these six domains is one important attributal data on multilateral treaties. At the dawn of national independence after decolonization, many policy domains must be taken seriously yet pragmatically. First, labor and health often takes the first and continuous priority. Even prior to labor and health, peace and disarmament needs to be handled. After peace is settled, governments need to invigorate trade, commerce and communications. Also after war and other kinds of tumultuous years, priority has to be placed on human rights to establish free and stable society. Gross national product must go up. Depending on the stage of industrial modernization, the kind of policy domains that need to be prioritized differs. If pollution is getting out of hand, the environment has to be prioritized. Accordingly, globally coordinated efforts must be undertaken in sync with multilateral treaties. If intellectual property is violated, that domain has to be prioritized.

Civilization refers to the ten geographical, historical and cultural regions of the world (Welzel 2013): Old West, New West, Reformed West, Returned West, Orthodox East, Islamic East, Indic East, Sinic East, Latin America, and Sub-Saharan Africa. Old West is defined as those states whose state-building originated from the Roman Empire. New West is defined as those states that originated from English-speaking white settlers' societies and their offshoot former colonies. Reformed West is defined as those whose state-building endeavors originated the Reformation in Europe. Returned West refers to those states in Central and Western Europe which switched from the Soviet bloc to the Western bloc in 1989. Orthodox East is defined as the amalgamation of orthodox Russia, Soviet Union bloc, and Ottoman Empire. Islamic East refers to those states where Islam pervades life and society, covering the Middle East and North Africa. Indic East is defined as those states whose cultural and religious influence originated from India, ancient, medieval, modern, and contemporary. Sinic East is defined as those states influenced by Chinese culture and institutions. Latin America is seen as the whole of the Americas except the United States and Canada. Sub-Saharan Africa is defined as the whole Africa minus North Africa. Geographical proximity often means similarity in outlook. This civilizationally flavored regions are no less important attributal variables in characterizing multilateral treaties despite all the claimed universality and globality of multilateral treaties. Geography gives often distinctive flavors in the modes of participation in multilateral treaties.

All these variables are on 600 multilateral treaties around whose participation 193 sovereign states play their global legislative politics. We summarize all these data by factor analysis with varimax rotation. The idea is to statistically simplify the 600 × 193 data by decomposing the sum of correlation coefficients of six variables step by step dimensionally. We have got three key dimensions. The names of these dimensions are related to the decision's speed, the angle of decision, and the strategy of decision. In other words, most pronounced are speed. Thirty percent of variance is explained. Second is angle. Twenty-five percent of variance is explained. Third is strategy, explaining 17%. In total 75% of variance is explained. The first dimension is loaded heavily by variables of year of deposit and year of membership. The second dimension is loaded heavily by variables of the number of current members, ten regions and six policy domains. The third dimension is loaded heavily by variables of treaty participation index and ten regions.

The labels of the three dimensions are:

1. agile vs. cautious,
2. global commons vs. individual interests, and
3. aspirational bonding vs. mutual binding.

To explain, the speed of decision always means something. What causes procrastination? What is behind a rash decision? The angle of decision means which perspective is stressed: globalist vs. nationalist. The strategy of decision means which strategy is preferred: the developing South vs. the developed North.

Using three capitalized A or B or C and three non-capitalized a, b, c to denote two sides of each dimension, we have eight types, i.e., abc, aBC, aBc, abC, Abc, AbC, ABc, ABC. In table format, some of those states, which fit each one of the eight types are indicated:

abc	Japan, Indonesia, Iran, Morocco, Singapore
aBC	Laos, Syria, Jordan, Ecuador, Mexico,
aBc	Uruguay, Zimbabwe, Ghana, Algeria, Argentina, Bahamas, Burkina Faso, Cameroon, DR Congo, Dominica, Ethiopia, Iraq, Kuwait, Lebanon, Libya, Nepal, Nigeria, Peru, Rwanda, Senegal, Somalia, Uganda, Tanzania, Yemen, Venezuela
abC	France, US, UK, Solomon Islands, Spain, Sweden, Switzerland, Thailand, Netherlands, New Zealand, Norway, Pakistan, Papua New Guinea, Philippines, Poland, Romania, Tunisia, Germany, China, Israel,
Abc	Albania, Montenegro, Armenia, Georgia, Kazakhstan, Kyrgyzstan, Uzbekistan, Turkey,
AbC	Belarus, Croatia, Czech Republic, Estonia, Latvia, Lithuania, Portugal, R Korea
ABc	Bahrain, Benin, Burundi, Chad, DPR Korea, El Salvador, Guinea-Bissau, Mongolia, Mozambique, Namibia, Oman, Qatar, Saudi Arabia, South Africa, South Sudan,
ABC	Bangladesh, Bhutan, Maldives, Panama

How do we decipher these combinations of three alphabetical characters attached to 193 states with the label of global quasi-legislative behavior? We turn to these matters in Parts II and Part III. Part II explains how we conceptualize and operationalize multilateral treaties participation as *global quasi-social contract* whereas Part III explains how *a bundle of global quasi-legislative behavior*, exhibited by 193 sovereign states, are interpreted.

References

Alston, Philip, and Ryan Goodman. 2012. *International Human Rights*. 2nd ed. Oxford: Oxford University Press.

Alston, Philip. 2017. "The Populist Challenge to Human Rights." *Journal of Human Rights Practice* 9 (1): 1–15.

Annan, Kofi. 2002. "Problems without Passports." *Foreign Policy* 132: 30–31.

Baldwin, Richard. 2016. *The Great Convergence*. Cambridge, MA: Harvard University Press.

Baldwin, Richard. 2019. *Globotics Upheaval: Globalization, Robotics and the Future of Work*. Oxford: Oxford University Press.

Blackwill, Robert D., and Jennifer Harris. 2016. *War by Other Means: Geoeconomics and Statecraft*. Cambridge, MA: Harvard University Press.

Fairbank, John (ed.). 1968. *The Chinese World Order: Traditional China's Relations*. Harvard University Press.

Fairbank, John and S.Y. Teng. 1941. "On The Ch'ing Tributary System." *Harvard Journal of Asiatic Studies* 6 (2): 135–246.

Fettweis, C. 2018. *Psychology of a Superpower: Security and Dominance in U.S. Foreign Policy*. New York, NY: Columbia University Press, p. 1.

Foot, Rosemary. 2020a. "Shaping from Within: A UN with Chinese Characteristics?" *East Asia Forum*, August 10, pp. 1–2.

Foot, Rosemary. 2020b. *China, the UN, and Human Protection: Beliefs, Power, Image*. Oxford: Oxford University Press.

Galloway, Eilene. 1960. "World Security and the Peaceful Use of Outer Space." XIth International Astronomical Cooperation Stockholm.

Gilani, B.I. (2020). "Gilani Gallopedia's Initiative on a Global Survey on Covid-19 to WAPOR: The World Association for Public Opinion Research." Islamabad, Pakistan.

Gilpin, Robert. 1983. *War and Change in World Politics*. Princeton: Princeton University Press.

Hale, Thomas, and David Held. 2017. *Beyond Gridlock*. Cambridge: Polity Press.

Hale, Thomas, David Held, and Kevin Young. 2012. *Gridlock: Why Global Cooperation Is Failing When We Need It Most*. Cambridge: Polity Press.

Harari, Yuval Noah. 2018. *Sapiens: A Brief History of Humankind*. New York: Harper Perennial, reprint edtion.

Hidalgo, César. 2016. *Why Information Grows: The Evolution of Order, from Atoms to Economies*. New York: Penguin Books.

Huntington, Samuel. 1997. *The Clash of Civilizations and the Remaking of World Order*. New York: Simon and Schuster.

Ikenberry, G. John. 2011. *Liberal Leviathan: The Origins, Crisis, and Transformation of the American World Order*. Princeton: Princeton University Press.

Ikenberry, G. John. 2020. *A World Safe for Democracy: Liberal Internationalism and the Crises of Global Order*. New Haven: Yale University Press.

Inoguchi, Takashi and Lien Thi Quynh Le. 2019. *The Development of Global Legislative Politics: Rousseau and Locke Writ Global*. Singapore: Springer Nature.

Inoguchi, Takashi and Lien Thi Quynh Le. 2021. *Digitized Statecraft in Multilateral Treaty Participation: Global Quasi-Legislative Behavior of 193 Sovereign States*. Singapore: Springer Nature.

Kissinger, Henry. 1985. *Observations: Selected Speeches and Essays 1982–1984*. London: Michael Joseph and Weidenfeld & Nicolson.
Lipset, Seymore Martin, and Stein Rokkan (eds.). 1967. *Party Systems and Voter Alignments*. New York: Free Press.
Mainichi Shimbun. 2020. "Korona kade Kurasu Doitsu:/ge Shiken seigen teiko nezuyoku (Living under the Shadow of the Covid-19 Infectious Disease Diffusion in Germany: 2nd part: Deep-Rooted Resistance Against Curtailing Private Rights)," May 22, 2020, p. 8.
Nihonkeizai Shimbun. 2018. Horei no eiyaku ichiwari domari: junenme okure kokusaika nokabeni (The English Translation of Domestic Laws and Acts Has Remained 10 Percent: Posing Barriers to Japan's Internationalization Since the Translation Task Started 10 Years ago), October 22 (morning ed.), p. 11.
Nye, Joseph S. 2004. *Soft Power: The Means to Success in World Politics*. New York: Public Affairs.
Pouliot, Vincent. 2016. *International Pecking Orders: The Politics and Practice of Multilateral Diplomacy*. Cambridge: Cambridge University Press.
Putnam, Robert and Nicholas Bayne. 1988. *Hanging Together: Cooperation and Conflict in the Seven-Power Summits, Revised and Enlarged Edition*. Cambridge, MA: Harvard University Press.
Roberts, Adam. 2010. "An 'Incredibly Swift Transition': Reflections on the End of the Cold War." In *The Cambridge History of the Cold War*, edited by M. P. Leffler and O. A. Westad, Vol. III, pp. 513–534. Cambridge: Cambridge University Press.
Saint Exupéry, Antoine de. 2011. *Le Petit Prince*. Oakham: Omillia Languages, 79.
Simmons, Beth. 2009. *Mobilizing for Human Rights: International Law in Domestic Politics*. New York: Cambridge University Press.
Suzuki, Shogo. 2009. *Civilization and Empire: China and Japan's Encounter with European International Society*. London: Routledge.
Teske, Sven (ed.). 2019. *Achieving the Paris Climate Agreement Goals*. Springer Nature Switzerland AG.
United Nations. 2020. *Multilateral Treaties Deposited with the Secretary-General*. New York (ST/LEG/SER.E), as available on https://treaties.un.org/Pages/ParticipationStatus.aspx. Accessed 2 March 2020.
Vaidhyanathan, Siva. 2017. *Intellectual Property: A Very Short Introduction*. Oxford: Oxford University Press.
Welzel, Christian. 2013. *Freedom Rising: Human Empowerment and the Quest for Emancipation*. New York: Cambridge University Press.

Part II
One Hundred Ninety-Three Calculi of Statecraft

Abstract

Taking 600 multilateral treaties out of United Nations Secretary-General's Depository plus two sub-depositories of International Labor Organization and World Intellectual Property Organization, and focusing on treaty participation modes (e.g., number of elapsed years, sovereign state's group attribute, treaty's policy domain attribute), we digitize statecraft in 193 ways by factor analysis via varimax rotation. Chapter 3 carries out this operation. Factor analyzing six variables yields three elements of speed, angle and strategy. Bifurcating each of the three-dimensional locations, we have eight types of multilateral treaty participation modes, which we call digitized statecraft. Speed means agile versus cautious, angle means global commons versus individual citizens' interests, and strategy means aspirational bonding versus mutual binding. Chapter 4 shows the three-dimensional locations of each of the 193 sovereign states which are members of the United Nations. We call these three-dimensional locations global quasi-legislative behavior when we conceptualize multilateral treaty participation as global quasi-social contract as a whole and each of 193 sovereign states' behavior as a bundle of global quasi-legislation (Inoguchi and Le 2019). Chapter 4 provides global quasi-legislative behavior of 193 sovereign states by regional groups, namely, Sinic East, Indic East, Islamic East, Orthodox East, Sub-Saharan Africa, Latin America, Old West, New West, Reformed West, and Returned West. Chapter 5 provides systemic explanation focusing on eight types of statecraft.

Reference

Inoguchi, Takashi, and Lien Thi Quynh Le. 2019. *The Development of Global Legislative Politics: Rousseau and Locke Writ Global*. Singapore: Springer Nature.

Chapter 3
The Development of Multilateral Treaty Participation

Abstract In this chapter we argue that sovereign states' physical action bespeaks itself eloquently and the following six instrumental variables are used for their action and their attributes of sovereign states and treaty's policy domains:

1. Year of membership (meaning the year when a state ratified a treaty is identified),
2. Year of deposit (meaning the year when a treaty is deposited to the relevant international body),
3. Number of current members (meaning the number of current member countries of treaty as of 2019),
4. Treaty participation index (meaning a quantitative index to measure how quickly a state participates in a treaty and is calculated based on the number of elapsed years between the promulgation of a treaty and a state's ratification),
5. Modified Welzel regional group (meaning that a country is classified in one of the ten geo-historico-cultural groups by Christian Welzel (2013) in its modified form by the Le/Inoguchi scheme) (see Appendix B), and
6. Policy domain (meaning the six policy domain categorizations based on the main purpose of a treaty).

Factor analyzing 600 multilateral treaty participation by 193 sovereign states yields the three dimensions of speed (cautious vs. agile), angle (global commons vs. individual citizens' interests), and strategy (aspirational bonding vs. mutual binding). These three dimensions are called digitized statecraft–speed, angle, and strategy. Bifurcating 193 sovereign states' scores and locating them generates eight types of digitized statecraft.

3.1 The Scope of Multilateral Treaties Examined

While we were preparing to publish *The Development of Global Legislative Politics: Rousseau and Locke Writ Global*, we encountered the barrage of comments. To those

T. Inoguchi and L. T. Q. Le, *Digitized Statecraft in Multilateral Treaty Participation*, Evidence-Based Approaches to Peace and Conflict Studies 1,
https://doi.org/10.1007/978-981-33-4485-3_3

who have not been quite persuaded by our argument that global politics can be framed as Jean-Jacques Rousseau and John Locke Writ Global and that global politics can be reformulated as a group of global quasi-social contracts and sovereign states' global quasi-legislative behavior, we have decided to do two things in this volume. They have two sets of things.

Six hundred multilateral treaties have been chosen this time. First, in addition to the United Nations Treaty Collection, the World Intellectual Property Organization (WIPO) and, the International Labor Organization (ILO) have been included as sources of our data. The WIPO is one of the newest international organizations. It deals with international property rights and the number of multilateral treaties dealing with intellectual property right has steadily increased as the expansion of the developing South vis-à-vis the developed North especially in the 1970s through 2010s. ILO, one of the oldest international organizations dating back in the mid-nineteenth century, has been keeping its own depository.

Second, the two criteria, primarily procedure-focused and primarily region-focused treaties have been less strict. The reason is simple: The number of multilateral treaties has grown as the number of those states called the developing South has increased especially in the 1970s through the 2000s. Those multilateral treaties categorized as trade, commerce, and communications have dramatically increased in the 1970s through the 2000s. Likewise multilateral treaties categorized as intellectual property as the transactions and communications have also increased dramatically, not only between the developing South and the developed North but also among the developing South. Moreover, those multilateral treaties categorized as labor and health have steadily increased during the same period. It is very important to note that those multilateral treaties categorized as trade, commerce and communications and as labor and health have increased in number but not in terms of the percentage of treaty joiners among member-states of the United Nations. Why? Those multilateral treaties are not necessarily easy to join. First, a very large number of those sovereign states in the developing South do not necessarily want to be deprived of the privileged right of the developing South in terms of tariffs and quotas in free trade. In a similar vein but in the opposite direction, those sovereign states categorized as the developing South cannot improve the labor and health conditions under which their nationals work their earnings safely and healthily. Only twenty percent of UN member-states join those multilateral treaties categorized as trade, commerce and communications. For instance, the Republic of Korea agreed to be deprived the status of the developing South in trade, commerce, and communications in October 2019 but does not want to be deprived of all the privilege of being the developing South despite having the world's eleventh-largest economy. A large number of those sovereign states whose populations have been afflicted by infectious diseases do not want to join those multilateral treaties categorized as health and labor, because membership would compel those joiners to improve those labor and health conditions in light of those labor and health standards of their nationals even by revising relevant domestic laws. Only thirty percent of UN member states have joined such multilateral treaties. It is striking that only in the categories of trade, commerce, and communications and of labor and health the percentage of UN member states which have joined those multilateral treaties has not increased beyond 30% of UN member-states for the long period between 1945 and 2019. In such policy domains as human rights, the environment, peace and disarmament, and intellectual property, those joiner states represent around 40% of UN member states. Hence, the distinction between less procedurally focused and less regionally focused needs to be loosened. Underlying the trend of getting "tougher" to the developing South is the spirit of self-sustaining development. By contrast, when the United Nations as founded in 1945, national self-determination (national independence from colonialism) and the aspirational solidarity of all UN member-states helping each other were predominant in terms of the developed North led by the United States.

Third, the United Nations Depository has changed the way of categorization from the largely hexagonal system of policy domains of multilateral treaties to an ad hoc categorization of policy domains of multilateral treaties. This change is in part a response to the dramatic increase in the policy domain in trade, commerce, and communications, especially in transport and communications in the 2000s and 2010s (as of 2019, the number of multilateral treaties in this subdomain is 197) as well as the development of semi-autonomously managed policy domains by the World Intellectual Property Organization and the International Labor Organization, with the number of multilateral treaties being 26 and 78 respectively.

The data set of 600 multilateral treaties for this book has been resulted as such major factors as shown above. To summarize the distribution of six policy domains in terms of the number of multilateral treaties, it is 52 for the environment, 53 for human rights, 36 for intellectual property, 110 for labor and health, 84 for peace and disarmament, 265 treaties for trade, commerce, and communications.

Two contentions made in our previous book, *The Development of Global Legislative Politics: Rousseau and Locke Writ Global* (2019) are that global politics during the 30 years' crisis between 1989 and 2019 are arguably best fathomed through multilateral treaties—first in terms of a bundle of global quasi-social contracts, and second in terms of global quasi-legislative behavior of the UN's 193 sovereign states. The former part of the argument relies on and makes use of Christian Welzel's most comprehensive, solid, and balanced analysis of the global citizens' values and norms (2013) along with our analysis of the modes of participation by and attributes to 193 sovereign states in relation to their multilateral treaties. The conclusions of Welzel (2013) have been further generalized and enhanced by Ronald Inglehart (2018) in terms of global citizens' value horizons. The latter part of the argument is further enhanced by the expansion of the data set used in this volume. The data set used in this volume has expanded to 600 multilateral treaties from 120 treaties analyzed in the Inoguchi and Le (2019) along the threefold change of the definition of multilateral treaties. These definitional changes have resulted in the further enhancement of the Inoguchi and Le (2019) argument, which will be shown later in this volume.

3.2 Who Joins Multilateral Treaties Most Actively and Least Actively over the Years Between 1945 and 2019?

One hundred ninety-three sovereign states have joined multilateral treaties during the period between 1945 and 2019. Out of the 600 multilateral treaties we have examined in this volume, the most active joiner is the Netherlands, registering 436. The least active joiner is South Sudan, registering 32. The Dutch proclivity for participation in multilateral treaties is exemplified recently by casting the yea vote in the Treaty on the Prohibition of Nuclear Weapons in 2019. All the nuclear weapons states abstained. All the allies of the United States abstained in the vote except for the Netherlands. It participates in the treaty but expresses its negative opinion of the treaty in treaty meetings. South Sudan is the least active because it has been almost totally preoccupied with incessant strife at home and interventions from outside the country since its declared independence. As you see above, one can see that the distribution of most and least frequent joiners ranging from 436 to 32 is very widespread.

A second striking fact is that the first-tier joiners of 1st–10th sovereign states are concentrated geographically in western Europe—namely, the Netherlands, Belgium, Finland, Slovakia, Czech Republic, Luxemburg, Norway, Germany, France, and Sweden. The second-tier joiners are also all European, although geographically they are more widespread. They are Hungary, Italy, Serbia, Romania, Spain, the Russian Federation, the United Kingdom, Poland, Switzerland, and Montenegro. The third-tier joiners of 21–30 sovereign states are almost all European. Only the 29th and 30th sovereign states joiners, Turkey and Egypt in the Middle East, are very close to Europe but outside Europe. The fourth-tier joiners are Latvia, Belarus, Bosnia and Herzegovina, Greece, Estonia, Bulgaria, Portugal, Nigeria, Armenia, and Malaysia. One only finds non-West countries (Nigeria, Armenia, and Malaysia) at the 38th–40th ranks and registering joining 274, 271 and 265 multilateral treaties respectively. One can further enhance the impression that multilateral treaties are dominated in number by European sovereign states.

Then one can ask which sovereign states are participants other than Europeans? Let us take a look at P5 (United Nations Security Council Permanent Members: that is, the United States, the United Kingdom, France, Russia, and China), G7 (the United States, the United Kingdom, France, Germany, Japan, Canada, Italy, and the European Union), G20 (the United States, the United Kingdom, France, Germany, Japan, Canada, Italy, Brazil, the Russian Federation, India, China, the Republic of South Africa, Saudi Arabia, Mexico, the Republic of Korea, Indonesia, Nigeria, Australia, Turkey, and Argentina), ASEAN plus Three (the Philippines, Thailand, Indonesia, Cambodia, Vietnam, Laos, Singapore, Myanmar, Brunei Darussalam, plus China, Japan, and the Republic of Korea) in this order.

P5

The United States	joiner in 133 multilateral treaties

The United Kingdom	joiner in 370 multilateral treaties
France	joiner in 401 multilateral treaties
The Russian Federation	joiner in 370 multilateral treaties
China	joiner in 166 multilateral treaties

G7

The United States	joiner in 133 multilateral treaties
The United Kingdom	joiner in 370 multilateral treaties
France	joiner in 401 multilateral treaties
Germany	joiner in 403 multilateral treaties
Japan	joiner in 243 multilateral treaties
Canada	joiner in 177 multilateral treaties
Italy	joiner in 394 multilateral treaties

G20 (G7 above plus the European Union and the Russian Federation plus 11 emerging states)

G7 shown above

The Russian Federation	joiner in 370 multilateral treaties
Brazil	joiner in 214 multilateral treaties
China	joiner in 166 multilateral treaties
India	joiner in 194 multilateral treaties
Mexico	joiner in 208 multilateral treaties
Republic of Korea	joiner in 189 multilateral treaties
South Africa	joiner in 210 multilateral treaties
Saudi Arabia	joiner in 118 multilateral treaties
Australia	joiner in 236 multilateral treaties
Indonesia	joiner in 136 multilateral treaties
Turkey	joiner in 320 multilateral treaties
Argentina	joiner in 193 multilateral treaties

ASEAN plus Three

The Philippines	joiner in 181 multilateral treaties
Singapore	joiner in 122 multilateral treaties
Thailand	joiner in 145 multilateral treaties
Indonesia	joiner in 136 multilateral treaties
Cambodia	joiner in 130 multilateral treaties
Vietnam	joiner in 129 multilateral treaties
Laos	joiner in 124 multilateral treaties
Myanmar	joiner in 89 multilateral treaties
Brunei	joiner in 83 multilateral treaties
Malaysia	joiner in 265 multilateral treaties
China	joiner in 166 multilateral treaties
Japan	joiner in 243 multilateral treaties
Republic of Korea	joiner in 189 multilateral treaties

Glancing at P5, one may be struck at the United States registering one of the very low figures of joining multilateral treaties (133). It looks as if in the United States the "disentanglement policy" spirit first enunciated by President George Washington in the late 18th century is alive and well. It is not the monopoly of President Donald Trump. All US presidents seem to share Washington's view to some degree. Most recently, Dwight Eisenhower did not start wars or interventions during his terms of 1953–1961. Donald Trump is not alone in his isolationism. The US figure, 133, is comparable to that of Indonesia (136), Vietnam (129), Laos (124), Saudi Arabia (118), and Singapore (122). However, it is overwhelmed by those of France (401), Germany (403), the United Kingdom (370), the Russian Federation (370), and even that of China (166). Needless to say, those enjoying hegemonic positions as the United States during the Cold War period do not need to be bound by multilateral treaties' limits to exercise power.

Glancing at G7 and G20, one can see the similar configuration of the world map: European powers have registered highest the accumulated figures of joining multilateral treaties. The United States has been enhancing the proclivity of taking distance from multilateral commitments, economic, security, and otherwise. This approach can be seen by the withdrawal from such binding commitments as the Paris climate accord, the 12-country Trans Pacific Pact, the unwillingness to renew the Nuclear Power Pact, the unwillingness to protect Kurds from Turkey, Afghans from Taliban, and possibly the Baltic states from Russia etc.

Glancing at ASEAN plus Three (China, Japan, and South Korea) gives a configuration in good contrast to Europe, where the European Union has accumulated the high level of multilateral treaty participation over years attracting adjacent states. ASEAN plus Three, i.e., the Association of Southeast Asian Nations and Northeast Asian Three, are both fragmentary and fluctuated over years. First, the former has hailed the principle of non-interference in internal affairs of ASEAN members. This has effectively prevented the ASEAN from more effectively acting together on, for instance, infrastructure development, communications and transportations across members, coordination of power generations across borders. The three, i.e., China, Japan and South Korea, have been at odds among them over years. Such issues as cooperative resource explorations and exploitations under seas, territorial issues in East China, South China and Japan seas, issues of intellectual property in relation to business enterprises' operations in China, issues of history issues in relation to the rallying to the flag at hard times, armed buildups in China and North Korea and related moves in South Korea, Japan, Taiwan, and Hong Kong. The economic vigor of the ASEAN plus Three has not been translated efficiently into external bargaining power vis-à-vis China or the United States. The ASEAN's declaration of building the ASEAN community in 2015 has not effectively materialized with the expected speed and necessary coordination. The United States has been imposing tariffs on goods and services from China for their high trade surpluses vis-à-vis the United States and effectively imposing economic sanctions on North Korea.

3.3 Global Quasi-Legislative Behavior: Eight Types

How to measure patterns of global quasi-legislative behavior of 193 sovereign states? Here we use the following instrumental variables:

1. Year of deposit (the year when a treaty is deposited to the relevant international body),
2. Year of membership (the year when a certain number of sovereign states have ratified as prescribed in a multilateral treaty),
3. The number of current members as of 2019,
4. Six policy domains,
5. Treaty participation index, and
6. Ten geo-historico-cultural groups of regions.

The idea underlying this operation is that the willingness of sovereign states to join multilateral treaties is captured by the treaty participation index, the core of which is the elapsed number of years between promulgation and ratification, inversed after adding one to the elapsed number of years between promulgation and ratification. The treaty participation index (5) and those instrumental variables (1) through (3) are modes of treaty participation of sovereign states. The instrumental variables (4) and (6) are attributes to sovereign states' proclivity to be associated well or not. The instrumental variable (4) is the proclivity to be associated well or not with one of six policy domains. The instrumental variable (6) is the proclivity to be associated with one of ten geo-historico-cultural regional groups. Both the modes of participation and the attributes to the sovereign states when carrying out treaty participation are simultaneously taken into account.

This use of instrumental variables is ingenious and innovative in gauging global quasi-legislative behavior. The underlying philosophy is that in the analysis of communications, both interpersonal and institutional, communication messages and communication modes are two important aspects and that communication modes are often no less important than communication messages. The use of instrumental variables has been familiar to one of the coauthors of this volume. Formal exchanges of congratulatory messages and their publications on *Renmin Ribao* (People's Daily), *Pravda* (Truth), and *Rodong Shinmun* (Labor News) among top communist leaders, Inoguchi (1969, 1972) skillfully and statistically analyzed both contents and modes of then-widely considered esoteric communication.

Factor-analyzing these six instrumental variables yields three dimensions: speed, angle, and strategy. Speed means that sovereign states' calculi of their statecraft of joining or not joining multilateral treaties are swiftly carried out or not. This is the dimension of agile judgment and action versus of caution and hesitation. Angle means that sovereign state's looking glass of perceiving and analyzing its participation or non-participation in multilateral treaties, weighing up global commons (shared) versus individual interests. In other words, it addresses which aspects of multilateral treaties sovereign states tend to focus on. Strategy is the dimension of prioritizing the aspirational bonding with similar hearted sovereign states or the mutual binding among similar minded sovereign states. In other words, the former strategy focuses on expanding those ideals like national independence, freedom of speech, income equality, national development without attaching some binding or constraining causes in treaties whereas the latter strategy focusing on binding joiners on certain standards and commitments with attaching some punishing and constraining clauses in treaties.

Speed matters in studying multilateral treaties or their drafts because it needs a great amount of time processing treaties and/or drafts and coming up with judgment and action in sync with not only domestic preferences of national citizens but also the preferences of other states and global conditions favoring joining multilateral treaties or not. English proficiency matters. General awareness of global affairs matters. The size of eigenvalues associated with the first dimension, speed, matters most. Angle carried the secondary weight of eigenvalues. Here those fixed and sticky mindsets or those with the same routinized looking-glass wearers sometimes fail to see the crux of the matter, stressing global commons versus sticking to individual interests, national or sectorial or personal. Strategy carries a third weight of eigenvalues. In an era of digitized globalization, global calculus is not easy to figure out. Complex calculi are often needed. The strategy of cooperation with many other sovereign states by joining multilateral treaties is gaining traction year by year. Yet the practice of joining multilateral treaties is steadily stalled in the latter half of the post-Cold War period between 2008 and 2019.

The first dimensional value of item 1 (year of deposit) is large and positive (in the direction of fast and agile). The first dimensional value of item 2 (year of membership) is large and positive similarly. With these two values, the first dimension is termed that of speed. The second dimensional values of item 3 (number of current members) is large and positive in the direction of leaning to individual interests rather than to global commons. The two attributes to sovereign states, items 4 (six policy domains) and 6 (ten geo-historico-cultural regional groups), need to be explained. To some sovereign states, some policy domains are not easy to handle. For example, health and labor treaties often have the clauses whereby the standards of medical care of patients are made explicit and which are difficult to carry it out in current medical standards and currently practiced laws. Policy domains carry large and negative in the direction of leaning to individual interests rather than to global commons. To many sovereign states, item 6 (ten geo-historico-cultural regional groups) are almost given conditions whereby their angle is almost destined to be determined. If a state belongs to the European Union, national parliaments of member states often semi-automatically legislate EU-legitimized laws as national laws. If a state is sandwiched by large, rich and strong neighbors, you must tread carefully your path. In the third dimension, the dimensional value of geo-historico-cultural regional groups is large and negative in the direction of leaning to the aspirational bonding rather than the mutual binding. The dimensional value of the treaty participant index (item 5) carries large and positive in the direction of leaning to the aspirational bonding. With the increase is the number of multilateral treaties with our setting standards to live up to or punishing clauses of violation, this value is large but positive, learning to the aspirational bonding. The steady dominance in number of the developing South has changed the sign of the value to the treaty participation index from negative leaning

Table 3.1 Factor analysis of six variables on 600 multilateral treaty dataset

Total variance explained					
Component	Initial eigenvalues			Rotation sums of squared loadings	
	Total	% of variance	Cumulative %	% of variance	Cumulative %
1	1.787	29.790	29.790	28.178	28.178
2	1.570	26.167	55.957	25.371	53.549
3	1.024	17.075	73.032	19.483	73.032
4	.801	13.356	86.388		
5	.611	10.187	96.575		
6	.206	3.425	100.000		

to the mutual binding to positive leaning to the aspirational bonding (Cf. Inoguchi and Le 2019, p. 78).

The figures of eigenvalues of each dimension are before rotation are 1.787, 1.570, and 1.024 in this order. The rotation sums of squared loadings are 28.178, 25.371, and 19.483 in this order. The cumulative percent of the three dimensions is 73.032%. In other words, explanatory power is sufficiently large (Table 3.1).

References

Inglehart, Ronald. 2018. *Cultural Evolution: People's Motivations are Changing, and Reshaping the World*. New York: Cambridge University Press.

Inoguchi, Takashi. 1969. *Kokusai Kankei no suryobunseki: Peking, Pyongyang and Moscow, 1961–1966 nen* (A Quantitative Analysis of International Relations: Peking, Pyongyang and Moscow, 1961–1966). Tokyo: Gannando Publishers.

Inoguchi, Takashi. 1972. "Measuring Friendship and Hostility among Communist Powers: Some Unobtrusive Measures of Esoteric Communication". *Social Science Research* 1(1): 79–105.

Inoguchi, Takashi, and Lien Thi Quynh Le. 2019. *The Development of Global Legislative Politics: Rousseau and Locke Writ Global*. Singapore: Springer Nature.

Welzel, Christian. 2013. *Freedom Rising: Human Empowerment and the Quest for Emancipation*. New York: Cambridge University Press.

Chapter 4
Three Dimensions of Global Legislative Politics: Ten Regional Groups

Abstract One hundred ninety-three sovereign states are assigned to ten regional groups. They are Sinic East, Indic East, Islamic East, Orthodox East, Sub-Saharan Africa, Latin America, Old West, New West, Reformed West, and Returned West. Each sovereign state's statecraft is profiled in terms of speed, angle and strategy.

4.1 How Can Three-Dimensional Locations Reveal and Illuminate Sovereign States' Global Quasi-Legislative Behavior?

As Chapter 3 has shown, three key dimensions are speed, angle, and strategy. In this chapter, we go from general analysis to national and regional analysis. In analysis we go from Sinic East, Indic East, Orthodox East, Islamic East, Sub-Saharan Africa, Latin America, Old West, New West, Reformed West, and Returned West in this order. In each of the ten regional groups, our description starts from the highlighting of geo-historico-cultural backgrounds of the ten groups and some three to seven sovereign states in each of the ten groups. Then the three-dimensional locations of selected sovereign states' global quasi-legislative behavior are analyzed. On the basis of the above descriptions, we discuss on what we call global statecraft, a new evidence-based concept of global politics.

4.2 Location of Sinic East Members

Here by Sinic East are meant the People's Republic of China, the Socialist Republic of Vietnam, the Democratic People's Republic of Korea, the Republic of Korea, and Japan. Their three-dimensional locations are presented:

In terms of speed, China and Japan are fast runners. Japan looks slightly more cautious than China on average. Pascal Lamy, former director of the World Trade Organization, once noted the trilateral meeting of the United States, the European

T. Inoguchi and L. T. Q. Le, *Digitized Statecraft in Multilateral Treaty Participation*, Evidence-Based Approaches to Peace and Conflict Studies 1,
https://doi.org/10.1007/978-981-33-4485-3_4

Union, and Japan evolved three distinctive ways of announcing their message (Lamy 2005). The United States representative uses the megaphone fairly unilaterally. The European Union representative tries to present a single voice by consulting multilaterally. The Japanese representatives call home to their respective bureaucratic agency of origin to legitimize their respective position on the issue with the resulting announcement tending to be a loosely amalgamated government position. Japan's style may be called multilateralism with each agency's voice substantially annihilating each other while the European Union's multilateralism and the United States' unilateralism move faster than Japanese. The Chinese representatives seem to have more unified positions than Japanese counterparts. Singapore is more agile than China or Japan. In the competitive Southeast Asian environment, speed seems to be the norm. Singapore is no exception. The Philippines is fastest whereas Indonesia and Thailand are on a par with China or Japan (Fig 4.1).

The Republic of Korea are much slower than China and Japan. Although it belongs to the developing South category, it has most recently relinquished its developing country status in principle. But its operationalization has yet to come. The most cautious are the Socialist Republic of Vietnam and the Democratic People's Republic of Korea. It makes sense in that they both are run by communist parties. Furthermore, having joined the United Nations quite late, they have been active only after the new Chinese scheme of what Milanovic (2019) calls "political capitalism" has been partially adopted like *Doi Moi* (reform and opening) by Vietnam (Thayer 1989) and

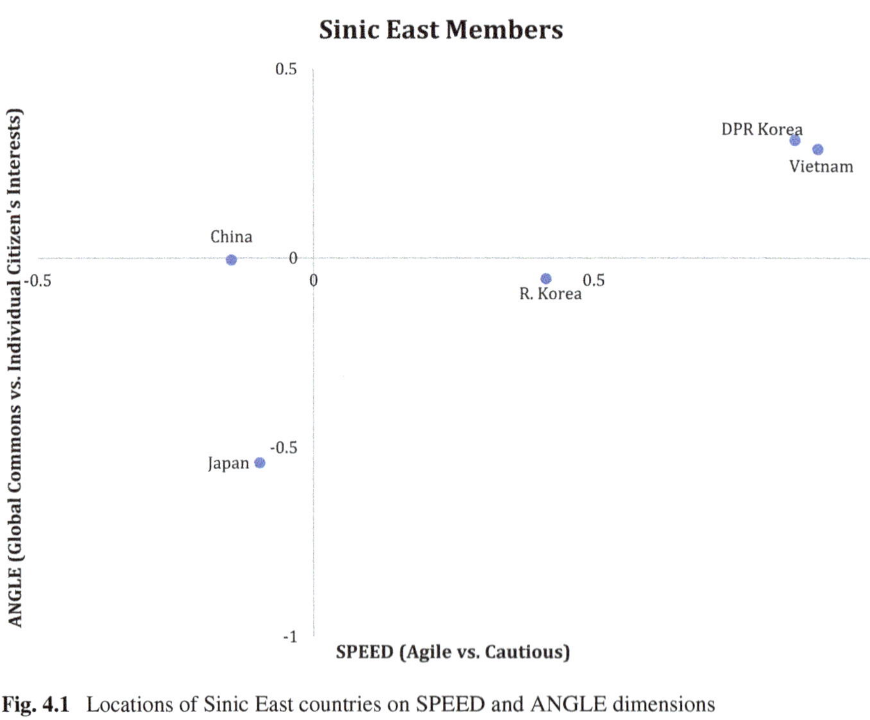

Fig. 4.1 Locations of Sinic East countries on SPEED and ANGLE dimensions

two-wheel strategy of military first (or nuclear weapons first) and (*janmadan*) small markets by North Korea (Baek 2013)—that is, in the 1990s and 2000s. In terms of angle, the angle of global commons is the strongest with Japan among Sinic East members. The Republic of Korea is on a par with China in terms of angle. They both contain the attributes of the developing South and the developed North. So are those Southeast Asian states, the Philippines, Indonesia, Thailand. The rest, namely the Socialist Republic of Vietnam and the Democratic People's Republic of Korea are more strongly preoccupied with individual interests, whether it is national or sectoral. It makes sense in that they were not been exposed to the rest of the world until only recently (1989) and thereafter, despite the amazingly fast development thereafter.

In terms of strategy, mutual binding orientation is strong with the Democratic People's Republic of Korea. Although its value is far less strong than those values of the Reformed West, it is not surprising that the DPR Korea is the strongest in mutual binding orientation among Sinic East members. After all, the Republic of Korea boasts of being the country of bilateral free trade agreements with many countries whose total space in terms of square kilometers being the largest in comparison to its national territorial space next to the United States (President Yi Myung Bak 2010). China and Japan are both big countries and many worry if they adopt strictly mutual binding orientation. They have both experienced the agony of "intimidation" with the United States,

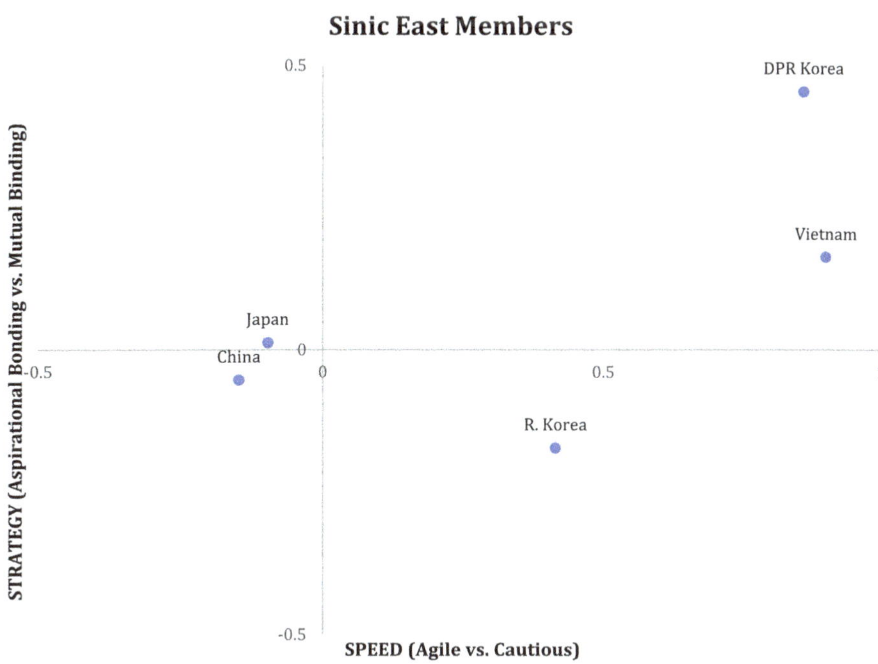

Fig. 4.2 Locations of Sinic East countries on SPEED and STRATEGY dimensions

with accusations of currency manipulation, strategic impediments, tariff wars, intellectual property theft, and structural corruption. China and Japan ironically register similar values in strategy. Some ASEAN countries, such as Singapore and Indonesia, cannot determine their strategy. They bend like willow trees in the mutual binding and aspirational bonding orientations.

4.3 Location of Indic East Members

In terms of speed, those large South and Southeast Asian states such as Pakistan, India, and the Philippines (which achieved its independence earliest in 1946 among Indic East and Sinic East groups) register speedy judgment and action. Those small states that achieved their independence somewhat late, such as Timor-Leste, Brunei, Bhutan, and the Maldives, take time. In terms of global commons vs. individual interests, former British colonies such as India, Pakistan, Sri Lanka, Malaysia, and Singapore, and Indonesia (a former Dutch colony) and Thailand (which kept independence through the modern era) register high scores in terms of angle of global commons. The South and Southeast Asian small states of Timor-Leste, the Maldives, Brunei, Bhutan, Cambodia, Laos, Nepal, Bangladesh, and Myanmar register low scores in terms of

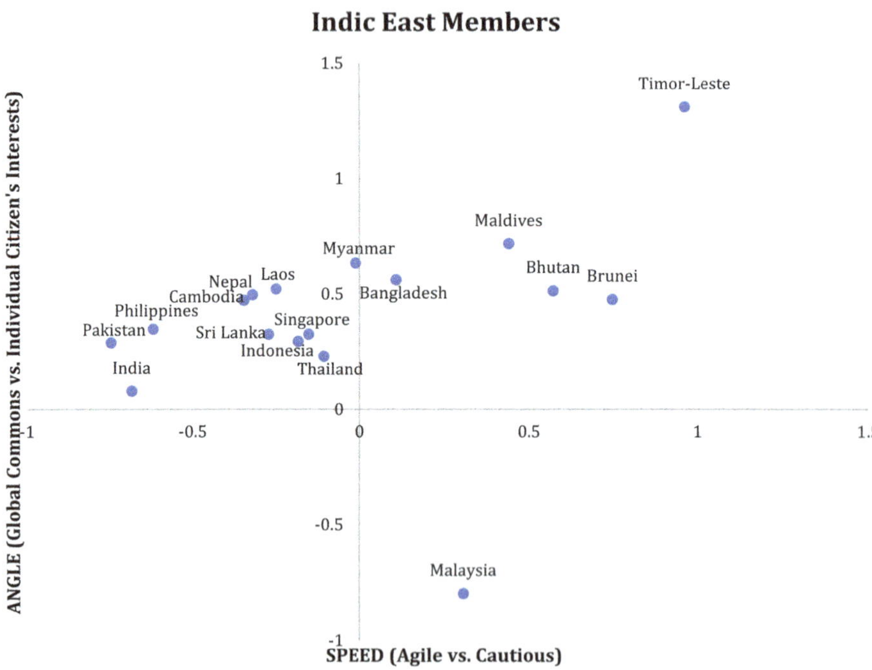

Fig. 4.3 Locations of Indic East countries on SPEED and ANGLE dimensions

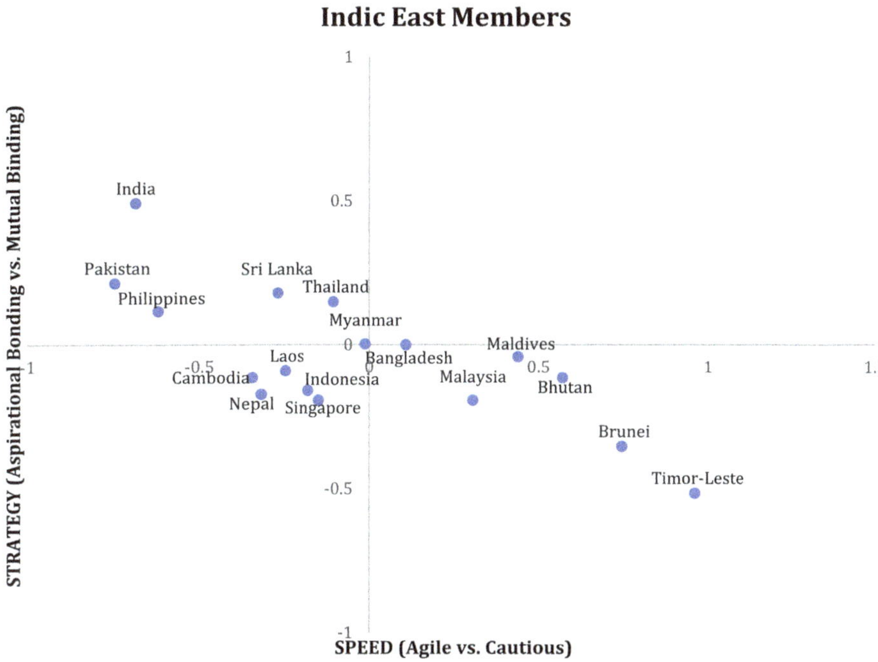

Fig. 4.4 Locations of Indic East countries on SPEED and STRATEGY dimensions

angle, global commons vs. individual interests. In terms of strategy, aspirational bonding vs. mutual binding, those small states often surrounded by big neighbors like Nepal (located between India and China), Singapore (by Islamic Indonesia and Malaysia), Brunei (by Indonesia and Malaysia), and Cambodia and Laos (both sandwiched by Thailand and Vietnam), Bhutan (sandwiched between India and China) register moderately aspirational bonding strategy which seek compassion with larger developing South. Those which adopt mutual binding strategy consist of two subgroups: those small states which cannot afford spending time for resources that might come from bonding with developing South and those states which commit themselves with those treaties only so far as they are more or less strictly mutually binding. The latter includes India, Malaysia, Sri Lanka, Pakistan, Myanmar, Bangladesh, and the Philippines. The former includes the Maldives, Bhutan, Cambodia, and Laos. Not to be forgotten is the unique strategy of Indonesia. It registers the self-restraining strategy within the regional group of the Association of South-East Asian Nations (Figs. 4.3 and 4.4).

4.4 Location of Islamic East Members

Islamic East is the broad areas of the Middle East and North Africa. Most states especially Arab states are cautious on the speed dimension of being agile vs. cautious. Turkey and Egypt are relatively agile because of geographical proximity, cultural exposure and economic connectedness as seen from Europe. Qatar, Bahrain, Saudi Arabia, Oman, United Arab Emirates are all cautious because they tend to focus on oil. On the dimension of global commons vs. individual interests, Saudi-dominated Gulf Cooperation Council member states and massive oil producers and exporters such as Saudi Arabia, Qatar, United Arab Emirates, Oman, and Bahrain exhibit their individual interests more strongly whereas most of the Middle East and North African Arab states are exposed to all the vicissitudes of the world and stick to individual interests. On the dimension of aspirational bonding vs. mutual binding, those states leaning to aspirational bonding strategy are Iran, Turkey, Morocco, Algeria, Libya, Yemen, Bahrain, Lebanon, United Arab Emirates, Oman, Afghanistan, Qatar, Iraq, Kuwait, and Saudi Arabia whereas those leaning moderately to mutual binding strategy are Egypt, Tunisia, Jordan and Syria, i.e., those states historically closer to Europe (Figs. 4.5 and 4.6).

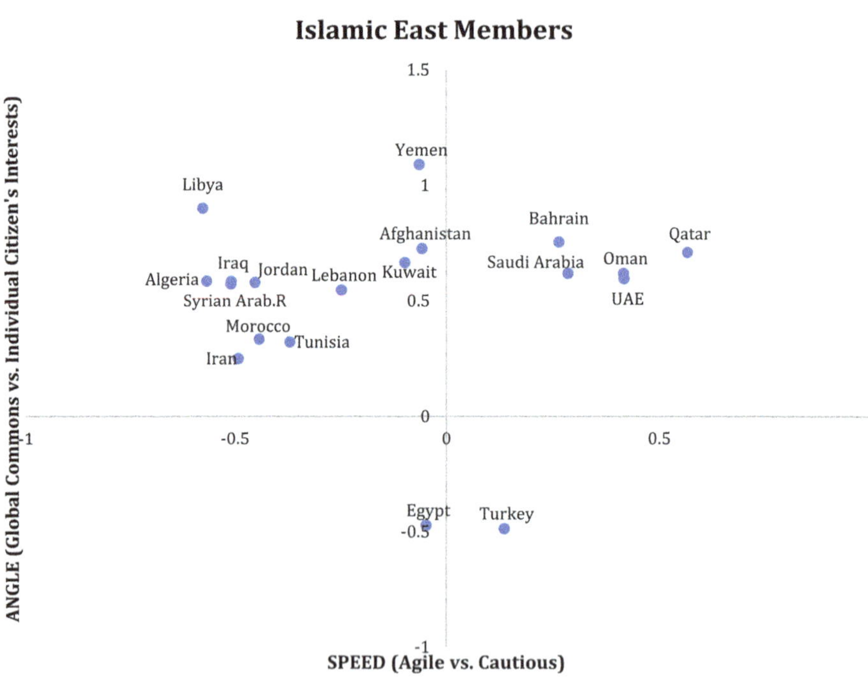

Fig. 4.5 Locations of Islamic East countries on SPEED and ANGLE dimensions

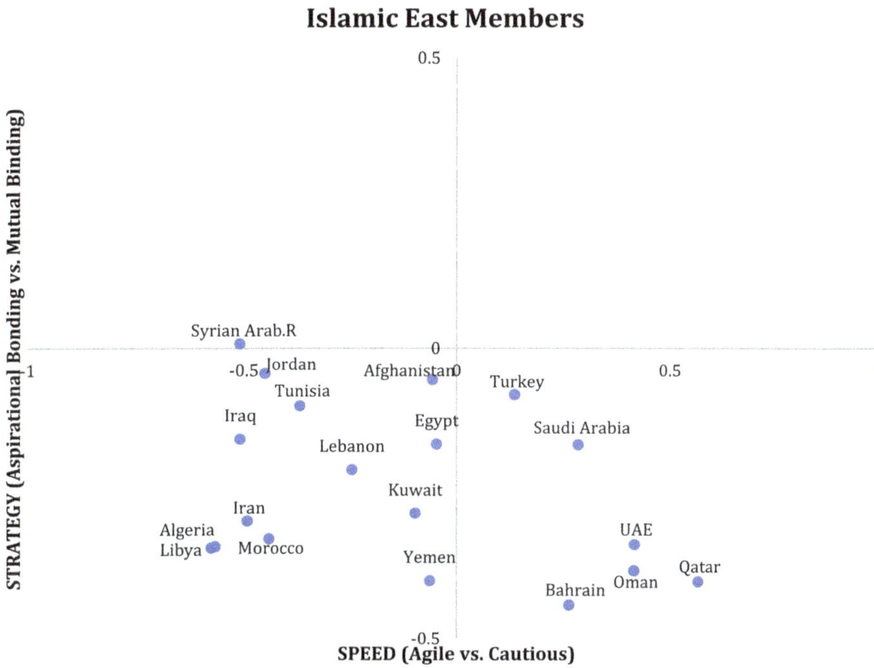

Fig. 4.6 Locations of Islamic East countries on SPEED and STRATEGY dimensions

4.5 Location of Orthodox East Members

Orthodox East consists of three broad influences: Russian-Ukrainian Orthodox, Byzantine-Greek Orthodox, and former Soviet Central Asia. In terms of speed, almost all states are cautious in their legislative behavior. At least until the fall of the Berlin Wall, Orthodox East members were more or less felt constrained in global legislative behavior. Even thereafter other factors than the Cold War have been held sway. Russia, Romania and Bulgaria are three outliers in the direction of independence. In terms of angle, division is demarcated between Europe and Asia. Europe uses more global commons angle whereas Asia uses more individual interests angle. In terms of strategy, Europe adopts mutual binding strategy. Europe here includes Russia, Bulgaria, Romania, Belarus, Ukraine, Serbia, North Macedonia, and Azerbaijan. Central Asians, that is, Kazakhstan, Turkmenistan, Armenia, Georgia, Tajikistan, Uzbekistan, and Kyrgyzstan are located in the aspirational bonding strategy. They are characterized by caution, global commons angle, and aspirational bonding strategy (Figs. 4.7 and 4.8).

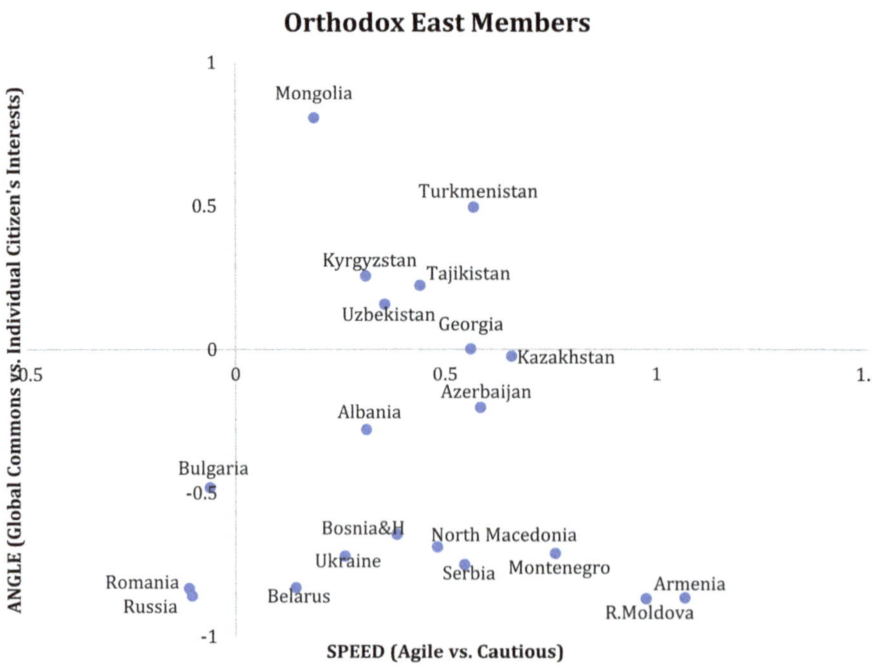

Fig. 4.7 Locations of Orthodox East countries on SPEED and ANGLE dimensions

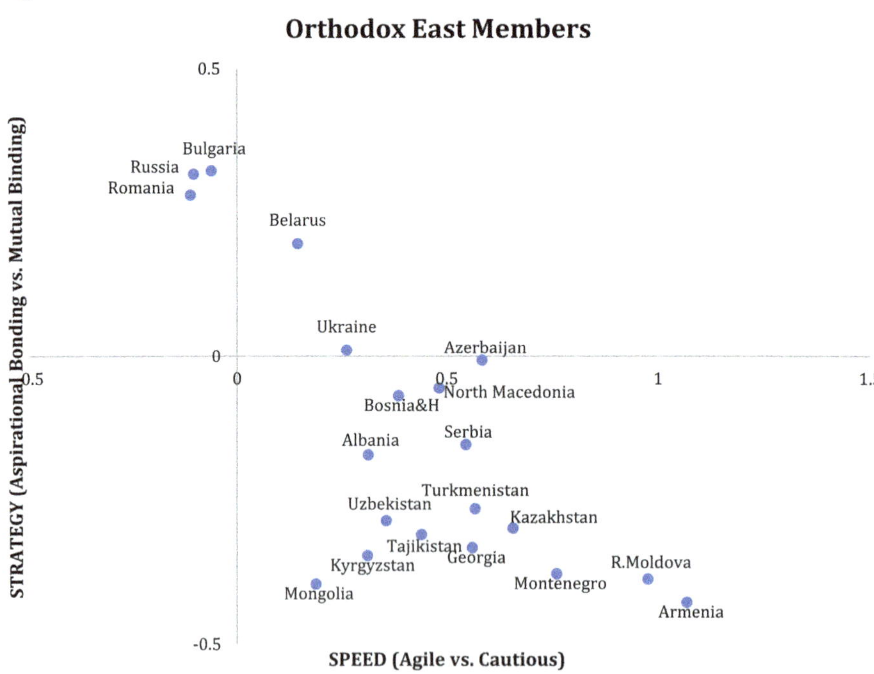

Fig. 4.8 Locations of Orthodox East countries on SPEED and STRATEGY dimensions

4.6 Location of Sub-Saharan Africa Members

On the speed dimension of agile vs. cautious, those Western-Central African states such as Democratic Republic of Congo, Sierra Leone, Senegal, Malawi, and Ghana lean to being agile whereas South Sudan, Eritrea, Guinea-Bissau, Namibia, South Africa, Benin, and Liberia are cautious. Whether it is due primarily to domestic dictatorship or external vulnerability or something else is not easy to tell. South Sudan, Eritrea, and Somalia registering most strongly individual interests because of extreme instability. South Africa, Liberia, Nigeria, and Ghana, all the four English-speaking and with close ties with Britain or the United States. On the aspirational bonding vs. mutual binding dimension, those leaning to aspirational bonding seem to include those states that are authoritarian-prone, sharing strong regional identity such as Zimbabwe, Eritrea, Angola, Democratic Republic of Congo, Central African Republic, Rwanda, Congo, and Mozambique whereas those leaning to mutual bonding include Ghana, Kenya, Senegal, Ethiopia, Nigeria, Tanzania, and Burkina Faso—all of which are geographically focused in western coastal Africa and eastern coastal Africa (Figs. 4.9 and 4.10).

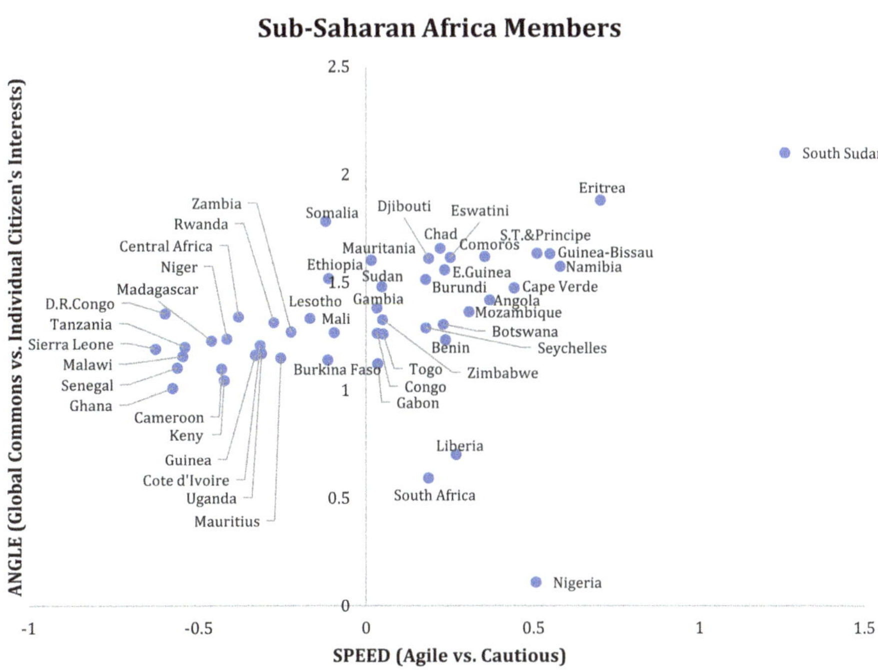

Fig. 4.9 Locations of Sub-Saharan Africa countries on SPEED and ANGLE dimensions

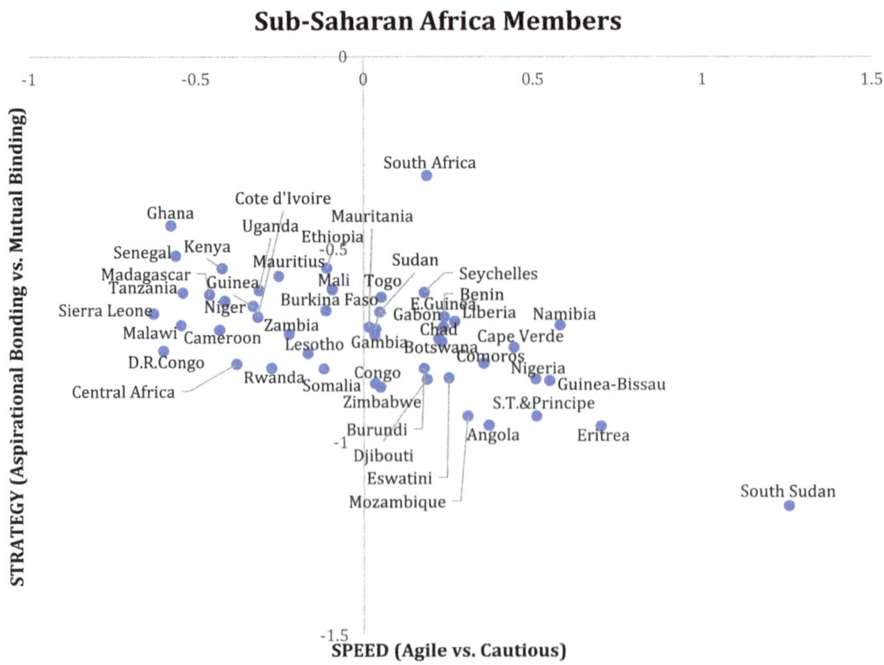

Fig. 4.10 Locations of Sub-Saharan Africa countries on SPEED and STRATEGY dimensions

4.7 Location of Latin America Members

On the speed dimension, agile vs. cautious, being agile include Haiti, Cuba, Barbados, Trinidad and Tobago, Bahamas, Jamaica, Brazil, Mexico, Argentina, Chile, and Venezuela, some of which are very close geographically to the United States and others are major Latin American states, whereas cautious examples include Saint Kitts and Nevis, Belize, Saint Vincent and the Grenadines, Antigua and Barbuda, Guyana, Honduras, El Salvador, some of which are geographically located close to the United States whether it is tiny states in the Caribbean or Central American. On the angle dimension of global commons vs. individual interests, most exhibit strongly individual interests angle. Some major Latin American states such as Cuba, Brazil, Mexico, Argentina, Peru and Chile are moderate among them. Those leaning to individual interests include many small states in the Caribbean and northeastern South America like Guyana, Grenada, Saint Kitts and Nevis, Belize, Suriname, Dominica, Bahamas, Saint Vincent and the Grenadines, and Antigua and Barbuda. On the dimension of strategy, aspirational bonding vs. mutual binding, those leaning to aspirational bonding are a majority in Latin America like many small states in the Caribbean, central Latin America, and northeastern South America and most importantly, major Latin American states such as Colombia, Venezuela, Bolivia, Uruguay, Brazil, Argentina, Chile, Cuba, and Peru. Those moderately leaning to mutual bonding are Panama and Mexico, which are so close to the United States geographically, politically, and economically that unless demanding mutually tying each other they are bound to lose (Figs. 4.11 and 4.12).

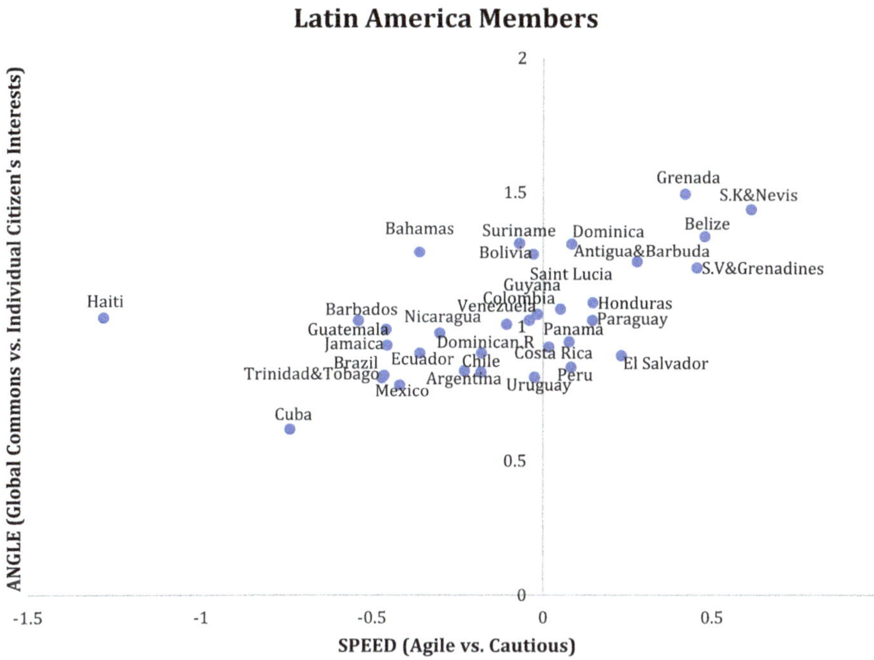

Fig. 4.11 Locations of Latin America countries on SPEED and ANGLE dimensions

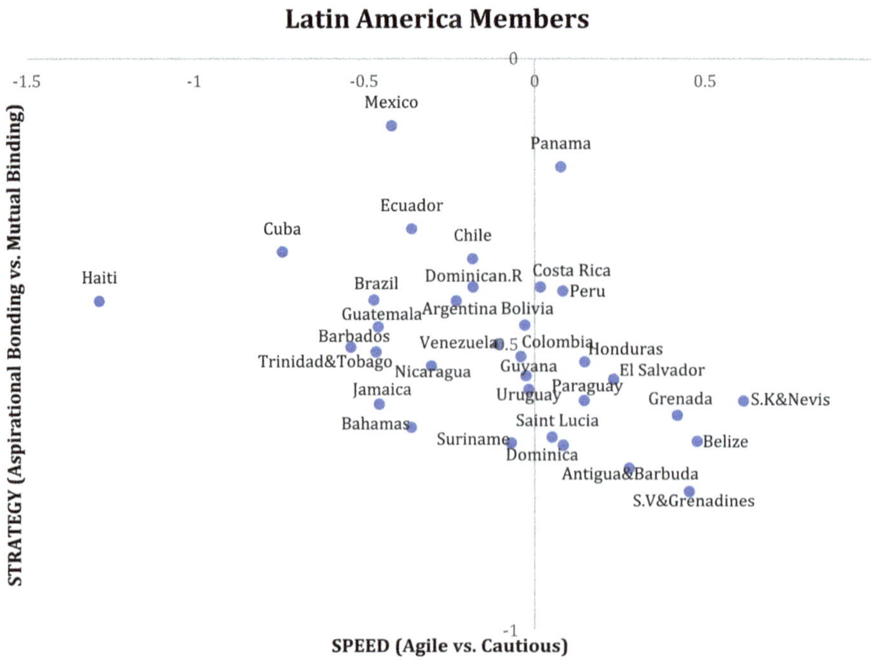

Fig. 4.12 Locations of Latin America countries on SPEED and STRATEGY dimensions

4.8 Location of Old West Members

Old West means those states that originated at the times of the Roman empire, i.e., Italy, Spain, France, Greece, Austria, Belgium, Luxembourg, Portugal, Cyprus, Malta, Israel, Monaco, Liechtenstein, San Marino, and Andorra. On the speed dimension, agile vs. cautious, the majority are agile: Israel, Italy, Austria, France, Spain. Belgium, Greece, Luxembourg. Cyprus, Malta, and Monaco. The rest are cautious: Andorra, San Marino, Liechtenstein, and Portugal. On the angle dimension, global commons vs. individual interests, those leaning to global commons are Luxembourg, Belgium, Italy, France, Austria, Spain, and Greece whereas the sticking to individual interests are Monaco, Israel, Malta, Liechtenstein, San Marino, Andorra, and Portugal. On the strategy dimension, aspirational bonding vs. mutual binding, those sticking to mutual binding are those members of the core European Union, France, Italy, Austria, Belgium, Spain, and Luxembourg, whereas those members moderately leaning to aspirational bonding are Greece, Monaco, Liechtenstein, Cyprus, Malta, San Marino, and Andorra (Figs. 4.13 and 4.14).

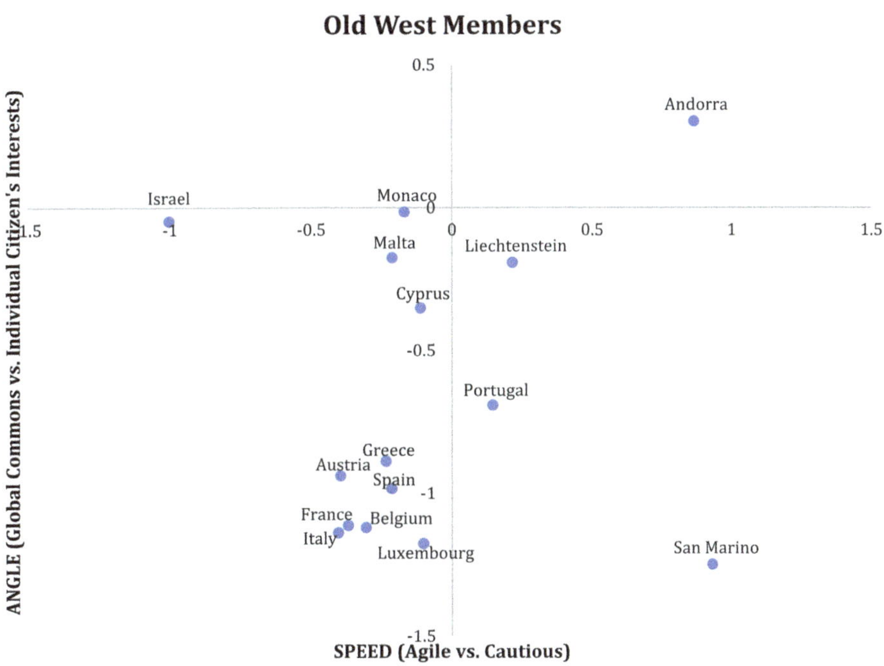

Fig. 4.13 Locations of Old West countries on SPEED and ANGLE dimensions

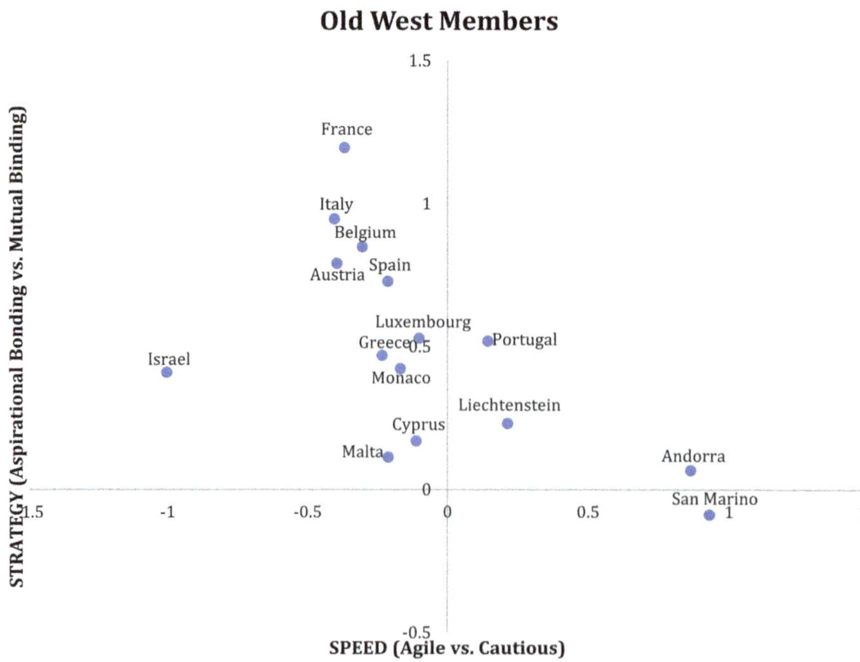

Fig. 4.14 Locations of Old West countries on SPEED and STRATEGY dimensions

4.9 Location of New West Members

New West means the white settler states outside Europe and their newly born small states in the Pacific: the United States, Australia, New Zealand, Canada, Fiji, Tonga, Papua New Guinea, Solomon Islands, Vanuatu, Samoa, Micronesia, Kiribati, Tuvalu, Nauru, Marshall Islands, and Palau. For the speed dimension of being agile vs. cautious, New Zealand, Australia, the United States, and Canada belong to the agile group whereas the rest belong to the cautious group. On the angle dimension of global commons vs. individual interests, those learning to global commons are New Zealand, Australia, and the United States whereas the rest including Canada belong to those moderately learning to individual interests group. On the strategy dimension of aspirational bonding vs. mutual binding, all exhibit aspirational bonding strategy: Canada, the United States, New Zealand, Australia, Palau, Micronesia, Samoa, Marshall Islands, Nauru, Solomon Islands, Papua New Guinea, Tonga, Vanuatu, Kiribati, and Tuvalu (Figs. 4.15 and 4.16).

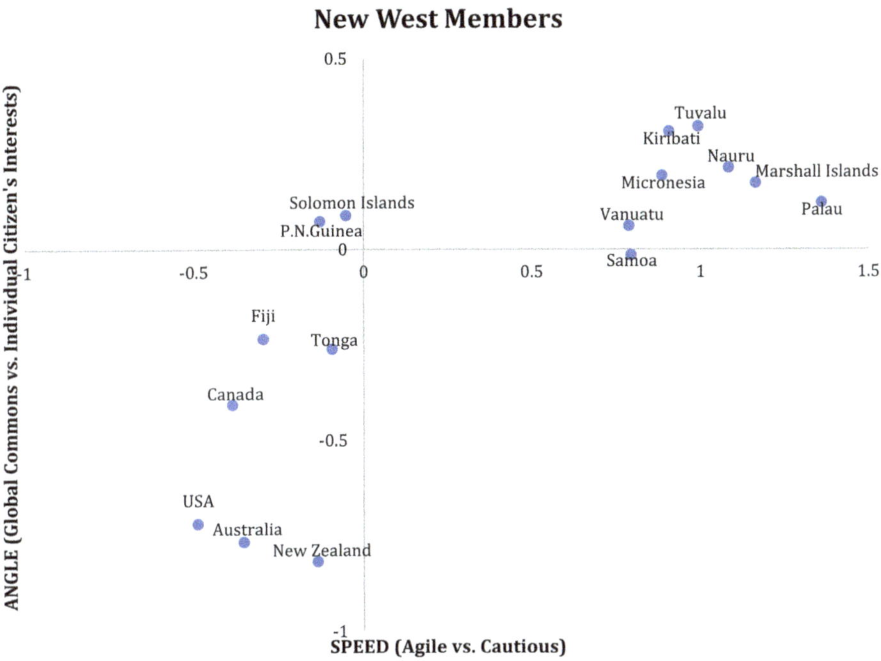

Fig. 4.15 Locations of New West countries on SPEED and ANGLE dimensions

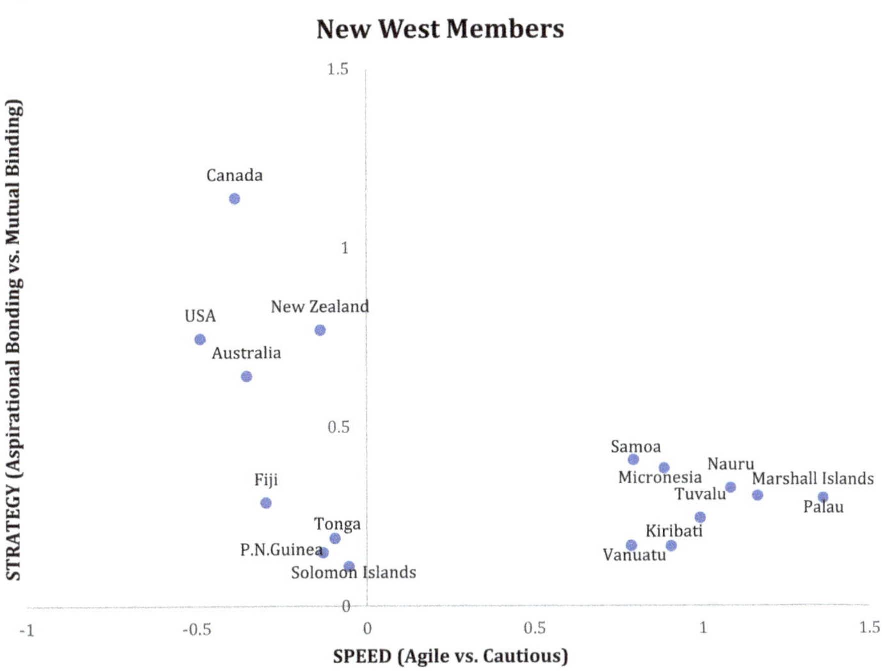

Fig. 4.16 Locations of New West countries on SPEED and STRATEGY dimensions

4.10 Location of Reformed West Members

Reformed West means those states whose state foundations are found in the Reformation: Germany, the Netherlands, the United Kingdom, Norway, Sweden, Finland, Switzerland, Denmark, Ireland, and Iceland. On the speed dimension of agile vs. cautious, Denmark, Ireland, Sweden and the United Kingdom are agile whereas Switzerland and Iceland are cautious. In between lie such states as Germany, Finland, Norway, and the Netherlands. On the angle dimension of global commons vs. individual interests, most states exhibit solid global commons whereas Iceland and Switzerland stick to individual interests. On the strategy dimension, aspirational bonding vs. mutual binding, all exhibit aspirational bonding (Figs. 4.17 and 4.18).

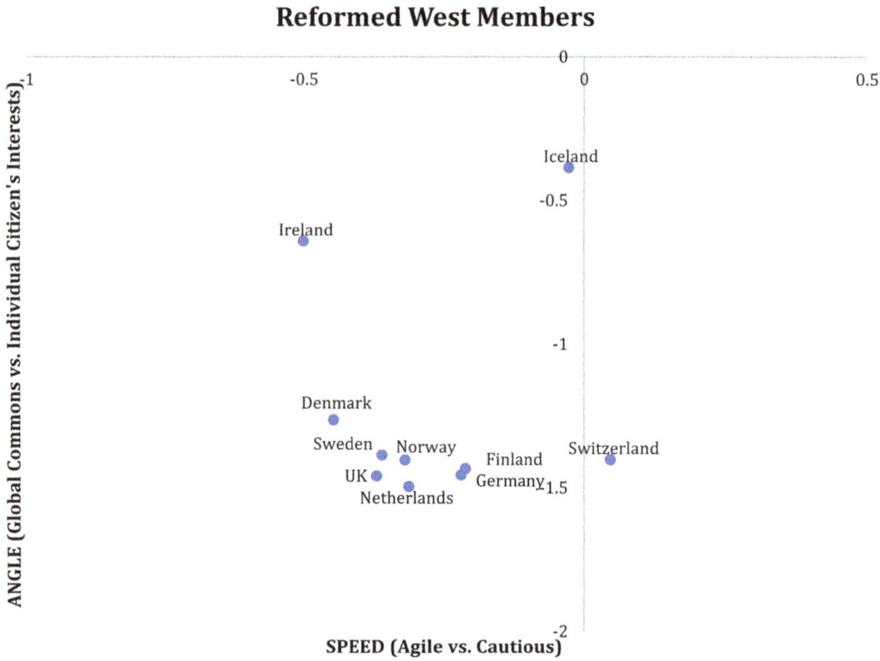

Fig. 4.17 Locations of Reformed West countries on SPEED and ANGLE dimensions

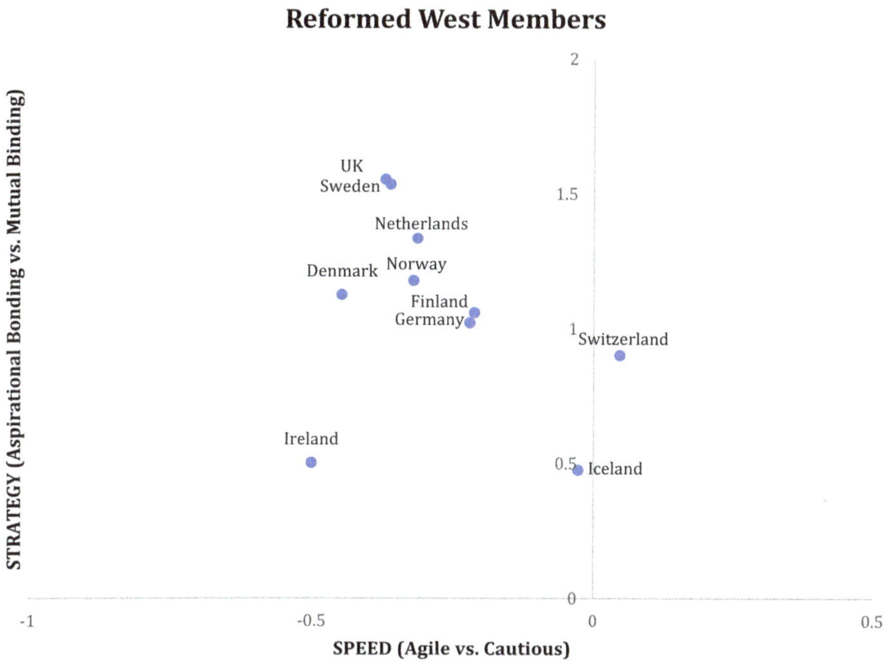

Fig. 4.18 Locations of Reformed West countries on SPEED and STRATEGY dimensions

4.11 Location of Returned West Members

Returned West means those states coming back to the West from the East after the end of the Cold War: Hungary, Poland, Czech Republic, Slovakia, Croatia, Latvia, Estonia, and Lithuania. On the speed dimension of being agile vs. cautious, Hungary and Poland act fast whereas Latvia, Estonia, Lithuania, Croatia, and Slovenia move slowly. In between them are the Czech Republic and Slovakia. Those in between seem to recognize the forces both from Germany and Russia evenly and strongly. On the angle dimension of global commons vs. individual interests, all exhibit individual interests angle: Hungary, Poland, Estonia, Latvia, Lithuania, the Czech Republic, Slovakia, Croatia, and Slovenia. On the dimension of strategy, aspirational bonding vs. mutual binding, Lithuania is the only state leaning to mutual binding. The rest exhibit all aspirational bonding strategy. The balance between the European Union member and the former Soviet bloc member is not sometimes easy to keep (Figs. 4.19 and 4.20).

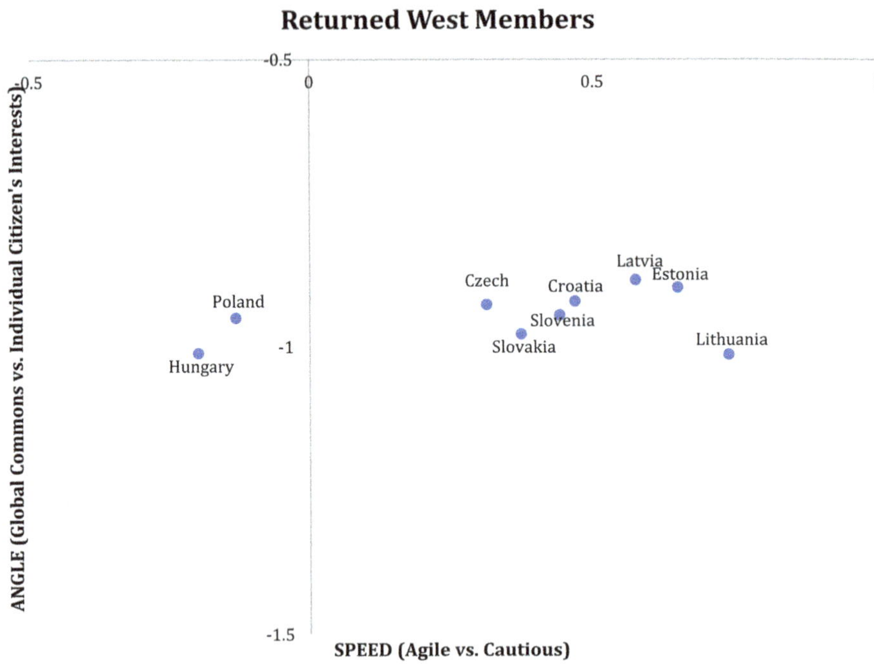

Fig. 4.19 Locations of Returned West countries on SPEED and ANGLE dimensions

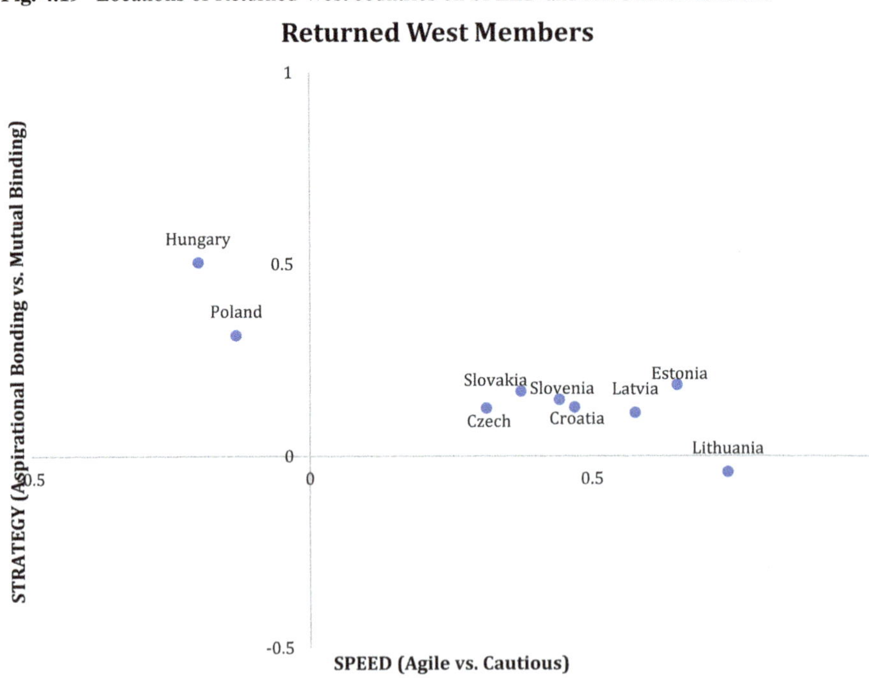

Fig. 4.20 Locations of Returned West countries on SPEED and STRATEGY dimensions

References

Baek, Jieun. 2013. *North Korea's Hidden Revolution: How the Information Underground Is Transforming a Closed Society*. Cambridge, MA: Harvard University Press.

Lamy, Pascal. 2005. "Beikoku daitoryo sengo" (After the U.S. Presidential Election), *Mainichi Shimbun*, 20 November.

Milanovic, Branko. 2019. *Capitalism, Alone: The Future of the System That Rules the World*. Cambridge, MA: Harvard University Press.

Thayer, Carlyle. 1989. *War by Other Means: National Liberation and Revolution in Viet-Nam, 1954–60*, Sydney, London, and Boston: Allen & Unwin.

Yi, Myung Bak. 2010. "Keizai ryodo wa sekai ichi: Bei-Kan FTA guide ROK daitoryo (ROK'S Economic Territory Is No. 1 in the World: ROK President Says on Occasion of the Agreement of Bilateral Free Trade Between the ROK and the US)". *Nihon Keizai Shimbun*, 8 December 8.

Chapter 5
Global Quasi-Legislative Behavior: Eight Types

Abstract In this chapter all the 193 sovereign states' digitized statecraft is profiled. It is called global quasi-legislative behavior of each sovereign state and reveals that each sovereign state shows a distinctive pattern constrained both by its internal preferences and global preferences. It demonstrates that multilateral treaties themselves are transformative in forcing sovereign states to revise their choice by changing internal preferences like revising their domestic laws and by changing global preferences like alluring some other sovereign states to share such global preferences.

In analyzing the global quasi-legislative behavior of 193 sovereign states, we have used six instrumental variables of sorts:

1. The year of deposit in which a multilateral treaty concerned goes effective and put into the United Nations Depository and those tailored to the International Labor Organization and the World Intellectual Property Organization;
2. The year on which a multilateral treaty joiner concerned obtains a membership in a multilateral treaty concerned;
3. The number of members of a multilateral treaty concerned as of 2019;
4. The treaty participation indicator whereby the metric of a given country concerned will take account of the delayed time of the state's decision by the inverse in the number of year lapsed plus one with the raw index has been the normalized with zero means and one standard variance across the 600 treaties and the 193 sovereign states;
5. The policy domain that a treaty concerned aims to solve a given issue of global governance; and
6. The name of the ten geo-historico-cultural groups by Christian Welzel (2013) in a modified and extended form: (1) Indic East, (2) Islamic East, (3) Latin America, (4) New West, (5) Old West, (6) Orthodox East, (7) Reformed West, (8) Sinic East, (9) Sub-Saharan Africa, and (10) Returned West (see Appendix B).

T. Inoguchi and L. T. Q. Le, *Digitized Statecraft in Multilateral Treaty Participation*, Evidence-Based Approaches to Peace and Conflict Studies 1,
https://doi.org/10.1007/978-981-33-4485-3_5

Table 5.1 Six variables of the factor analysis on multilateral treaties data

Variable	Description
Year of membership [YrMember]	The year when a state ratified a treaty is identified
Year of deposit [YrDeposit]	The year when a treaty is deposited to the relevant international body
Number of current members [CurrentMember]	The number of current member countries of a treaty as of 2019
Treaty participation index [TPI]	A quantitative index to measure how quickly a state participates in a treaty and is calculated based on the number of elapsed years between the promulgation of a treaty and a state's ratification act
Geo-historico-cultural regions [Region]	A country is classified in one of the ten geo-historico-cultural groups by Christian Welzel (2013) in its modified form by the Le/Inoguchi scheme (see Appendix B)
Policy domain [Domain]	The six policy domain categorizations based on the main purpose of a treaty

Why do we use instrumental variables? Because we do not use three kinds of possible alternatives. First, we often do not get hold of decision-makers' accounts of the kinds of key reasons for their decision to "join or not to join" a multilateral treaty concerned. Even if we can get hold of such accounts of a certain number of states, doing so for the 193 states multiplied by the 600 multilateral treaties examined in this book would be difficult. Second, also we do not use experimental variables. The number of the 193 sovereign states multiplied by the 600 multilateral treaties is prohibitive in carrying out experimental designs of relevant actors, factors and backgrounds. Third, having done our literature review of evidence-based works on multilateral treaties since 1945, we have been dissuaded from emulating those works which examine the phenomena with a simple, solid and elegant fashion. There have been no such works to meet our criteria: reasonably comprehensive in coverage, reasonably solid in methodology, and reasonably evidence-based.

To identify the key dimensions of the multilateral treaty participation modes of the 193 sovereign states examined in this book, we have used factor analysis with varimax rotation. The results—initial factors with initial eigenvalues, rotated factors with percentage of variance, rotated component matrix and some other related figures—are as set out in Tables 5.1 and 5.2.

A glance at rotated component matrix enables us to confirm the basic congruence with the results of our previous book (Inoguchi and Le 2019) in which the number of multilateral treaties examined was 120 key and most important ones. That is, the first dimension is that of speed with the agile vs. caution differences is deemed the most important factor explaining 28 percent of rotated variance; those components most contributing to the first dimension are year of deposit and year of membership; the second dimension is that of angle with the difference between global commons vs. individual interests; the third dimension is that of strategy with the difference

Table 5.2 Factor analysis using principal component analysis with varimax rotation and Kaiser normalization: Rotated component matrix

	Component		
	1	2	3
Year of deposit	.904		
Year of membership	.923		
Number of current members		.804	
Treaty participation index			.943
Geo-historico-cultural regions		.513	−.376
Policy domain		−.777	

between aspirational bonding vs. mutual trust. Those components most contributing to the third dimension are number of current members, geo-historico-cultural regions. Policy domain diverges from the book results where the 120 multilateral treaties are examined. Our explanation is as follows: The number of multilateral treaties has increased dramatically in those domains of trade, commerce, and communications in the 1980s and especially in the 1990s and the 2010s before 2008. Those multilateral treaties which have registered an extraordinary increase after the Cold War are the domains of human rights, the environment, intellectual property, peace and disarmament. But the increase in the domain of trade, commerce, and communications has shown almost astronomical by two digit increase. Digitized globalization means the deep penetration into every part and parcel on the earth, face-to-face or group communications, instantaneous transactions for trade, investment, sanctions, and patent acquisitions, and supersonic diffusions of ideas and emotions the world over. The possibility of subdividing the six policy domains came to our mind at one time. But we did not adopt this idea of redividing the original six policy domains of the UN Depository. Because the UN seems to have given up keeping the original scheme of having the six policy domains and categorized each multilateral treaty deposited in UN Depository and some other UN agencies such as the International Labor Organization and the World Intellectual Property Organization. Instead, each new multilateral treaty has been deposited without the main categories. Turning back to the third dimensional component loadings, treaty participation index and regions (10 geo-historico-cultural regions) are congruent with the results when 120 treaties were examined. In sum, our decisions are retrospectively sound given the extraordinary difficulties executing some alternative ideas.

In terms of speed, angle and strategy, global quasi-legislative behavior consists of eight types:

1.	abc	Agile	Global commons	Mutual binding
2.	aBC	Agile	Individual interests	Aspirational bonding
3.	aBc	Agile	Individual interests	Mutual binding
4.	abC	Agile	Global commons	Aspirational bonding
5.	Abc	Cautious	Global commons	Mutual binding

(continued)

(continued)

6.	AbC	Cautious	Global commons	Aspirational bonding
7.	ABc	Cautious	Individual interests	Mutual binding
8.	ABC	Cautious	Individual interests	Aspirational bonding

Some of those states that fit each of the eight types are as follows:

1.	abc	Japan, Indonesia, Iran, Singapore
2.	aBC	Laos, Syria, Jordan, Mexico, Ecuador
3.	aBc	Algeria, Argentina, DR of Congo, Nepal, Nigeria
4.	abC	US, UK, France, Germany, Sweden, Netherlands, Thailand, Philippines, China, Israel, India
5.	Abc	Albania, Georgia, Kazakhstan, Kyrgyzstan, Uzbekistan, Turkey
6.	AbC	Republic of Korea, Portugal, Lithuania, Estonia, Czech Republic, Croatia
7.	ABc	Bahrain, DPR Korea, Qatar, Saudi Arabia, Oman, South Africa
8.	ABC	Bangladesh, Bhutan, Maldives, Panama

Those multilateral treaties we examine have evolved in the Cold War period (1945–1989) and the post-Cold War period (1989–2019) with the key division between capitalism and communism in the first period and with the key division in the latter between the developed North and the developing South. With the fall of the Berlin Wall it looked that democracy won over communism. Francis Fukuyama (1992) propounded that democracy is the only game in town. Communism in Europe disappeared. Elsewhere communism dies hard in China and North Korea and elsewhere such as Vietnam, Cuba, and Laos. However, numerically speaking, if what Milanovic (2019) calls political capitalism is included in capitalism, there is "capitalism, alone." In other words, the East–West confrontation ceased in the world more or less. What has become a key division seems the stalled developed North (or OECD club) and the emerging developing South. Roughly speaking the developed North amounts to 44 states whereas the developing South amounts to 149. If we look back to the immediate postwar period, the developed North kept cohesion vis-à-vis the Soviet bloc. Most of the developed North were battered by wars in the former half of the twentieth century. Yet its nations learned the lesson of the division among themselves. Consequently their organizing efforts since 1945 have been termed the liberal world order. The so-called the OECD club did not expand much. It used to have only 25–30 members, mostly on either side of the Atlantic Ocean. In contrast the developing South has kept expanding numerically as well. The United Nations Organization, born of the lesson of the League of Nations in the pre-1945 period, ardently wanted to be a universal organization comprising former colonies and newly independent states as well. They have grown by leaps and bounds. The architect designer of the United Nations Headquarters along the Hudson River in New York envisaged the building accommodating some 50 states. But the growth of newly independent states has been staggering. In the 1950s and 1960s those in Asia, in the 1960s and 1970s in

Africa and the Middle East, in the 1970s and 1980s in those southern Pacific, those in the Caribbean, and those in the former Soviet Union members in Central Asia and the Caucasus have become independent. As of 2020, the number of United Nations members is 193.

Here let us briefly examine the kinds of tasks multilateral treaties deal with in order to see the staggering increase in number of the emerging developing South as well as in the developed and stalled North in the United Nations. Those newly sovereign states must strive to attain the key ingredients as a sovereign state. They include:

1. Human rights and dignity, liberating slaves, women, non-whites, those with all kinds of handicaps, and reducing all kinds of inequalities and discriminations;
2. Peace and disarmament, liberating all mankind from war, reducing all kinds of instruments of terminating and injuring people;
3. Trade, commerce, and communications, improving the opportunities of trade and commerce so that people's welfare is increased, upgrading the instruments of communications whereby the opportunities of getting and emitting information increases for keeping up the bursting of knowledge;
4. The environment, reducing the deterioration of living environments on the Earth, keeping energy consumption safe for daily life, and developing human space in sync with other species and in harmony under changing geological, meteorological, and planetary conditions;
5. Intellectual property, encouraging sharing discovery of new scientific laws, inventing useful ways of human living, innovating efficient and effective ways of keeping society abreast of social change, discouraging new discovery, invention, and innovation to be used without showing minimum respect for risk-taking courage and costs; and
6. Labor and health, improving working conditions in terms of hours per day, per week, per year, keeping health—physical, mental, and societal—in good conditions, upgrading quality of life and well-being.

The list is endless. Yet the purpose of this brief examination is to remind one of the facts that those problems are, as Kofi Annan says, issues without passports, i.e., not only narrowly national solutions but also broadly global solutions must be found and implemented. For the developing South, human rights and dignity comes first for a sovereign state and its citizen to feel that it is a sovereign state and a citizen. In a similar vein, peace and disarmament should be a starting point for many developing South since with virtually endless wars and strife at home and abroad nothing can be done. UN peacekeeping and building efforts are often essential. Labor and health are essential to human beings emancipated from yokes of all kinds, which national independence aims at achieving step by step not only formally but substantively to survive and sustain as a sovereign state and as a citizen; trade, commerce, and communications are like nerves and bloods and thus indispensable. Since the earth's singularity is information and knowledge, whereby human beings can deteriorate or improve with virtually endless knowledge of the environmental conditions of human species, as contrasted to stars whose singularity is matter and to blackholes whose singularity is energy. Intellectual property can both sustain vigorous human society by encouraging the innovation or aggravate its stagnation and deterioration by virtually monopolizing the fruits of invention and innovation. Multilateral treaties as a bundle of quasi-social contracts play an essential role in initiating and implementing such tasks; however, it is occasionally done only modestly or insufficiently or inappropriately.

In carrying out those tasks, two things become increasingly essential:

1. Setting measurements common and universal: sticking national measurement schemes may hinder efficiency across states (Seaman 2020) and
2. Cooperation among member states requires well-thought out smart design and pragmatically rational dispute settlement rules (Koremenos 2016). We do not enter into these two because they are a little too far from the main subject of this volume. But it is very important to be aware of these two things because they penetrate all the six policy domains. One example each would be sufficient here. China has become very keen on the subject given two backgrounds:

    a. China's thirty decade-long two-digit economic growth and
    b. China's increasing influence in trade with, investment in, aid to some developing and stagnant South and some developed and stalled North countries especially in Africa, Latin America, Asia, Europe, and the southern Pacific and the Caribbean.

To return to the main subject, the rebalancing between the developed North and the developing South has been steadily favorable to the latter. The sheer number of 44 vis-à-vis 149 for three decades, given the majority decision rule for UN agencies' collective decision except the UN Security Council in which five powers (the US, the UK, France, Russia, and China) possess and sometimes exercise vetoes. The picture of the three decades' evolution of the developing South and the developed North is schematized as follows: the developed North has been more or less stagnant at a high income level whereas the developing South has registered more or less strident economic development from the very low or lower levels with some poverty-stricken populations remaining stuck to the lowest strata. Of the eight types of sovereign state's multilateral treatment participation the developed North states take the type of abC, agile, global commons and aspirational bonding. Under Pax Americana whether it is under Donald Trump or not, American allies seem to adopt the strategy of C in big capital, i.e., aspirational bonding among US allies and friends as if to restrain US demands to them to pay higher duties of alliance and free market beyond what they regard the reasonable degree of America-firstism. The strategy of the developing South seems to mean more of rejecting what they regard unreasonably high duties expected of the developing South. The abc type in the developing South appears in Indonesia, Iran and Singapore. The abc type in the developed North appears in Japan. Japan's strategy seems to mean sticking to the strategy of mutual binding so that it can keep binding with non-US members of the OECD club like trying to reduce those tariff rates of the free trade agreement with the UK after the exit from the EU and of the free trade agreement with the EU. Vis-à-vis the US, Japan can pay some of the cost-sharing with the US in different forms like

a. The government asking Toyota to build more automobile factories in the US, or
b. The government paying less by comparing the US-demanded tariff rate of beef under a proposed bilateral free trade agreement with the US and the 11-country Pacific Partnership agreement after the US withdrew after promulgation.

In short, the developed North's speed is more or less cautious, the angle is more or less individual interests, and the strategy is mostly aspirational bonding except Japan.

The developing South's speed is cautious. Its angle is individual interests. Its strategy is predominantly aspirational bonding. A little surprisingly, the digital statecrafts of the developed and stalled North and the developing and stagnant South are getting similar when compared as the two groups under globalization. The divisions both within the North and within the South have grown very divergent. Yet those adopt the strategy of mutual binding is due to different reasons.

To sum up, the eight types of global legislative behavior and two-three representative sovereign states are indicated here.

Japan, Indonesia, Iran	abc
Mexico, Jordan, Laos	aBC
Nigeria, Argentina, Nepal	aBc
US, Germany, China, India	abC
Kazakhstan, Turkey	Abc
South Korea, Portugal	AbC
Saudi Arabia, North Korea	ABc
Bangladesh, Bhutan	ABC

References

Fukuyama, Francis. 1992. *The End of History and the Last Man*. London: Penguin.

Inoguchi, Takashi, and Lien Thi Quynh Le. 2019. *The Development of Global Legislative Politics: Rousseau and Locke Writ Global*. Singapore: Springer Nature.

Koremenos, Barbara. 2016. *The Continent of International Law: Explaining Agreement Design*. Cambridge: Cambridge University Press.

Milanovic, Branko. 2019. *Capitalism, Alone: The Future of the System That Rules the World*. Cambridge, MA: Harvard University Press.

Seaman, John. 2020. "China and the New Geopolitics of Technical Standardization," *Notes de l'Ifri*, Ifri (Institut français des relations internationals), January 2020.

Welzel, Christian. 2013. *Freedom Rising: Human Empowerment and the Quest for Emancipation*. New York: Cambridge University Press.

Part III
Sinic Calculi of Statecraft

Abstract

In Part III we focus on Sinic East in multilateral treaty participation. Sinic East here means the People's Republic of China, Japan, the Republic of Korea, the Democratic People's Republic of Korea, and the Socialist Republic of Vietnam. Chapter 6 provides the adaptation by Sinic East to multilateral treaties in the broader context of rebalancing between East and West (Milanovic 2019). In Sections 6.3 and 6.4, we analyze each state's societal preferences about people's daily satisfaction about life domains in conjunction with global quasi-legislative behavior. Chapter 7 examines Sinic East's changing priorities of six policy domains: peace, human rights, trade, commerce, and communications, the environment, intellectual property, labor and health. Chapter 8 shows how multilateral treaty participation triggers an upward leap in Sinic East, country by country and regional dynamics. Chapter 9 examines both the typology of global quasi-legislative behavior and the typology of societies in the whole Asia, i.e., East Asia, Southeast Asia, South Asia and Central Asia (Inoguchi 2019), showing that the two typologies, global quasi-legislative behavior and societies, are connected in each own way.

Reference

Milanovic, Branko. 2019. *Capitalism Alone: The Future of the System That Rules the World*. Cambridge, MA: Harvard University Press.

Chapter 6
Adaptation to Multilateral Treaties

Abstract This chapters and 7–9 focus on Sinic East's global quasi-legislative behavior. Sinic East means China, Japan, South Korea, North Korea, and Vietnam. Taiwan and Hong Kong are not members of the United Nations, and thus not examined in this volume. This chapter examines Sinic East's adaptation to multilateral treaties since 1945. A sub-chapter examines daily life satisfaction in each of the four Sinic East societies and another focuses on the preference for global or national solutions to "problems without passports" (Annan 2002).

6.1 The East Learn from the West in Multilateral Treaties

The history of the adaptation of the Sinic East to multilateral treaties is very interesting, not only for its similarity but also for its immense diversity (for example, the divergence between "obstinate" China sticking to its traditional order and "shameless" Japan flexibly adapting to the Western order; cf. Suzuki 2009). In this chapter, similarities are highlighted. But diversities are also noted. For the purposes of this book, the Sinic East consists of the People's Republic of China, the Socialist Republic of Vietnam, Japan, the Republic of Korea, and the Democratic People's Republic of Korea. Neither the Republic of China (Taiwan) nor Hong Kong is included for our investigation. Taiwan is not a member of the United Nations since 1972, Hong Kong has been a special administrative region of the People's Republic of China since 1997.

First of all, one notices that the Sinic East's behavior in multilateral treaties participation is active in comparison to other regional groups in terms of the number of multilateral treaties joined by sovereign states in each of the ten regional groups. Controlled by the number of states in each of the ten regional groups and the number of years during which it is a member of the United Nations, the number of multilateral treaties they join is comparable to that of the Reformed West (northwestern Europe). In terms of the number of multilateral treaties, the Reformed West captures the top seven, including the Netherlands (436), Germany (403), and Sweden (401). Reformed West states or their precursors developed after the Reformation led by Martin Luther

T. Inoguchi and L. T. Q. Le, *Digitized Statecraft in Multilateral Treaty Participation*, Evidence-Based Approaches to Peace and Conflict Studies 1,
https://doi.org/10.1007/978-981-33-4485-3_6

and others. Sinic East is noted by secular societies more or less in comparison to most other geo-historico-cultural groups. Sinic East societies are more or less fairly meritocratic. Rather than developing in Europe 200-odd years ago (Young 2017), they trace their origins to 2,000 years ago when ancient Chinese bureaucracy first invented institutions on meritocratic recruitment (Woodside 2006). In terms of the number of multilateral treaties they join, they register 243 (Japan), 189 (Republic of Korea), 166 (China), 129 (Vietnam), and 74 (Democratic People's Republic of Korea). Given their years of UN membership, these countries' figures are more like that of the United States, which registers 133 during the three quarters of a century.

Second, the number of diplomatic representations of Sinic East countries in terms of total posts (embassies/high commissions, consulates/consulates-general, permanent missions and other representations) is formidable (Lowy Diplomacy Index 2019). Of all the 61 countries under the umbrellas of G20, OECD, and/or Asia, Sinic East represents itself very highly. It is 276 for China, surpassing the US figure by three for the first time in 2019. It is 247 for Japan, next to France, registering 267 and surpassing the Russian Federation registering 242. Other Sinic East countries register 183 for the Republic of Korea, (107 for Taiwan), 96 for Vietnam, and 52 for Democratic People's Republic of Korea.

Third, Sinic East includes those states whose economic dynamism in terms of the size of Gross Domestic Product in the latter half of the last century and the first quarter of the twenty-first century has been the core driving force of what is called the Rebalancing between the West and the East (Milanovic 2019, p. 212). The idea comes from the comparison of the size of GDP of China over GDP of England (1) in the late 18th and early nineteenth century, (2) the early twentieth century, and (3) the early twenty-first century. It traces the large China vis-à-vis England at (1), say, when King George V sent his emissary to Emperor Jianlong, the nadir of China vis-à-vis England at (2), say, the Opium war (1841) when China was defeated by England, and the rebalance of China vis-à-vis England at (3), say, in the fourth quarter of the last century through the first quarter of the twenty-first century. Sinic East in the early twenty-first century comprises this resurgent China. The global rebalancing of the "Rest" (as distinguished from the West) has been following the lead of the Sinic East.

Fourth, what is called "East Asian Peace" has been the core of stability and prosperity of broader East Asia and Southeast Asia during the period between 1979 and 2019 (Kivimaki 2012). After Asia's two big wars—the Korean War of 1950–1953 (Cumings 1981, 1990) and the Vietnam War of 1965–1975, and the Chinese military intervention in Vietnam of 1978–1979 (Inoguchi 1980), this East Asian peace has accelerated and accommodated this further rebalancing.

Fifth, in the twentieth century, world wars were waged, internal strifes took place, and national independence was achieved in the Sinic East at long last. The last century was a tumultuous era for the Sinic East. A number of multilateral treaties were succeeded by a new regime replacing an ancient regime. The Republic of China was succeeded by the People's Republic of China in 1972. The Republic of Vietnam was succeeded by the Socialist Republic of Vietnam in 1975. When the United Nations came into being in 1945, its spirit was full of welcoming and accommodating newly independent nations and championed the spirit of aspirational bonding among all the members, especially newly independent nations. Here are some tricky points. Both capitalist and communist regimes joined the United Nations in 1945 and shortly thereafter. The ratio of communist and capitalist regimes was 15 and 40–50 in the 1950s respectively. East–West confrontation disappeared formally in 1989–1991 in Europe. In the 1950s onward many newly independent states joined the United Nations. By 2019 the membership figures of the developing South and the developed North had become something like 149 and 44 respectively. If the UN Security Council is semi-monopolized by the five permanent members (the United States, the United Kingdom, France, Russia, China) because of its veto power, other UN councils, such as the Human Rights Council and the Social and Economic Council, have been semi-dominated by the developing South. Unlike the Security Council, these councils and some specialized agencies make it a rule of "one country – one vote" with a majority decision. While the Security Council has been frozen with respect to the collective security provision after the Korean War of 1950–1953, replaced by economic sanctions provision (Biersteker et al. 2016; Hufbauer et al. 2007; Wallensteen and Staibano 2005), the Human Rights Council and the Social and Economic Council deal with many other issues affecting the developing South in various directions without vocal council members often from the developed North.

6.2 History of Sinic East's Adaptation to Multilateral Treaties

6.2.1 People's Republic of China

China has gone through its dynamic external policy metamorphosis since 1949. First, it is the "policy of leaning to one side," that is, the USSR-led communist line, which coincided with anti-US policy. It peaked when China waged war in Korea against the US. Second, the policy of leaning to the Third World through sharing compassion of national independence and extending help thereto. It coincided with the Chinese domestic policy of self-reliance. Third, the policy of confronting the revisionist line, namely the anti-Soviet line. It coincided the gradual rapprochement of China with the US. Fourth has been the policy of assisting the Third World with trade, investment, and technical assistance symbolized by "One Belt, One Road" policy, whereby the Chinese surplus capacity of infrastructure construction through state-owned-enterprises with money and labor surplus (The Economist 2020). It coincided with the tariff and technology disputes with the US. Branko Milanovic (2019) is a world-famous economist known for his insight into various forms of capitalism, especially China's political capitalism. Traditionally and even today, he observes that China is aloof and alone, thinking that its long history and its high culture do not lead them to think about assiduously seeking friends near and afar. In the 1940s and 1950s Mao Zedong trusted neither Joseph Stalin nor Kim Il Sung. In the 1950s and in the 1960s China had some distance from the non-alignment movement led by Nehru, Tito, Nasser, and Sukarno. Before the fall of the Berlin Wall, Albania was the only ally of China. Since its fall, the Democratic People's Republic of Korea has been the only ally of China, if the word is justified. China's "One Belt, One Road" policy has been sometimes characterized by China's own industrial policy with domestic surpluses in money and labor used for infrastructure constructing in and destined for many countries in Africa, the Middle East, Latin America, Europe, and Central Asia with Khorgas on the Chinese–Kazakh border, which houses the International Center for Border Cooperation. China's international policy seems to be designed deliberately to invigorate inter-firm competition in technological innovation and productivity against state-owned-firms, which tend to become stagnant. At the same time, it is China's foreign policy of international cooperation assists the economically stalled developed North as well as the developing South (Macaes 2018).

A glance at the calendar of China joining multilateral treaties enables one to identify a few blind pockets when no multilateral treaty interested China: 1950–1953, 1955–1957, 1959–1972, and 1978. All of this was before Deng Xiaoping's dramatic comeback in 1978 (Vogel 2013), Maoist China was isolationist and protectionist under the slogan of *zili gengsheng* (self-reliance or self-sustainment).

Since the People's Republic of China succeeded the Republic of China (Taiwan) in the United Nations in 1972 when the United States normalized its diplomatic relations with it (Kissinger 2012). Yet there are a number of multilateral treaties joined by the Republic of China in both the League of Nations and the United Nations eras, before the declaration of the People's Republic of China in October 1949. There are 17 such treaties the Republic of China joined and succeeded by the People's Republic of China. The policy domains were dominated by labor and health, and human rights. Those on labor and health are mostly about how to deal with narcotic drugs. Those on labor and health include the Constitution of the World Health Organization (1946). One relevant multilateral treaty in the trade, commerce, and communications domain was the General Agreement on Tariffs and Trade (1947). In 1954 the treaty was the Protocol for Limiting and Regulating the Cultivation of the Poppy Plant, the Production of, International and Wholesale Trade in, and Use of Opium. In 1958 it was the Convention on the Nationality of Married Women. Besides the World Health Organization and the General Agreement on Tariffs and Trade, during the civil war period between 1945 and 1949, most pronounced was the opium production and trade. In 1958 when the Maoist gamble of the entire nation was filled up by people's communes not allowing even small-scale privately owned firms spectacularly failed, whereby millions of peasants starved to death in the year and thereafter (MacFarquar and Schoenhas 2008).

6.2.2 Japan

Japan was the only country in the East in its quest for survival in the mid-nineteenth century when the West was seeking to open the ports and the country. Westernization, in the words of Kaoru Inoue, who led the large delegation of investigating the West before the Meiji Restoration of 1868, means: "We must make our empire a European-style empire; make our people a European-style people, create a new, European-style empire in the Orient. Only by doing so can our empire climb to an equal position in terms of treaties with the Occidental states" (quoted by Suzuki 2009, p. 114). Before those unequal treaties in terms of extraterritorial rights and tariff non-autonomy were revised, by 1873 and by 1911 respectively, Japan was most eager to assiduously comply with whatever international treaties joined by Japan. Its consistent policy was carried out more or less before and during the inter-war period between 1894 and 1922 with the foreign policy principle of what Sasaki (2017) calls the exchange of equivalence of interest and legitimacy combined.

First, Japan was one of the four major powers supplying the secretary-generals in the League of Nations (Mimaki 2014). Second, Japan assiduously participated in many of the multilateral treaties: peace (Versailles), peace (Washington), war prohibition (Paris), disarmament (London), and labor (Geneva) (Inoguchi 2018). With the establishment of the United Nations in 1945, Japan along with West Germany was categorized as a sinful country in World War II (Macmillan 2003; Shinohara 2012). West Germany and Japan joined the United Nations later than any of the victorious powers. The United Nations started with all the states that stood on the side of Allied powers led by the United States, the Soviet Union, the United Kingdom, France, China, and all the independent states mostly in Europe and Latin America. The number was some 43 states. All the Asian, Middle Eastern, African, Caribbean, and South Pacific colonies or areas under the League of Nations trusteeship were to achieve national independence subsequently. Asia did it mostly in the 1940s, 1950s, and 1960s. The Middle East did it in the 1950s, 1960s, and 1970s, and African did it in the 1960s, 1970s, and 1980s. The Caribbean did it in the 1960s, 1970s, and 1980s, and the South Pacific in the 1970s, 1980s, and 1990s. The number of United Nations member states grew out of the estimated number of 50 member states by the end of the 1950s, estimated by an architect of the United Nations headquarter buildings on the Hudson: 193 member states as of 2019.

Japan was permitted to join the United Nations in 1955 but it did participate in multilateral treaties even before 1955. Throughout in the 1950s they were mostly in the policy domains of labor and health, measurements and standards, intellectual property, trade, commerce, and communications, and human rights. In 1964, the year of the Tokyo Olympic Games, Japan returned all the debts to the International Bank of Reconstruction and Development. Also, this was the year when Japan became a member of the Organization of Economic Cooperation and Development (OECD). Also, by 1964 Japan joined many multilateral treaties, attached especially to many United Nations special agencies including International Labor

Organization, World Meteorological Organization, International Maritime Organization, International Finance Organization, International Development Organization, Food and Agricultural Organization, International Civil Aviation Organization, United Nations Educational, Scientific and Cultural Organizations, International Monetary Fund, International Bank for Reconstruction and Development, World Health Organization, Universal Postal Union, and International Telecommunication Union.

In the 1970s Japan formed with the other six (the United States, the United Kingdom, France, Germany, Canada, and Italy plus the European Community or later the European Union) what is called the Group of Seven or G7, with the initiative of France under Giscard d'Estaing confronting and coping with the first oil crisis of 1973–1974 with G7 (Putnam and Bayne 1988). The number of multilateral treaties grew by leaps and bounds since the 1970s through 1990s. The need for multilateral treaties to take care of "problems without passports" (Annan 2002) dramatically increased in the last quarter of the last century. After all, of all the member states of the United Nations the number of the developing South has become predominant in number and in influence to a certain extent, vis-à-vis the developed North, given the accommodating spirit of the United Nations Charter. In the United Nations the Security Council with veto-exercising power of P5 (the United States, the Russian Federation, the United Kingdom, France, and China) has been regarded very strong. But with the demise of the Soviet Union bloc confronting the United States bloc with nuclear weapons and with the dramatic decline of wars among sovereign states (Inoguchi and Le 2019, p. xvi; Russett 1993), the Social and Economic Council and the Human Rights Council have gained enormous power voicing the developing South's grievances and dissatisfactions vis-à-vis the developed North in terms of income gaps, poverty alleviation, infectious diseases prevention, development infrastructure building, and racial and religious discriminations. The developing South has been on the ride of "Rebalancing between the West and the East" in the last quarter of the last century led by Sinic East, Indic East and Africa (Milanovic 2019; Gray and Murphy 2015). Japan's legislative behavior type is *abc*, meaning agile in judgment and action, global commons angle, and mutual binding strategy.

6.2.3 Republic of Korea

Korea was colonized by Japan in 1911. Japan's surrender in World War II placed Korea in an ambivalent position in 1945. The Japanese defeat in the war was accelerated by the US' use of atomic bombs at Hiroshima and Nagasaki on 6 and 9 August respectively (Alperovitz 1965; Gallicchio 2020). The United States was vaguely thinking about a collective trusteeship area set up in Korea after the Japanese defeat like the one envisaged about occupied Germany (Kim 2013; Okonogi 2019). However, the atomic bombs not only accelerated the Japanese acceptance of defeat after the Potsdam declaration of Allied powers but also, more seriously from the view of Korea's national independence, the Soviet Union accelerated its use of military advance into the East, notably Kurile, Kamchatka, Manchuria, northern China, all of Korea, and northern Japan, starting on 8 August 1945. The race of military advance of the US and the Soviet Union into Japan and Korea ended up with the division of Korea on the 38 degree line (Cumings 1981; Hasegawa 2006; Okonogi 2019).

The predicament of Korea is that the northern half was occupied by the Soviet Union whereas the southern half was occupied by the United States. In 1948 both the Republic of Korea and the Democratic People's Republic of Korea declared their respective independence amidst chaos, poverty and vehement internal fighting in the divided south and north (Okonogi 2019; Armstrong 2003; Lankov 2013; Suh 1995), then prevailing in Korean society. Amid the nationwide mobilization and contestation of communist and anti-communist forces in the form of an internationalizing quasi-civil war, in June 1950 the Democratic People's Republic of Korea attacked the Republic of Korea to unify Korea by military means (Cumings 1981, 1990). North Korean forces pushed South Korean forces down to the pocket surrounding Busan, a major southern city. Then the United Nations forces landed on Inchon, a port city one-hour tank ride to Seoul, pushed North Korean forces back near the border of the People's Republic of China. Then China's People's Liberation Army intervened to help North Korea and the combined forces of North Korea's People's Army and China's People's Liberation Army and the combined forces of South Korea' Army and the United Nations Armed Forces reached the stalemate around 38 degree latitude line, which became the Armistice Line until today (Whiting 1960). With this Korean War (1950–1953) long frozen thereafter, neither North Korea nor South Korea was a member of the United Nations until 1992, when both became a member simultaneously.

In the Republic of Korea, a vehemently nationalist, anti-Japanese and anti-communist President Synmang Rhee was toppled in 1960 by non-violent student protests. He was succeeded by an interim and incompetent president till 1961 when a bunch of military officers led by Chung Hee Park struck a coup d'etat and took power. Chung Hee Park was a former Japanese Imperial Army officer assigned in Manchukuo, later trained in the United States Armed Forces became a Korean Army officer. His dictatorship brought about economic stability and triggered what was called the miracle of Hangan (Han River), a river flowing in Seoul (Kim and Vogel 2013).

Before the South Korean economic miracle brought about double-digit economic growth in the 1970s, South Korea joined multilateral treaties mostly in the policy domains of labor and health, human rights, and trade, commerce, and communications. Once the Basic Treaty between South Korea and Japan was concluded in 1965 and ratified soon thereafter, South Korea joined multilateral treaties in the policy domain of trade, commerce, and communications like the Agreement establishing the Asian Development Bank (1965) wherefrom South Korea borrowed massive capital for consolidation of infrastructure and manufacturing industry. By 1977 South Korea joined multilateral treaties *en bloc*, including the World Health Organization, International Maritime Organization, World Meteorological Organization, Food and Agricultural Organization, International Civil Aviation Organization, United Nations Educational, Scientific and Cultural Organization, International Monetary

Fund, International Bank for Reconstruction and Development, World Health Organization, and Vienna Convention on Diplomatic Relations. In 1978 South Korea joined the World Intellectual Property Organization and in 1984 it also joined Patent Cooperation Treaty.

With the entry into the United Nations in 1992, South Korea joined many multilateral treaties in such domains as peace and disarmament, intellectual property, human rights, the environment, labor and health. South Korea has registered participating in 123 multilateral treaties till 2019. That means that South Korea joined average 15 treaties per year. The Republic of Korea's legislative behavior type is *AbC*, meaning cautious in judgment and action, individual interest oriented and aspirational bonding oriented.

6.2.4 Democratic People's Republic of Korea

The Democratic People's Republic of Korea was born in 1948 as Kim Il Sung declared its independence in 1948 when the northern half of Korea was occupied by the Soviet Union since 1945 (Suh 1995; Okonogi 2019). In June 1950 it entered into war against the Republic of Korea, the southern half. It looked as if South Korea would fall into the hands of North Korea by the end of 1950. But the United Nations forces commanded by General Douglas MacArthur landed on Inchon, east of Seoul, and moved north upward. The combined forces of the United Nations and South Korea moved close to the border of China near the Yalu or Amnok river. Then the Chinese People's Liberation Army "volunteer forces" moved down to repel the combined forces of the UN and the Republic of Korea. The war continued at the stalemate around the 38 degree latitude since then until 1953, when the armistice was concluded and continued to be frozen for a long time. Thus, the DPRK had been isolated in the world of multilateral treaties for a long period of time. Since 1948 till 1972 the DPRK did not join any multilateral treaties. In 1973 it joined the Constitution of the World Health Organization and in 1974 the World Intellectual Property Organization. These two treaties are basic to the survival of the DPRK. First, large-scale famines have been taking place once a decade on average, especially since the 1970s onward. Since the late 1960s the DPRK lost aid from the Soviet Union and China because of their poor economic performance and the countries' feuding (Inoguchi 1969). Second, to keep up the level of technology and industry with the slogan of *chuche* (autonomous, independent, self-reliant) despite the basic protectionist stance, being part of the World Intellectual Property Organization has been seen to help the DPRK keep up with the frontier knowledge of science, medicine, and industry. The ROK under the military dictatorship of Park Chung Hee moved up its industry and economy steadily since the late 1960s and the DPRK started to recognize that otherwise they would be left far behind the ROK (Baek 2014).

In the latter half of the 1970s, the DPRK showed the period of a void in joining multilateral treaties. However, as if making up for the void of the 1970s, the DPRK started to keep itself busy with joining multilateral treaties in the 1980s. The DPRK started its participation from the basics. It was exemplified by its joining the three treaties: Vienna Convention on Diplomatic Relations (effective as of 1961), Paris Convention for the Protection of Industrial Property (effective as of 1883), and Madrid Agreement Concerning the International Registration of Marks (effective as of 1891). Then it joined many multilateral treaties in such policy domains as human rights, trade, commerce and communications, labor and health, peace and disarmament. Moving onto the 1990s and the 2000s it further participated in many multilateral treaties in such policy domains as the environment, intellectual property, human rights, labor and health, in tandem with the increasing weight of UN Human Rights Council, UN Social and Economic Council. The trend of the DPRK's participation is broadly in tandem with its proactive diplomacy when the neighboring countries of China, South Korea, Japan, Taiwan, Hong Kong, Vietnam, and Singapore visibly and tangibly moved up in the ladder of economic development. In the 2000s and 2010s it joined multilateral treaties in the domain of intellectual property: the Convention for the Safeguarding of the Intangible Cultural Heritage (2003), Singapore Treaty on the Law of Trademarks (2016), Beijing Treaty on Audiovisual Performances (Treaty not in force, 2012), and Patent Law Treaty (2018).

Although the DPRK started late among Sinic East's race of joint rebalancing between the West and the East, it has been struggling hard to make its presence felt. Kim Il Sung tried to manufacture nuclear bombs by way of first "seducing" the US, the Soviet Union, China, South Korea, Japan into helping his country manufacture light-water power-generation facilities. Kim Jong Il, one of his sons, adopted the military firstism whereby nuclear weapons development were accorded the highest priority. Kim Jong Un tried to advance both the military and to develop market mechanisms albeit of very limited kind and scope. The military priority was highest whereas market mechanism was auxiliary. The result was the remarkable success of weapons and missiles development. Market mechanism introduction was a partial success in that it made up for the inadequacies of tightly regulated and protectionist economic policy to raise capital for the survival of the nation (Milanovic 2019). The Democratic People's Republic of Korea's legislative behavior type is *ABc*, meaning cautious in judgment and action, individual interest angle, and mutual binding strategy strongly. It is the broadly same type with the Socialist Republic of Vietnam.

6.2.5 Socialist Republic of Vietnam

The independence of Vietnam was hard won. After the defeat of Japan in World War II, the Communist Party of Vietnam declared independence in 1945 and the Democratic Republic of Vietnam (North Vietnam) were born (Tai 1996). After peace with France was achieved in 1955, Emperor Baodai fell and the Republic of Vietnam was set up. However, France refused to surrender and the liberation war of Vietnam began. In 1956 the two countries concluded an armistice on the northern latitude of 18 degrees. In nation-building efforts South Vietnam was assisted by the United States while North Vietnam was assisted by the Soviet Union. The Vietnamese Liberation

Front backed by North Vietnam was formed to wage a protracted guerrilla war in South Vietnam against the US-backed southern regime. In 1965 the United States, allegedly provoked by North Vietnam, started to militarily attack North Vietnam and suppress what was called the Viet Cong on a large scale. The Vietnam War began but with the withdrawal of the United States ended in 1973. North Vietnam subsequently unified the countries by force in 1975. The Socialist Republic of Vietnam was born (Tønnesson 2019).

The Republic of Vietnam (South Vietnam) joined multilateral treaties before 1975. Constitution of World Health Organization (1950), Agreement on the Importation of Educational Scientific and Cultural Materials (1952), Convention on Road Traffic (1953), Convention concerning Customs Facilities for Touring (1956), Madrid Agreement Concerning the International Registration on Marks (1956), Amendments to articles 24 and 25 of the Constitution of World Health Organization (1959), Agreement establishing the Asian Development Bank (1966), Single Convention on Narcotic Drugs (1970), and Optional Protocol to the Vienna Convention on Consular Relations concerning Acquisition of Nationality (1973).

After the unification of 1975, the Socialist Republic of Vietnam participated multilateral treaties head-on. The number of multilateral treaties under the Republic of Vietnam and the Democratic Republic of Vietnam was 14 while that under the Socialist Republic of Vietnam was 115. In comparison to North Korea, Vietnam is in terms of proclivity of joining multilateral treaties, far more active. In comparison to China, the United States (defeated by Vietnam) was slower to return to Vietnam with investment than to China. Once China began facing heavy tariffs by the United States, foreign investment started to divert away from China: Hong Kong, Taiwan, Vietnam, Malaysia, and Singapore are major countries receiving diverted investment from China. Vietnam has been one of the priority target countries for foreign investors. The Socialist Republic of Vietnam's global legislative type is *ABc*, meaning cautious in judgment and action, individual interest angle, and mutual binding orientation.

6.3 Daily Life Satisfaction 2019 in Sinic East Countries

We have described and analyzed how the Sinic East countries have participated in multilateral treaties system in Sects. 6.1 and 6.2. Sinic multilateral treaties' policy domains have a lot to do with daily life satisfaction with life domains, areas and styles. As such, this section digresses to offer a brief glimpse at daily satisfaction in Sinic East societies based on the survey carried out in 2019 (Appendix E). The question is: Please tell me how satisfied or dissatisfied you are with the following aspects of your life (aspects: housing, friendship, marriage (if married), standard of living, household income, health, education, job, neighbors, public safety, the condition of the environment, social welfare system, democratic system, family life, leisure, spiritual life). Choose one of the six options: very satisfied, somewhat satisfied, neither satisfied nor dissatisfied, somewhat dissatisfied, very unsatisfied, don't know.

The satisfaction score is calculated as (very satisfied + somewhat satisfied)—(very dissatisfied + somewhat dissatisfied). We examine daily life satisfaction of each of the 16 daily life aspects one by one.

Housing: Life satisfaction with housing in Sinic East countries is the highest in Japan. Yet a large majority of those satisfied with housing register "somewhat satisfied" rather than "very satisfied." Vietnam, registering 7% annual economic growth rate, is second highest. Rapid improvement in housing over the 2010s has satisfied the nearly one half of the sampled population. South Korea and Taiwan registering next highest satisfaction with housing registering "somewhat satisfied" rather than "very satisfied." China and Hong Kong come in the last category of lower satisfaction with housing. China has been steady slowdown of annual economic growth rate in the 2010s and on top of that, the tariff and technology war with the United States over tariff rates, intellectual property rights and "unfair competition" using state-owned enterprises have reduced satisfaction level and increased dissatisfaction. Hong Kong has been filled with protests in the streets in 2019, which has partially paralyzed the Hong Kong economy and plagued the impoverished lower strata of population further.

Friendship: Friendship is often nourished at hard times when those extending help to those in difficulty in business and those among protesting movements against the government in 2019. Japan has long been in "elegant decline" (Leheny 2018). Hong Kong's majority population have been fairly solidly united in protest movements. Those who have experienced daily life in democratic societies such as Canada, Australia, and the United States after 1997 and some of them after a while came back to Hong Kong possibly erroneously perceiving the 'one country-two systems' formula to work longer (The Economist 2020). South Korea and Taiwan, two of the formerly four Asian Tigers, has been sometimes playing top goose role after Japan reduced the magnetic force of its manufacturing sector (The Economist 2019; Inoguchi 2006).

Marriage: Respondents in China and in Vietnam are the happiest on average of the Sinic East countries. Is it in part because private life in communist societies can be lived only between a couple, thus marriage reinforcing solidarity and love between a couple? Is it in part because the annual economic growth rates in Vietnam and in China have been the highest of all the Sinic East countries? Taiwan and South Korea register the lower figures of marriage satisfaction. Is it in part because both economies undergo through steady threat or magnet from China to be drawn into the Chinese economic orbit on top of their economic transitional difficulties? Hong Kong and Japan register similar figures. Is it in part because of solidarity against the Chinese interpretation of the "one country-two systems" for Hong Kong? Is it in part because of slow but "elegant decline" for Japan (Leheny 2018)?

Standard of living: Communist societies such as China and Vietnam register the highest satisfaction. Their annual economic growth rates are much higher than in capitalist societies. It seems that in capitalist societies as if the higher per capita national income, the less satisfied with standard of living: Hong Kong, Taiwan, Japan, South Korea, in descending order of satisfaction. Is it in part because of the growing income gaps generated to "neo-liberal" economic dynamics?

Household income: Sinic East countries' respondents register low-level satisfaction with household income. China and Vietnam may feel that their income should keep expanding much faster. Respondents in South Korea, Japan, Taiwan, Hong Kong may feel that their household income should be larger because they should belong to the club of advanced economies.

Health: Heath satisfaction is puzzling. Some may think that the longer the longevity the happier. Hong Kong and Japan are two of the longest-living peoples in the whole world, along with Iceland. Hong Kong respondents are the happiest while Japanese respondents are the least happy, along with Taiwanese respondents. It may also have to do with the increasing medical expenditures in the national government budget. Japan's social welfare-related expenditure (of which medical insurance expenditure has been of late the highest budget item) is a concern, along with national debt-related expenditure. If we compare the budget size of Japan and the United States (at federal level), Japan looks like a maximalist social welfare, and minimalist defense budget while the United States looks like a minimalist social welfare government and maximalist war-ready government. Taiwan may be close to Japan's high medical expenditure in national government budget. The Taiwanese are the unhappiest of all Sinic East countries. South Korea respondents perceive that the longevity is one of the high dreams which seem to them to have been realized (Shin and Inoguchi 2008). The figure in the 2019 mini-survey shows that they are the happiest. China registers high figure in part because of rapid advancement in medical care system throughout the country however inadequate it might be seen in the vast countryside of the country from outside.

Education: The meritocratic system of education with Chinese characteristics seems to emphasize rote memory, familiarity with old Chinese classics, high mathematical literacy, and some socialist philosophy (PISA 2019). Sinic East inherits much of this even without familiarity with old Chinese classics and socialist philosophy. South Korea, Vietnam, and to a lesser degree Japan are societies Confucianism has some influences on their education indirectly at least. China and Taiwan register the least happy responses. Too much competition at entrance examinations, especially highlight gaps in terms of preparations for entrance examinations in the countryside and big urban centers breed dissatisfaction widely. Taiwan registers "somewhat satisfied" rather than "very satisfied" and "somewhat dissatisfied" rather than "very dissatisfied." Hong Kong has British thinking about education and American influence especially the exit option available to high IQ and TOEFL students, for both of which dissatisfaction with education has been somewhat deflated in Hong Kong.

Job: The job satisfaction figures are low on the whole among Sinic East countries. It makes sense to understand that both the high per-capita income (Hong Kong, Japan, Taiwan, South Korea) and large Gross Domestic Product countries (China, Japan, South Korea) suffer from low annual economic growth rates since the 2008 American originated deflation permeated all the Sinic East countries as well. Most important is the similarly high figures across Sinic East countries (except Vietnam), of the "somewhat dissatisfied." Vietnam registers a very high figure of unemployed youth, but not in this survey perhaps in part because of the survey method of relying on quota sampling and face-to face interview at home (the sample size of 400 and areas covered being Hanoi, Danang, Ho Chi Minh and Can Tho) (Appendix E: Metholodogical Notes of Social Survey Used for the Book: The AsiaBarometer Quality of Life Survey; The Asia-Europe Democracy Survey; The Sinic East Survey [Asian Poll] of this book).

Neighbors: Satisfaction with neighbors in Sinic East countries is on the whole high. The contrast between Taiwan and Hong Kong is startling. In Taiwan satisfaction with neighbors is very low. It may have something to do with the split of policy line on how to deal with China's threat-cum-attraction vis-à-vis Taiwan. The Presidential election campaign is the clear evidence of the split between Tsai Ing-wen, with Taiwan-born parents and the leader of the Democratic Progressive Party, and Han Kuo-yu, with Taiwan-born parents based on southern Taiwan, and the candidate of the Kuomintang Party. The division between Taiwanese support for the Democratic Progressive Party and Continental support for the Kuomintang Party has ceased to be the key dividing line. The division is not along ethnic lines but along how to cope with China's charm economic offensive line. Even those neighbors in southern Taiwan, traditionally Taiwan-born parents and dominantly supporters of the Democratic Progressive Party are not fully trusted especially at economic difficulties. The contrast between Taiwanese satisfaction with neighbors and that of Hong Kong is sharp. In Hong Kong, those protesting to abolish the sending of crime suspects to Chinese authorities are united against the Hong Kong Executive Head, Carrie Lam, with those parents and grandparents fleeing from the communist continent to the British colony of Hong Kong and then those parents who migrated to Canada, Australia and the United States after the transfer of Hong Kong to China in 1997. But with the lure of many splendored Hong Kong under the "one country-two systems" many of those parents and their children came back to Hong Kong to discover the policy change in Beijing negatively affecting Hong Kong. Besides Taiwan and Hong Kong, other Sinic East countries seem to be satisfied with neighbors although steady urbanization seems to weaken the neighborhood based community spirit in Sinic East societies as well.

Public Safety: China and Japan enjoy the high level of satisfaction with public safety, registering 60.0 and 58.6 respectively. The low level of satisfaction with public safety in Taiwan and Hong Kong is alarming, registering 10.4 and minus 34.3 respectively. These societies are divided seriously. South Korea and Vietnam register intermediate level of satisfaction with neighbors. A large bulk of young people in both societies are unemployed, increasing the level of dissatisfaction with public safety, registering 44.6 and 38.3 respectively.

Conditions of the Environment: Satisfaction with conditions of the environment in Sinic East varies tremendously. Japan enjoys the high level of satisfaction with the environment although the weaknesses remaining to be resolved with respect to nuclear power plant safety, the coal-based power station technology transfer to developing countries and the plan to increase coal-based power stations at home and most tangibly global climate emergency like frequent floods and semitropical summer temperature. South Korea comes next at a high level of satisfaction with some unresolved problems remaining to be tackled. Taiwan and China come third and fourth after South Korea with regard to satisfaction with the environment with some serious problems of coal-based power stations and nuclear power stations remaining to be tackled. Vietnam suffers from the low level of satisfaction with the environment. Hong Kong suffers from the lowest level of satisfaction with the environment because its water and energy are both dependent on supply from China mainland. On the whole Sinic East societies, economic giants of the world, are destined to cope with problems of fossil-based and nuclear-based societies.

Social Welfare System: On the whole Sinic East societies register the low level of satisfaction with social welfare system for various reasons. South Korea, Vietnam and China register 28.7, 22.7 and 18.8 respectively for satisfaction with social welfare system. These three figures are not high by world standards. But among Sinic East societies their figures are relatively high. It may as well be interpreted that extended family networks and their assistance among themselves have been relatively kept strong in these societies despite urbanization and globalization. Taiwan and Japan register the lower figures of 9.2 and 4.7 respectively. Family nuclearization in both societies may as well be stronger than China, Vietnam and South Korea. China's threat-cum-magnet for Taiwan may be another fragmenting factor. Japan's sky-rocketing increase in medical expenditure in family budget may be another important factor reducing satisfaction with social welfare system. Hong Kong's figure is minus 33.8. Beijing's integration attempt has been a divisive factor weakening satisfaction with social welfare system.

Democratic System: Satisfaction with the democratic system among Sinic East societies is on the whole low. South Korea, Taiwan, China and Vietnam register 37.8, 36.3, 34.5, and 23.5 respectively. Hong Kong is the lowest, registering minus 50.4 and Japan registers plus 14.5. It is not necessarily distinguished characteristic of Sinic East societies but it has been fairly universal that democratic system is not highly satisfactorily functioning the world over especially in the developed North. Sinic East societies in the developed North in terms of per capita income level are Japan, Taiwan, Hong Kong, and South Korea.

Family Life: Sinic East societies used to register high satisfaction with family life. Taiwan and Hong Kong register lower figures than the rest. Urbanization, globalization and fragmentation work against family networks especially in these two cases. China's threat-cum-magnet policy seems to contribute to the further fragmentation in extended family networks. Vietnam registers relatively high satisfaction with family life despite the rapid advent of globalization and urbanization.

Leisure: Satisfaction with leisure is relatively high in Sinic East societies except for South Korea. South Korean government policy of raising wages in small scale industries which occupy 95% of South Korean industrial enterprises in terms of the population has forced them to lay off substantial number of employees there. China's middle class has been enjoying leisure time despite the slow but steady decline of annual economic growth rates in the 2010s.

Spiritual Life: Satisfaction with spiritual life in Sinic East is puzzling. In China and Vietnam register 58.8 and 57.5, higher than the rest. What Branko Milanovic (2019) calls "political capitalism" in China and Vietnam leads people to seek quiet spiritual moment more strongly than the rest. In China, for instance, 100 million Christians are on a par with Communist Party members, registering 95 millions. Christians in Hong Kong, Taiwan, and South Korea register 37.8, 30.1, and 21.6 respectively, showing that they cannot afford to indulge in spiritual life further. Japan registers 44.5. Is it an example of "elegant decline" (Leheny 2018) with samurai spirit spending time on *zen*?

6.4 Preference for Global or National Solutions

We examine multilateral treaties in 1956–2019 in this book in which so far we have not asked the questions about the global or national solutions to "problems without passports." In 2000 the AsiaEurope Survey (Appendix E) was carried out in nine countries in Asia and nine countries in Europe in which one of the questions asked is: Of the following eight issues, which do you prefer, global solutions or national solutions?

In 2019 the same question was asked in Sinic East countries. The 2019 survey on national or global solutions for the following eight policy issues was carried out in summer 2019 in the following societies: Japan, Vietnam, China, Taiwan, Hong Kong, and South Korea:

1. human rights,
2. the environment,
3. women's rights,
4. unemployment,
5. developing countries,
6. migrants and refugees,
7. danger and military conflicts (Asia), and
8. danger and military conflicts (the world).

Sinic East's mean figures of preference for global solution are in the descending order as follows:

1. 9.5% on danger in military conflict (the world),
2. 12.2% on danger in military conflict (Asia),
3. 17.4% on migrants and refugees,
4. 24.1% on the environment,
5. 26.3% on developing countries,
6. 27.8% on human rights,
7. 34.5% on women's rights, and
8. 62.2% on unemployment.

These eight policy issues belong to what Kofi Annan calls "problems without passports." Yet Sinic East's overall preference is clearly for national solutions. Their pride in national capacity and apprehension about external interference in what they regard sovereign states' prerogatives seem to lead them to register these figures on military conflict, Asia and otherwise. Sinic East prefers national solutions than global solutions. In other words, even when military conflict is to take place, their preferred position is not to interfere excessively, and to somehow maintain peace and to constrain it to bilateral solutions. What is called the East Asian peace (Tønnesson 2019) has been achieved in the region since the Sino-Vietnamese war of 1979 ended.

On migrants and refugees, the picture is different, with Sinic East's clear position being to minimize migrants and refugees into their homelands. Until recently, Sinic East was worried more about demographic growth rather than demographic decline. In the first quarter of the twenty-first century, excessive demographic decline has become a universal issue of Sinic East (Haas 2007; Inoguchi 2009): South Korea registers below the one percent figure of reproductive ratio of a couple: On top of unemployment issues, national security issues loom large; furthermore, gender issues have led younger, well educated females to exit. Taiwan registers a similar figure for a bundle of similar issues with South Korea. Hong Kong does have a lower figure than Taiwan and South Korea; it is a special administrative region of China in which the interpretations of what is called the "one country-two systems" scheme has diverged dramatically, triggered by the clash between Hong Kong's executive head and citizens at large after the executive head's order to send suspected lawbreakers to China. With China's recent imposition on the National Security Law on Hong Kong, migrating out to Taiwan and Britain may register the increasingly high number (The Economist 2020, pp. 22–23). China, alarmed by demographic decline by its one child policy, switched to demographic growth allowing a couple to have two children. Yet its reproductive ratio does not go up much, since couples worry about the very high educational expenses of having more than one child in all Sinic East societies. Vietnam also registers demographic decline. Although it registers a higher economic growth rate annually (around 7%), lower per capita income level prompts some young ambitious men and women to migrate to high income countries.

On the environment, Sinic East preferences diverge widely: Japan registers least global solutions 5.5% whereas Hong Kong does it most strongly, at 53. 6%. Japan's environmental consciousness peaked toward the end of the 1990s. The manufacturing sector peaked its competitiveness internationally by the 1980s and their success in reducing environmental pollution arising from manufacturing industrial products remarkably by the 1990s. The new phase started with the global emphasis on non-fossil and non-nuclear energy utilization such as wind, sun, wave, water. The renewed global emphasis on non-fossil energy utilization has arisen with the growing awareness of the alarming increase in the emission of carbon dioxide. That increase has been causing the global climate emergency with the steady rise of air temperature, the rise of temperature and level of sea water, and unusually frequent violent floods, winds, and geological changes on large scale. Japan's memory of success in reducing pollution in the recent past has been slowing down its action in anti-pollution in the new phase of climate emergency. Japan has been resisting swift adaptation to non-fossil energy utilization policies in the new millennium by sticking to retaining the residual fossil materials use for power generation. Japan's annual GDP growth of almost 1–2% for the last three decades has been underlying all this slow and hesitant speed in struggling climate emergency.

China, Taiwan, South Korea, and Vietnam register those figures in between Japan's and Hong Kong's: 26.8%, 32.1%, 33.5%, and 28.0% respectively. China, Taiwan, and South Korea are confronted by a difficult choice. Their status is superior to many of advanced countries in terms of Gross Domestic Product. Yet they do not necessarily want to immediately throw away their developing South category completely. China's GDP will surpass that of the United States soon while Taiwan and South Korea are good matches with Japan in terms of per capita national income (The Economist 2019). China's dilemma illustrates Sinic East's dilemma. It is not comfortably endowed with petroleum or coal. China has been importing petroleum massively from the Middle East and it has been massively importing coal from Australia and to a lesser degree from Brazil. Coal-related air pollution has been reduced dramatically in Beijing by the government's draconian measures of forbidding coal use for heating residences in Beijing and on nationwide with less draconian measures. China struck a big deal in 2016 with the United States to effectuate the Paris climate accord successfully because these two powers' combined carbon dioxide emission surpass one half of global emission. However, President Donald Trump assumed office in 2017 and ordered the exit of the United States from the Paris climate accord.

On developing countries especially on aid, investment, technology transfer, and infrastructure, Sinic East has the developed South dilemma. They are mostly very advanced industrially even compared to many of the 40-odd OECD members; many enjoy fairly high per capita income level; Three of them, China, Japan, and South Korea, will be ranked the first, third, and ninth in terms of GDP soon. But except Japan, they are categorized as the developing South. Thus, Sinic East's responses to global solutions or national solutions on the developing South are very divergent. Their responses register 4.3%, 27.5%, 30.3%, 31.8%, 45.9%, and 61.3% in the descending order of Japan, Vietnam, Taiwan, South Korea, China, and Hong Kong. Taiwan, South Korea, and China face the developed South dilemma. Hong Kong follows China's position on this question. Vietnam's response must be similar to Taiwan and South Korea perhaps because Vietnam has been more used to rely on its resilience to changes at home and abroad (especially as a member of the Association of the South-East Asian Nations).

On human rights, Sinic East registers global solutions by 11.6%, 28.8%, 30.5%, 34.3%, 37.6%, and 54.5% for Japan, Taiwan, South Korea, Vietnam, Hong Kong, and China respectively. Japan's thinking on human rights seems to be that the more democratic, the more emphasis on national solutions. In other words, on human rights the developed North had better trust the developing South to become more sensitive to human rights and to grow more democratic by themselves. Taiwan, South Korea, and Vietnam give the impression that East Asian tigers and to-be-tiger follow Japan's pattern that the developed North had better trust the developing South to become more sensitive to human rights. Hong Kong's response, given the survey data in summer 2019, seems to be saying that the rise of human rights voice in the developed South (for example, Hong Kong, Taipei, Shanghai) as well as in the developing North (such as Guangdong, Zhejiang, Jiangsi) may as well help trigger accelerating democratic breakthrough if it ever is to take place. China's response can be interpreted in both ways (Ci 2015; Zhang 2008). First, the human rights issue needs global solutions because its practice differs tremendously country by country. The developing South knows it. In encouraging their improved practice, they had better rely on the voices of the developing South and their number registering 149 countries dominating the

United Nations Human Rights Council and the United Nations Social Economic Council. Second, the human rights issue will evolve as market mechanism inside China advances or recedes. If it advances, then the voice of human rights improves. If it recedes, it will be further suppressed. Yet it is bound to rebound in due course. In sum, voting for the voice of global solutions instead of national solutions seems to be the easy way to go for some time to come.

On women's human rights issue, the voice of global solutions is registered as 24.1% for Japan, 32.0% for Vietnam, 41.0% for China, 33.2% for Taiwan, 45.9% for Hong Kong, and 51.8% for South Korea. Given the oft-noted strong Confucian traditions in Sinic East societies, the figures for global solutions on women's rights issue are somewhat puzzling. Important to interpret the responses are two variables: gender discrimination, said to be inherent to Confucian tradition, and degree of democratization. First, in terms of the sacred versus secular orientation of the World Value Survey (Welzel 2013) and the Multilateral Treaties Survey (Inoguchi and Le 2019) both point to the fact that Sinic East registers on the whole most secular, next to Reformed West (e.g., Scandinavia, Germany, the Netherlands, Switzerland) among the ten geo-historico-cultural groups in the whole world. This does not necessarily mean that Sinic East societies are not free from gender discrimination. Rather other gender-biases do exist strongly, such as strong parental authority over children and strong male biases against females in terms of job recruitment, inheritance, divorce and education. Second, the degree of democratization affects gender biases. In this respect, it is important to note that gender biases are apparent or at least hidden in civil law, family law, inheritance law, punitive law, and business transaction law. It is no less important to note that Sinic East had experienced big turmoils including world wars and civil-cum-international wars before and after the current regimes captured power. Centuries-long gender biases may die hard in many societies somehow irrespective of current regime types.

Japan's low response on global solutions in women's human rights may as well indicate a number of probable interpretations: less strong Confucian influence among Sinic East members (Inoguchi 2015; Inoguchi and Fujii 2013), more democratic values permeated (Inoguchi and Fujii 2013). Since the question asks respondents about their society primarily in mind, they may mean that they have pride and capacity in carrying out such tasks. On the other hand, many domestic laws since the late 1890s have been kept largely intact during the Allied Powers' occupation of 1945–1952 except for blatantly anti-democratic laws and practices involving the Imperial Army, the Police, and some of the Home Ministries oppressing practices. More recently the United Nations has encouraged its members to make the English language translation available. But while South Korea has done so by 60%, Japan has done so about 10% (Nihon keizai Shimbun 2018).

The Ministry of Justice's home page, called the Database System of Foreign Language Translations of Japanese Laws and Acts, registers the very high frequencies of access to such laws and acts: corporate law, commodity exchange law, bank law, civil rehabilitation act, code of civil procedure, law on cooperative society of medium and small scale enterprises, law on special measures on taxes, anti-monopoly law, law on bankruptcy, foreign exchange act, patent law. As seen in this access frequency list, business laws and acts are most frequently needed in English translation. No less important is the frequency of civil law, civil rehabilitation law, code of civil procedure. The Hague treaty of international arbitration places emphasis on a third party's judgment in arbitrating and mediating process of taking care of children when a couple is divorced and when a couple are from different nationalities.

Vietnam registers medium figures of global solutions on gender human rights. Just like Russian and British wartime heroic works of women fighting at battle fronts (Russian) and on the home front (British), Vietnamese women may have achieved strong positions vis-à-vis men. Also important to note is that southern Vietnam has been widely using market mechanisms since the *doi moi* reform and opening policy was adopted in the mid-1980s, in comparison to northern Vietnam where socialist bureaucratic planning tradition are resilient. Both of the two factors-cum-backgrounds point to their pride and capacity. From these figures, South Korean and Hong Kong respondents more strongly call for rectification of gender discrimination of the Asian tigers. South Korea has been characterized to be stronger Confucian influences than socialist China or Vietnam (Woodside 2006; Shin and Inoguchi 2008). Hong Kong respondents seem to call for more democracy in conjunction to the just scrapped Hong Kong law of sending criminal suspects in Hong Kong to China. In 2020 China legislated the National Security Legal System and imposed it in Hong Kong as well.

The unemployment issue registers divergent responses among Sinic East members. Sinic East members register 50.8% for Japan, 50.0 for Vietnam, 61.1% for Taiwan, 73.0% for China, 76.8% for South Korea, and 73.0% for China. Japan registers the lowest figure among Sinic East for global solutions. Vietnam follows next. The Japanese and Vietnamese possibly have common traits, such as being able to take hard times with perseverance and endurance whether it is wartime or peacetime.

References

Alperovitz, Gar. 1965. *Atomic Diplomacy: Hiroshima and Potsdam*. New York: Simon and Schuster.

Annan, Kofi. 2002. "Problems Without Passports." *Foreign Policy* 132: 30–31.

Armstrong, Charles. 2003. *The North Korean Revolution, 1945–1950*. New York: Columbia University Press.

Baek, Jieun. 2014. *North Korea's Hidden Revolution: How the Information Underground Is Transforming a Closed Society*. New Haven, CT: Yale University Press.

Biersteker, Thomas, Sue E. Eckert, and Marcos Tourinho (eds.). 2016. *Targeted Sanctions: The Impacts and Effectiveness of United Nations Action*. Cambridge: Cambridge University Press.

Bowden, Mark. 2017. *Hue 1968: A Turning Point of the American War in Vietnam*. New York: Atlantic Monthly Press.

Ci, Jiwei. 2015. *Democracy in China: The Coming Crisis*. Cambridge, MA: Harvard University Press.

Cumings, Bruce. 1981. *The Origins of the Korean War, vol. 1: Liberation and the Emergence of Separate Regimes 1945–1947*. Princeton: Princeton University Press.

Cumings, Bruce. 1990. *The Origins of the Korean War vol. 2: The Roaring of the Cataract, 1947–1950*. Princeton: Princeton University Press.

The Economist. 2019. Special Report: Asia Tigers, December 7: 1–10.

The Economist. 2020. One Country, Two Passports: Voting with Their Feet. August 15: 22–23.

Galicchio, Marc. 2020. *Unconditional: The Japanese Surrender in World War II*. Oxford: Oxford University Press.
Gray, Keven, and Craig Murphy. 2015. *Rising Powers and the Future of Global Governance*. London: Routledge.
Haas, Mark L. 2007. "A Geriatric Peace? The Future of U.S. Power in a World of Aging Populations." *International Security* 32 (1) (Summer): 112–147.
Hasegawa, Tsuyoshi. 2006. *Racing the Enemy: Stalin, Truman, and the Surrender of Japan*. Cambridge, MA: Belknap Press of Harvard University Press.
Hufbauer, Gary C., Jeffrey J. Schott, Kimberly A. Elliott, and Barbara Oegg. 2007. *Economic Sanctions Reconsidered*, 3rd ed. Washington, DC: Peterson Institute for International Economics.
Inoguchi, Takashi. 1969. *Kokusai Kankei no suryobunseki: Peking, Pyongyang and Moscow, 1961–1966 nen* (A Quantitative Analysis of International Relations: Peking, Pyongyang and Moscow, 1961–1966). Tokyo: Gannando Publishers.
Inoguchi, Takashi. 1980. "Chugoku no Vietnam kansho, 1789 nen to 1979 nen (Chinese Interventions in Vietnam, 1789 and 1979)." *Ajia Kenkyu* (*Asian Studies*) 27 (2): 1–42.
Inoguchi, Takashi. 2006. "Has the Japanese Model Ceased to be a Magnet in Asia?" In *Democratization, Governance and Regionalism in East and Southeast Asia*, edited by Ian Marsh, 204–222. London: Routledge.
Inoguchi, Takashi. 2009. "Demographic Change and Asia Dynamics: Social and Economic Implications." *Asian Economic Policy Review* 4 (19): 142–157.
Inoguchi, Takashi. 2015. "Asia Barometer." In *Wiley Blackwell Encyclopedia of Sociology*, edited by George Ritzer. London: Wiley-Blackwell.
Inoguchi, Takashi. 2018. "The Wilsonian Moment: Japan 1912–1952." *Japanese Journal of Political Science* 19 (4): 565–570.
Inoguchi, Takashi, and Seiji Fujii. 2013. *The Quality of Life in Asia: A Comparison of Quality of Life in Asia*. Dordrecht: Springer.
Inoguchi, Takashi, and Lien Thi Quynh Le. 2019. *The Development of Global Legislative Politics: Rousseau and Locke Writ Global*. Singapore: Springer Nature.
Kim, Seung-Young. 2013. "The Rise and Fall of the United States Trusteeship Plan for Korea as a Peace-maintenance Scheme." *Diplomacy and Statecraft* 24 (2): 227–252.
Kim, Byung-Kook, and Ezra Vogel. 2013. *The Park Chung Hee Era: The Transformation of Korea*. Cambridge, MA: Harvard University Press.
Kissinger, Henry. 2012. *On China*. New York: Penguin Books.
Kivimaki, Timo. 2012. *Can Peace Research Make Peace? Lesson in Academic Diplomacy*. London: Ashgate.
Lankov, Andrei. 2013. *The Real North Korea: Life and Politics in the Failed Stalinist Utopia*. Oxford: Oxford University Press.
Leheny, David. 2018. *Empire of Hope: The Sentimental Politics of Japanese Decline*. Ithaca, NY: Cornell University Press.
Lowy Institute. 2019. *Lowy Global Diplomacy Index*. Sydney: Lowy Institute.
Macaes, Bruno. 2018. *The Dawn of Eurasia*. New York: Penguin Books.
MacFarquar, Roderick, and Micharl Schoenhas. 2008. *Mao's Last Revolution*. Cambridge: Belknap Press of Harvard University Press.
Macmillan, Margaret. 2003. *Paris in 1919: Six Months That Changed the World*. New York: Random House.
Milanovic, Branko. 2019. *Capitalism, Alone: The Future of the System That Rules the World*. Cambridge, MA: Harvard University Press.
Mimaki, Seiko. 2014. *Senso ihoka undo no jidai (The Age of the Movement of Outlawing Wars)*. Nagoya: Nagoya University Press.
Nihon keizai Shimbun. 2018. Horei no eiyaku ichiwari domari: junenme okure kokusaika nokabeni (The English Translation of Domestic Laws and Acts Has Remained 10 Percent: Posing Barriers to Japan's Internationalization Since the Translation Task Started 10 Years ago), October 22 (morning ed.), p. 11.

Nihon keizai Shimbun. 2019. Nihon no 15-sai no dokkairyoku, sekai 15-i ni koutai (15 Years' Old Japanese Ability to Comprehend Japanese Has Declined to the 15th in the World (according to the OECD's PISA report), December 3 (evening ed.), p. 5.

Okonogi, Masao. 2019. *Chosen bundan no kigen* (The Origins of Divided Korea). Tokyo: Keio University Press.

Putnam, Robert, and Nicholas Bayne. 1988. *Hanging Together: Cooperation and Conflict Among Seven-Power Summit, Revised and Enlarged Edition.* Cambridge, MA: Harvard University Press.

Russett, Bruce M. 1993. *Grasping the Democratic Peace: Principles for a Post-Cold War Period.* Princeton: Princeton University Press.

Sasaki, Yuichi. 2017. *Teikoku Nihon no gaiko, 1894–1922: Naze hanto wa kakudai shitanoka* (The Diplomacy of Imperial Japan, 1894–1922: Why Its Territory Expanded?), 3–9. Tokyo: University of Tokyo Press.

Shinohara, Hatsue. 2012. *US International Lawyers in The Interwar Years: A Forgotten Crusade.* Cambridge, NY: Cambridge University Press.

Shin, Doh Chull and Takashi Inoguchi (eds.). 2008. *The Quality of Life in Confucian Asia: From Physical Strength to Subjective Well-Being.* Dordrecht: Springer.

Suh, Dae-sook. 1995. *Kim Il Sung: The North Korean Leader.* New York: Columbia University Press.

Suzuki, Shogo. 2009. *Civilization and Empire: China and Japan's Encounter with the Western International Society.* London: Routledge.

Tai, Hue-Tam Ho. 1996. *Radicalism and the Origins of the Vietnamese Revolution.* Cambridge, MA: Harvard University Press.

Tønnesson, Stein. 2019. "East Asian Peace." In *The Sage Handbook of Asian Foreign Policy*, 2 vols., edited by Takashi Inoguchi. London: Sage.

Vogel, Ezra. 2013. *Deng Xiaoping and the Transformation of China.* Cambridge, MA: Belknap Press of Harvard University Press.

Wallensteen, Peter, and Carina Staibano (eds.). 2005. *International Sanctions: Between Words and Wars in the Global System.* London: Routledge.

Welzel, Christian. 2013. *Freedom Rising: Human Empowerment and the Quest for Emancipation.* New York: Cambridge University Press.

Whiting, Allen. 1960. *China Crosses the Yalu.* Stanford: Stanford University Press.

Woodside, Alexander. 2006. *Lost Modernities: China, Vietnam, Korea and the Hazards of World History.* Cambridge, MA: Harvard University Press.

Young, Michael. 2017. *The Rise of Meritocracy*, 2nd ed. London: Routledge.

Zhang, Jianjun. 2008. *Marketization and Democracy in China.* London: Routledge.

Chapter 7
Comparative Statecraft in Sinic East

Abstract This chapter shows how Sinic East's multilateral treaty participation fits with one of the eight types of global quasi-legislative behavior: China's statecraft being agile in speed, global commons in angle, and aspirational bonding in strategy; North Korea's statecraft being cautious in speed, individual interests in angle, and mutual binding in strategy; Japan's statecraft being agile in speed, global commons in angle, and mutual binding in strategy; South Korea's statecraft being cautious in speed, global commons in angle, and aspirational bonding in strategy; Vietnam's statecraft being cautious in speed, individual interests in angle, and mutual binding in strategy. We emphasize Sinic East's diversity in multilateral treaty participation modes and thus statecraft.

Let us take a look at Table 7.1.

China is agile in decision; its angle is that of global commons; its strategy is that of aspirational bonding. DPR Korea is cautious in decision; its angle is that of individual interests; its strategy is that of mutual binding. Japan is agile in terms of decision to join or not to join; its angle is that of global commons; its strategy is that of mutual binding. R Korea is cautious in decision; its angle is that of global commons; its strategy is that of aspirational bonding. Vietnam is cautious in decision; its angle is that of individual interests; its strategy is that of mutual binding.

China befits a great power with three features. Its decision is fast. Its policy direction is highly centralized in the central committee of the Chinese Communist Party. Being the number one GNP power, China pays utmost attention to global issues. Its investment abroad is literally global. Its foreign language education is serious. At Peking University of Foreign Languages, for instance, 108 foreign languages are taught regularly with their native speakers. (At Korea University of Foreign Languages, the number is 78. At Tokyo University of Foreign Studies, the number is 27. At Pyongyang University of Foreign Languages, the number is 21.) Its strategy is that of aspirational bonding. After the 1979–2012 period Deng Xiaoping's slogan, "Hide your strength, bide your time" was replaced by more self-assertive slogans emphasizing China's strength, its globalizing endeavor and pride in international

T. Inoguchi and L. T. Q. Le, *Digitized Statecraft in Multilateral Treaty Participation*, Evidence-Based Approaches to Peace and Conflict Studies 1,
https://doi.org/10.1007/978-981-33-4485-3_7

Table 7.1 Typology of global quasi-legislative behavior of Sinic East countries

China	abC	agile, global commons, aspirational bonding
DPR Korea	ABc	cautious, individual interests, mutual binding
Japan	abc	agile, global commons, mutual binding
R Korea	AbC	cautious, global commons, aspirational bonding
Vietnam	ABc	cautious, individual interests, mutual binding

cooperation. With gradual changes in rules of world order in mind, China has been trying to make new and many friends from near and afar.

DPR Korea is slow in making decisions on joining multilateral treaties. Decision is highly centralized and hereditary in the founding father's family nested in the Korean Workers' Party. The country has been poverty-stricken since the 1970s and 1980s, during which time Soviet and Chinese assistance dwindled whereas large and periodic famines in the 1970s and onward led North Korea to focus on economic and military enhancement through the assistance of five major powers (the US, China, the Soviet Union, South Korea, Japan) assistance on nuclear power stations, then on military firstism, further onto nuclear weapons and *janmadan* capitalism. North Korea is fast in making decision but fast in changing decision as well. The withdrawal from the treaty banning intermediate range nuclear weapons is the case in point. One of the most important goals of DPR Korea is to remove US armed forces sitting on the southern part of the Korean Peninsula. First, obtaining nuclear power stations from the five powers ended in failure. Second, manufacturing nuclear weapons by themselves to compel the United States to withdraw by threatening intercontinental ballistic missiles to the US mainland and intermediate-and short-range missiles to the US forces in the vicinities of the Korean Peninsula and Japan. This combination has halted efforts to achieve peace between DPR Korea and R Korea. Its angle is that of individual interests, especially to get US dollars to buy necessary technology and manufacturing parts. Its strategy is that of aspirational bonding. It sells weapons to many countries in the developing South, especially in Africa and the Middle East.

Japan's decision is relatively slow among Group of Seven Countries. But it has been a member of the United Nations since 1956, a member of the developed North since 1964, and is a member of Group of Seven Powers since 1974. It is agile in making decision on participation. Its strategy is mutual binding, being bound by many rules and obligations of the developed North, OECD's Development Assistance Committee, International Energy Agency, International Monetary Fund, Bank for Economic Development and International Cooperation etc. China is number one in GNP in the world; R Korea is number 11 in GNP in the world; both of them have been unwilling to exit from the status of the developing South. Japan's GNP is number three in the world. Japan's angle is that of global commons. Japan's strategy is that of mutual binding. Thus, Japan befits the developed North in all features.

R Korea is slow in making decisions. It is cautious for internal and external reasons. Internally Korean society has been divided by two forces, conservative and capitalist on the one hand, and progressive and communist on the other after Japan surrendered and Korea was occupied by the United States armed forces and the Soviet armed forces in southern and northern half of the peninsula respectively. In North Korea conservative, progressive and anti-Kim Il Sung-led communist forces were wiped out more or less. In South Korea both right-wing and left-wing forces have remained alive and well, adapting themselves both to dictatorship or democracy. Only during the military dictatorship (1961–1988) were both left-wing and right-wing forces oppressed more or less equally. Yet gradually the military moderated its authoritarian character after Park Chung Hee's assassination in 1979. In 1988 Kim Dae-Jung, a civil movement activist, won the presidential election, overwhelming the former military general candidate. After Kim Dae-Jung, Roh Moo-Hyun became a left-wing President, who, worried about his relatives' corruption, committed suicide. Then Park Chung Hee's daughter, Park Geun-hye, became President representing right-wing forces. She was also arrested and jailed for bribing. The current President, Moon Jae Yin, was supported by left-wing forces. This kind of divisiveness is one of the causes of slow decision. Externally, South Korea has been sandwiched by China, bordering North Korea on Amnok (Yalu) and Tuman (Douman) rivers and the United States, stationing both in South Korea and Japan. China and the United States put pressure on South Korea to accept their demands, which are often mutually contradictory. South Korea's angle is that of global commons, being Number 11 of GNP size in the world, exporting advanced manufactured products especially IT products massively to the rest of the world, and investing in many foreign countries. Former President Lee Myung Bak boasted of South Korea's having the largest combined space under bilateral free trade agreements in the world. South Korea's strategy is that of aspirational bonding. It is the strategy of the developing South despite retaining the Number 11 GNP size in the world. It is also because the contestation in the UN and outside with North Korea has been harsh, needing as many friends as possible from near and afar.

Vietnam is slow in making decision on participation in multilateral treaties. The Socialist Republic of Vietnam was born of the military overwhelming force of North Vietnam and its foe, the US's own withdrawal from the war in 1973. Northern Vietnam has been continuously governed by the Vietnamese Communist Party whereas southern Vietnam used to be governed by the Republic of Vietnam and a more importantly market economy has been practiced. The government seems to be differentiated between governing north with orthodox central planning and governing south with market mechanism. Since the *Doi Moi* (reform) policy has been adopted and carried out in all Vietnam, it has become "political capitalism" (Milanovic 2019) more or less akin to Chinese or Singaporean. Its angle is that of individual interests as contrasted to global commons. Its strategy is that of mutual binding. It is that of the developing South. Since 1995 Vietnam has been a member of the Association of South-East Asian Nations (ASEAN) and in 2015 it performed its chairman's role very well.

Reference

Milanovic, Branko. 2019. *Capitalism, alone: The future of the system that rules the world.* Cambridge, MA: Harvard University Press.

Chapter 8
Multilateral Treaty Participation Triggers Upward Leap in Sinic East

Abstract This chapter traces the Sinic East's patterns of joining multilateral treaties by six policy domains country by country. The strong finding is that in Sinic East multilateral treaty participation has registered an upward leap. Japan's multilateral treaty participation came very early after the defeat in 1945. Japan's development was orchestrated by joining in the United Nations in 1956 and the multilateral treaties such as the International Monetary Fund, the International Bank of Economic Recovery and Development, and the OECD in the early and mid-1960s, leading *The Economist* magazine to publish a "Consider Japan" editorial in 1962. In early and mid-1970s Japan's elevation to the developed North club position was established with the its becoming a founder member of Group of Seven. Policy domain-wise, Japan's good footing in the International Labor Organization and General Agreements on Tariffs and Trade cannot be underestimated. While the four Asian tigers (South Korea, Taiwan, Singapore, and Hong Kong) dramatically and nimbly solidified their economic position in the 1970s through 1990s, China evolved through waves of upward leaps: first, by opening to Japan and the United States through the 1970s, second through lifting economic sanctions by Japan followed by the rest of the West in the early 1990s after the massacre of the Tiananmen square protesters, and finally with the joining and acquiring privileged status in the World Trade Organization in the early 2000s. All of these advances have been dramatic. After Vietnam's very long years of war-footings, internal and external, it has benefited from the long East Asian peace (Tønnesson 2019), from the peace agreement between the United States and Vietnam in 1973, the peace agreement between China and Vietnam in 1984 to the reform policy starting in 1986 and the joining in the Association of South-East Asian Nations (ASEAN) in 1991 through the US-led economic sanctions against China in 2017 onward. Its development has also been noteworthy. Multilateral treaties have been very transformative in themselves. Sinic East has been very adaptive to the changing internal preferences and global preferences, orchestrating has worked well. Even North Korea has been moving dexterously: Even after many years of absence in multilateral treaties, North Korea was early in joining multilateral treaties dealing with intellectual property and the environment and once joining the United Nations in 1992 it has joined more multilateral treaties per year than the United States since 1945.

T. Inoguchi and L. T. Q. Le, *Digitized Statecraft in Multilateral Treaty Participation*, Evidence-Based Approaches to Peace and Conflict Studies 1,
https://doi.org/10.1007/978-981-33-4485-3_8

8.1 Multilateral Treaty Participation Are in Sync with Economic Development

We have examined how sovereign states' participation in multilateral treaties has triggered upward leap broadly in terms of economic, social, and political development. Our focus is on Sinic East countries, Japan, South Korea, China, North Korea and Vietnam. To show how multilateral treaty participation has much to do with economic development in the East Asian region, we first start with the flying geese developmental paradigm (Akamatsu 1962; Korhonen 1994; Ozawa 1994, 2005). Akamatsu's idea started with his observation on Japan's woolen goods industry in 1930s. Japan excelled itself in producing silk in the pre-modern eighteenth and nineteenth centuries (Hayami 1992, 2015). Once cotton-weaving technology was introduced, cotton cloth became Japan's most cash-earning product. Then Japan shifted to woolen products while relocating some of cotton production to its neighboring places such as China in the 1920s and 1930s. His idea is to focus on a labor-intensive product such as cotton at an early developmental stage. But once labor productivity goes down in terms of comparative advantage or changes in other circumstances, there was a need to shift to more profitable products such as woolen goods or automobiles in the 1930s. Toyota, a large automobile producer in the twenty-first century, was one of the most profit-making firms in the production of cotton cloths in the 1930s. Already in the 1930s Toyota had begun producing automobiles with the cotton-weaving machine metamorphosed into automobile driving engine. An empirical testing ground was now opened once the turmoils and whirlwinds of the interwar period was over in 1945. Under the Pax Americana structure, East Asia offered an ideal testing ground for the empirical testing and further reformulation of his idea.

8.2 Japan

After 1945 Japan was the only country of the five Sinic East which was not war-torn (Inoguchi 2020). The rest were all torn by war, both civil and international, after 1945. Furthermore, World War II forced Japan to start afresh, at least on the surface. The accumulated technological advances before 1945 were not underestimated (Hayami 2015; Gordon 2018; Nakamura 1983, 1994). The redeployment of cotton-weaving machinery to automobile production by the 1930s is one of the best examples. Therefore, Japan's recovery from ashes of war was fast thanks to the seven-year-long American occupation, which got rid of potentially destabilizing forces, extreme right and extreme left (Dower 2012), and deflating government expenditures on security and defense by the asymmetric alliance with Japan, whereby, the US defends Japan whereas Japan keeps the no-war constitution, which was not to be amended (Smith 2019). Japan started to export simple, crude, and cheap products, then more value-added manufactured goods such as TV, automobiles, and machines. Joining multilateral treaties came step by step. Initially the treaties and agreements with the United States were literally everything. No other Asian countries had much to do with Japan since many Asian countries were either not yet independent or barely independent but soon drawn into civil and international wars; moreover, many Asian peoples were negatively affected by Japanese wars in Asia. The triggering mechanism of multilateral treaties came step by step on key occasions: first, regaining national independence in 1952; second, being admitted to enter the United Nations in 1956; third, paying back of all loans to the World Bank and obtaining developed country status (joining the OECD and hosting the Tokyo Olympic Games) in 1964; fourth, overcoming the oil crisis and joining the Group of Seven in 1974; fifth, joining the Plaza accord with Group of Seven on allowing the selling and purchasing of major currencies, to assist the US to keep the leading position; sixth, enduring the Asian monetary crisis of 1997–1998 offering financial and technological transfer assistance; seventh, overcoming the great depression of 2008 and helping to alleviate negative impacts of globalization by envigorating global, regional and bilateral arrangements with developing and developed countries. In sum, Japan was the lead goose regionally in a happy environment under the Pax Americana.

It should be noted that the global "lead goose" was the United States. Other geese followed Japan, and some of them replaced Japan's lead-goose position by excelling themselves, focusing on advanced service manufacturing. They are the Four Tigers (South Korea, Taiwan, Singapore, and Hong Kong). Having received Japan's trade and investment massively in China's manufacturing and infrastructure after the joint uplifting economic sanctions against China's suppression of protests in 1989, China resumed its two-digit economic growth, which lasted three decades thereafter. Following up the lead-goose formation pattern, they were able to spend less on research and investment than the United States and so were the Four Tigers in Asia. Most striking in the graph for Japan in Multilateral Treaties Participation (Fig. 8.1) were:

(1) Participation in all the six domains, especially those in peace and disarmament, labor and health, trade, commerce, and communications increased in parallel more or less;
(2) In the post-Cold War period the domain in trade registered a very active and astronomical increase in participation.
(3) The post-Cold War trio domains—intellectual property, human rights, and the environment—expanded steadily.

Summing up, Japan has been helped immensely by its steadfast participation in and compliance with multilateral treaties despite all the shortcomings. As the "oasis" of stability now so noted in the turbulent world of digitized globalization, Japan is linked to proactive policies. In sum, Japan was able to spearhead manufacturing products in the latter half of the twentieth century. But into the new millennium, 30 years' stagnation has prevailed: demographic decline, stagnant innovation and patent acquisition, and organizationally stalled society under the surface of peace and stability, Japan as the leading goose in East Asia has been replaced by China challenging the US, the Four Tigers leading advanced service-sector projects (The Economist 2019).

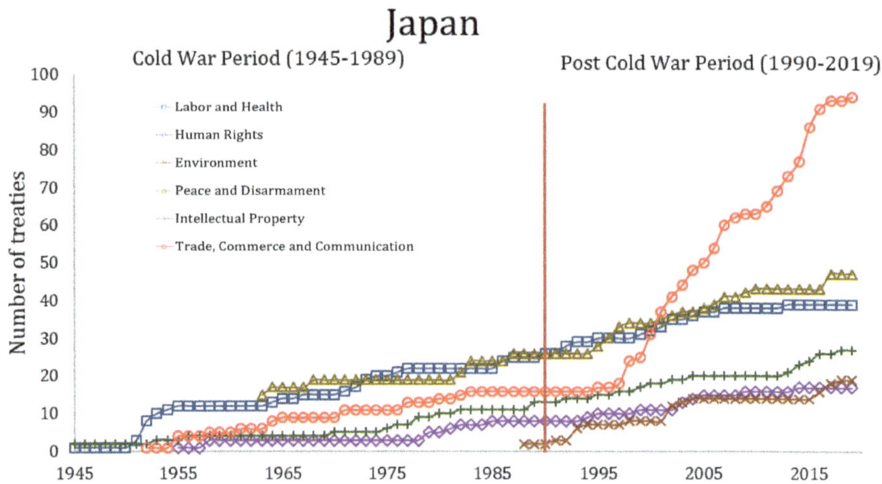

Fig. 8.1 The participation in UN multilateral treaties of Japan

8.3 China

The most striking feature of China's graph of Multilateral Treaties Participation (Fig. 8.2) is that the its position in 1978 and beyond resembles that of Japan in 1956

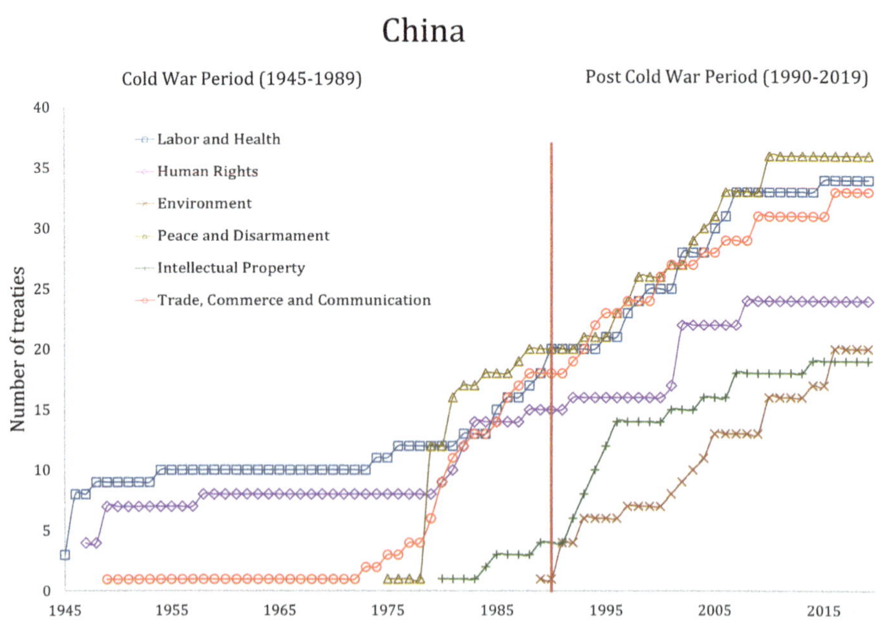

Fig. 8.2 The participation in UN multilateral treaties of China

and beyond. What is meant by that? As Japan opened itself to the outside world in 1956, China did so in 1978. Before 1956 when Japan entered into the United Nations Organization, it was alone and apart from the rest of the world except for the United States. No less important is the per-capita income level of Japan in the first decade after the war. It was recovering and developing fast from the lowest level. In 1950, in terms of per-capita national income, Japan was ranked almost at the bottom of Asia when the Philippines was one of the richest in the region. In 1978 China was one of the poorest in Asia. Deng Xiaoping stood high with the slogan of "hiding oneself and biding time." In three decades the picture seems similar between Japan 1986 and China 2008. In 1986 Japan was at the height of "Japan as Number One" (Vogel 1983) whereas in 2008 China was at the height of its hidden ambition laid bare by publishing "China 2025," in which China made it clear that its economic strengths would overtake the US by 2025 (Gabriele 2020). In 2019 Japan was sometimes reputed to be the oasis in the turbulent world. Yet it faces a society that is increasingly aging, decreasing patent-acquisition, and resignation-cum-satisfaction in a stalled society. In 2019 China still registered a 6% annual growth rate. Yet the hyper-regulations of what Branko Milanovic calls "political capitalism" (2019) practiced in China generate bureaucrats with tight lips, one of the consequences of which being the tardy response to the outburst of coronavirus epidemic in Wuhan. The one-and-half-month delay in publicly recognizing its outburst (and thus triggering a prompt response), resulted in some close to 60,000 persons killed by the epidemic as of the end of April 2020, the figure surpassing those American soldiers killed in the Vietnam War. The efficient and effective characteristic of "political capitalism" is exemplified by the construction of a few hospitals, in each of which 1000 beds were installed, in half a month at Wuhan. Tracing China's rise and fall and analyzing three decisive issues from an international perspective, Wei (2019) lists energy, territory, environmental problem, and human rights and anti-corruption. All four domains are decisive. But Wei (2019) gives Part IV: Human Rights and Anti-Corruption the subtitle "Key Elements for China's rise as a great Nation."

8.4 South Korea

In 1945 South Korea was sprouting a lot of political and social movements liberated from Japanese colonial rule. All sorts of actors were involved. Out of the chaotic uncertainty emerged two declarations of independence: the Democratic People's Republic of Korea and the Republic of Korea. The latter was headed by Synmang Rhee, a right-wing nationalist ideologue and emigre from Hawaii whereas the former was headed by Kim Il Sung, a communist active in the pre-independence Manchukuo brought in with the Soviet Army from the Soviet Far East in 1945. The fierce competition between them resulted in North Korea's all-out military attack on South Korea to militarily unify the country in 1950. Although the armistice was signed in 1953, the land was left ruined and both governments continued to place themselves on war footings for many years till now. Focusing on South Korea, one is struck by the similarity of industrial growth between South Korea and Japan. Both recovered swiftly from war devastation. Then multilateral treaty participation in the labor domain and in the human rights domain prepared good industrialization in the mid-1950s through in the mid-1970s (Fig. 8.3). Both started with elementary manufactured products for export like "cotton shirts, plastic flowers and black wigs" (The Economist 2019). Then they moved on to "memory chips, laptops and equity derivatives." It was in the latter half of the 1970s that South Korea vigorously activated infrastructure (subway and airway) and heavy industrial sectors (steel, chemicals) thanks in part to the basic treaty between South Korea and Japan in 1965 and South Korea's multilateral treaty participation thereafter, including the treaty on the Asian Development Bank. It is most interesting to note that multilateral treaty participation in the peace domain and in the trade domain ran in parallel since the mid-1970s. These parallel movements coincided with the self-confidence in economic strength vis-à-vis North Korea. South Korea has maintained steady participation in the labor and human rights domains since the mid-1970s despite authoritarian politics. The Asian monetary crisis in 1997–1998 transformed South Korea dramatically in two fronts: South Korea was under the guidance of the International Monetary Fund, which transformed the economy in line with the "neo-liberal" policy and its electorates leaned to the progressive direction, which was evidenced in the renewed increase of those multilateral treaties in the labor and human rights domains and the strident increase on the multilateral treaty participation in the environment and intellectual property domains. The global recession, originating in the US in 2008 onward, and Japan's big earthquake-cum-tsunami-cum nuclear power meltdown in 2011 created the vacuum of global markets into which the developing South spearheaded by BRICS (Brazil, Russia, India, China, and South Africa) and the MIKTA (Mexico, Indonesia, South Korea, Turkey, and Australia)

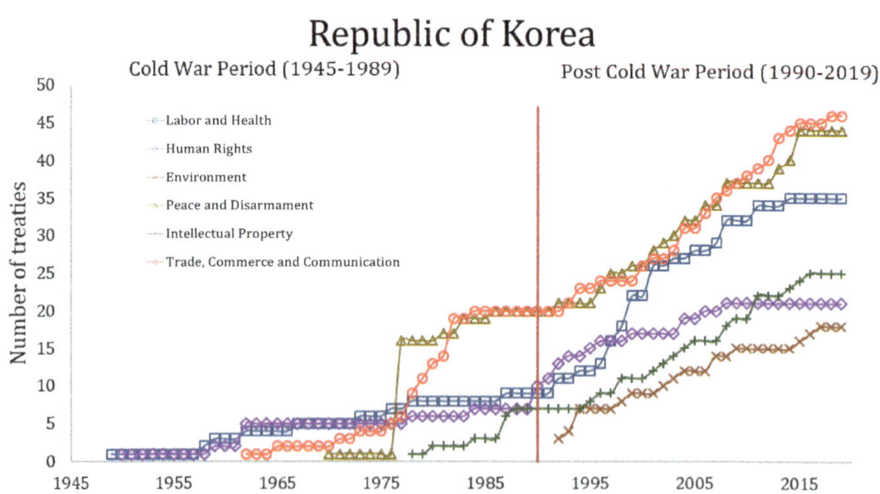

Fig. 8.3 The participation in UN multilateral treaties of South Korea

expanded its share in the global market. The rise of the US–China tariff-tech war in 2017 has had a negative impact on the South Korean economy, especially in the further improvement of social security and poverty-stricken strata. Yet the rise of South Korea has been quite admirable all the more because of its great vulnerability to the outside environmental forces like the sandwiched between great powers the US and China and facing the hostile North Korea. Its per capita GDP is on a par with that of Japan (The Economist 2019).

8.5 North Korea

Self-reliance ideology and a centralized system long dominated North Korea without multilateral treaty participation (1953–1975); *Janmadam* market informal capitalism since the 1970s rose while the strict centralized system was somewhat relaxed and weakened (Baek 2016). Multilateral treaty participation in the labor and human rights domains increased as the centralized system weakened (Fig. 8.4). Then in the 1980s onward, both peace and trade domain participation increased; the latter half of the 1990s saw frequent intermittent famines; science education was emphasized, and science and technology were directly linked to economic development. (One of the most striking findings of multilateral treaty participation is the leading profile of those participation in the intellectual property and the environment domains throughout all the periods especially in the post-Cold War period.) Whereas the priority on

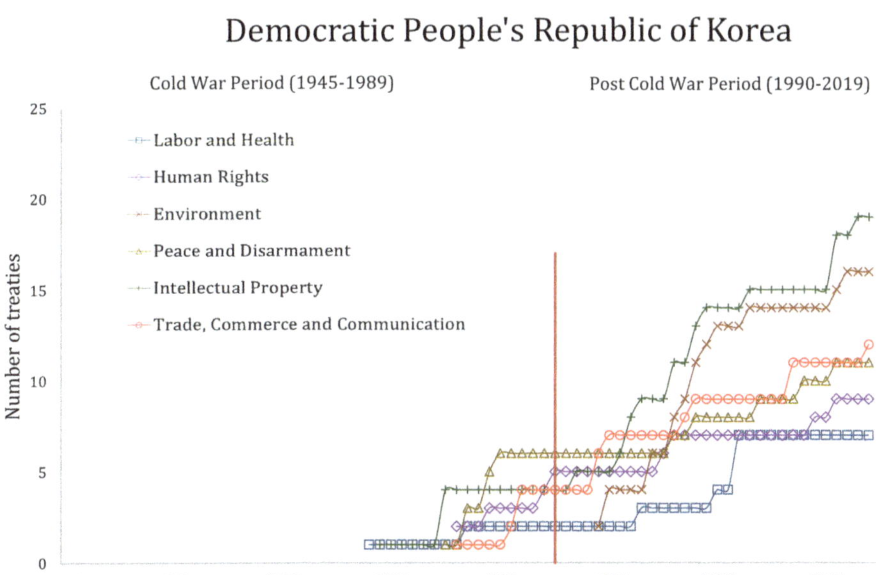

Fig. 8.4 The participation in UN multilateral treaties of North Korea

people's livelihood was emphasized, national security or more narrowly regime security remained vital, according to *Sungun* ideology (the military is paramount among all sectoral priorities); hence priority goes to study science and technology especially in nuclear and rocketry technology for deterrence. Kim Il Sung first wanted to get nuclear power stations with agreement with Bill Clinton in 1994. But the agreement collapsed in 2009. Then Kim Jong Il searched for *Sungun* policy (the military first). Kim Jong Il died from a heart attack in 2011. Kim Jong Un then more narrowly focused on nuclear weapons, which led him to test nuclear missiles and nuclear bombs in the 2010s. That led to the US–North Korean denuclearization talks in 2017 through 2019 between Donald Trump and Kim Jong Un. The Summit talks had stalled by 2019. To sum up, North Korea was basically reluctant to join the multilateral treaties system because doing so was in total opposition to its principle, *juche* (independence, autonomy, self-reliance) especially in the 1950s, 1960s, and 1970s. Yet recognizing South Korea's rise, especially in the manufacturing sector and in the military build-up under the dictatorship and its *Nordpolitik*, North Korea has been very proactive in mobilizing support from the developed South, especially those weapons-purchasing Middle East and African countries. North Korea has been quite active in trying to build nuclear power stations by the Six Party talks headed by the US along with South Korea, China, Russia, and Japan. North Korea joined and after the Six Party's failure withdrew from the Treaty on the Non-Proliferation of Nuclear Weapons. Subsequently focusing on ICBM with nuclear bombs loaded, North Korea has been trying to wipe out the US from the Korean Peninsula, so far to no avail. The fact that North Korea's participation in multilateral treaties per number of years in the UN is much larger than the corresponding figure of the US.

8.6 Vietnam

The prevalence of war in Vietnamese life before and after 1945 until the border with China was calmed down in 1984 with the peace settlement of the Chinese-Vietnamese war of 1979. During the long war-cum-peace period during 1945 and 1984 a small number of multilateral treaties were joined by Vietnam in the domains of trade, commerce, and communications, labor and health, intellectual property, and human rights (Fig. 8.5). The collapse of the Soviet Union and the US post-war embargoes negatively affected the Vietnamese economy. Trade liberalization was implemented by devaluing its exchange rate to increase exports and reform embarkation started. In 1986 the *Doi Moi* reform was officially announced and implemented. The US embargo stopped in 1994, but the Asian monetary crisis of 1997–1998 caused the Vietnamese economy to slow down. But by 1999 annual economic growth rate came back to around 7%, making Vietnam's one of the world's fastest-growing economies. With the accelerated *Doi Moi* reform policy, multilateral treaties in all domains increased in number, especially those in the trade domain and the labor domain. Since the mid-1980s those multilateral treaties in such domains as human rights, the environment, intellectual property, and peace domains have registered a

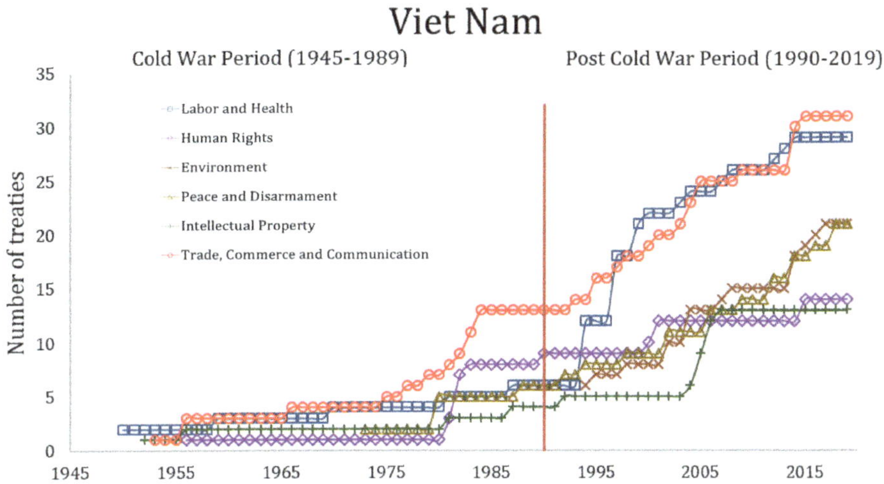

Fig. 8.5 The participation in UN multilateral treaties of Vietnam

steady increase. To sum up, Vietnam has been one of the most active states in the developing South. In terms of the member of multilateral treaties joined by Vietnam per the number of years in the United Nations, Vietnam overtakes that of the US even more than North Korea. With the adoption of "political capitalism" with Vietnamese characteristics, *Doi Moi*, Vietnam has been quite constructively active in the regional organization as well.

8.7 Throughout Sinic East

One notices from Figs. 8.1, 8.2, 8.3 and 8.5 (Japan, South Korea, China, and Vietnam) that participation in a bundle of multilateral treaties in six policy domains triggered developmental leaps upward. The timing of such participation depends on circumstances in which each Sinic East country was placed. By circumstances are meant a number of things: developmental stages (early starter, late comer), developmental principles (nationalist, protectionist, internationalist, universalist), regime characteristics (dictatorship, authoritarianism, democracy), popular life satisfaction (satisfied, dissatisfied), and global (and regional) systemic breakdowns (the first and second oil crisis, Asian monetary crisis, global recession, economic sanctions, and the Covid-19 pandemic assault world over).

8.8 Regional Dynamics of Sinic East

Before examining each Sinic East country's graphs of multilateral treaties participation, a brief summary of regional dynamism is given here. From a long-term perspective, Sinic Asia or East Asia has been most significantly characterized by three trends: (1) East Asia was one of the two key battlefields of World War II along with Europe; (2) The localized Cold War was waged in East Asia, the Korean War and the Vietnam War; (3) The global end of the Cold War precipitated East Asian communist regimes not to be prevailed by its capitalist brothers and sisters, thus creating "the East Asian peace" (Tønnesson 2019) and the era of the "capitalism, alone" (Milanovic 2019). In this section we summarize how the first trend was succeeded by the second trend. From Sect. 8.10 we will summarize what came as the second and third trends country by country with multilateral treaties functioning transformatively as vehicles and agents. The peace settlement of World War II was precipitated by Germany's surrender, Europe was left in ashes and faced division into western and eastern Europe by the US and the USSR respectively. However, the peace settlement of World War II in East Asia was partial peace with the US-led Western bloc, that is, Japan's surrender with the US-led allied powers. What happened after the East Asia's partial peace settlement was the struggle between communist forces and capitalist forces in all East Asian societies, especially Korea, Vietnam, China, and Taiwan, with Japan being an exception. What triggered these struggles in East Asia? It was the accelerated destruction of East Asian societies by the Japanese imperial armed forces. The European war was waged with the breakdown of the fragile Versailles peace (Macmillan 2007). The East Asian war started in one sense by the subjectively preemptive preparatory consolidation of war footings, which was foresightedly envisaged by Lieutenant Kanji Ishihara against the emerging hegemon, the US. For that purpose, Japan enhanced its aggressions in one region after another in Asia. The US imposed the economic embargoes in the spirit of war prohibition specified by the Kellogg-Brian Treaty (1928) further consolidated with "teeth" added to guard against Japanese aggression in East Asia (Hathaway and Shapiro 2007). What happened toward the end of the war in East Asia? It is the Japanese destruction of East Asian societies to fight against the US by brutally and relentlessly mobilizing resources in occupied territories, human and material, and Japanese and other Asian. Anticipating the Japanese defeat and surrender to the Allied powers, Joseph Stalin rushed his soldiers and weapons from the West to the East with the German surrender in May 1945. Stalin and Franklin D. Roosevelt raced to the East for Japan and surrounding East Asia in order to become the occupying power (Hasegawa 2006; Okonogi 2019).

In China in 1945, Chiang Kaishek, President of the Republic of China, announced clemency to the Japanese imperial forces to surrender their weapons to the Chinese government forces, saying China would not seek revenge against Japan but would offer clemency to all the Japanese soldiers and peoples. Chiang's clemency was Christian, meaning love your former enemy. Mao Zedong, representing Communist forces in China, announced clemency to the surrendered Japanese imperial armed forces on the grounds that the war was led by the Japanese military and that Japanese people were the no less victims of the military cliques than the Chinese people. All the Japanese military forces in China, then amounting to 2 million soldiers, surrendered their weapons either to the Chinese Communist forces and to the Kuomintang government forces. Communist and government forces competed to get massive caches of Japanese weapons wherever they were. In 1945–1949 the civil war was waged between them. It was in former Manchuria where communist forces overwhelmed the government forces: the first massive head-on confrontation between them in Shenyang, Liaoning province in Manchuria which ended with the overwhelming victory of the Communists. Civil wars in 1945–1949 experienced new factors. First, the Soviet Union activated its operations throughout Sinic East: China, Korea, and Japan. In China, the Soviet military guidance and assistance to the Chinese communists were not underestimated. Second, the United States policy toward China changed dramatically: from Roosevelt to Truman; from its pro-Chiang Kaishek policy to elevate China as the center of US far eastern policy to its policy cool and critical to the Kuomintang China (Van de Ven 2017). Then Communists drove the Kuomintang's forces to southern waters and Taiwan.

In Vietnam earlier in autumn 1941, and before Japan's attack on Pearl Harbor on 7 December 1941, French Indochina and shortly thereafter British Malaya and Singapore were occupied by the Japanese imperial armed forces, which wanted to negate and nullify the colonial French and colonial British power in Southeast Asia. In 1945, as soon as Japanese surrendered, Ho Chi Minh, leading Vietnamese Communists and representing the Vietnamese people, declared national independence, with the Constitution vividly reminding people of the American Declaration of Independence in 1776. Ho Chi Minh's most famous words were "Nothing is more precious than national independence." However, the colonial war came back with the French fighting Vietnamese in 1945–1953. In 1953, a fragile peace settlement called the Geneva agreement was signed between them. In the south the Republic of Vietnam was born whereas in the north the Democratic Republic of Vietnam was born. The guerrilla war resumed in the south in the mid-1950s and then the US intervened massively in mid-1960s and the war ended in 1973 with the fragile peace agreement was signed. In 1975 both Vietnams were militarily united with the Communists emerging as victors in this long-fought struggle.

In Korea the race between the US and the USSR was the struggle of speed of not only moving soldiers and sailors closer to Japan and its vicinities. Soviet soldiers needed recuperation after the German surrender, but were sent out shortly after May 1945 from the West to the Far East. Americas soldiers and sailors skipped from one island to another in the Pacific Ocean, defeating the remaining Japanese imperial forces one by one. The competition between two US militaries, Chester Nimitz (navy) and Douglas MacArthur (army), took the two parallel forms:

(1) Nimitz chose the strategy of massive aerial strikes on Japanese cities, factories, ports, railways, and
(2) MacArthur chose the strategy of unprecedented bombing of civilians, targeting Hiroshima and Nagasaki with atomic bombs to accelerate the Japanese surrender

and thereby reduce the anticipated massive amount of American soldiers and sailors needed to land at Japan and face heavy Japanese resistance.

Those atomic bombs were dropped on 6 and 9 August, 1945. Soviet soldiers had reached Kurile islands and northern Korea. In northern and southern Korea the latent struggle between Communists and non-Communists commenced, anticipating the Japanese imminent defeat and surrender. It involved not only competition between Communists and non-Communists but also between home nationalists and nationalists abroad (like Moscow, Beijing and the Soviet Far East and Manchukuo, Hawaii, and Shanghai). The initiative of consolidating power was taken by Communists in the Soviet Fast East and Manchukuo and in northern Korea (that is, Kim Il Sung), whereas the initiative of consolidating power in southern Korea was taken by nationalist in Hawaii (Synman Rhee). To Joseph Stalin the US atomic bombs were dropped too early whereas to Truman they were surprisingly fast in persuading Japanese emperor to nod his surrender—but not soon enough to free the US of complications in Korea, including the latent seed of triggering the Korean war in 1950.

8.9 Japan

Japan's participation in multilateral treaties is most active among Sinic East states. It makes sense because it has been one of the few OECD club countries in the non-West with many multilateral commitments. In the Cold War period those treaties in the peace domain and the trade domain were steadily on the rise whereas those multilateral treaties in the labor and health domain have risen steadily during the Cold War period and more so beyond. Multilateral treaties in the environment, intellectual property and human rights have risen during the late Cold War period, and most importantly during the post-Cold War period.

Those multilateral treaties in the trade domain registered an upward slope when epoch-making events took place. In the mid-1950s Japan entered the United Nations, the World Health Organization and the General Agreement of Tariffs and Trade, and the Bank of International Reconstruction and Development. In the mid-1960s Japan's participation in the trade domain registered in conjunction with the Tokyo Olympic Games, the joining of OECD, and International Monetary Organization and other international financial institutions. In the mid-1970s they joined of Group of Seven Powers in post-first oil crises in the 1970s and 1980s (Putnam and Bayne 1988). These two constituted the foundation of the Japan as Number 1 (Vogel 1983), which lasted by around mid-1990s. Beyond 1995 those multilateral treaties registered by leaps and bounds in the broad harmony of the advent and acceleration of globalization. Important to note here was the Asian monetary crisis (1997–1998). Thereafter those multilateral treaties jumped upward in a striking fashion. The pattern was repeated in 2008 and beyond, after another economic upheaval. While in the 1950s and 1960s multilateral treaties in the trade domain were meant to accelerate economic development by enhancing infrastructure and alleviating conflicting arrangements on foreign trade, investment and technology transfer with foreign states, those in the mid-1990s and beyond the late 2000s were meant more to alleviate the negative impacts of regional and global crises. Japan's participation in multilateral treaties domain by domain for each period, Cold War and post-Cold War are illustrated from Figs. 8.6, 8.7, 8.8, 8.9, 8.10 and 8.11.

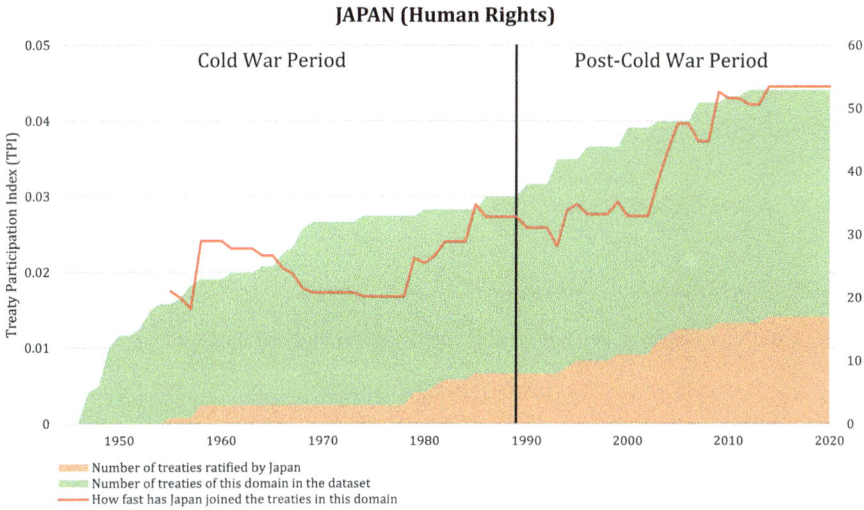

Fig. 8.6 Japan's participation in human rights multilateral treaties

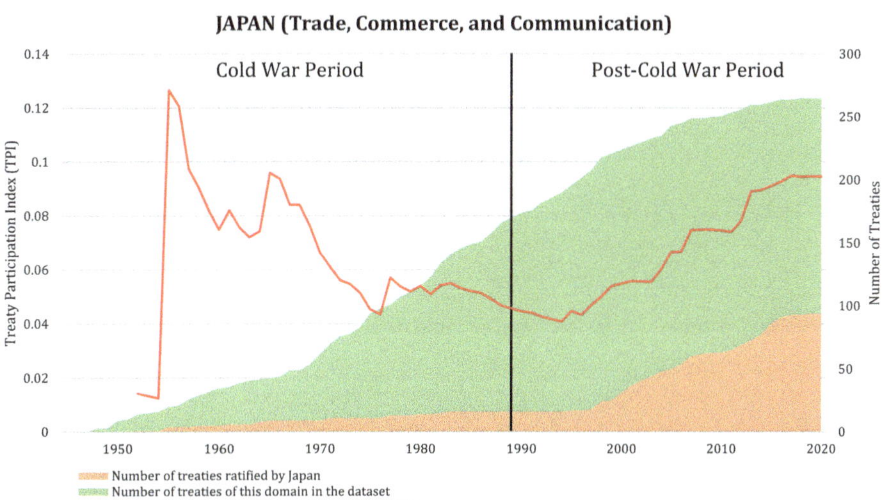

Fig. 8.7 Japan's participation in trade, commerce, and communication multilateral treaties

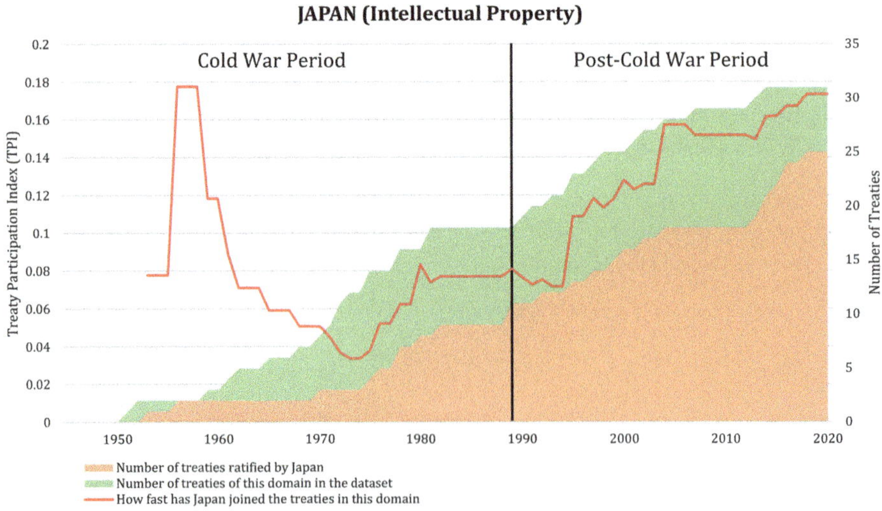

Fig. 8.8 Japan's participation in intellectual property rights multilateral treaties

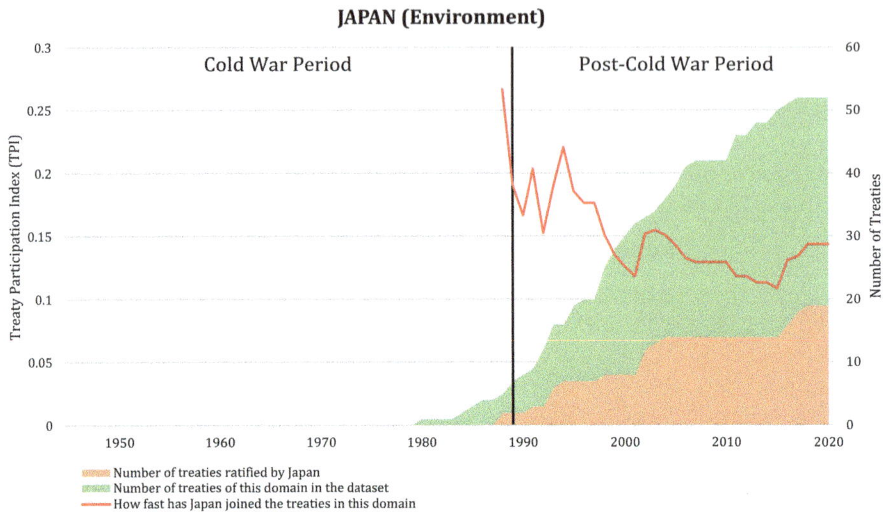

Fig. 8.9 Japan's participation in environment multilateral treaties

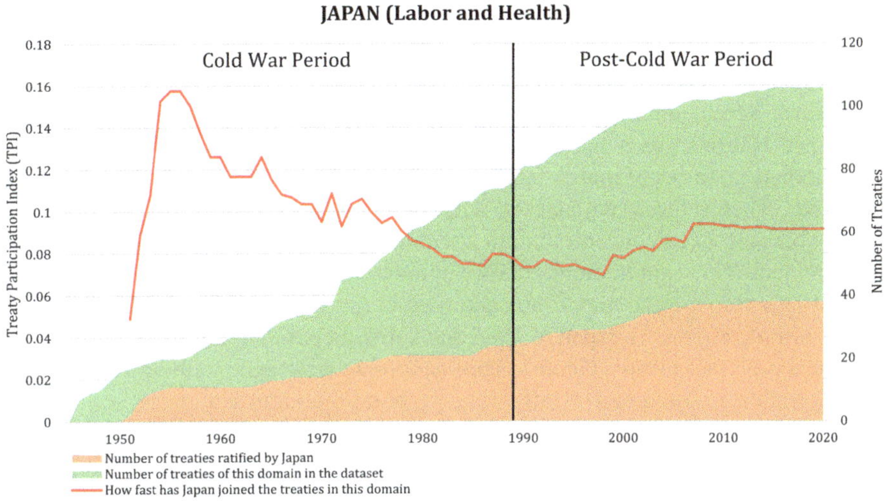

Fig. 8.10 Japan's participation in labor and health multilateral treaties

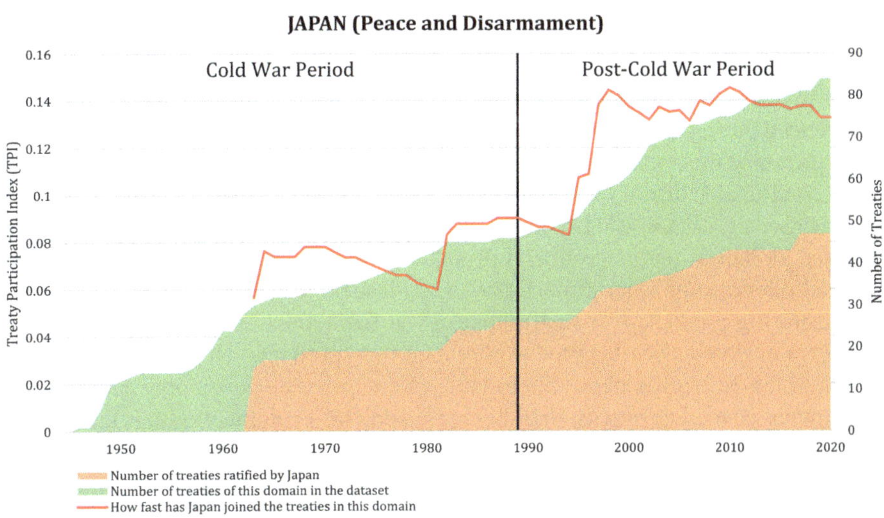

Fig. 8.11 Japan's participation in peace and disarmament multilateral treaties

8.10 South Korea

The Korean war (1950–1953) ended with the armistice agreement in 1953 between the US-ROK-UN forces and the DPRK-PRC forces. But it was not a peace treaty. Therefore, occurrence of non-major confrontations was not excluded thereafter. That is why number of multilateral treaties in the peace domain jumped twice: in the mid-1970s when South Korea adopted *Nordpolitik* establishing the diplomatic normalization with the Soviet Union and thus meant to push its diplomatic offensive vis-à-vis North Korea; and in 1992 when the simultaneous entry of the two Koreas into the United Nations was achieved. To adapt its diplomacy to a new situation South Korea joined a number of multilateral treaties for the subsequent few years thereafter each time. Then a few years elapsed without any multilateral treaties in the peace domain because of its concentration in attention to economic development and arms enhancement. Those multilateral treaties in the trade domain increased dramatically in the 1970s through the mid-1980s and then in the late 1990s onward. The diplomatic normalization with Japan in 1965 and subsequent bilateral treaties with Japan were meant de facto war-reparation-cum-economic assistance without the name of war reparation in the areas of infrastructure building, industrial construction such as automobiles, technology transfer such as manufacturing of the advanced kind of steel products and financial assistance. Before multilateral treaties placed important roles to South Korea, those bilateral agreements were instrumental to push South Korea to the position of "four flying geese" (South Korea, Taiwan, Hong Kong, and Singapore) between the mid-1970s and mid-1980s. "Four flying geese" was meant to denote a flock of geese flying as a group. It is headed by a leader of navigation in economic development like Japan as the first flying goose. The next sub-leaders are the four flying geese. Because of its brand, multilateral treaties the four flying tigers joined by leaps and bounds during the mid-1970s and mid-1990s. Some excesses experienced during this period caused the Asian monetary crisis of 1997–1998. One consequence of this crisis was that South Korea was subordinated to the guidance of the International Monetary Fund, which forced too many mini-scale industrial firms to be merged by what would become very few mammoth *chebols*. Riding high on the digitized globalization in neo-liberal persuasion South Korea and other flying tigers changed the order of seats, from followers to leaders, especially in special service manufacturing products like smartphones (The Economist 2019) where Japan was slower to develop service-targeted worldwide export products. This is admirable even though South Korea has been able to take advantage of its developing South status for so many years. Despite its GDP being ranked No. 11 in the world, it has not yet discarded its developing status in the World Trade Organization, the International Energy Agency and other international institutions despite its promise to do so.

Because South Korea was late in joining, its membership of multilateral treaties in all domains was one half of Japan's during the entire Cold War and Post-Cold War period. But South Korea's accumulated number is twice as many as North Korea. Even North Korea's number is, when the accumulated number is divided by the number of years in the United Nations, on a par with that of the United States! The United States has been following the Washingtonian principle of disentanglement all the way since 1945 despite its role as leader of the liberal world order. Donald Trump is not an exception. It is normal, American style of multilateral treaty participation! In the intellectual property, the environment and human rights domains, South Korea has registered a similar pattern with Japan in that during the post-Cold War period they have joined such treaties eagerly although because of the developing South status they do not necessarily shoulder much of its burdens, as in the Paris climate change accord. South Korea's participation in multilateral treaties domain by domain for each period, post-armistice and post-Asian monetary crisis period (1997–1998) are illustrated from Figs. 8.12, 8.13, 8.14, 8.15, 8.16 and 8.17.

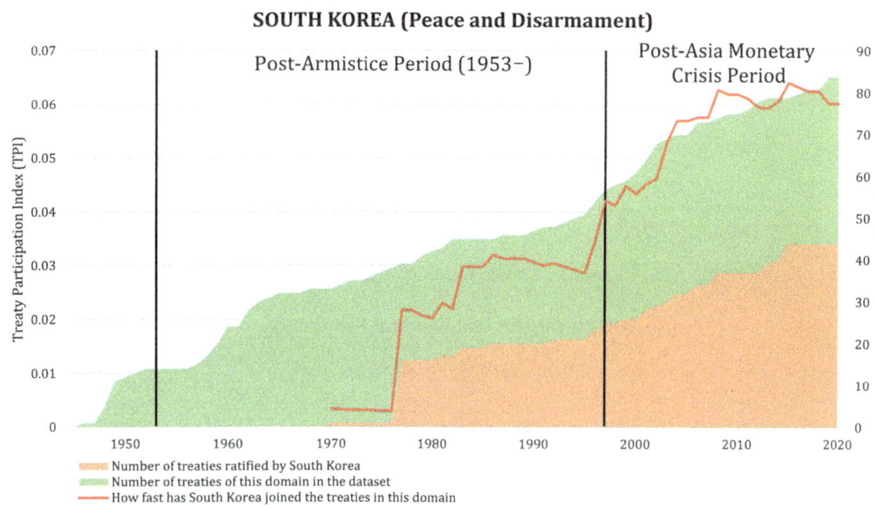

Fig. 8.12 South Korea's participation in peace and disarmament multilateral treaties

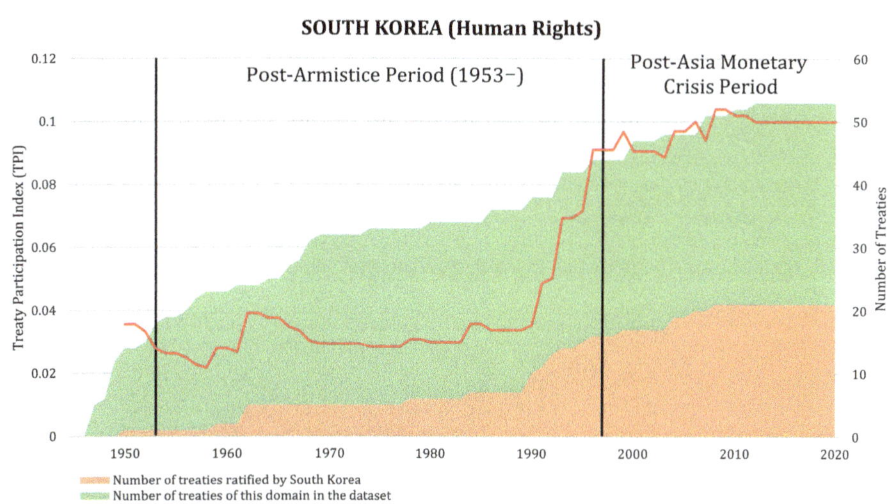

Fig. 8.13 South Korea's participation in human rights multilateral treaties

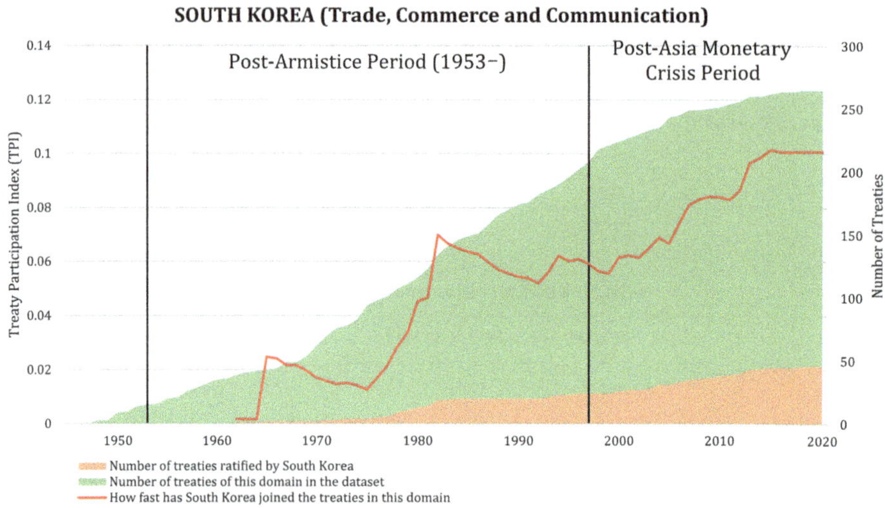

Fig. 8.14 South Korea's participation in trade, commerce, and communication multilateral treaties

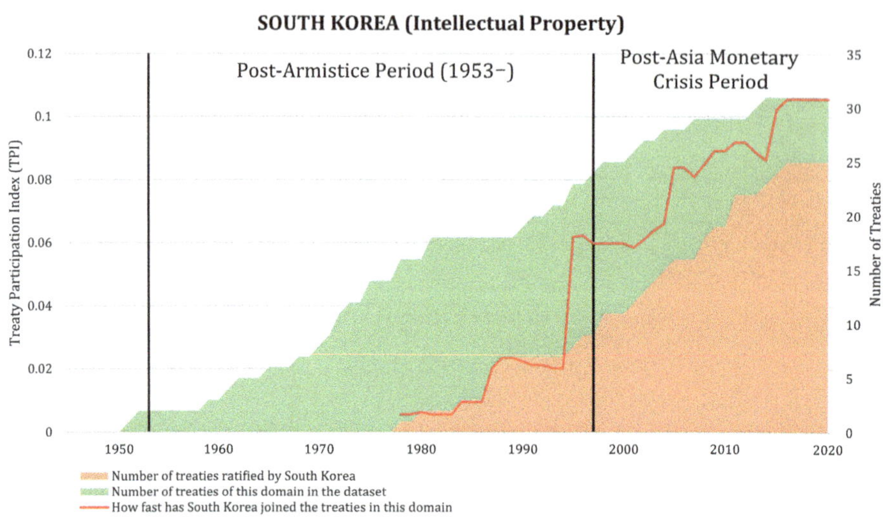

Fig. 8.15 South Korea's participation in intellectual property multilateral treaties

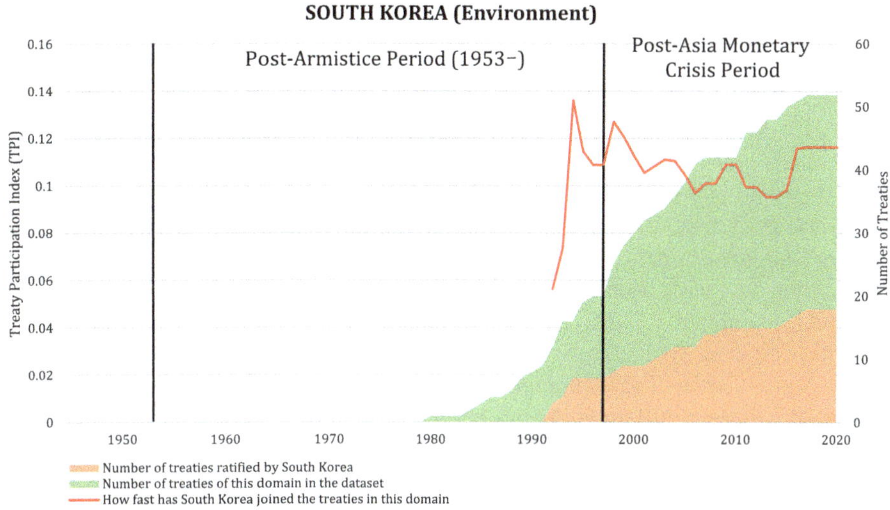

Fig. 8.16 South Korea's participation in environment multilateral treaties

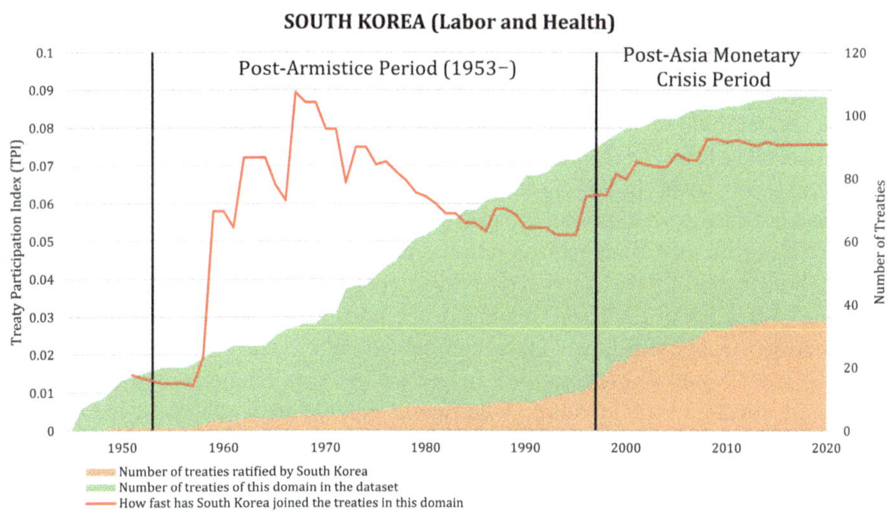

Fig. 8.17 South Korea's participation in labor and health multilateral treaties

8.11 China

Civil war divided China, with its Kuomintang Government led by Chiang Kaishek, until 1945. After Japan surrendered to the Allied powers led by the United States, Communists and Kuomintang forces resumed the civil war after they captured as many weapons as possible from the surrendered Japanese armed forces throughout China and East Asia. The resumed civil war ended with Communist victory. The Kuomintang government captured Taiwan in 1949, a former Japanese colony, proclaiming the same Republic of China and retaining United Nations membership and remaining a Security Council permanent member until 1972. The People's Republic of China replaced the Republic of China on Taiwan in 1972, when the United States normalized diplomatic relationship with Beijing at the sacrifice of Taiwan. Yet those multilateral treaties earlier signed and ratified by the Republic of China were acknowledged by the People's Republic of China in 1972 through 1979. The Republic of China on Taiwan subsequently behaved in international organizations such as the World Health Organization as an "as if" observer. The practice was permitted until recently. More recently, since the independence-leaning Democratic Progressive Party President Chen Shui Bian assumed the office in 2006, China has been rejecting Taiwan's observer's participation. Before 1972 those domains in which multilateral treaties China joined were mostly those domains in labor and health, and human rights. China since 1949 adopted a policy of self-reliance of economic development and national security, so it had not much to do in multilateral treaties except those succeeded from the Republic of China, Nanjing. With the diplomatic normalization first with Japan (in 1972) and then with the United States (1973), and with the peace and friendship treaties with Japan (1978) and with the United States (1979), the People's Republic of China entered into the multilateral treaty arena (Soeya 1998; Vogel 2019; Hattori 2011; Smith 2015). Most noteworthy is the jump start of those multilateral treaties in the trade domain in the mid-1970s and beyond. The diplomatic normalization with Japan was accompanied with a massive dose of economic assistance (not called war reparation). In late 1970s Deng Xiaoping came to power, initiating reform and the opening to the world policy line in 1978—what Branko Milanovic (2019) called "political capitalism" in full fashion. The 1989 suppression of Tianmen protestors led the West and Japan to impose strong economic sanctions. In 1991 Japan lifted economic sanctions and the West followed shortly thereafter. That led China to join key multilateral treaties in the trade domain thereafter until Donald Trump started to impose economic sanctions vis-à-vis China from 2017 onward. The entry into the World Trade Organization was admitted by Barak Obama in 2000 (Steinberg, January 2020). Since China was categorized as a developing South country in the WTO, rules and regulations were leniently applied. Hence China registered two-digit developmental achievement—three decades of annual economic growth rate. When the world economy stagnated in 2008 and, thereafter what Branko Milanovic calls the "rebalancing between the West and the East" became very visible and tangible, with the West or the developed North stagnating and declining whereas the East or the developing South surging forward with annual economic growth rates registering 6–8% growth rates spearheaded in India and China. All these led to the United States carry out economic sanctions for the reasons of violation of intellectual property rights, technology transfer, and massive use of state-owned-enterprise ability to amass investment capital through state possession of land, global construction of value chains *sans frontier*. Those multilateral treaties in the trade domain have kept growing despite Trump. But China has discovered the global infrastructure-enhancing project called the One Belt, One Road project, consolidating roads and ports throughout the rest of the world using its surplus capital and labor for linking China and the neighbors near and afar. Multilateral treaties in the peace domain have been registering near astronomical military expenditure almost reaching US counterpart in 40 years period if including personnel costs. During the post-Cold War period the four domains have increased those multilateral treaties in such domains as labor and health, human rights, the environment and intellectual property. The priority of labor and health has been evinced by the total change of style of words used for describing what is on the demand side of people (beautiful good life) and on the supply side of government and enterprises (insufficient provision of products and services declared in the Central Committee policy line in 2016). Although many multilateral treaties in the domains of intellectual property, human rights and the environment have clauses of duties, regulations and burdens, China has been bereft of paying so much due to the developing South country status provision (Wei 2019). China's participation in multilateral treaties domain by domain for each period, pre-normalization period (1950s–1960s), normalization period (1970s) and post-Cold War period are illustrated from Figs. 8.18, 8.19, 8.20, 8.21, 8.22 and 8.23.

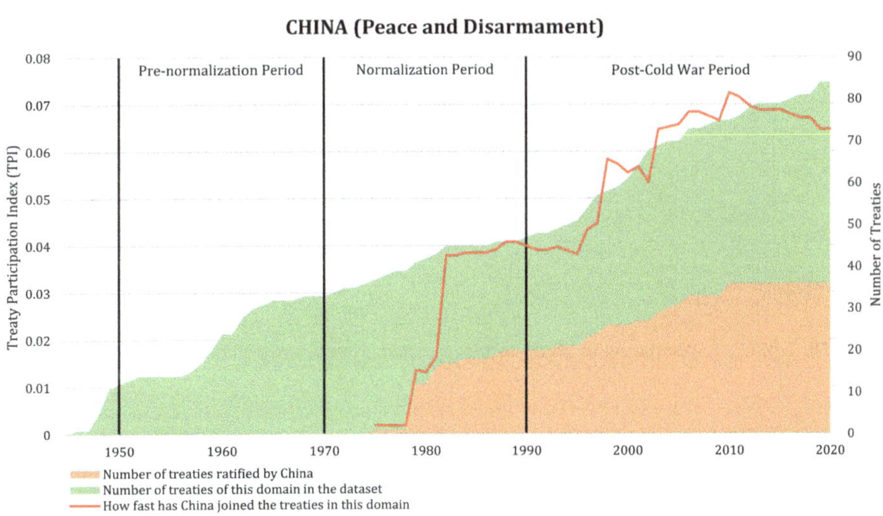

Fig. 8.18 China's participation in peace and disarmament multilateral treaties

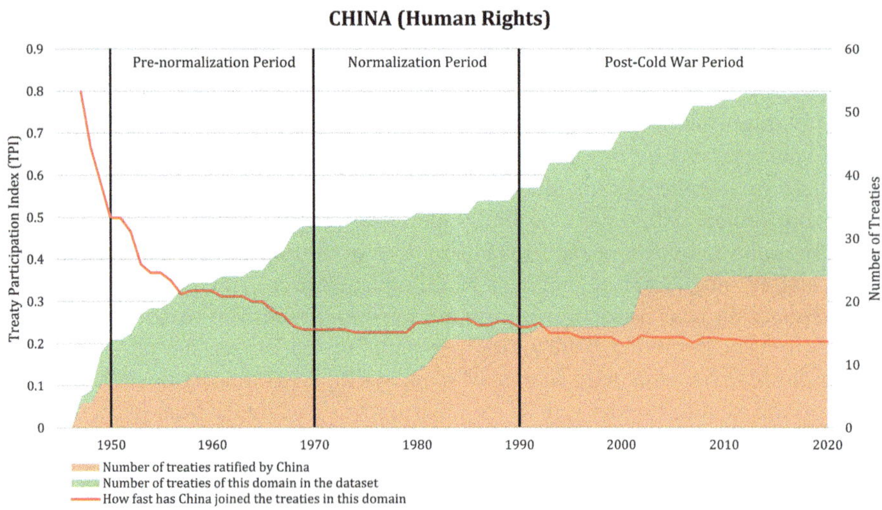

Fig. 8.19 China's participation in human rights multilateral treaties

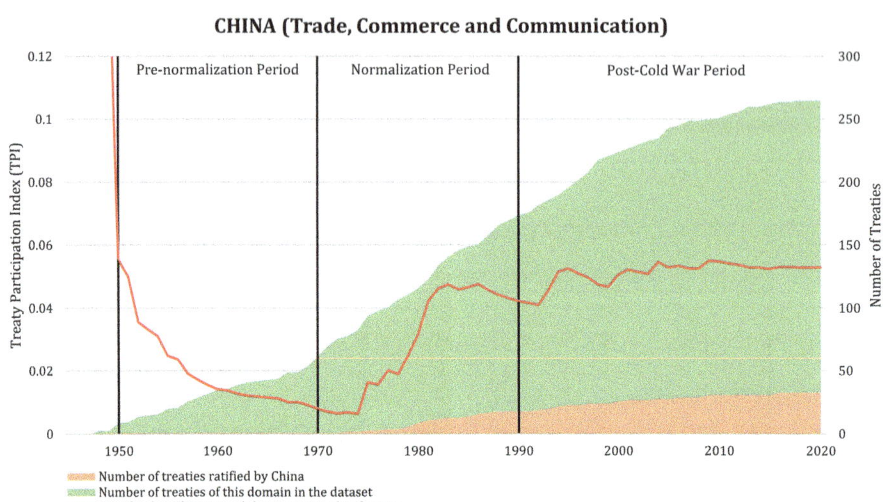

Fig. 8.20 China's participation in trade, commerce, and communication multilateral treaties

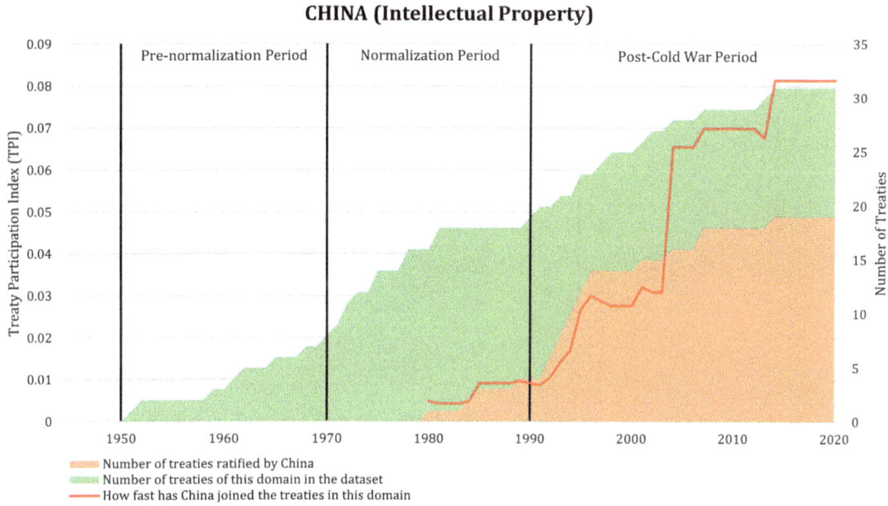

Fig. 8.21 China's participation in intellectual property multilateral treaties

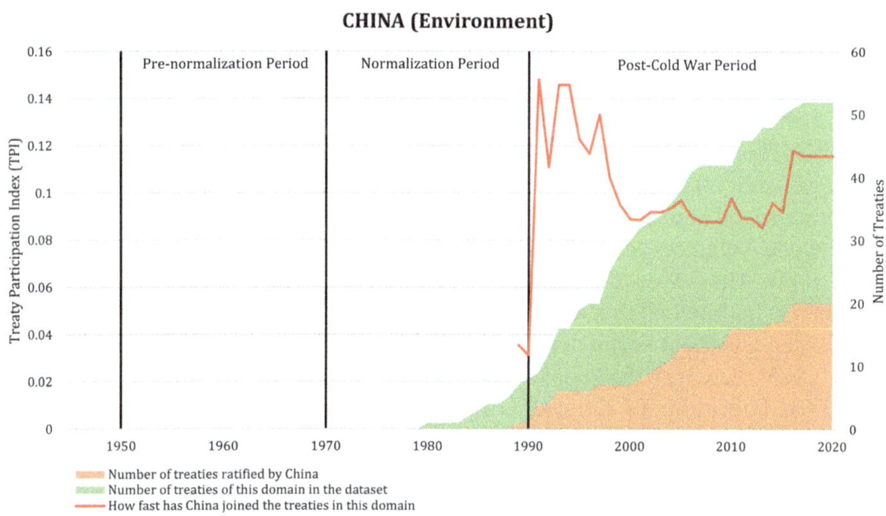

Fig. 8.22 China's participation in environment multilateral treaties

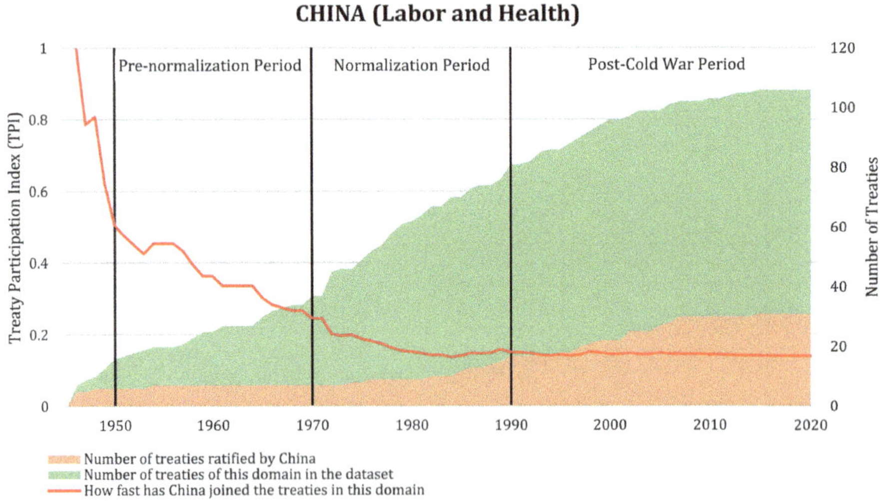

Fig. 8.23 China's participation in labor and health multilateral treaties

8.12 North Korea

North Korea was long regarded as a country totally secluding itself from the rest of the world. Having declared independence in 1948 it entered into war for the 1950–1953 against South Korea and the US-led United Nations forces. The war battered each other's land almost completely and killed not only Koreans from both sides but also Chinese Volunteer armed forces and American armed forces and their allies such as the Turks. Thus, even after the armistice agreement was signed, North Korea did not join any multilateral treaties until in the early 1970s when it joined a multilateral treaty in the labor and health domain. Its important ties during its isolationist period (1948–1968) were with the People's Republic of China and the Soviet Union plus the pro-DPRK Federation of Koreans in Japan and its predecessors. Most noteworthy of North Korean participation in multilateral treaties is that its joining multilateral treaties in the intellectual property domain was the first big action in the early 1980s along with its joining multilateral treaties in the peace domain. While those treaties in the peace domain were more erratic, those in the intellectual property domain have leaped since 1980. Joining those multilateral treaties in the environment domain has been on a steep, continuous rise whereas joining those multilateral treaties in the trade domain has been in the staccato-like fashion, each time moving up by one octave or two higher. Those multilateral treaties in the peace and trade domains have been influenced by more political considerations rather than those in intellectual property and environment domains. North Korea's participation in multilateral treaties domain by domain for each period, post-armistice period (1953–), post-Nordpolitik period and post-Cold War period are illustrated from Figs. 8.24, 8.25, 8.26, 8.27, 8.28 and 8.29.

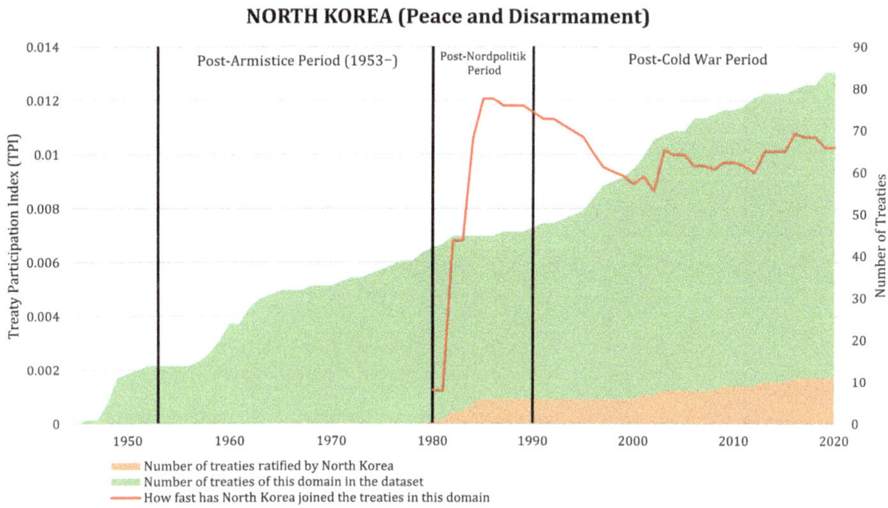

Fig. 8.24 North Korea's participation in peace and disarmament multilateral treaties

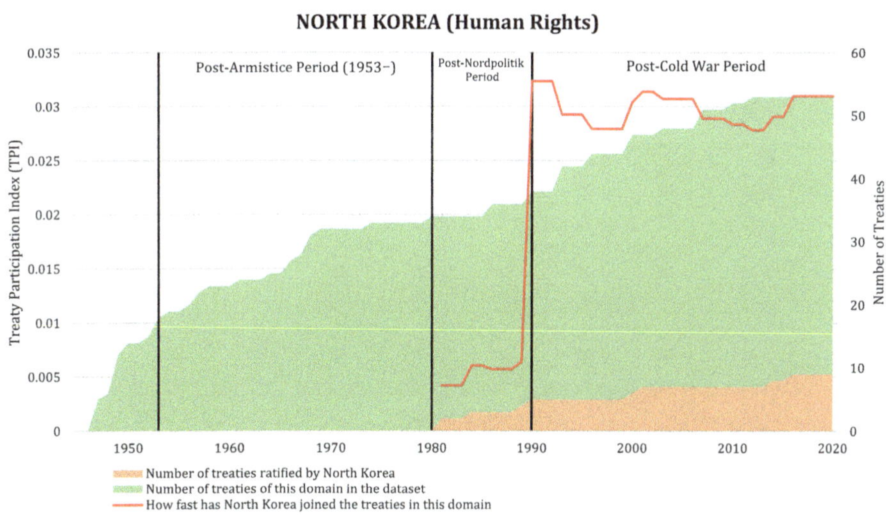

Fig. 8.25 North Korea's participation in human rights multilateral treaties

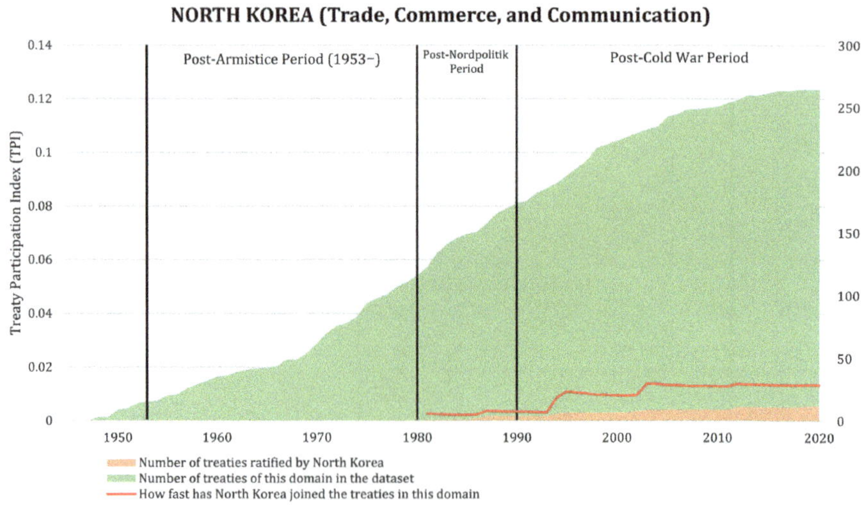

Fig. 8.26 North Korea's participation in trade, commerce, and communication multilateral treaties

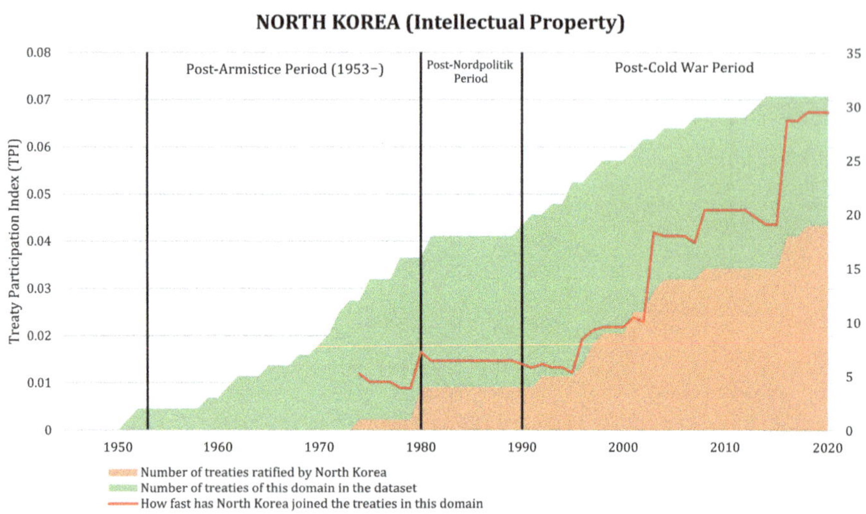

Fig. 8.27 North Korea's participation in intellectual property multilateral treaties

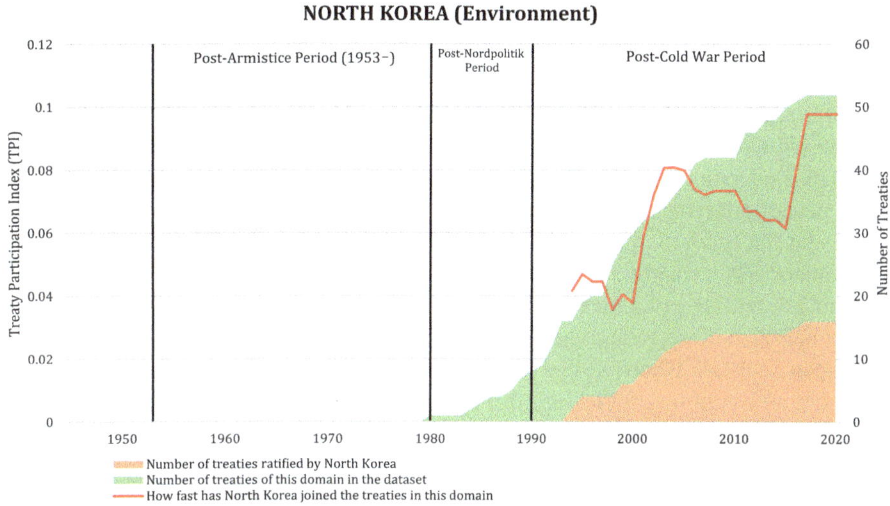

Fig. 8.28 North Korea's participation in environment multilateral treaties

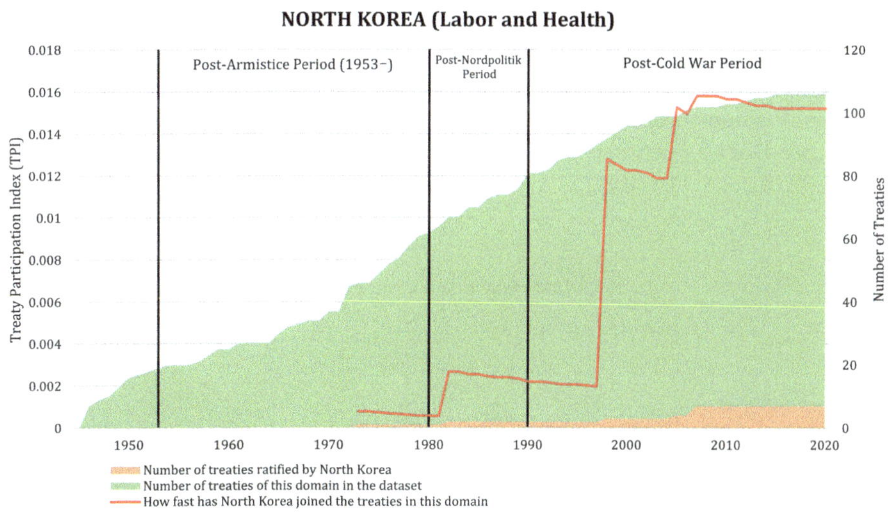

Fig. 8.29 North Korea's participation in labor and health multilateral treaties

8.13 Vietnam

Vietnam was long placed on a war footing—before, during, and after wars of many kinds, even before 1954 when the Geneva peace accords between the Democratic Republic of Vietnam and France were signed. But the national election stipulated in the Geneva accords was not carried out. South Vietnam's prime minister Ngo Dinh Diem said that the Republic of Vietnam had not signed the Geneva accords and therefore South Vietnam was not bound by it. The guerrilla war started in South Vietnam thereafter. It was in mid-1960s when the United States decided to militarily intervene in South Vietnam in support of the Republic of Vietnam. In 1973 the United States decided to withdraw its forces. The Democratic Republic of Vietnam and the United States signed the peace accords. In 1975 Saigon fell to the armed forces of the Democratic Republic of Vietnam. The Republic of Vietnam collapsed. Thus, peace looked arrived. Yet, even before the peace in Vietnam against the US, China and the Soviet Union were extremely at odds over what China called Soviet revisionism. They fought a brief but bloody war in 1969 on the Amur River flowing on their border. Nearly a decade thereafter, China was led by Deng Xiaoping with the banner of the reform and the opening to the world. He visited the United States and Japan in 1978. Shortly after his trips abroad, China intervened militarily into the Socialist Republic of Vietnam in February 1979. Vietnam had been occupying Cambodia where anti-Vietnamese forces were emerging strong. China withdrew from Vietnam whereas Vietnam withdrew from Cambodia. An accord was signed in 1984 between Vietnam and China, so that peace arrived in Vietnam at long last. After 1975 and especially from1984 onward Vietnam joined many multilateral treaties. Those policy domains of Vietnam joining multilateral treaties were the trade domain and the labor and health domain. These two domains have been overwhelming in number vis-à-vis other domains like the peace domain, the human rights domain and the intellectual property domain. This is very different in North Korea, where the intellectual property domain and the environment domain overshadow the other domains. Vietnam's participation in multilateral treaties domain by domain for each period, pre-Doi Moi period (1986) and post-Cold War are illustrated from Figs. 8.30, 8.31, 8.32, 8.33, 8.34 and 8.35.

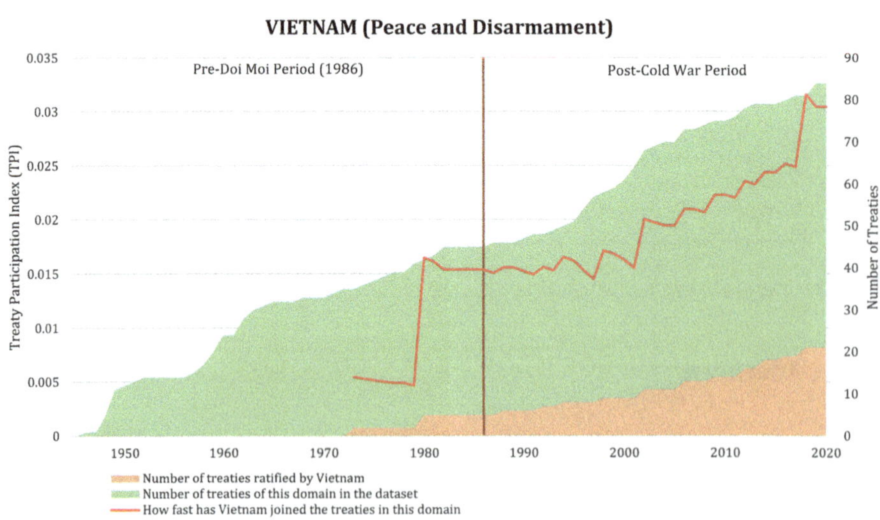

Fig. 8.30 Vietnam's participation in peace and disarmament multilateral treaties

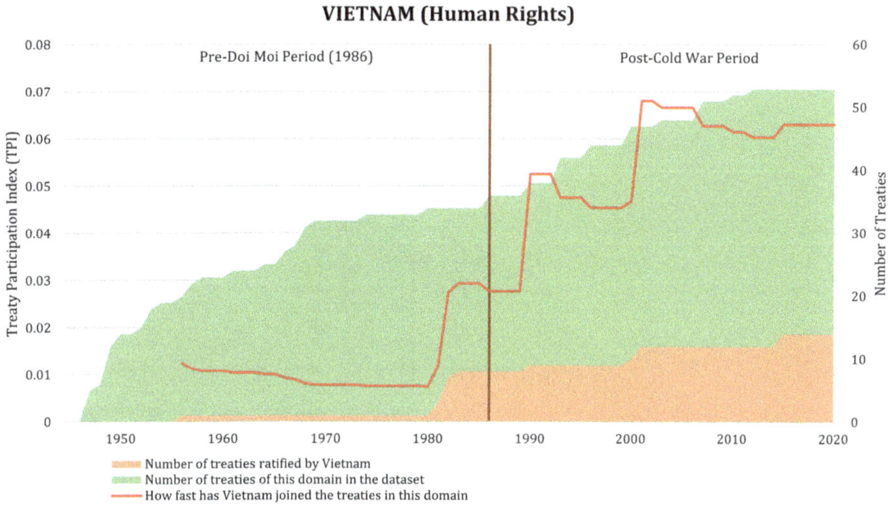

Fig. 8.31 Vietnam's participation in human rights multilateral treaties

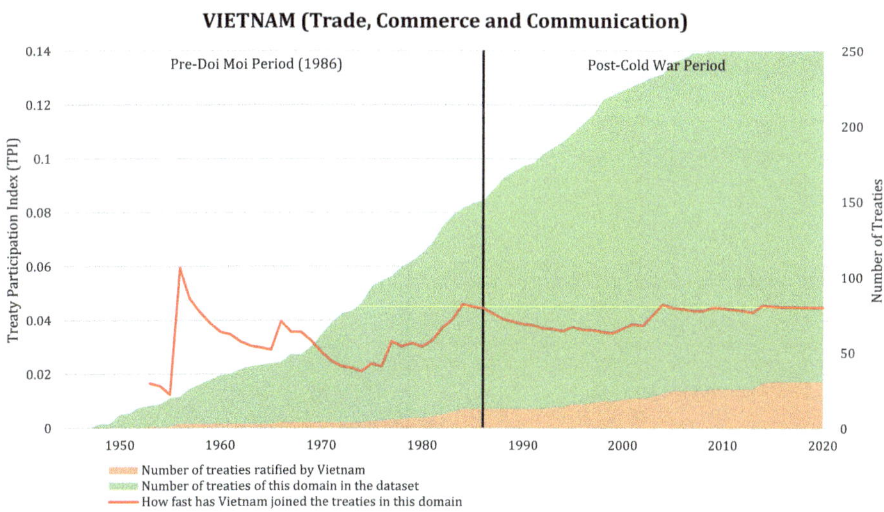

Fig. 8.32 Vietnam's participation in trade, commerce, and communication multilateral treaties

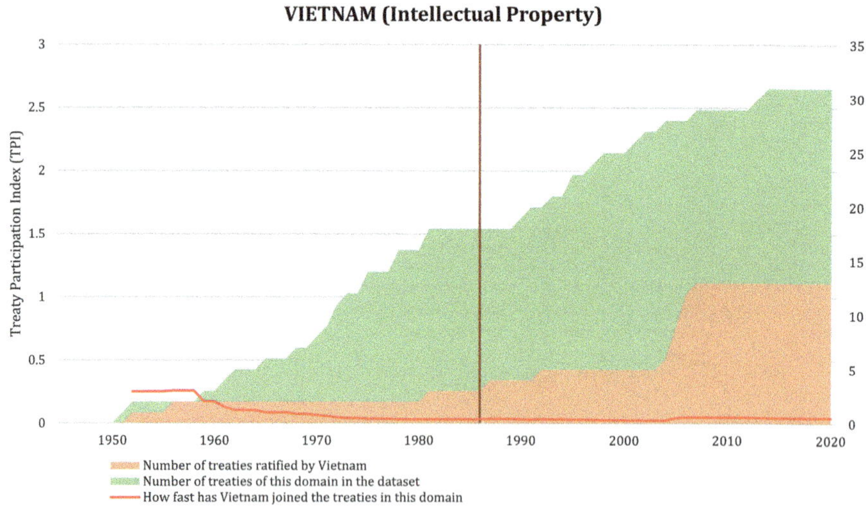

Fig. 8.33 Vietnam's participation in intellectual property multilateral treaties

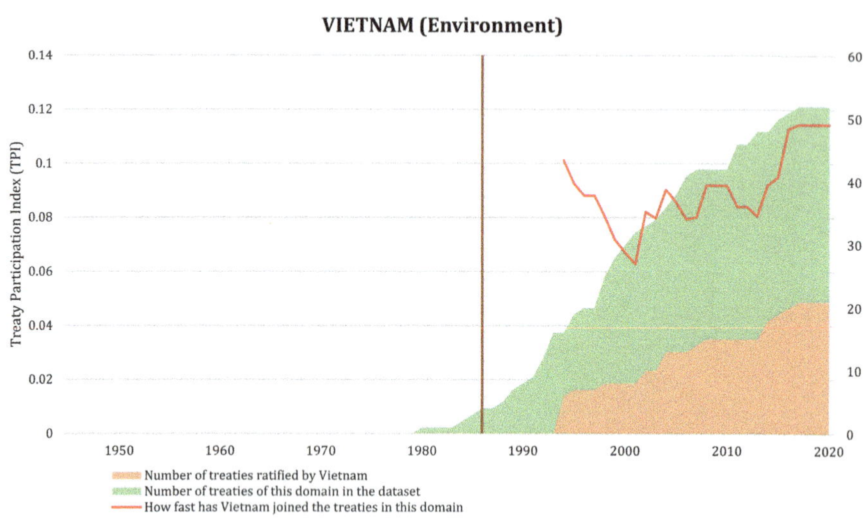

Fig. 8.34 Vietnam's participation in environment multilateral treaties

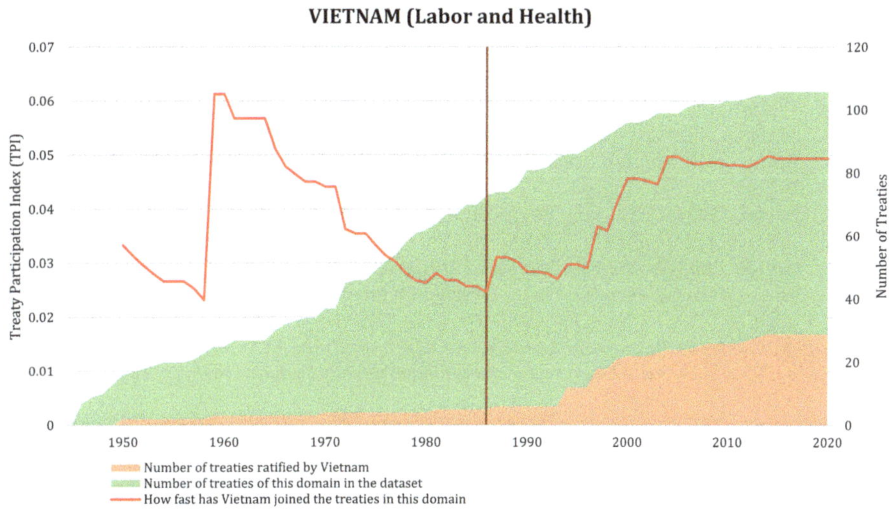

Fig. 8.35 Vietnam's participation in labor and health multilateral treaties

References

Akamatsu, Kaname. 1962. A Historical Pattern of Economic Growth in Developing Countries. *The Developing Economies* 1 (1): 3–25.

Baek, Jieun. 2016. *North Korea's Hidden Revolution: How the Information Underground Is Transforming a Closed Society*. New Haven: Yale University Press.

Dower, John. 2012. *Embracing Defeat: Japan in the Wake of World War II*. New York: W. W. Norton.

Gabriele, Alberto. 2020. *Enterprises, Industry and Innovation in the People's Republic of China: Questioning Socialism from Deng to the Trade and Tech War*. Singapore: Springer Nature.

Gordon, Andrew. 2018. *A Modern History of Japan: From Tokugawa Times to the Present*. Oxford: Oxford University Press.

Hasegawa, Tsuyoshi. 2006. *Racing the Enemy: Stalin, Truman, and the Surrender of Japan*. Belknap Press of the Imprint of Harvard University Press.

Hathaway, Oona, and Scott Shapiro. 2007. *The Internationalists: How a Radical Plan to Outlaw War Remade the World*. New Haven, CT: Yale University Press.

Hattori, Ryuji. 2011. *Nitchu kokko seijoka: Tanaka Kakuei, Ohira Masayoshi, kanryotachi no chosen* (The Normalization of Japan and China: Tanaka Kakuei, Ohira Masayoshi, and Bureaucrtats' Challenge). Tokyo: Chuko shinsho.

Hayami, Akira. 1992. *Kinsei Nobi chiho no jinko, keiai, shakai* (The Population, the Economy, and the Society in Early Modern Nobi Region). Tokyo: Sobunsha.

Hayami, Akira. 2015. *Japan's Industrious Revolution: Economic and Social Transformations in the Early Modern Period*. London: Springer.

Inoguchi, Takashi. 2020. "Japanese Foreign Policy as an 'Asian Country'." In *Japanese Foreign Policy in the Twenty-First Century: Continuity and Change*, edited by Peng Er Lam and Purnendra Jain. Lexington Books, 55–72.

Korhonen, Pekka. 1994. *Japan and Asia Pacific Integration: Pacific Romances 1968–1996*. London: Routledge.

Macmillan, Margaret. 2007. *Paris 1919: Six Months That Changed the World*. New York: Random House.

Milanovic, Branko. 2019. *Capitalism, Alone: The Future of the System That Rules the World*. Cambridge, MA: Harvard University Press.
Nakamura, Takafusa. 1983. *Economic Growth in Prewar Japan*. Ithaca, NY: Yale University Press.
Nakamura, Takafusa. 1994. *Lectures on Modern Japanese Economic History: 1926–1994*. Tokyo: LTCB International Library Foundation.
Okonogi, Masao. 2019. *Chosen bundan no kigen* (The Origins of Divided Korea). Tokyo: Keio University Press.
Ozawa, Terutomo. 1994. "Exploring the Asian Economic Miracle: Politics, Economics, Society. Culture and History." *Journal of Asian Studies* 53(1) (February 1994).
Ozawa, Terutomo. 2005. *Institutions, Industrial Upgrading and Economic Performance in Japan: The Flying Geese Paradigm of Catch-Up Growth*. Cheltenham: Edward Elgar.
Putnam, Robert and Bayne, Nicholas. 1988. *Hanging Together: Cooperation and Conflict in the Seven-Power Summits, Revised and Enlarged Edition*. Cambridge, MA: Harvard University Press.
Smith, Sheila A. 2015. *Intimate Rivals: Japanese Domestic Politics and a Rising China*. New York: Columbia University Press.
Smith, Sheila A. 2019. *Japan Rearmed: The Politics of Military Power*. Cambridge, MA: Harvard University Press.
Soeya, Yoshihide. 1998. *Japan's Economic Diplomacy with China, 1945–1978*. Oxford: Clarendon Press.
The Economist. 2019. Special Report: Asian Tigers, December 7, 1–10.
Tønnesson, Stein. 2019. "The East Asian Peace." in *The SAGE Handbook of Asian Foreign Policy*, 2 vols., edited by Takashi Inoguchi, London: SAGE reference (1097–1117).
Van de Ven, Hans. 2017. *China at War: Triumph and Tragedy in the Emergence of the New China*. Cambridge, Mass.: Harvard University Press.
Vogel, Ezra. 1983. *Japan as No. 1: Lessons for America*, Ithaca, NY: Yale University Press.
Vogel, Ezra. 2019. *China and Japan: Facing History*. Cambridge, MA: Harvard University Press.
Wei, Yuwa. 2019. *Issues Decisive for China's Rise or Fall: An International Law Perspective*. Singapore: Springer Nature.

Chapter 9
Typology of Global Quasi-Legislative Behavior and Typology of Societies Focusing on Sinic East

Abstract In this chapter we attempt relating the typology of global quasi-legislative behavior (in this volume) to the typology of societies (Inoguchi 2019) focusing on Sinic East. The latter, the typology of societies, is based on daily life satisfaction surveyed by the AsiaBarometer quality of life research carried out in 29 Asian societies with face-to-face interviewing and with the sample size of 800 to 2,000 in each of 29 Asian societies (Inoguchi and Fujii 2013; see also Appendix E). The typology of societies is based on factor analyzing people's daily life satisfaction with 16 life items (domains, aspects and styles). It is a profile of societies from the bottom up rather than top down. Since both the typology of global quasi-legislative behavior has proved to be reasonably strongly related to the internal preferences of each society obtained by the World Value Survey through the world data used in Welzel 2013 and statistically examined positively in Inoguchi and Le, 2019, another data set of domestic daily life satisfaction collected in Sinic East societies in 2019 has been examined and proved to be reasonably related each other. One strong finding here is that those domestic preferences gauged on the experts' assessment of regimes' nature like democratic vs. authoritarian does not seem to work well in comparison to the daily life satisfaction in 16 items of domains, aspects and styles and the values and norms in concrete life situations.

Typology of societies has been constructed from the angle of bottom up to characterize 29 societies by the degree of human daily life satisfaction in the AsiaBarometer Survey (Inoguchi 2019 and forthcoming). The idea that prompted me to construct the typology of Asian societies from the bottom up rather than top down is that Asian societies have been so often seen and typologized from the top-down perspective (Hegel, Marx, Wittfogel, Weber). The task was carried out by collecting empirical data derived from face-to-face interviews on people's daily life satisfaction in 29 societies in East Asia, Southeast Asia, South Asia, and Central Asia with each of national sample sizes ranging between 800 (for example, Brunei, Bhutan, the Maldives) and 2,000 (for example, India, China, Japan) during the 2003–2008 period (Inoguchi and Fujii 2013). The sixteen items of daily life domains, aspects, and styles are: housing, friendship, marriage, standard of living, household income,

T. Inoguchi and L. T. Q. Le, *Digitized Statecraft in Multilateral Treaty Participation*, Evidence-Based Approaches to Peace and Conflict Studies 1,
https://doi.org/10.1007/978-981-33-4485-3_9

health, education, job, neighbors, public safety, conditions of the environment, social welfare system, democratic system, family life, spiritual life, and leisure. What are the key dimensions of daily life satisfaction? How are Asian societies as seen from the bottom up different? With these two questions in mind, my operation of typologizing Asian societies is: First, factor analyzing each of 29 national data with 16 daily life satisfaction items has yielded three key dimensions—survival, social relations, and public-policy dominance. What comes a small surprise in the findings is that each of 29 Asian societies differs tremendously from one to another in the order of the size of each of three key dimensions. For instance, the Inglehartian dimensions are two, materialism and post-materialism or survival and social relations. With 16 items we have got the three key dimensions of survival, social relations, and public-policy dominance. What is most important and interesting from our perspective is that the three dimensions' order among themselves in terms of their explanatory power (i.e., dimensional eigenvalues) is of eight varieties. In other words, if survival is called a, if social relations is called b, and if public-policy dominance is called c, and if the largest explanatory power-exhibiting dimension is capitalized like A, B, or C, then there are six such types of Asian societies: Abc, Acb, Bac, Bca, Cab, Cba. In other words, a society characterized Abc is a society in which people get daily satisfaction most on the dimension of survival, next on the dimension of social relations, and last on public-policy dominance. This is a standard Inglehartian type bar the last dimension (public-policy dominance). Japan (Gordon 2018) and Indonesia (Kim 2019) were societies experienced feudalism which means the centripetal nature of the state is weak. Taiwan was a settler society. Uzbekistan and Tajikistan are sparsely populated and geographically dispersed. Common to them is that power centralization is minimized in getting daily life satisfaction from our bottom up perspective. Acb is represented by China (Zhang 2008; Economy 2018; Ci 2019), India (Roy 1997), South Korea, Mongolia. The public-policy dominance dimension comes the second. People get daily life satisfaction more in the Acb society from that dimension than the Abc society. Authoritarian-tinged leadership is required. In the Bac society comes atop the social relations dimension. In other words, it is a networked society among new diverse settlers. Hong Kong, Malaysia (Tajuddin 2012), Thailand (Glassman 2019), Vietnam (Nguyen 2012), and Kyrgyzstan fall into this type. The Bca society does not exist in the 29 Asian societies. My wild but reasonably educated guess is that North Korea might be close to this type although there is no systematic evidence or empirical survey data to back up that guess (Baek 2016). The Cab society is the society in which public-policy dominance comes to the fore. A fractured society though it is, it is the way in which order is restored. Pakistan (Lieven 2012), Brunei (Cheung 2017), the Philippines, Bhutan, Kazakhstan fall into this type. The Cba society includes Singapore (Chua 2017) and Sri Lanka. It is illustrated by Singapore. Public-policy dominance comes to the fore like the Cab society. One difference from the Cab society is that not only at the higher level of society but also at the lower level of society, social relations and survival dimensions tend to be routinely affected by public-policy dimension.

Although this book is about global quasi-legislative behavior, a sovereign state's decision about participation in multilateral treaties depends not only what the rest of

Table 9.1 Domestic societal types and global quasi-legislative behavior types

Sinic East	Domestic societal types	Global quasi-legislative behavior types
Japan	Abc	abc
China	Acb	abC
Vietnam	Bac	ABc
DPR Korea	(Cab)	ABc
R Korea	Acb	AbC
Taiwan	Abc	(abC)
Hong Kong	Bac	(abC)
Singapore	Cba	abc
Mongolia	Acb	ABc

the world thinks about values and norms multilateral treaties represent and exemplify, but also how its people feel about daily life satisfaction, the sum of which can be aggregated into societal types. Therefore, taking a glance at the relationship between global quasi-legislative behavior types and societal types may add more credence to the hypothesis that national citizens' preference and global citizens' preference converge at reasonably high level, which have been affirmed positively in Inoguchi and Le (2019).

Looking at Table 9.1, two things should be noted. First, among Sinic East's societal types, diversity is most striking. The parenthesized DPR Korea's societal type is my guess. With this included for regional observation, Sinic East enlarged to nine members with Singapore (see Fig. 4.3 and Fig. 4.4) and Mongolia (see Fig. 4.7 and Fig. 4.8) also included, Sinic East has every variety of eight types: Abc, Acb, Bac, Cab, Acb, Abc, Bac, Cba, and Acb when we use the bottom-up perspective. This is an important point when the more common perspective of looking at political systems, democratic vs. authoritarian, an approach used by the Economist Intelligence Unit (2020) in reporting that Sinic East or enlarged East Asia has no full democracy, with both Japan and South Korea sliding down from full democracy down to partial democracy in 2019. Although the general trend in East Asia in the dawn of the third Millennium is authoritarian backsliding (cf. Mikami and Inoguchi 2010; Croissant and Hellmann 2020) the perspective from the bottom up gives an astonishing variety as shown in the societal types. This point is doubly important because in gauging multilateral treaty participation chosen by a sovereign state, the indicator of societal preference must be based on randomly sampled, face-to-face interviews of citizens in each Sinic East society and thus not including a sovereign state's preference or proclivity must be assured. Coming back to the main point, the Inglehartian paradigm may not easily apply to Sinic East when Sinic East's societal characteristics are to be revealed and illuminated.

Second, on quasi-legislative behavior types, most striking is the prevalence of mutual binding strategy of Japan, Vietnam, DPR Korea, Singapore, and Mongolia. This preponderance of mutual binding strategy among Sinic East is striking when compared to the dominance of aspirational bonding strategy both among the developed and stalled North and the developing and stagnant South. China and R Korea are the only two states in Sinic East exhibiting the strategy of aspirational bonding. (Taiwan and Hong Kong are not members of the United Nations. Therefore, we do not have empirical data for them. The parenthesized types of Taiwan and Hong Kong are merely my guess.) China and R Korea show their strategy of aspirational bonding. Milanovic (2019) argues that China has difficulties in keeping many friends and allies because it has been aloof and alone even during the non-align movement's heady time in the 1950s. R Korea has been torn into two groups, conservative vs. progressive, which befriend two different sets of neighbors: conservatives with the US and Japan whereas progressives prefer DPR Korea, Russia, and China. Both are inclined to bond with the developing South rather than the developed North because R Korea's maneuverability is much larger with the developing South status when coping with the developed North's demand for burden sharing. Next most striking is the prevalence of the global commons angle in Sinic East countries, notably Japan, China, R Korea, and Singapore. They need to be exposed to the rest of the world with market access to energy, technology, and agricultural and mineral products. Those not characterized by the angle of global commons are Vietnam, DPR Korea, and Mongolia, all are run by political capitalism (Milanovic 2019).

Japan is of the Inglehartian ideal type of materialism and post-materialism exhibited in this order. First, satisfaction with survival-related daily life dominates. Second, satisfaction with social relations-related daily life aspects follows survival-related daily life satisfaction. Third, satisfaction with public-policy dominance comes last. In the Inglehartian scheme the public-policy dominance dimension never appears. But the survival and social relations aspects do appear consistently for the last four decades (Inglehart 2018; Inglehart and Welzel 2016; Welzel 2013). This is largely because the World Values Survey focuses on values and norms. Inoguchi (2019) argues that people's perception of society contains public institutions and activities by the state. Especially seen from the bottom up, that is, from ordinary people's daily life perspective, so this angle cannot be disregarded. Bringing in their perception of public-policy-related aspects of daily life allows to reveal the varieties of societal types. Whether the role of public policy is large or small or in which order the dimension on which public-policy-related categories are loaded strongly interests us. Not surprisingly the weight of public-policy dominance varies from one society to another. That is fascinating in itself and in relation to a sovereign state's global legislative behavior. In Japan's case, the order of the three dimensions is materialism, post-materialism, and public-policy dominance. How does Japan's societal type relates to global legislative behavior? Japan's type of global legislative behavior is abc, meaning that its speed is agile as contrasted to slow, that its angle is global commons as contrasted to individual interests, and that its strategy is mutual binding as contrasted to aspirational bonding. Then is the hypothesis accepted or rejected? It seems that the initial hypothesis is more or less moderately accepted. Japan's semi-sovereign status or what some people call a semi-vassal status is sync with the fairly small defense expenditure per GNP. It also is harmonious with the large percentage of government budget allocated to those expenditure items related to social welfare, public infrastructure, and government debt repayment. Calling for global leadership on the global assault of Covid-19, former prime ministers of the UK and Australia, Robert Brown and Kevin Rudd, named Shinzo Abe to lead. Japan's strategy of mutual binding is a good strategy for this opportune time to ride on this call (Brown and Rudd 2020).

China's societal type is Acb. That is, the weight of satisfaction with survival-related daily life aspects matters most. The second dimension is public-policy dominance. That is interesting in the sense that the state's role carries the secondary importance in the eyes of ordinary people. In other words, Chinese society has a certain strength of resistance and resilience vis-à-vis the Chinese state's exercising its muscle. The third is the satisfaction with daily life aspects related to social relations primarily among themselves. China's global legislative behavioral type is abC. That is, its speed is agile. It is befitting a global power's status, handling thousands of issues. Its angle is global commons. China's slogan is that of advancing globalization and international cooperation on the basis of what Milanovic calls political capitalism (2019). Its strategy is aspirational bonding. Deng Xiaoping called the approach "hiding your strength and biding your time." For the last decade or so, its strategy has got more self-assertive within the slogan of aspirational bonding with friends from near and afar. In running Chinese society from above, what counts most is whether its two-digit economic growth rates slow down visibly for three decades if from 2020 (Economy 2018).

Vietnam's societal type is Bac. What is most important in ordinary people's eyes is social relations. With constant war and strife, people need to rely on family, community, and workplace for assurance and assistance for safety and survival. Next important is satisfaction with daily life aspects for material survival. Family, relatives, friends, and neighbors go a long way. What comes next? Vietnam developed from incessant battlefield to prosperous market. By 2019 it boasted of registering one of the world highest annual economic growth rates. Once peace with China came at long last in 1984, Vietnamese reform policy, or *Doi Moi*, commenced in 1986. This is the Vietnamese version of Milanovic's political capitalism. China has always been presence at Vietnam's northern border, naturally leading to a combination of vigilance and trade. The southern territory is now inside the Socialist Republic of Vietnam and the Southeast Asian continental competitive animal spirit has been burning there (Woodside 1971). The third dimension is public-policy dominance. Vietnam's societal type is the same as Thailand, Malaysia, and the Philippines with good, wide, and deep social relations mattering most whether it is family, colleagues, or friends. What about Vietnam's legislative behavior? It is ABc. Its speed is slow and cautious. Its angle is individual interests. Its strategy is mutual binding. When contestation and competition are ubiquitous in one's neighborhood, one cannot afford sloganeering on aspirational bonding. The fact that China has been an immediate neighbor in the north while in the south and on the hills Mons, Chams, Khmers, many ethnic Chinese, and other ethnic minorities have been settlers, old and new, with Vietnamese themselves being ancient settlers, leads theVietnamese to adopt mutual binding.

North Korea's societal type is unknown. Surveys cannot be carried out within and from without. One survey results of refugees were published (Haggard and

Noland 2011). My educated comparative estimate is that of Bca. The first dimension is that of post-materialism or social relations-dominant. The reason is that the Kim dynastic hereditary system has been kept unbroken for more than seven decades over three generations and that the Kim dynasty has been kept with the very tightly knit family-centered elites with autocratic control from one person. The second dimension is public-policy predominance. That means that neighborhood, workplace, government, and armed forces are all centrally managed. Politics takes command. *Janmadan* (small black market) capitalism has become ubiquitous and been slowly changing society by loosening the implementation of central order. The third dimension is materialism, survival-related daily life satisfaction. This carries the least weight. That is why with no other alternative to *janmadan* market, has *janmadan* capitalism spread out. The combination of tight government regulations and ubiquitous needs to use bribes and other services to get commodities for survival generates *janmadan* market. How does the societal type relate to the global legislative type? North Korea's type is ABc. Its speed of decision is cautious and slow. Given the country's complex relations with major powers(China, the US, Russia, South Korea, and Japan) North Korea is perennially vulnerable in energy, food, the environment, poverty, nutrition, hygiene, advanced technology, and security. The ways out of extreme difficulty has been tried three times:

1. Under Kim Il Son and Kim Jong Il, North Korea was about to be successful in getting light-water nuclear power stations half-constructed in the six power talks, but ended in failure. But North Korea got good knowledge and practice on nuclear power generation.
2. Kim Jong Il was able to further shift its resources to armed buildup (*sungun* politics) along with economic development loosening to use a modicum of market forces.
3. Kim Jong Un was able to use the fanfare of denuclearization of the Korean peninsula along with President Donald Trump, he bought the time to advance production of nuclear weapons in order to dissuade the US and South Korea from attacking North Korea.

What is North Korea's angle of global legislative type? It is individual interests, that is, nuclear weapons to dissuade from around Japan and its vicinity. Its strategy is mutual binding. North Korea is minimalist in participating in multilateral treaties. It has joined multilateral treaties as many as the perhaps most minimalist US. The US has been the leading power since 1945 but in terms of keeping the Washingtonian principle of disentanglement from external affairs has been well kept thereafter as well, registering 133 such treaties whereas North Korea registering 77. However, the number of joining multilateral treaties per annual are about twice as many as that of the US.

South Korea's societal type is Acb. The first dimension is that of materialism, which is followed by c, meaning public-policy dominance. The division between the conservatives and the progressives or the right and the left, has been kept sharp despite its admirable democratization after the long authoritarian and military dictatorship. Public-policy dominance is located at the second dimension, meaning that

Table 9.2 Eight typologies of global quasi-legislative behavior

	Types	Speed	Angle	Strategy
1.	abc	Agile	Global commons	Mutual binding
2.	aBC	Agile	Individual interests	Aspirational bonding
3.	aBc	Agile	Individual interests	Mutual binding
4.	abC	Agile	Global commons	Aspirational bonding
5.	Abc	Cautious	Global commons	Mutual binding
6.	AbC	Cautious	Global commons	Aspirational bonding
7.	ABc	Cautious	Individual interests	Mutual binding
8.	ABC	Cautious	Individual interests	Aspirational bonding

Table 9.3 Types of societies

Societal types	1st dimension	2nd dimension	3rd dimension
Abc	1. Materialism	2. Post-materialism	3. Public sector dominance
Acb	1. Materialism	2. Public sector dominance	3. Post-materialism
Bac	1. Post-materialism	2. Materialism	3. Public sector dominance
Bca	1. Post-materialism	2. Public sector dominance	3. Materialism
Cab	1. Public sector dominance	2. Materialism	3. Post-materialism
Cba	1. Public sector dominance	2. Post-materialism	3. Materialism

authoritative inclinations, whether it is president or parliament or judiciary, tend to carry strong flavors. After 1998, when democratically elected presidents of non-military origin occupied the post, each outgoing president either smelled of bribery, committed suicide, or was sent to prison. The third dimension is post-materialism. Social relations-related life satisfaction tend to be given shadows of public-policy dominance. What is South Korea's global legislative behavioral type? It is that of Abs. Its speed is cautious and slow given the complexity of surrounding within and without. Its angle is that of global commons. As the world 11th greatest economic power, its angle is definitely that of global commons, without being globally oriented, South Korea cannot survive in prosperity. Its strategy is that of aspirational bonding. South Korean nationalism is very strong, whether it is left-leaning or right-leaning. Without campaigning for or at least seriously mentioning national reunification possibilities, no political leader aspirant can build a career (Tables 9.2, 9.3, 9.4, and 9.5).

Table 9.6 Subregional Asian Member States: East Asia, Southeast Asia, South Asia, Central Asia plus what is called the Orthodox East is defined to consist of the following states (or areas).

Table 9.4 Some representative Asian states based on typologies of global quasi-legislative behavior

	Types	Some representative Asian states
1.	abc	Japan, Indonesia, Iran, Singapore
2.	aBC	Laos, Syria, Jordan, Mexico, Ecuador
3.	aBc	Algeria, Argentina, DR Congo, Nepal, Nigeria
4.	abC	US, UK, France, Germany, Sweden, Netherlands, Thailand, Philippines, China, Israel, India
5.	Abc	Albania, Georgia, Kazakhstan, Kyrgiztan, Uzbekistan, Turkey
6.	AbC	R Korea, Portugal, Lithuania, Estonia, Czech R., Croatia
7.	ABc	Bahrain, DPR Korea, Qatar, Sandi Arabia, Oman, South Africa
8.	ABC	Bangladesh, Bhutan, Maldives, Panama

Table 9.5 Some representative Asian states based on daily life satisfaction

	Societal types	Asian societies
1.	Abc	Japan, Indonesia, Taiwan, Afghanistan, Uzbekistan, Tajikistan
2.	Acb	China, South Korea, Cambodia, Laos, Myanmar, Bangladesh, India, Nepal, Mongolia
3.	Bac	Hong Kong, Malaysia, Thailand, Vietnam, Kyrgyzstan
4.	Bca	not found in 29 Asian societies
5.	Cab	Pakistan, Brunei, the Philippines, Bhutan, Kazakhstan
6.	Cba	Singapore, Sri Lanka

Table 9.6 Subregional Asian Member States

East Asia	Japan, China, R Korea, DPR Korea, Vietnam, Singapore, Mongolia, Hong Kong, Taiwan
Southeast Asia	Philippines, Thailand, Vietnam, Laos, Cambodia, Myanmar, Singapore, Indonesia, Timor Leste, Malaysia, Brunei
South Asia	India, Pakistan, Nepal, Bangladesh, Sri Lanka, Maldives, Bhutan, Maldives
Central Asia	Kazakhstan, Kyrgyzstan, Tajikistan, Turkmenistan, Uzbekistan, Mongolia, Afghanistan, Azerbaijan, Armenia, Georgia
Orthodox East	Russia, Ukraine, Turkey, Syria, Jordan, Israel, Greece, Serbia, Croatia

Table 9.7 Daily life satisfaction and multilateral treaty participation across Asia

		Society types Daily life satisfaction	Global quasi-legislative behavior types multilateral treaty participation
East Asia			
1.	Japan	Abc	abc
2.	China	Acb	abC
3.	Vietnam	Bac	ABc
4.	DPR Korea		ABc
5.	R Korea	Acb	AbC
6.	Taiwan	Abc	
7.	Hong Kong	Bac	
Southeast Asia			
1.	Philippines	Cab	abC
2.	Thailand	Bac	abC
3.	Vietnam	Bac	ABc
4.	Laos	Acb	aBC
5.	Cambodia	Acb	abC
6.	Myanmar	Acb	ABC
7.	Singapore	Cba	abc
8.	Indonesia	Abc	abc
9.	Timor Leste		ABc
10.	Malaysia	Bac	AbC
11.	Brunei	Cab	ABc

(continued)

Table 9.7 (continued)

		Society types Daily life satisfaction	Global quasi-legislative behavior types multilateral treaty participation
South Asia			
1.	India	Acb	abC
2.	Pakistan	Cab	abC
3.	Nepal	Acb	aBc
4.	Bangladesh	Acb	ABC
5.	Sri Lanka	Cab	AbC
6.	Maldives		ABC
7.	Bhutan	Cab	ABC
8.	Afghanistan	Abc	ABc
Central Asia plus Orthodox East			
1.	Kazakhstan	Cab	Abc
2.	Kyrgyzstan	Bac	Abc
3.	Tajikistan	Abc	Abc
4.	Uzbekistan	Abc	Abc
5.	Turkmenistan		ABc
6.	Mongolia	Acb	ABc

References

Baek, Jieun. 2016. *North Korea's Hidden Revolution: How the Information Underground Is Transforming a Closed Society*. New Haven, CT: Yale University Press.

Brown, Robert, and Kevin Rudd. 2020. "Japan Should Lead G20 in Devising Global Coronavirus Rescue Package." *Nikkei Asian Review*, April 10.

Chua, Beng Huat. 2017. *Liberalism Disavowed: Communitarianism and State Capitalism in Singapore*. Ithaca, NY: Cornell University Press.

Cheung, Johnson Chung-Sing. 2017. "Rentier Welfare States in Hydrocarbon-Based Economies: Brunei Darussalam and Islamic Republic of Iran in Comparative Context." *Journal of Asian Public Policy* 10 (3): 287–301.

Ci, Jiwei. 2019. *Democracy in China: The Coming Crisis*. Cambridge, MA: Harvard University Press.
Croissant, Aurel, and Olli Hellmann. 2020. *Stateness and Democracy in East Asia*. New York: Cambridge University Press.
Economy, Elizabeth C. 2018. *The Third Revolution: Xi Jinping and the New Chinese State*. Oxford: Oxford University Press.
Glassman, Jim. 2019. "Lineages of the Authoritarian State in Thailand: Military Dictatorship, Lazy Capitalism and the Cold War Past as Post-Cold War Prologue." *Journal of Contemporary Asia* 50 (4): 571–592.
Gordon, Andrew. 2018. *A Modern History of Japan: From Tokugawa Times to the Present*. Oxford: Oxford University Press.
Haggard, Stephan, and Markus Noland. 2011. *Witness to Transformation: Refugee Insights into North Korea*. Washington, DC: Peterson Institute for International Economics.
Inglehart, Ronald. 2018. *Cultural Evolution: People's Motivations are Changing, and Reshaping the World*. New York: Cambridge University Press.
Inglehart, Ronald, and Christian Welzel. 2016. *Modernization, Cultural Change, and Democracy: The Human Development Sequence*. Cambridge University Press.
Inoguchi, Takashi. 2019. "An Evidence-Based Typology of Asian Societies: What Do Asian Societies Look Like from the Bottom Up instead of Top Down?" In *The SAGE Handbook of Asian Foreign Policy*, 2 vols., London: Sage Publications, vol. 1, pp. 443–461.
Inoguchi, Takashi. (forthcoming) *Typology of Asian Societies: Evidence-Based Approach and Bottom Up Perspective*.
Inoguchi, Takashi, and Lien Thi Quynh Le. 2019. *The Development of Global Legislative Politics: Rousseau and Locke Writ Global*. Singapore: Springer Nature.
Inoguchi, Takashi, and Seiji Fujii. 2013. *The Quality of Life in Asia: A Comparison of Quality of Life in Asia*. Dordrecht: Springer.
Kim, Kyunghoon. 2019. "Indonesia's Restrained State Capitalism: Development and Policy Challenges." *Journal of Contemporary Asia* (online version).
Lieven, Aatol. 2012. *Pakistan: A Hard Country*. London: Penguin Pocket Book.
Mikami, Satoru, and Takashi Inoguchi. 2010. "Diagnosing the Micro Foundation of Democracy in Asia: Evidence from the AsiaBarometer Survey 2003–2008." In *East Asia's New Democracies: Deepening, Reversal, Non-Liberal Alternatives*, edited by Yin-wah Chu and Siu-lun Wong. New York: Routledge, pp. 246–292.
Milanovic, Branko. 2019. *Capitalism, Alone: The Future of the System That Rules the World*. Cambridge, MA: Harvard University Press.
Nguyen, Lan. 2012. *Guerilla Capitalism: The State in the Market in Vietnam*. Oxford: Chandos.
Roy, Arundhati. 1997. *The God of Small Things*. London: Flamingo.
Tajuddin, Azlan. 2012. *Malaysia in the World Economy (1824–2011): Capitalism, Ethnic Divisions, and "Managed" Democracy*. Lamham: Lexington Books.
The Economist Intelligence Unit. 2020. *Democracy Index 2020*. London: The Economist Intelligence Unit.
Welzel, Christian. 2013. *Freedom Rising: Human Empowerment and the Quest for Emancipation*. New York: Cambridge University Press.
Woodside, Alexander. 1971. *Vietnam and the Chinese Model: A Comparative Study of Nguyen and Ching Civil Government in the First Half of the Nineteenth Century*. Cambridge, MA: Harvard University Press.
Zhang, Jianjun. 2008. *Marketization and Democracy in China*. London: Routledge.

Conclusion

When Chanakya Kautilya (Kautilya and Shamashastry 1915) in the third–fourth-century BC ancient India and Niccolò Machiavelli (Skinner 2000) in the fifteenth–sixteenth-century Florentine Italy AD articulated their thoughts about statecraft for the monarchs and kings. They are well read by their aspirants to emulate their advice. Kautilya preached how imaginatively and mercilessly mobilize and deploy power resources to suppress rebels and conquer rivals. Machiavelli prepared the Florentine prince to be awed and admired by subjects and usurpers. They were the times before the Westphalian sovereign states were key actors in the world. Statecraft was considered for monarchs and kings mostly in the form of aphorism.

In the new millennium an entirely new world has been developing. It is the Earth under digitized globalization (Inoguchi and Le 2019). Communications, transportations, and transactions are carried out across the globe with speed, costs, and comfort unthinkable even a quarter of a century ago. Thus the degree of connectivity and vulnerability has increased through digitized action. It is called digitized globalization.

The concept of globalization may also be somewhat inappropriate in the sense that phenomena often go beyond the scope of globalization. Climate change means that the difficulty of the earth emitting carbon dioxide preventing the earth heat from being cooled down in relation to the planetary environment. It might as well be conceptualized as planetization. Infectious disease is another phenomenon often seen as a form of globalization. The physicist César Hidalgo (2013) argues that the Earth's singularity is information, in contrast to the stars' singularity (matter) and the black holes' singularity (energy). Homo sapiens have come to pump out incessantly an incredible amount of information, with the rising population surpassing 7.5 billion and with the steady progress of science and technology helping produce and diffuse information on Earth. Information has been the vehicle of vast human activities with communications, transportation, and transactions. One result is the growth of economic products and another is the growth of multilateral treaty participation. The latter is the subject of this book. If economic growth is one form of global actors working together to

T. Inoguchi and L. T. Q. Le, *Digitized Statecraft in Multilateral Treaty Participation*, Evidence-Based Approaches to Peace and Conflict Studies 1,
https://doi.org/10.1007/978-981-33-4485-3

manufacture products (Hidalgo 2013), the growth of multilateral treaties is another form of global actors working together toward solving problems without passports (Annan 2002). Seen this way, it is a little surprising to find that there has never been a systematic evidence-based analysis of as many as 600 substantive and substantial multilateral treaties that have been effective since 1945 before like this volume and Inoguchi and Le (2019). After all, if economic products represent the sum of global human economic activities, multilateral treaty participation represents the sum of global human legal agreements on how to solve problems without passports. The latter is no less important than the former. Digitized statecraft is the concept used to characterize multilateral treaty participation modes of 193 sovereign states. The three dimensions of these modes have been found to be speed, angle, and strategy. Each sovereign state watches and thinks about whether to join or not about a multilateral treaty or its draft. This book shows that how the 193 sovereign state under digitized globalization behave vis-à-vis multilateral treaties with the speed (agile vs. cautious), the angle (global commons vs. individual interests), and the strategy (aspirational bonding vs. mutual binding). Digitized statecraft is numerically shown for each sovereign state with the vast number of 600 multilateral treaties that meet the two criteria, being primarily substantive rather than narrowly procedural and being primarily universal rather than narrowly regional. The six instrumental variables are gauged by sovereign states' physical actions (for example, the gap between promulgation and ratification, and the number of other joiners in the year of joining) and attributable characteristics such as the policy domain of multilateral treaty and the group affiliation attributes such as the geo-historico-cultural regional group. All the variables are drawn from the United Nations Secretary-General's Depository and two other UN agencies' sub-depositories, which are open to access to anyone willing to use them.

How is digitized statecraft used for academic and policy making purposes? The method is basically that of artificial intelligence (cf. Russell and Norvig 2010; Goodfellow et al. 2016). With three parameters determined by the six instrumental variables as preference and proclivity, what one needs to prepare are backgrounds about and knowledge of a concerned sovereign state, of other sovereign states, and of voices of non-governmental organizations and transnational social movements and of a concerned multilateral treaty or its draft. Three examples are the Paris climate change accord, Trans-Pacific partnership, and the Treaty on the Prohibition of Nuclear Weapons. The Paris accord has not been moving toward implementation with the US having withdrawn and the developing South's no or little payment of cost sharing remaining to be very serious. The TPP with the US withdrawn needs to recruit and persuade some other regional states to join. India has given it up while China may be closely watching it. The Treaty on the Prohibition of Nuclear Weapons needs some abstainers to change the position to joiners if it wants to become effective. As of August 6, 2020, the 75th anniversary of dropping a nuclear bomb over Hiroshima, Ireland, Nigeria, and Niue ratified the Treaty on the Prohibition of Nuclear Weapons. Those ratified countries amount to 43, awaiting 7 states to ratify before the treaty goes effective (Mainichi shimbun 2020). There are so many ways to concretize artificial intelligence models of multilateral treaties in relation to each of 193 sovereign states' different preference and proclivity. But that is our future agenda. What we have done in this volume as well as in Inoguchi and Le (2019) is to show logically and empirically how important it is to understand ways in which sovereign states decide to join multilateral treaties or not. Under digitized globalization this Earth needs to have more agreements as to how human activities accommodate both diversity and inclusiveness as well as ensuring sustainability.

References

Annan, Kofi. 2002. "Problems Without Passports." *Foreign Policy* 132: 30–31.

Goodfellow, Ian, Yoshua Bengio, and Aaron Courville. 2016. *Deep Learning*. Cambridge, MA: MIT Press.

Hidalgo, César. 2013. *Why Information Grows: The Evolution of Order, from Atoms to Economics*. New York: Penguin.

Inoguchi, Takashi, and Lien Thi Quynh Le. 2019. *The Development of Global Legislative Politics: Rousseau and Locke Writ Global*. Singapore: Springer.

Kautilya, Chanakya, and R.M. Shamashastry. 1915. *Arthashastra*, translated by R.M. Shamashastry. India.

Mainichi shimbun. 2020. "Kakukin joyaku hijun aratani 3 ka koku (the Treaty on the Prohibition of Nuclear Weapons Ratified by Three More New States)," August 6: 8.

Russell, S., and P. Norvig. 2010. *Artificial Intelligence: A Modern Approach*. Upper Saddle River, NJ: Prentice Hall.

Skinner, Quentin. 2000. *Machiavelli: A Very Short Introduction*. Oxford: Oxford University Press.

Appendix A
List of 600 Multilateral Treaties by Domain

Domain	Treaty name	Place of conclusion	Date of conclusion
Environment	Convention on Long-Range Transboundary Air Pollution. Geneva, 13 November 1979	Geneva	13/11/1979
Environment	Protocol to the 1979 Convention on Long-range Transboundary Air Pollution on Long-term Financing of the Cooperative Programme for Monitoring and Evaluation of the Long-range Transmission of Air Pollutants in Europe (EMEP). Geneva, 28 September 1984	Geneva	28/09/1984
Environment	Vienna Convention for the Protection of the Ozone Layer. Vienna, 22 March 1985	Vienna	22/03/1985
Environment	Protocol to the 1979 Convention on Long-Range Transboundary Air Pollution on the Reduction of Sulphur Emissions or their Transboundary Fluxes by at least 30 per cent. Helsinki, 8 July 1985	Helsinki	08/07/1985
Environment	Montreal Protocol on Substances that Deplete the Ozone Layer. Montreal, 16 September 1987	Montreal	16/09/1987

(continued)

T. Inoguchi and L. T. Q. Le, *Digitized Statecraft in Multilateral Treaty Participation*, Evidence-Based Approaches to Peace and Conflict Studies 1,
https://doi.org/10.1007/978-981-33-4485-3

(continued)

Domain	Treaty name	Place of conclusion	Date of conclusion
Environment	Protocol to the 1979 Convention on long-range transboundary air pollution concerning the control of emissions of nitrogen oxides or their transboundary fluxes. Sofia, 31 October 1988	Sofia	31/10/1988
Environment	Basel Convention on the Control of Transboundary Movements of Hazardous Wastes and their Disposal. Basel, 22 March 1989	Basel	22/03/1989
Environment	Amendment to the Montreal Protocol on Substances that Deplete the Ozone Layer. London, 29 June 1990	London	29/06/1990
Environment	Convention on Environmental Impact Assessment in a Transboundary Context. Espoo, Finland, 25 February 1991	Espoo	25/02/1991
Environment	Protocol to the 1979 Convention on Long-Range Transboundary Air Pollution concerning the Control of Emissions of Volatile Organic Compounds or their Transboundary Fluxes. Geneva, 18 November 1991	Geneva	18/11/1991
Environment	Agreement on the Conservation of Small Cetaceans of the Baltic, North East Atlantic, Irish and North Seas. New York, 17 March 1992	New York	17/03/1992
Environment	Convention on the Protection and Use of Transboundary Watercourses and International Lakes. Helsinki, 17 March 1992	Helsinki	17/03/1992
Environment	Convention on the Transboundary Effects of Industrial Accidents. Helsinki, 17 March 1992	Helsinki	17/03/1992
Environment	United Nations Framework Convention on Climate Change. New York, 9 May 1992	New York	09/05/1992
Environment	Convention on Biological Diversity. Rio de Janeiro, 5 June 1992	Rio de Janeiro	05/06/1992
Environment	Amendment to the Montreal Protocol on Substances that Deplete the Ozone Layer. Copenhagen, 25 November 1992	Copenhagen	25/11/1992

(continued)

(continued)

Domain	Treaty name	Place of conclusion	Date of conclusion
Environment	Protocol to the 1979 Convention on Long-Range Transboundary Air Pollution on Further Reduction of Sulphur Emissions. Oslo, 14 June 1994	Oslo	14/06/1994
Environment	Lusaka Agreement on Cooperative Enforcement Operations Directed at Illegal Trade in Wild Fauna and Flora. Lusaka, 8 September 1994	Lusaka	08/09/1994
Environment	United Nations Convention to Combat Desertification in those Countries Experiencing Serious Drought and/or Desertification, Particularly in Africa. Paris, 14 October 1994	Paris	14/10/1994
Environment	Amendment to the Basel Convention on the Control of Transboundary Movements of Hazardous Wastes and their Disposal. Geneva, 22 September 1995	Geneva	22/09/1995
Environment	Convention on the Law of the Non-Navigational Uses of International Watercourses. New York, 21 May 1997	New York	21/05/1997
Environment	Amendment to the Montreal Protocol on Substances that Deplete the Ozone Layer adopted by the Ninth Meeting of the Parties. Montreal, 17 September 1997	Montreal	17/09/1997
Environment	Kyoto Protocol to the United Nations Framework Convention on Climate Change. Kyoto, 11 December 1997	Kyoto	11/12/1997
Environment	Protocol to the 1979 Convention on Long-Range Transboundary Air Pollution on Heavy Metals. Aarhus, 24 June 1998	Aarhus	24/06/1998
Environment	Protocol to the 1979 Convention on Long-Range Transboundary Air Pollution on Persistent Organic Pollutants. Aarhus, 24 June 1998	Aarhus	24/06/1998

(continued)

(continued)

Domain	Treaty name	Place of conclusion	Date of conclusion
Environment	Convention on Access to Information, Public Participation in Decision-Making and Access to Justice in Environmental Matters. Aarhus, Denmark, 25 June 1998	Aarhus	25/06/1998
Environment	Rotterdam Convention on the Prior Informed Consent Procedure for Certain Hazardous Chemicals and Pesticides in International Trade. Rotterdam, 10 September 1998	Rotterdam	10/09/1998
Environment	Protocol on Water and Health to the 1992 Convention on the Protection and Use of Transboundary Watercourses and International Lakes. London, 17 June 1999	London	17/06/1999
Environment	Protocol to the 1979 Convention on Long-range Transboundary Air Pollution to Abate Acidification, Eutrophication and Ground-level Ozone. Gothenburg (Sweden), 30 November 1999	Gothenburg (Sweden)	30/11/1999
Environment	Amendment to the Montreal Protocol on Substances that Deplete the Ozone Layer. Beijing, 3 December 1999	Beijing	03/12/1999
Environment	Basel Protocol on Liability and Compensation for Damage Resulting from Transboundary Movements of Hazardous Wastes and their Disposal. Basel, 10 December 1999	Basel	10/12/1999
Environment	Cartagena Protocol on Biosafety to the Convention on Biological Diversity. Montreal, 29 January 2000	Montreal	29/01/2000
Environment	Amendment to the Convention on Environmental Impact Assessment in a Transboundary Context. Sofia, 27 February 2001	Sofia	27/02/2001
Environment	Stockholm Convention on Persistent Organic Pollutants. Stockholm, 22 May 2001	Stockholm	22/05/2001

(continued)

(continued)

Domain	Treaty name	Place of conclusion	Date of conclusion
Environment	Protocol on Civil Liability and Compensation for Damage Caused by the Transboundary Effects of Industrial Accidents on Transboundary Waters to the 1992 Convention on the Protection and Use of Transboundary Watercourses and International Lakes and to the 1992 Convention on the Transboundary Effects of Industrial Accidents. Kiev, 21 May 2003	Kiev	21/05/2003
Environment	Protocol on Pollutant Release and Transfer Registers to the Convention on Access to Information, Public Participation in Decision-Making and Access to Justice in Environmental Matters. Kiev, 21 May 2003	Kiev	21/05/2003
Environment	Protocol on Strategic Environmental Assessment to the Convention on Environmental Impact Assessment in a Transboundary Context. Kiev, 21 May 2003	Kiev	21/05/2003
Environment	Amendment to the Agreement on the Conservation of Small Cetaceans of the Baltic and North Seas. Esbjerg, 22 August 2003	Esbjerg	22/08/2003
Environment	Amendments to Articles 25 and 26 of the Convention on the Protection and Use of Transboundary Watercourses and International Lakes. Madrid, 28 November 2003	Madrid	28/11/2003
Environment	Amendment to the Convention on Environmental Impact Assessment in a Transboundary Context. Cavtat, 4 June 2004	Cavtat	04/06/2004
Environment	Amendment to the Convention on Access to Information, Public Participation in Decision-Making and Access to Justice in Environmental Matters. Almaty, 27 May 2005	Almaty	27/05/2005

(continued)

(continued)

Domain	Treaty name	Place of conclusion	Date of conclusion
Environment	Amendment to Annex B of the Kyoto Protocol to the United Nations Framework Convention on Climate Change. Nairobi, 17 November 2006	Nairobi	17/11/2006
Environment	Amendments to Annexes I and II to the 1998 Protocol on Persistent Organic Pollutants. Geneva, 18 December 2009	Geneva	18/12/2009
Environment	Amendments to the Text and to Annexes I, II, III, IV, VI and VIII to the 1998 Protocol on Persistent Organic Pollutants. Geneva, 18 December 2009	Geneva	18/12/2009
Environment	Nagoya–Kuala Lumpur Supplementary Protocol on Liability and Redress to the Cartagena Protocol on Biosafety. Nagoya, 15 October 2010	Nagoya	15/10/2010
Environment	Nagoya Protocol on Access to Genetic Resources and the Fair and Equitable Sharing of Benefits Arising from their Utilization to the Convention on Biological Diversity. Nagoya, 29 October 2010	Nagoya	29/10/2010
Environment	Amendment of the text and annexes II to IX to the Protocol to the 1979 Convention on Long-range Transboundary Air Pollution to Abate Acidification, Eutrophication and Ground-level Ozone and the addition of new annexes X and XI. Geneva, 4 May 2012	Geneva	04/05/2012
Environment	Doha Amendment to the Kyoto Protocol. Doha, 8 December 2012	Doha	08/12/2012
Environment	Amendments to the Text of and Annexes Other than III and VII to the 1998 Protocol on Heavy Metals. Geneva, 13 December 2012	Geneva	13/12/2012
Environment	Minamata Convention on Mercury. Kumamoto, 10 October 2013	Kumamoto	10/10/2013
Environment	Paris Agreement. Paris, 12 December 2015	Paris	12/12/2015

(continued)

(continued)

Domain	Treaty name	Place of conclusion	Date of conclusion
Environment	Amendment to the Montreal Protocol on Substances that Deplete the Ozone Layer. Kigali, 15 October 2016	Kigali	15/10/2016
Human Rights	International Convention for the Suppression of the Traffic in Women and Children. Geneva, 30 September 1921	Geneva	30/09/1921
Human Rights	International Convention for the Suppression of the Circulation of and Traffic in Obscene Publications. Geneva, 12 September 1923	Geneva	12/09/1923
Human Rights	International Convention for the Suppression of the Traffic in Women of Full Age. Geneva, 11 October 1933	Geneva	11/10/1933
Human Rights	Convention for the Suppression of the Circulation of, and Traffic in, Obscene Publications, concluded at Geneva on 12 September 1923 and amended by the Protocol signed at Lake Success, New York, on 12 November 1947. New York, 12 November 1947	New York	12/11/1947
Human Rights	International Convention for the Suppression of the Traffic in Women and Children, concluded at Geneva on 30 September 1921, as amended by the Protocol signed at Lake Success, New York, on 12 November 1947. Lake Success, 12 November 1947	Lake Success	12/11/1947
Human Rights	International Convention for the Suppression of the Traffic in Women of Full Age, concluded at Geneva on 11 October 1933, as amended by the Protocol signed at Lake Success, New York, on 12 November 1947. Lake Success, 12 November 1947	Lake Success	12/11/1947

(continued)

(continued)

Domain	Treaty name	Place of conclusion	Date of conclusion
Human Rights	Protocol signed at Lake Success, New York, on 12 November 1947, to amend the Convention for the Suppression of the Traffic in Women and Children, concluded at Geneva on 30 September 1921, and the Convention for the Suppression of the Traffic in Women of Full Age, concluded at Geneva on 11 October 1933. Lake Success, New York, 12 November 1947	New York	12/11/1947
Human Rights	Protocol to amend the Convention for the suppression of the circulation of, and traffic in, obscene publications, concluded at Geneva on 12 September 1923. Lake Success, New York, 12 November 1947	New York	12/11/1947
Human Rights	Convention on the Prevention and Punishment of the Crime of Genocide. Paris, 9 December 1948	Paris	09/12/1948
Human Rights	Agreement for the Suppression of the Circulation of Obscene Publications, signed at Paris on 4 May 1910, amended by the Protocol signed at Lake Success, New York, 4 May 1949. New York, 4 May 1949	New York	04/05/1949
Human Rights	International Agreement for the Suppression of the White Slave Traffic, signed at Paris on 18 May 1904, amended by the Protocol signed at Lake Success, New York, 4 May 1949. Lake Success, New York, 4 May 1949	New York	04/05/1949
Human Rights	International Convention for the Suppression of the White Slave Traffic, signed at Paris on 4 May 1910, amended by the Protocol signed at Lake Success, New York, 4 May 1949. Lake Success, New York, 4 May 1949	New York	04/05/1949
Human Rights	Protocol amending the Agreement for the Suppression of the Circulation of Obscene Publications, signed at Paris, on 4 May 1910. Lake Success, New York, 4 May 1949	New York	04/05/1949

(continued)

(continued)

Domain	Treaty name	Place of conclusion	Date of conclusion
Human Rights	Protocol amending the International Agreement for the Suppression of the White Slave Traffic, signed at Paris on 18 May 1904, and the International Convention for the Suppression of the White Slave Traffic, signed at Paris on 4 May 1910. Lake Success, New York, 4 May 1949	New York	04/05/1949
Human Rights	Convention for the Suppression of the Traffic in Persons and of the Exploitation of the Prostitution of Others. Lake Success, New York, 21 March 1950	New York	21/03/1950
Human Rights	Final Protocol to the Convention for the Suppression of the Traffic in Persons and of the Exploitation of the Prostitution of Others. Lake Success, New York, 21 March 1950	New York	21/03/1950
Human Rights	Convention relating to the Status of Refugees. Geneva, 28 July 1951	Geneva	28/07/1951
Human Rights	Protocol amending the Slavery Convention signed at Geneva on 25 September 1926. New York, 7 December 1953	New York	1953
Human Rights	Convention on the International Right of Correction. New York, 31 March 1953	New York	31/03/1953
Human Rights	Convention on the Political Rights of Women. New York, 31 March 1953	New York	31/03/1953
Human Rights	Slavery Convention, signed at Geneva on 25 September 1926 and amended by the Protocol. New York, 7 December 1953	New York	07/12/1953
Human Rights	Convention relating to the Status of Stateless Persons. New York, 28 September 1954	New York	28/09/1954
Human Rights	Supplementary Convention on the Abolition of Slavery, the Slave Trade, and Institutions and Practices Similar to Slavery. Geneva, 7 September 1956	Geneva	07/09/1956

(continued)

(continued)

Domain	Treaty name	Place of conclusion	Date of conclusion
Human Rights	Convention on the Nationality of Married Women. New York, 20 February 1957	New York	20/02/1957
Human Rights	Convention on the Reduction of Statelessness. New York, 30 August 1961	New York	30/08/1961
Human Rights	Convention on Consent to Marriage, Minimum Age for Marriage and Registration of Marriages. New York, 10 December 1962	New York	10/12/1962
Human Rights	International Convention on the Elimination of All Forms of Racial Discrimination. New York, 7 March 1966	New York	07/03/1966
Human Rights	International Covenant on Civil and Political Rights. New York, 16 December 1966	New York	16/12/1966
Human Rights	International Covenant on Economic, Social and Cultural Rights. New York, 16 December 1966	New York	16/12/1966
Human Rights	Optional Protocol to the International Covenant on Civil and Political Rights. New York, 16 December 1966	New York	16/12/1966
Human Rights	Protocol relating to the Status of Refugees. New York, 31 January 1967	New York	31/01/1967
Human Rights	Convention on the non-applicability of statutory limitations to war crimes and crimes against humanity. New York, 26 November 1968	New York	26/11/1968
Human Rights	International Convention on the Suppression and Punishment of the Crime of Apartheid. New York, 30 November 1973	New York	30/11/1973
Human Rights	Convention on the Elimination of All Forms of Discrimination against Women. New York, 18 December 1979	New York	18/12/1979
Human Rights	Convention against Torture and Other Cruel, Inhuman or Degrading Treatment or Punishment. New York, 10 December 1984	New York	10/12/1984

(continued)

(continued)

Domain	Treaty name	Place of conclusion	Date of conclusion
Human Rights	International Convention against Apartheid in Sports. New York, 10 December 1985	New York	10/12/1985
Human Rights	Convention on the Rights of the Child. New York, 20 November 1989	New York	20/11/1989
Human Rights	Second Optional Protocol to the International Covenant on Civil and Political Rights, aiming at the abolition of the death penalty. New York, 15 December 1989	New York	15/12/1989
Human Rights	International Convention on the Protection of the Rights of All Migrant Workers and Members of their Families. New York, 18 December 1990	New York	18/12/1990
Human Rights	Amendment to article 8 of the International Convention on the Elimination of All Forms of Racial Discrimination. New York, 15 January 1992	New York	15/01/1992
Human Rights	Agreement establishing the Fund for the Development of the Indigenous Peoples of Latin America and the Caribbean. Madrid, 24 July 1992	Madrid	24/07/1992
Human Rights	Amendments to articles 17 (7) and 18 (5) of the Convention against Torture and Other Cruel, Inhuman or Degrading Treatment or Punishment . New York, 8 September 1992	New York	08/09/1992
Human Rights	Amendment to article 43 (2) of the Convention on the Rights of the Child. New York, 12 December 1995	New York	12/12/1995
Human Rights	Amendment to article 20, paragraph 1 of the Convention on the Elimination of All Forms of Discrimination against Women. New York, 22 December 1995	New York	22/12/1995
Human Rights	Optional Protocol to the Convention on the Elimination of All Forms of Discrimination against Women. New York, 6 October 1999	New York	06/10/1999

(continued)

(continued)

Domain	Treaty name	Place of conclusion	Date of conclusion
Human Rights	Optional Protocol to the Convention on the Rights of the Child on the involvement of children in armed conflict. New York, 25 May 2000	New York	25/05/2000
Human Rights	Optional Protocol to the Convention on the Rights of the Child on the sale of children, child prostitution and child pornography. New York, 25 May 2000	New York	25/05/2000
Human Rights	Optional Protocol to the Convention against Torture and Other Cruel, Inhuman or Degrading Treatment or Punishment. New York, 18 December 2002	New York	18/12/2002
Human Rights	Convention on the Rights of Persons with Disabilities. New York, 13 December 2006	New York	13/12/2006
Human Rights	Optional Protocol to the Convention on the Rights of Persons with Disabilities. New York, 13 December 2006	New York	13/12/2006
Human Rights	International Convention for the Protection of All Persons from Enforced Disappearance. New York, 20 December 2006	New York	20/12/2006
Human Rights	Optional Protocol to the International Covenant on Economic, Social and Cultural Rights. New York, 10 December 2008	New York	10/12/2008
Human Rights	Optional Protocol to the Convention on the Rights of the Child on a communications procedure. New York, 19 December 2011	New York	19/12/2011
Intellectual Property	Paris Convention for the Protection of Industrial Property		1883
Intellectual Property	Berne Convention (Total Contracting Parties : 177)	Berne	1886
Intellectual Property	Madrid Agreement Concerning the International Registration of Marks	Madrid	1891
Intellectual Property	Madrid Agreement for the Repression of False or Deceptive Indications of Source on Goods	Madrid	1891

(continued)

(continued)

Domain	Treaty name	Place of conclusion	Date of conclusion
Intellectual Property	Hague Agreement Concerning the International Registration of Industrial Designs	Hague	1925
Intellectual Property	Agreement on the Importation of Educational, Scientific and Cultural Materials. Lake Success, New York, 22 November 1950	Lake Success	22/11/1950
Intellectual Property	Universal Copyright Convention		1952
Intellectual Property	Nice Agreement Concerning the International Classification of Goods and Services for the Purposes of the Registration of Marks	Nice	1957
Intellectual Property	Lisbon Agreement for the Protection of Appellations of Origin and their International Registration	Lisbon	1958
Intellectual Property	International Convention for the Protection of New Varieties of Plants (UPOV)	Paris	1961
Intellectual Property	International Convention for the Protection of Performers, Producers of Phonograms and Broadcasting Organisations. Rome, 26 October 1961	Rome	26/10/1961
Intellectual Property	WIPO Convention	Stockholm	1967
Intellectual Property	Locarno Agreement Establishing an International Classification for Industrial Designs	Locarno	1968
Intellectual Property	Patent Cooperation Treaty (PCT)		1970
Intellectual Property	Strasbourg Agreement Concerning the International Patent Classification	Strasbourg	1971
Intellectual Property	Convention for the Protection of Producers of Phonograms against Unauthorized Duplication of their Phonograms. Geneva, 29 October 1971	Geneva	29/10/1971
Intellectual Property	Convention concerning the Protection of the World Cultural and Natural Heritage		1972
Intellectual Property	Vienna Agreement Establishing an International Classification of the Figurative Elements of Marks	Vienna	1973

(continued)

(continued)

Domain	Treaty name	Place of conclusion	Date of conclusion
Intellectual Property	Brussels Convention Relating to the Distribution of Programme-Carrying Signals Transmitted by Satellite	Brussels	1974
Intellectual Property	Protocol to the Agreement on the Importation of Educational, Scientific and Cultural Materials of 22 November 1950. Nairobi, 26 November 1976	Nairobi	26/11/1976
Intellectual Property	Budapest Treaty on the International Recognition of the Deposit of Microorganisms for the Purposes of Patent Procedure	Budapest	1977
Intellectual Property	Additional Protocol to the Multilateral Convention for the Avoidance of Double Taxation of Copyright Royalties. Madrid, 13 December 1979	Madrid	13/12/1979
Intellectual Property	Multilateral Convention for the Avoidance of Double Taxation of Copyright Royalties. Madrid, 13 December 1979	Madrid	13/12/1979
Intellectual Property	Nairobi Treaty on the Protection of the Olympic Symbol	Nairobi	1981
Intellectual Property	Protocol Relating to the Madrid Agreement Concerning the International Registration of Marks	Madrid	1989
Intellectual Property	Washington Treaty on Intellectual Property in Respect of Integrated Circuits	Washington	1989
Intellectual Property	Agreement on Trade-Related Aspects of Intellectual Property Rights (TRIPS)		1994
Intellectual Property	Trademark Law Treaty (TLT)		1994
Intellectual Property	WIPO Copyright Treaty (WCT)		1996
Intellectual Property	WIPO Performances and Phonograms Treaty		1996
Intellectual Property	Patent Law Treaty (PLT)		2000
Intellectual Property	International Treaty on Plant Genetic Resources for Food and Agriculture (November 3, 2001)		03/11/2001
Intellectual Property	Convention for the Safeguarding of the Intangible Cultural Heritage (October 17, 2003)		17/10/2003

(continued)

(continued)

Domain	Treaty name	Place of conclusion	Date of conclusion
Intellectual Property	Singapore Treaty on the Law of Trademarks	Singapore	2006
Intellectual Property	Beijing Treaty on Audiovisual Performances (Treaty not yet in force)	Beijing	2012
Intellectual Property	Marrakesh Treaty to Facilitate Access to Published Works for Persons Who Are Blind, Visually Impaired or Otherwise Print Disabled	Marrakesh	2013
Labor and Health	International Opium Convention. The Hague, 23 January 1912	The Hague	23/01/1912
Labor and Health	C014—Weekly Rest (Industry) Convention, 1921 (No. 14)		1921
Labor and Health	International Opium Convention. Geneva, 19 February 1925	Geneva	19/02/1925
Labor and Health	Protocol to the International Opium Convention. Geneva, 19 February 1925	Geneva	19/02/1925
Labor and Health	C029—Forced Labour Convention, 1930 (No. 29)		1930
Labor and Health	P029—Protocol of 2014 to the Forced Labour Convention, 1930		1930
Labor and Health	Convention for limiting the Manufacture and regulating the Distribution of Narcotic Drugs. Geneva, 13 July 1931	Geneva	13/07/1931
Labor and Health	Protocol of Signature. Geneva, 13 July 1931	Geneva	13/07/1931
Labor and Health	Convention of 1936 for the Suppression of the Illicit Traffic in Dangerous Drugs. Geneva, 26 June 1936	Geneva	26/06/1936
Labor and Health	Protocol of Signature. Geneva, 26 June 1936	Geneva	26/06/1936
Labor and Health	Constitution of the World Health Organization. New York, 22 July 1946	New York	22/07/1946
Labor and Health	Protocol concerning the Office international d'hygiène publique. New York, 22 July 1946	New York	22/07/1946

(continued)

(continued)

Domain	Treaty name	Place of conclusion	Date of conclusion
Labor and Health	Agreement concerning the Suppression of the Manufacture of, Internal Trade in, and Use of, Prepared Opium. Geneva, 11 February 1925, and Lake Success, New York, 11 December 1946	New York	11/12/1946
Labor and Health	Convention for Limiting the Manufacture and Regulating the Distribution of Narcotic Drugs. Geneva, 13 July 1931, and Lake Success, New York, 11 December 1946	New York	11/12/1946
Labor and Health	Convention for the Suppression of the Illicit Traffic in Dangerous Drugs. Geneva, 26 June 1936, and Lake Success, New York, 11 December 1946	New York	11/12/1946
Labor and Health	International Opium Convention. Geneva, 19 February 1925, and Lake Success, New York, 11 December 1946	New York	11/12/1946
Labor and Health	Protocol amending the Agreements, Conventions and Protocols on Narcotic Drugs, concluded at The Hague on 23 January 1912, at Geneva on 11 February 1925 and 19 February 1925, and 13 July 1931, at Bangkok on 27 November 1931 and at Geneva on 26 June 1936. Lake Success, New York, 11 December 1946	New York	11/12/1946
Labor and Health	C077—Medical Examination of Young Persons (Industry) Convention, 1946 (No. 77)		1946
Labor and Health	C078—Medical Examination of Young Persons (Non-Industrial Occupations) Convention, 1946 (No. 78)		1946
Labor and Health	C081—Labour Inspection Convention, 1947 (No. 81)		1947
Labor and Health	P081—Protocol of 1995 to the Labour Inspection Convention, 1947		1947

(continued)

(continued)

Domain	Treaty name	Place of conclusion	Date of conclusion
Labor and Health	Protocol Bringing under International Control Drugs Outside the Scope of the Convention of 13 July 1931 for Limiting the Manufacture and Regulating the Distribution of Narcotic Drugs, as amended by the Protocol signed at Lake Success, New York, on 11 December 1946. Paris, 19 November 1948	Paris	19/11/1948
Labor and Health	C087—Freedom of Association and Protection of the Right to Organise Convention, 1948 (No. 87)		1948
Labor and Health	P089—Protocol of 1990 to the Night Work (Women) Convention (Revised), 1948		1948
Labor and Health	C094—Labor Clauses (Public Contracts) Convention, 1949 (No. 94)		1949
Labor and Health	C095—Protection of Wages Convention, 1949 (No. 95)		1949
Labor and Health	C097—Migration for Employment Convention (Revised), 1949 (No. 97)		1949
Labor and Health	C098—Right to Organise and Collective Bargaining Convention, 1949 (No. 98)		1949
Labor and Health	C100—Equal Remuneration Convention, 1951 (No. 100)		1951
Labor and Health	C102—Social Security (Minimum Standards) Convention, 1952 (No. 102)		1952
Labor and Health	Protocol for Limiting and Regulating the Cultivation of the Poppy Plant, the Production of, International and Wholesale Trade in, and use of Opium. New York, 23 June 1953	New York	23/06/1953
Labor and Health	C105—Abolition of Forced Labour Convention, 1957 (No. 105)		1957
Labor and Health	C106—Weekly Rest (Commerce and Offices) Convention, 1957 (No. 106)		1957
Labor and Health	C110—Plantations Convention, 1958 (No. 110)		1958

(continued)

(continued)

Domain	Treaty name	Place of conclusion	Date of conclusion
Labor and Health	C111—Discrimination (Employment and Occupation) Convention, 1958 (No. 111)		1958
Labor and Health	P110—Protocol of 1982 to the Plantations Convention, 1958		1958
Labor and Health	Amendments to articles 24 and 25 of the Constitution of the World Health Organization. Geneva, 28 May 1959	Geneva	28/05/1959
Labor and Health	C115—Radiation Protection Convention, 1960 (No. 115)		1960
Labor and Health	Single Convention on Narcotic Drugs, 1961. New York, 30 March 1961	New York	30/03/1961
Labor and Health	C118—Equality of Treatment (Social Security) Convention, 1962 (No. 118)		1962
Labor and Health	C120—Hygiene (Commerce and Offices) Convention, 1964 (No. 120)		1964
Labor and Health	C121—Employment Injury Benefits Convention, 1964 [Schedule I amended in 1980] (No. 121)		1964
Labor and Health	C122—Employment Policy Convention, 1964 (No. 122)		1964
Labor and Health	Amendment to article 7 of the Constitution of the World Health Organization. Geneva, 20 May 1965	Geneva	20/05/1965
Labor and Health	C124—Medical Examination of Young Persons (Underground Work) Convention, 1965 (No. 124)		1965
Labor and Health	Amendments to articles 24 and 25 of the Constitution of the World Health Organization. Geneva, 23 May 1967	Geneva	23/05/1967
Labor and Health	C128—Invalidity, Old-Age and Survivors' Benefits Convention, 1967 (No. 128)		1967
Labor and Health	C129—Labour Inspection (Agriculture) Convention, 1969 (No. 129)		1969
Labor and Health	C130—Medical Care and Sickness Benefits Convention, 1969 (No. 130)		1969
Labor and Health	C131—Minimum Wage Fixing Convention, 1970 (No. 131)		1970

(continued)

(continued)

Domain	Treaty name	Place of conclusion	Date of conclusion
Labor and Health	Convention on psychotropic substances. Vienna, 21 February 1971	Vienna	21/02/1971
Labor and Health	C135—Workers' Representatives Convention, 1971 (No. 135)		1971
Labor and Health	Protocol amending the Single Convention on Narcotic Drugs, 1961. Geneva, 25 March 1972	Geneva	25/03/1972
Labor and Health	Amendments to articles 34 and 55 of the Constitution of the World Health Organization. Geneva, 22 May 1973	Geneva	22/05/1973
Labor and Health	C138—Minimum Age Convention, 1973 (No. 138)		1973
Labor and Health	C139—Occupational Cancer Convention, 1974 (No. 139)		1974
Labor and Health	C140—Paid Educational Leave Convention, 1974 (No. 140)		1974
Labor and Health	Single Convention on Narcotic Drugs, 1961, as amended by the Protocol amending the Single Convention on Narcotic Drugs, 1961. New York, 8 August 1975	New York	08/08/1975
Labor and Health	C141—Rural Workers' Organisations Convention, 1975 (No. 141)		1975
Labor and Health	C142—Human Resources Development Convention, 1975 (No. 142)		1975
Labor and Health	C143—Migrant Workers (Supplementary Provisions) Convention, 1975 (No. 143)		1975
Labor and Health	Amendments to articles 24 and 25 of the Constitution of the World Health Organization. Geneva, 17 May 1976	Geneva	17/05/1976
Labor and Health	C144—Tripartite Consultation (International Labour Standards) Convention, 1976 (No. 144)		1976
Labor and Health	C145—Continuity of Employment (Seafarers) Convention, 1976 (No. 145)		1976
Labor and Health	C146—Seafarers' Annual Leave with Pay Convention, 1976 (No. 146)		1976

(continued)

(continued)

Domain	Treaty name	Place of conclusion	Date of conclusion
Labor and Health	C147—Merchant Shipping (Minimum Standards) Convention, 1976 (No. 147)		1976
Labor and Health	C148—Working Environment (Air Pollution, Noise and Vibration) Convention, 1977 (No. 148)		1977
Labor and Health	C149—Nursing Personnel Convention, 1977 (No. 149)		1977
Labor and Health	Amendment to article 74 of the Constitution of the World Health Organization. Geneva, 18 May 1978	Geneva	18/05/1978
Labor and Health	C150—Labour Administration Convention, 1978 (No. 150)		1978
Labor and Health	C151—Labour Relations (Public Service) Convention, 1978 (No. 151)		1978
Labor and Health	C152—Occupational Safety and Health (Dock Work) Convention, 1979 (No. 152)		1979
Labor and Health	C154—Collective Bargaining Convention, 1981 (No. 154)		1981
Labor and Health	C155—Occupational Safety and Health Convention, 1981 (No. 155)		1981
Labor and Health	C156—Workers with Family Responsibilities Convention, 1981 (No. 156)		1981
Labor and Health	P155—Protocol of 2002 to the Occupational Safety and Health Convention, 1981		1981
Labor and Health	C157—Maintenance of Social Security Rights Convention, 1982 (No. 157)		1982
Labor and Health	C159—Vocational Rehabilitation and Employment (Disabled Persons) Convention, 1983 (No. 159)		1983
Labor and Health	C160—Labour Statistics Convention, 1985 (No. 160)		1985
Labor and Health	C161—Occupational Health Services Convention, 1985 (No. 161)		1985
Labor and Health	Amendments to articles 24 and 25 of the Constitution of the World Health Organization. Geneva, 12 May 1986	Geneva	12/05/1986

(continued)

(continued)

Domain	Treaty name	Place of conclusion	Date of conclusion
Labor and Health	C162—Asbestos Convention, 1986 (No. 162)		1986
Labor and Health	C163—Seafarers' Welfare Convention, 1987 (No. 163)		1987
Labor and Health	C164—Health Protection and Medical Care (Seafarers) Convention, 1987 (No. 164)		1987
Labor and Health	C166—Repatriation of Seafarers Convention (Revised), 1987 (No. 166)		1987
Labor and Health	United Nations Convention against Illicit Traffic in Narcotic Drugs and Psychotropic Substances. Vienna, 20 December 1988	Vienna	20/12/1988
Labor and Health	C167—Safety and Health in Construction Convention, 1988 (No. 167)		1988
Labor and Health	C168—Employment Promotion and Protection against Unemployment Convention, 1988 (No. 168)		1988
Labor and Health	C169—Indigenous and Tribal Peoples Convention, 1989 (No. 169)		1989
Labor and Health	C170—Chemicals Convention, 1990 (No. 170)		1990
Labor and Health	C171—Night Work Convention, 1990 (No. 171)		1990
Labor and Health	C172—Working Conditions (Hotels and Restaurants) Convention, 1991 (No. 172)		1991
Labor and Health	C173—Protection of Workers' Claims (Employer's Insolvency) Convention, 1992 (No. 173)		1992
Labor and Health	C174—Prevention of Major Industrial Accidents Convention, 1993 (No. 174)		1993
Labor and Health	C175—Part-Time Work Convention, 1994 (No. 175)		1994
Labor and Health	C176—Safety and Health in Mines Convention, 1995 (No. 176)		1995
Labor and Health	Agreement on the establishment of the International Vaccine Institute. New York, 28 October 1996	New York	28/10/1996

(continued)

(continued)

Domain	Treaty name	Place of conclusion	Date of conclusion
Labor and Health	C177—Home Work Convention, 1996 (No. 177)		1996
Labor and Health	C178—Labour Inspection (Seafarers) Convention, 1996 (No. 178)		1996
Labor and Health	C181—Private Employment Agencies Convention, 1997 (No. 181)		1997
Labor and Health	Amendments to articles 24 and 25 of the Constitution of the World Health Organization. Geneva, 16 May 1998	Geneva	16/05/1998
Labor and Health	C182—Worst Forms of Child Labour Convention, 1999 (No. 182)		1999
Labor and Health	C183—Maternity Protection Convention, 2000 (No. 183)		2000
Labor and Health	C184—Safety and Health in Agriculture Convention, 2001 (No. 184)		2001
Labor and Health	WHO Framework Convention on Tobacco Control. Geneva, 21 May 2003	Geneva	21/05/2003
Labor and Health	C187—Promotional Framework for Occupational Safety and Health Convention, 2006 (No. 187)		2006
Labor and Health	MLC, 2006—Maritime Labour Convention, 2006 (MLC, 2006)		2006
Labor and Health	C188—Work in Fishing Convention, 2007 (No. 188)		2007
Labor and Health	C189—Domestic Workers Convention, 2011 (No. 189)		2011
Labor and Health	Protocol to Eliminate Illicit Trade in Tobacco Products. Seoul, 12 November 2012	Seoul	12/11/2012
Peace and Disarmament	Convention on the Privileges and Immunities of the United Nations. New York, 13 February 1946	New York	13/02/1946
Peace and Disarmament	Convention on the Privileges and Immunities of the Specialized Agencies. New York, 21 November 1947	New York	21/11/1947

(continued)

(continued)

Domain	Treaty name	Place of conclusion	Date of conclusion
Peace and Disarmament	Annex III—International Civil Aviation Organization (ICAO)—to the Convention on the Privileges and Immunities of the Specialized Agencies. Geneva, 21 June 1948	Geneva	21/06/1948
Peace and Disarmament	Annex I—International Labour Organisation (ILO)—to the Convention on the Privileges and Immunities of the Specialized Agencies. San Francisco, 10 July 1948	San Francisco	10/07/1948
Peace and Disarmament	Annex VII—World Health Organization (WHO)—to the Convention on the Privileges and Immunities of the Specialized Agencies. Geneva, 17 July 1948	Geneva	17/07/1948
Peace and Disarmament	Annex II—Food and Agriculture Organization of the United Nations (FAO)—to the Convention on the Privileges and Immunities of the Specialized Agencies. Washington, 29 November 1948	Washington	29/11/1948
Peace and Disarmament	Annex IV—United Nations Educational, Scientific and Cultural Organization (UNESCO)—to the Convention on the Privileges and Immunities of the Specialized Agencies. Paris, 7 February 1949	Paris	07/02/1949
Peace and Disarmament	Annex V—International Monetary Fund (IMF)—to the Convention on the Privileges and Immunities of the Specialized Agencies. Washington, 11 April 1949	Washington	11/04/1949
Peace and Disarmament	Annex VI—International Bank for Reconstruction and Development (IBRD)—to the Convention on the Privileges and Immunities of the Specialized Agencies. Washington, 19 April 1949	Washington	19/04/1949
Peace and Disarmament	Revised General Act for the Pacific Settlement of International Disputes. New York, 28 April 1949	New York	28/04/1949

(continued)

(continued)

Domain	Treaty name	Place of conclusion	Date of conclusion
Peace and Disarmament	Annex VIII—Universal Postal Union (UPU)—to the Convention on the Privileges and Immunities of the Specialized Agencies. Geneva, 25 May 1949	Geneva	25/05/1949
Peace and Disarmament	Revised text of Annex VII—World Health Organization (WHO)—to the Convention on the Privileges and Immunities of the Specialized Agencies. Geneva, 26 May 1950	Geneva	26/05/1950
Peace and Disarmament	Annex IX—International Telecommunication Union (ITU)—to the Convention on the Privileges and Immunities of the Specialized Agencies. Geneva, 6 October 1950	Geneva	06/10/1950
Peace and Disarmament	Annex XI—World Meteorological Organization (WMO)—to the Convention on the Privileges and Immunities of the Specialized Agencies. Paris, 17 April 1951	Paris	17/04/1951
Peace and Disarmament	Second revised text of Annex VII—World Health Organization (WHO)—to the Convention on the Privileges and Immunities of the Specialized Agencies. Geneva, 27 May 1957	Geneva	27/05/1957
Peace and Disarmament	Convention on Fishing and Conservation of the Living Resources of the High Seas. Geneva, 29 April 1958	Geneva	29/04/1958
Peace and Disarmament	Convention on the Continental Shelf. Geneva, 29 April 1958	Geneva	29/04/1958
Peace and Disarmament	Convention on the High Seas. Geneva, 29 April 1958	Geneva	29/04/1958
Peace and Disarmament	Convention on the Territorial Sea and the Contiguous Zone. Geneva, 29 April 1958	Geneva	29/04/1958
Peace and Disarmament	Optional Protocol of Signature concerning the Compulsory Settlement of Disputes. Geneva, 29 April 1958	Geneva	29/04/1958

(continued)

(continued)

Domain	Treaty name	Place of conclusion	Date of conclusion
Peace and Disarmament	Third revised text of Annex VII—World Health Organization (WHO)—to the Convention on the Privileges and Immunities of the Specialized Agencies. Minneapolis, 17 July 1958	Minneapolis	17/07/1958
Peace and Disarmament	Annex XII—International Maritime Organization (IMO)—to the Convention on the Privileges and Immunities of the Specialized Agencies. London, 16 January 1959	London	16/01/1959
Peace and Disarmament	Annex XIII—International Finance Corporation (IFC)—to the Convention on the Privileges and Immunities of the Specialized Agencies. Washington, 2 April 1959	Washington	02/04/1959
Peace and Disarmament	Revised text of Annex II—Food and Agriculture Organization of the United Nations (FAO)—to the Convention on the Privileges and Immunities of the Specialized Agencies. Rome, 20 November 1959	Rome	20/11/1959
Peace and Disarmament	Optional Protocol to the Vienna Convention on Diplomatic Relations, concerning Acquisition of Nationality. Vienna, 18 April 1961	Vienna	18/04/1961
Peace and Disarmament	Optional Protocol to the Vienna Convention on Diplomatic Relations, concerning the Compulsory Settlement of Disputes. Vienna, 18 April 1961	Vienna	18/04/1961
Peace and Disarmament	Vienna Convention on Diplomatic Relations. Vienna, 18 April 1961	Vienna	18/04/1961
Peace and Disarmament	Annex XIV—International Development Association (IDA)—to the Convention on the Privileges and Immunities of the Specialized Agencies. Washington, 13 February 1962	Washington	13/02/1962
Peace and Disarmament	Optional Protocol to the Vienna Convention on Consular Relations concerning Acquisition of Nationality. Vienna, 24 April 1963	Vienna	24/04/1963

(continued)

(continued)

Domain	Treaty name	Place of conclusion	Date of conclusion
Peace and Disarmament	Optional Protocol to the Vienna Convention on Consular Relations concerning the Compulsory Settlement of Disputes. Vienna, 24 April 1963	Vienna	24/04/1963
Peace and Disarmament	Vienna Convention on Consular Relations. Vienna, 24 April 1963	Vienna	24/04/1963
Peace and Disarmament	Second revised text of Annex II—Food and Agriculture Organization of the United Nations (FAO)—to the Convention on the Privileges and Immunities of the Specialized Agencies. Rome, 8 December 1965	Rome	08/12/1965
Peace and Disarmament	Revised text of Annex XII—International Maritime Organization (IMO)—to the Convention on the Privileges and Immunities of the Specialized Agencies. London, 16 May 1968	London	16/05/1968
Peace and Disarmament	Convention on special missions. New York, 8 December 1969	New York	08/12/1969
Peace and Disarmament	Optional Protocol to the Convention on Special Missions concerning the compulsory settlement of disputes. New York, 8 December 1969	New York	08/12/1969
Peace and Disarmament	Convention on the Prevention and Punishment of Crimes against Internationally Protected Persons, including Diplomatic Agents. New York, 14 December 1973	New York	14/12/1973
Peace and Disarmament	Convention on registration of objects launched into outer space. New York, 12 November 1974	New York	12/11/1974
Peace and Disarmament	Vienna Convention on the Representation of States in their Relations with International Organizations of a Universal Character. Vienna, 14 March 1975	Vienna	14/03/1975
Peace and Disarmament	Convention on the prohibition of military or any other hostile use of environmental modification techniques. New York, 10 December 1976	New York	10/12/1976

(continued)

(continued)

Domain	Treaty name	Place of conclusion	Date of conclusion
Peace and Disarmament	Annex XV—World Intellectual Property Organization (WIPO)—to the Convention on the Privileges and Immunities of the Specialized Agencies. Geneva, 4 October 1977	Geneva	04/10/1977
Peace and Disarmament	Annex XVI—International Fund for Agricultural Development (IFAD)—to the Convention on the Privileges and Immunities of the Specialized Agencies. Rome, 16 December 1977	Rome	16/12/1977
Peace and Disarmament	Agreement governing the Activities of States on the Moon and Other Celestial Bodies. New York, 5 December 1979	New York	05/12/1979
Peace and Disarmament	International Convention Against the Taking of Hostages. New York, 17 December 1979	New York	17/12/1979
Peace and Disarmament	Convention on Prohibitions or Restrictions on the Use of Certain Conventional Weapons which may be deemed to be Excessively Injurious or to have Indiscriminate Effects (with Protocols I, II and III). Geneva, 10 October 1980	Geneva	10/10/1980
Peace and Disarmament	United Nations Convention on the Law of the Sea. Montego Bay, 10 December 1982	Montego Bay	10/12/1982
Peace and Disarmament	Vienna Convention on Succession of States in Respect of State Property, Archives and Debts. Vienna, 8 April 1983	Vienna	08/04/1983
Peace and Disarmament	Annex XVII—United Nations Industrial Development Organization (UNIDO)—to the Convention on the Privileges and Immunities of the Specialized Agencies. Vienna, 3 July 1987	Vienna	03/07/1987
Peace and Disarmament	International Convention Against the Recruitment, Use, Financing and Training of Mercenaries. New York, 4 December 1989	New York	04/12/1989

(continued)

(continued)

Domain	Treaty name	Place of conclusion	Date of conclusion
Peace and Disarmament	Convention on the Prohibition of the Development, Production, Stockpiling and Use of Chemical Weapons and on their Destruction. Geneva, 3 September 1992	Geneva	03/09/1992
Peace and Disarmament	Agreement relating to the implementation of Part XI of the United Nations Convention on the Law of the Sea of 10 December 1982. New York, 28 July 1994	New York	28/07/1994
Peace and Disarmament	Convention on the Safety of United Nations and Associated Personnel. New York, 9 December 1994	New York	09/12/1994
Peace and Disarmament	Agreement for the Implementation of the Provisions of the United Nations Convention on the Law of the Sea of 10 December 1982 relating to the Conservation and Management of Straddling Fish Stocks and Highly Migratory Fish Stocks. New York, 4 August 1995	New York	04/08/1995
Peace and Disarmament	Additional Protocol to the Convention on Prohibitions or Restrictions on the Use of Certain Conventional Weapons which may be deemed to be Excessively Injurious or to have Indiscriminate Effects (Protocol IV, entitled Protocol on Blinding Laser Weapons). Vienna, 13 October 1995	Vienna	13/10/1995
Peace and Disarmament	Protocol on Prohibitions or Restrictions on the Use of Mines, Booby-Traps and Other Devices as amended on 3 May 1996 (Protocol II, as amended on 3 May 1996) annexed to the Convention on Prohibitions or Restrictions on the Use of Certain Conventional Weapons which may be deemed to be Excessively Injurious or to have Indiscriminate Effects. Geneva, 3 May 1996	Geneva	03/05/1996
Peace and Disarmament	Comprehensive Nuclear-Test-Ban Treaty. New York, 10 September 1996	New York	10/09/1996

(continued)

(continued)

Domain	Treaty name	Place of conclusion	Date of conclusion
Peace and Disarmament	Agreement on the Privileges and Immunities of the International Tribunal for the Law of the Sea. New York, 23 May 1997	New York	23/05/1997
Peace and Disarmament	Convention on the Prohibition of the Use, Stockpiling, Production and Transfer of Anti-Personnel Mines and on their Destruction. Oslo, 18 September 1997	Oslo	18/09/1997
Peace and Disarmament	International Convention for the Suppression of Terrorist Bombings. New York, 15 December 1997	New York	15/12/1997
Peace and Disarmament	Protocol on the Privileges and Immunities of the International Seabed Authority. Kingston, 27 March 1998	Kingston	27/03/1998
Peace and Disarmament	Rome Statute of the International Criminal Court. Rome, 17 July 1998	Rome	17/07/1998
Peace and Disarmament	International Convention for the Suppression of the Financing of Terrorism. New York, 9 December 1999	New York	09/12/1999
Peace and Disarmament	Protocol against the Smuggling of Migrants by Land, Sea and Air, supplementing the United Nations Convention against Transnational Organized Crime. New York, 15 November 2000	New York	15/11/2000
Peace and Disarmament	Protocol to Prevent, Suppress and Punish Trafficking in Persons, Especially Women and Children, supplementing the United Nations Convention against Transnational Organized Crime. New York, 15 November 2000	New York	15/11/2000
Peace and Disarmament	United Nations Convention against Transnational Organized Crime. New York, 15 November 2000	New York	15/11/2000
Peace and Disarmament	Protocol against the Illicit Manufacturing of and Trafficking in Firearms, Their Parts and Components and Ammunition, supplementing the United Nations Convention against Transnational Organized Crime. New York, 31 May 2001	New York	31/05/2001

(continued)

(continued)

Domain	Treaty name	Place of conclusion	Date of conclusion
Peace and Disarmament	Second Revised text of Annex XII—International Maritime Organization (IMO)—to the Convention on the Privileges and Immunities of the Specialized Agencies. London, 22 November 2001	London	22/11/2001
Peace and Disarmament	Amendment to Article I of the Convention on Prohibitions or Restrictions on the Use of Certain Conventional Weapons which may be deemed to be Excessively Injurious or to have Indiscriminate Effects. Geneva, 21 December 2001	Geneva	21/12/2001
Peace and Disarmament	Agreement on the Privileges and Immunities of the International Criminal Court. New York, 9 September 2002	New York	09/09/2002
Peace and Disarmament	United Nations Convention against Corruption. New York, 31 October 2003	New York	31/10/2003
Peace and Disarmament	Protocol on Explosive Remnants of War to the Convention on Prohibitions or Restrictions on the Use of Certain Conventional Weapons which may be deemed to be Excessively Injurious or to have Indiscriminate Effects (Protocol V). Geneva, 28 November 2003	Geneva	28/11/2003
Peace and Disarmament	United Nations Convention on Jurisdictional Immunities of States and Their Property. New York, 2 December 2004	New York	02/12/2004
Peace and Disarmament	International Convention for the Suppression of Acts of Nuclear Terrorism. New York, 13 April 2005	New York	13/04/2005
Peace and Disarmament	Optional Protocol to the Convention on the Safety of United Nations and Associated Personnel. New York, 8 December 2005	New York	08/12/2005
Peace and Disarmament	Convention on Cluster Munitions. Dublin, 30 May 2008	Dublin	30/05/2008

(continued)

(continued)

Domain	Treaty name	Place of conclusion	Date of conclusion
Peace and Disarmament	Annex XVIII—World Tourism Organization (WTO)—to the Convention on the Privileges and Immunities of the Specialized Agencies. Jeju, 30 July 2008	Jeju	30/07/2008
Peace and Disarmament	Central African Convention for the Control of Small Arms and Light Weapons, their Ammunition and all Parts and Components that can be used for their Manufacture, Repair and Assembly. Kinshasa, 30 April 2010	Kinshasa	30/04/2010
Peace and Disarmament	Amendment to article 8 of the Rome Statute of the International Criminal Court. Kampala, 10 June 2010	Kampala	10/06/2010
Peace and Disarmament	Amendments on the crime of aggression to the Rome Statute of the International Criminal Court. Kampala, 11 June 2010	Kampala	11/06/2010
Peace and Disarmament	Arms Trade Treaty. New York, 2 April 2013	New York	02/04/2013
Peace and Disarmament	Amendment to article 124 of the Rome Statute of the International Criminal Court. The Hague, 26 November 2015	The Hague	26/11/2015
Peace and Disarmament	Treaty on the Prohibition of Nuclear Weapons. New York, 7 July 2017	New York	07/07/2017
Peace and Disarmament	Amendment to article 8 of the Rome Statute of the International Criminal Court (Blinding laser weapons). New York, 14 December 2017	New York	14/12/2017
Peace and Disarmament	Amendment to article 8 of the Rome Statute of the International Criminal Court (Weapons the primary effect of which is to injure by fragments undetectable by x-rays in the human body) . New York, 14 December 2017	New York	14/12/2017
Peace and Disarmament	Amendment to article 8 of the Rome Statute of the International Criminal Court (Weapons which use microbial or other biological agents, or toxins). New York, 14 December 2017	New York	14/12/2017

(continued)

(continued)

Domain	Treaty name	Place of conclusion	Date of conclusion
Trade, commerce, and communication	General Agreement on Tariffs and Trade. Geneva, 30 October 1947	Geneva	30/10/1947
Trade, commerce, and communication	Convention on the International Maritime Organization. Geneva, 6 March 1948	Geneva	06/03/1948
Trade, commerce, and communication	International Convention relating to economic statistics, signed at Geneva on 14 December 1928, amended by the Protocol signed at Paris on 9 December 1948. Paris, 9 December 1948	Paris	09/12/1948
Trade, commerce, and communication	Protocol amending the International Convention relating to Economic Statistics, signed at Geneva on 14 December 1928. Paris, 9 December 1948	Paris	09/12/1948
Trade, commerce, and communication	Agreement for Facilitating the International Circulation of Visual and Auditory Materials of an Educational, Scientific and Cultural Character. Lake Success, New York, 15 July 1949	New York	15/07/1949
Trade, commerce, and communication	Convention on Road Traffic. Geneva, 19 September 1949	Geneva	19/09/1949
Trade, commerce, and communication	Protocol concerning countries or territories at present occupied. Geneva, 19 September 1949	Geneva	19/09/1949
Trade, commerce, and communication	Protocol on Road Signs and Signals. Geneva, 19 September 1949	Geneva	19/09/1949
Trade, commerce, and communication	Declaration on the construction of main international traffic arteries. Geneva, 16 September 1950	Geneva	16/09/1950
Trade, commerce, and communication	European Agreement on the application of article 23 of the 1949 Convention on road traffic, concerning the dimensions and weights of vehicles permitted to travel on certain roads of the Contracting Parties. Geneva, 16 September 1950	Geneva	16/09/1950

(continued)

(continued)

Domain	Treaty name	Place of conclusion	Date of conclusion
Trade, commerce, and communication	European Agreement on the application of article 3 of annex 7 of the 1949 Convention on Road Traffic Concerning the Dimensions and Weights of Vehicles Permitted to Travel on Certain Roads of the Contracting Parties. Geneva, 16 September 1950	Geneva	16/09/1950
Trade, commerce, and communication	European Agreement supplementing the 1949 Convention on road traffic and the 1949 Protocol on road signs and signals. Geneva, 16 September 1950	Geneva	16/09/1950
Trade, commerce, and communication	International Convention to facilitate the crossing of frontiers for goods carried by rail. Geneva, 10 January 1952	Geneva	10/01/1952
Trade, commerce, and communication	International Convention to facilitate the crossing of frontiers for passengers and baggage carried by rail. Geneva, 10 January 1952	Geneva	10/01/1952
Trade, commerce, and communication	International Convention to Facilitate the Importation of Commercial Samples and Advertising Material. Geneva, 7 November 1952	Geneva	07/11/1952
Trade, commerce, and communication	General Agreement on Economic Regulations for International Road transport (a) Additional Protocol (b) Protocol of Signature. Geneva, 17 March 1954	Geneva	17/03/1954
Trade, commerce, and communication	Additional Protocol to the Convention concerning Customs Facilities for Touring, relating to the Importation of Tourist Publicity Documents and Material. New York, 4 June 1954	New York	04/06/1954
Trade, commerce, and communication	Convention concerning Customs Facilities for Touring. New York, 4 June 1954	New York	04/06/1954
Trade, commerce, and communication	Customs Convention on the Temporary Importation of Private Road Vehicles. New York, 4 June 1954	New York	04/06/1954

(continued)

(continued)

Domain	Treaty name	Place of conclusion	Date of conclusion
Trade, commerce, and communication	Agreement on Signs for Road Works, amending the European Agreement of 16 September 1950 supplementing the 1949 Convention on Road Traffic and the 1949 Protocol on Road Signs and Signals. Geneva, 16 December 1955	Geneva	16/12/1955
Trade, commerce, and communication	Convention on the Taxation of Road Vehicles for Private Use in International Traffic. Geneva, 18 May 1956	Geneva	18/05/1956
Trade, commerce, and communication	Customs Convention on Containers. Geneva, 18 May 1956	Geneva	18/05/1956
Trade, commerce, and communication	Customs Convention on the Temporary Importation for Private Use of Aircraft and Pleasure Boats. Geneva, 18 May 1956	Geneva	18/05/1956
Trade, commerce, and communication	Customs Convention on the Temporary Importation of Commercial Road Vehicles. Geneva, 18 May 1956	Geneva	18/05/1956
Trade, commerce, and communication	Convention on the Contract for the International Carriage of Goods by Road (CMR). Geneva, 19 May 1956	Geneva	19/05/1956
Trade, commerce, and communication	Convention on the Taxation of Road Vehicles engaged in International Goods Transport. Geneva, 14 December 1956	Geneva	14/12/1956
Trade, commerce, and communication	Convention on the Taxation of Road Vehicles Engaged in International Passenger Transport. Geneva, 14 December 1956	Geneva	14/12/1956
Trade, commerce, and communication	European Agreement concerning the International Carriage of Dangerous Goods by Road (ADR). Geneva, 30 September 1957	Geneva	30/09/1957
Trade, commerce, and communication	European Agreement on Road Markings. Geneva, 13 December 1957	Geneva	13/12/1957
Trade, commerce, and communication	Customs Convention concerning spare parts used for repairing EUROP wagons. Geneva, 15 January 1958	Geneva	15/01/1958

(continued)

(continued)

Domain	Treaty name	Place of conclusion	Date of conclusion
Trade, commerce, and communication	Agreement concerning the Adoption of Harmonized Technical United Nations Regulations for Wheeled Vehicles, Equipment and Parts which can be Fitted and/or be Used on Wheeled Vehicles and the Conditions for Reciprocal Recognition of Approvals Granted on the Basis of these United Nations Regulations. Geneva, 20 March 1958	Geneva	20/03/1958
Trade, commerce, and communication	Convention on the Recognition and Enforcement of Foreign Arbitral Awards. New York, 10 June 1958	New York	10/06/1958
Trade, commerce, and communication	Customs Convention on the International Transport of Goods under Cover of TIR Carnets (TIR Convention). Geneva, 15 January 1959	Geneva	15/01/1959
Trade, commerce, and communication	Convention relating to the unification of certain rules concerning collisions in inland navigation. Geneva, 15 March 1960	Geneva	15/03/1960
Trade, commerce, and communication	United Nations Regulation No. 1. Uniform provisions concerning the approval of motor vehicle headlamps emitting an asymmetrical passing beam and/or a driving beam and equipped with filament lamps of categories R2 and/or HS1. 8 August 1960		08/08/1960
Trade, commerce, and communication	United Nations Regulation No. 2. Uniform provisions concerning the approval of incandescent electric lamps for headlamps emitting an asymmetrical passing beam or a driving beam or both. 8 August 1960		08/08/1960
Trade, commerce, and communication	European Convention on Customs Treatment of Pallets used in International Transport. Geneva, 9 December 1960	Geneva	09/12/1960
Trade, commerce, and communication	European Convention on International Commercial Arbitration. Geneva, 21 April 1961	Geneva	21/04/1961

(continued)

(continued)

Domain	Treaty name	Place of conclusion	Date of conclusion
Trade, commerce, and communication	Agreement on Special Equipment for the Transport of Perishable Foodstuffs and on the Use of such Equipment for the International Transport of some of those Foodstuffs. Geneva, 15 January 1962	Geneva	15/01/1962
Trade, commerce, and communication	Agreement establishing the African Development Bank. Khartoum, 4 August 1963	Khartoum	04/08/1963
Trade, commerce, and communication	United Nations Regulation No. 3. Uniform provisions concerning the approval of retro-reflecting devices for power-driven vehicles and their trailers. Geneva, 1 November 1963	Geneva	01/11/1963
Trade, commerce, and communication	United Nations Regulation No. 4. Uniform provisions concerning the approval of devices for the illumination of rear registration plates of power-driven vehicles and their trailers. Geneva, 15 April 1964	Geneva	15/04/1964
Trade, commerce, and communication	Convention on the registration of inland navigation vessels. Geneva, 25 January 1965	Geneva	25/01/1965
Trade, commerce, and communication	Convention on Transit Trade of Land-locked States. New York, 8 July 1965	New York	08/07/1965
Trade, commerce, and communication	Agreement establishing the Asian Development Bank. Manila, 4 December 1965	Manila	04/12/1965
Trade, commerce, and communication	Convention on the measurement of inland navigation vessels. Geneva, 15 February 1966	Geneva	15/02/1966
Trade, commerce, and communication	Articles of Association for the establishment of an Economic Community of West Africa. Accra, 4 May 1967	Accra	04/05/1967
Trade, commerce, and communication	United Nations Regulation No. 5. Uniform provisions concerning the approval of power-driven vehicle's "sealed beam" headlamps (SB) emitting a European asymmetrical passing beam or a driving beam or both. 30 September 1967		30/09/1967

(continued)

(continued)

Domain	Treaty name	Place of conclusion	Date of conclusion
Trade, commerce, and communication	United Nations Regulation No. 6. Uniform provisions concerning the approval of direction indicators for power-driven vehicles and their trailers. Geneva, 15 October 1967	Geneva	15/10/1967
Trade, commerce, and communication	United Nations Regulation No. 7. Uniform provisions concerning the approval of front and rear position lamps, stop-lamps and end-outline marker lamps for motor vehicles and their trailers. Geneva, 15 October 1967	Geneva	15/10/1967
Trade, commerce, and communication	United Nations Regulation No. 8. Uniform provisions concerning the approval of motor vehicle headlamps emitting an asymmetrical passing beam or a driving beam or both and equipped with halogen filament lamps (H1, H2, H3, HB3, HB4, H7, H8, H9, HIR1, HIR2 and/or H11). 15 November 1967		15/11/1967
Trade, commerce, and communication	Convention on Road Signs and Signals. Vienna, 8 November 1968	Vienna	08/11/1968
Trade, commerce, and communication	Convention on Road Traffic. Vienna, 8 November 1968	Vienna	08/11/1968
Trade, commerce, and communication	Agreement establishing the Asian Coconut Community. Bangkok, 12 December 1968	Bangkok	12/12/1968
Trade, commerce, and communication	United Nations Regulation No. 9. Uniform provisions concerning the approval of category L2, L4 and L5 vehicles with regard to sound emission.. 1 March 1969		01/03/1969
Trade, commerce, and communication	United Nations Regulation No. 10. Uniform provisions concerning the approval of vehicles with regard to electromagnetic compatibility. Geneva, 1 April 1969	Geneva	01/04/1969
Trade, commerce, and communication	United Nations Regulation No. 11. Uniform provisions concerning the approval of vehicles with regard to door latches and door retention components. 1 June 1969		01/06/1969

(continued)

(continued)

Domain	Treaty name	Place of conclusion	Date of conclusion
Trade, commerce, and communication	United Nations Regulation No. 12. Uniform provisions concerning the approval of vehicles with regard to the protection of the driver against the steering mechanism in the event of impact. Geneva, 1 July 1969	Geneva	01/07/1969
Trade, commerce, and communication	Agreement establishing the Caribbean Development Bank. Kingston, 18 October 1969	Kingston	18/10/1969
Trade, commerce, and communication	United Nations Regulation No. 14. Uniform provisions concerning the approval of vehicles with regard to safety-belt anchorages, ISOFIX anchorages systems and ISOFIX top tether anchorages. Geneva, 1 April 1970	Geneva	01/04/1970
Trade, commerce, and communication	United Nations Regulation No. 13. Uniform provisions concerning the approval of vehicles of categories M, N and O with regard to braking. Geneva, 1 June 1970	Geneva	01/06/1970
Trade, commerce, and communication	European Agreement concerning the Work of Crews of Vehicles Engaged in International Road Transport (AETR). Geneva, 1 July 1970	Geneva	01/07/1970
Trade, commerce, and communication	United Nations Regulation No. 15. Uniform provisions concerning the approval of vehicles equipped with a positive-ignition engine or with a compression-ignition engine with regard to the emission of gaseous pollutants by the engine—method of measuring the power of positive-ignition engines—method of measuring the fuel consumption of vehicles. 1 August 1970		01/08/1970
Trade, commerce, and communication	Agreement on the International Carriage of Perishable Foodstuffs and on the Special Equipment to be used for such Carriage (ATP). Geneva, 1 September 1970	Geneva	01/09/1970

(continued)

(continued)

Domain	Treaty name	Place of conclusion	Date of conclusion
Trade, commerce, and communication	United Nations Regulation No. 16. Uniform provisions concerning the approval of: I. Safety-belts, restraint systems, child restraint systems and ISOFIX child restraint systems for occupants of power-driven vehicles II. Vehicles equipped with safety-belts, safety-belt reminder, restraint systems, child restraint systems, ISOFIX child restraint systems and i-Size child restraint systems. Geneva, 1 December 1970	Geneva	01/12/1970
Trade, commerce, and communication	United Nations Regulation No. 17. Uniform provisions concerning the approval of vehicles with regard to the seats, their anchorages and any head restraints. 1 December 1970		01/12/1970
Trade, commerce, and communication	United Nations Regulation No. 18. Uniform provisions concerning the approval of motor vehicles with regard to their protection against unauthorized use. 1 March 1971		01/03/1971
Trade, commerce, and communication	United Nations Regulation No. 19. Uniform provisions concerning the approval of power-driven vehicle front fog lamps. Geneva, 1 March 1971	Geneva	01/03/1971
Trade, commerce, and communication	Agreement establishing the International Pepper Community. Bangkok, 16 April 1971	Bangkok	16/04/1971
Trade, commerce, and communication	European Agreement supplementing the Convention on Road Signs and Signals. Geneva, 1 May 1971	Geneva	01/05/1971
Trade, commerce, and communication	European Agreement supplementing the Convention on road traffic opened for signature at Vienna on 8 November 1968. Geneva, 1 May 1971	Geneva	01/05/1971
Trade, commerce, and communication	United Nations Regulation No. 20. Uniform provisions concerning the approval of motor vehicle headlamps emitting an asymmetrical passing beam or a driving beam or both and equipped with halogen filament lamps (H4 lamps). 1 May 1971		01/05/1971

(continued)

(continued)

Domain	Treaty name	Place of conclusion	Date of conclusion
Trade, commerce, and communication	United Nations Regulation No. 21. Uniform provisions concerning the approval of vehicles with regard to their interior fittings. Geneva, 1 December 1971	Geneva	01/12/1971
Trade, commerce, and communication	United Nations Regulation No. 23. Uniform provisions concerning the approval of reversing and manoeuvring lamps for power-driven vehicles and their trailers. Geneva, 1 December 1971	Geneva	01/12/1971
Trade, commerce, and communication	United Nations Regulation No. 25. Uniform provisions concerning the approval of head restraints (headrests), whether or not incorporated in vehicle seats. 1 March 1972		01/03/1972
Trade, commerce, and communication	United Nations Regulation No. 22. Uniform provisions concerning the approval of protective helmets and their visors for drivers and passengers of motor cycles and mopeds. 1 June 1972		01/06/1972
Trade, commerce, and communication	United Nations Regulation No. 26. Uniform provisions concerning the approval of vehicles with regard to their external projections. Geneva, 1 July 1972	Geneva	01/07/1972
Trade, commerce, and communication	United Nations Regulation No. 24. Uniform provisions concerning: I. The approval of compression ignition (C.I.) engines with regard to the emission of visible pollutants; II. The approval of motor vehicles with regard to the installation of C.I. engines of an approved type; III. The approval of motor vehicles equipped with C.I. engines with regard to the emission of visible pollutants by t.... 15 September 1972		15/09/1972
Trade, commerce, and communication	United Nations Regulation No. 27. Uniform provisions concerning the approval of advance-warning triangles. 15 September 1972		15/09/1972
Trade, commerce, and communication	Customs Convention on Containers, 1972. Geneva, 2 December 1972	Geneva	02/12/1972

(continued)

(continued)

Domain	Treaty name	Place of conclusion	Date of conclusion
Trade, commerce, and communication	United Nations Regulation No. 28. Uniform provisions concerning the approval of audible warning devices and of motor vehicles with regard to their audible warning signals. 15 January 1973		15/01/1973
Trade, commerce, and communication	Convention on the contract for the international carriage of passengers and luggage by road (CVR). Geneva, 1 March 1973	Geneva	01/03/1973
Trade, commerce, and communication	Protocol on Road Markings, additional to the European Agreement supplementing the Convention on Road Signs and Signals. Geneva, 1 March 1973	Geneva	01/03/1973
Trade, commerce, and communication	Agreement establishing the Asian Rice Trade Fund. Bangkok, 16 March 1973	Bangkok	16/03/1973
Trade, commerce, and communication	Convention on a Code of Conduct for Liner Conferences. Geneva, 6 April 1974	Geneva	06/04/1974
Trade, commerce, and communication	Convention relating to the distribution of programme-carrying signals transmitted by satellite. Brussels, 21 May 1974	Brussels	21/05/1974
Trade, commerce, and communication	Convention on the Limitation Period in the International Sale of Goods, as amended by the Protocol of 11 April 1980. New York, 14 June 1974	New York	14/06/1974
Trade, commerce, and communication	Convention on the Limitation Period in the International Sale of Goods. New York, 14 June 1974	New York	14/06/1974
Trade, commerce, and communication	United Nations Regulation No. 29. Uniform provisions concerning the approval of vehicles with regard to the protection of the occupants of the cab of a commercial vehicle. 15 June 1974		15/06/1974
Trade, commerce, and communication	Amendments to articles 10, 16, 17, 18, 20, 28, 31 and 32 of the Convention on the International Maritime Organization. London, 17 October 1974	London	17/10/1974

(continued)

(continued)

Domain	Treaty name	Place of conclusion	Date of conclusion
Trade, commerce, and communication	Agreement on minimum requirements for the issue and validity of driving permits (APC). Geneva, 1 April 1975	Geneva	01/04/1975
Trade, commerce, and communication	United Nations Regulation No. 30. Uniform provisions concerning the approval of pneumatic tyres for motor vehicles and their trailers. 1 April 1975		01/04/1975
Trade, commerce, and communication	United Nations Regulation No. 31. Uniform provisions concerning the approval of power-driven vehicle's halogen sealed-beam headlamps (HSB) emitting an European asymmetrical passing beam or a driving beam or both. Geneva, 1 May 1975	Geneva	01/05/1975
Trade, commerce, and communication	United Nations Regulation No. 32. Uniform provisions concerning the approval of vehicles with regard to the behaviour of the structure of the impacted vehicle in a rear-end collision. 1 July 1975		01/07/1975
Trade, commerce, and communication	United Nations Regulation No. 33. Uniform provisions concerning the approval of vehicles with regard to the behaviour of the structure of the impacted vehicle in a head-on collision. 1 July 1975		01/07/1975
Trade, commerce, and communication	United Nations Regulation No. 34. Uniform provisions concerning the approval of vehicles with regard to the prevention of fire risks. 1 July 1975		01/07/1975
Trade, commerce, and communication	Protocol amending article 14 (3) of the European Agreement of 30 September 1957 concerning the International Carriage of Dangerous Goods by Road (ADR). New York, 21 August 1975	New York	21/08/1975
Trade, commerce, and communication	United Nations Regulation No. 35. Uniform provisions concerning the approval of vehicles with regard to the arrangement of foot controls. 10 November 1975		10/11/1975

(continued)

(continued)

Domain	Treaty name	Place of conclusion	Date of conclusion
Trade, commerce, and communication	Amendments to the title and substantive provisions of the Convention on the International Maritime Organization. London, 14 November 1975 and 9 November 1977	London	14/11/1975
Trade, commerce, and communication	Customs Convention on the International Transport of Goods under Cover of TIR Carnets (TIR Convention). Geneva, 14 November 1975	Geneva	14/11/1975
Trade, commerce, and communication	European Agreement on main international traffic arteries (AGR). Geneva, 15 November 1975	Geneva	15/11/1975
Trade, commerce, and communication	United Nations Regulation No. 36. Uniform provisions concerning the approval of large passenger vehicles with regard to their general construction. 1 March 1976		01/03/1976
Trade, commerce, and communication	Constitution of the Asia-Pacific Telecommunity. Bangkok, 27 March 1976	Bangkok	27/03/1976
Trade, commerce, and communication	Agreement establishing the International Fund for Agricultural Development. Rome, 13 June 1976	Rome	13/06/1976
Trade, commerce, and communication	Agreement establishing the International Tea Promotion Association. Geneva, 31 March 1977	Geneva	31/03/1977
Trade, commerce, and communication	Agreement establishing the Southeast Asia Tin Research and Development Centre. Bangkok, 28 April 1977	Bangkok	28/04/1977
Trade, commerce, and communication	Agreement establishing the Asia-Pacific Institute for Broadcasting Development. Kuala Lumpur, 12 August 1977	Kuala Lumpur	12/08/1977
Trade, commerce, and communication	Amendments to the Convention on the International Maritime Organization relating to the institutionalization of the Committee on Technical Cooperation in the Convention . London, 17 November 1977	London	17/11/1977

(continued)

(continued)

Domain	Treaty name	Place of conclusion	Date of conclusion
Trade, commerce, and communication	United Nations Regulation No. 37. Uniform provisions concerning the approval of filament light sources for use in approved lamps of power-driven vehicles and of their trailers. Geneva, 1 February 1978	Geneva	01/02/1978
Trade, commerce, and communication	United Nations Convention on the Carriage of Goods by Sea, 1978. Hamburg, 31 March 1978	Hamburg	31/03/1978
Trade, commerce, and communication	Protocol to the Convention on the Contract for the International Carriage of Goods by Road (CMR). Geneva, 5 July 1978	Geneva	05/07/1978
Trade, commerce, and communication	Protocol to the Convention on the contract for the international carriage of passengers and luggage by road (CVR). Geneva, 5 July 1978	Geneva	05/07/1978
Trade, commerce, and communication	United Nations Regulation No. 38. Uniform provisions concerning the approval of rear fog lamps for power-driven vehicles and their trailers. Geneva, 1 August 1978	Geneva	01/08/1978
Trade, commerce, and communication	United Nations Regulation No. 39. Uniform provisions concerning the approval of vehicles with regard to the speedometer and odometer equipment including its installation. 20 November 1978		20/11/1978
Trade, commerce, and communication	Constitution of the United Nations Industrial Development Organization. Vienna, 8 April 1979	Vienna	08/04/1979
Trade, commerce, and communication	United Nations Regulation No. 40. Uniform provisions concerning the approval of motor cycles equipped with a positive-ignition engine with regard to the emission of gaseous pollutants by the engine. 1 September 1979		01/09/1979
Trade, commerce, and communication	Amendments to articles 17, 18, 20 and 51 of the Convention on the International Maritime Organization. London, 15 November 1979	London	15/11/1979

(continued)

(continued)

Domain	Treaty name	Place of conclusion	Date of conclusion
Trade, commerce, and communication	Protocol amending the Convention on the Limitation Period in the International Sale of Goods. Vienna, 11 April 1980	Vienna	11/04/1980
Trade, commerce, and communication	United Nations Convention on Contracts for the International Sale of Goods. Vienna, 11 April 1980	Vienna	11/04/1980
Trade, commerce, and communication	United Nations Convention on International Multimodal Transport of Goods. Geneva, 24 May 1980	Geneva	24/05/1980
Trade, commerce, and communication	United Nations Regulation No. 41. Uniform provisions concerning the approval of motor cycles with regard to noise. 1 June 1980		01/06/1980
Trade, commerce, and communication	United Nations Regulation No. 42. Uniform provisions concerning the approval of vehicles with regard to their front and rear protective devices (bumpers, etc). 1 June 1980		01/06/1980
Trade, commerce, and communication	Agreement Establishing The Common Fund For Commodities. Geneva, 27 June 1980	Geneva	27/06/1980
Trade, commerce, and communication	International Agreement for the Establishment of the University for Peace. New York, 5 December 1980	New York	05/12/1980
Trade, commerce, and communication	United Nations Regulation No. 44. Uniform provisions concerning the approval of restraining devices for child occupants of power-driven vehicles ("Child Restraint Systems"). Geneva, 1 February 1981	Geneva	01/02/1981
Trade, commerce, and communication	United Nations Regulation No. 43. Uniform provisions concerning the approval of safety glazing materials and their installation on vehicles. 15 February 1981		15/02/1981
Trade, commerce, and communication	United Nations Regulation No. 45. Uniform provisions concerning the approval of headlamp cleaners, and of power-driven vehicles with regard to headlamp cleaners. Geneva, 1 July 1981	Geneva	01/07/1981

(continued)

(continued)

Domain	Treaty name	Place of conclusion	Date of conclusion
Trade, commerce, and communication	United Nations Regulation No. 46. Uniform provisions concerning the approval of devices for indirect vision and of motor vehicles with regard to the installation of these devices. Geneva, 1 September 1981	Geneva	01/09/1981
Trade, commerce, and communication	United Nations Regulation No. 47. Uniform provisions concerning the approval of mopeds equipped with a positive-ignition engine with regard to the emission of gaseous pollutants by the engine. Geneva, 1 November 1981	Geneva	01/11/1981
Trade, Commerce, and Communication	Amendment to article 11, paragraph 2 (a), of the Constitution of the Asia-Pacific Telecommunity. Bangkok, 13 November 1981	Bangkok	13/11/1981
Trade, Commerce, and Communication	United Nations Regulation No. 48. Uniform provisions concerning the approval of vehicles with regard to the installation of lighting and light-signalling devices. Geneva, 1 January 1982	Geneva	01/01/1982
Trade, Commerce, and Communication	Charter of the Asian and Pacific Development Centre. Bangkok, 1 April 1982	Bangkok	01/04/1982
Trade, Commerce, and Communication	United Nations Regulation No. 49. Uniform provisions concerning the measures to be taken against the emission of gaseous and particulate pollutants from compression-ignition engines and positive ignition engines for use in vehicles. Geneva, 15 April 1982	Geneva	15/04/1982
Trade, Commerce, and Communication	Agreement establishing the African Development Bank done at Khartoum on 4 August 1963, as amended by resolution 05-79 adopted by the Board of Governors on 17 May 1979. Lusaka, 7 May 1982	Lusaka	07/05/1982

(continued)

(continued)

Domain	Treaty name	Place of conclusion	Date of conclusion
Trade, Commerce, and Communication	United Nations Regulation No. 50. Uniform provisions concerning the approval of front position lamps, rear position lamps, stop lamps, direction indicators and rear-registration-plate illuminating devices for vehicles of category L. Geneva, 1 June 1982	Geneva	01/06/1982
Trade, Commerce, and Communication	United Nations Regulation No. 51. Uniform provisions concerning the approval of motor vehicles having at least four wheels with regard to their sound emissions. 15 July 1982		15/07/1982
Trade, Commerce, and Communication	International Convention on the Harmonization of Frontier Controls of Goods. Geneva, 21 October 1982	Geneva	21/10/1982
Trade, Commerce, and Communication	United Nations Regulation No. 52. Uniform provisions concerning the approval of M2 and M3 small capacity vehicles with regard to their general construction. 1 November 1982		01/11/1982
Trade, Commerce, and Communication	United Nations Regulation No. 53. Uniform provisions concerning the approval of category L3 vehicles with regard to the installation of lighting and light-signalling devices. Geneva, 1 February 1983	Geneva	01/02/1983
Trade, Commerce, and Communication	United Nations Regulation No. 54. Uniform provisions concerning the approval of pneumatic tyres for commercial vehicles and their trailers. 1 March 1983		01/03/1983
Trade, Commerce, and Communication	United Nations Regulation No. 55. Uniform provisions concerning the approval of mechanical coupling components of combinations of vehicles. 1 March 1983		01/03/1983
Trade, Commerce, and Communication	United Nations Regulation No. 56. Uniform provisions concerning the approval of headlamps for mopeds and vehicles treated as such. 15 June 1983		15/06/1983

(continued)

(continued)

Domain	Treaty name	Place of conclusion	Date of conclusion
Trade, Commerce, and Communication	United Nations Regulation No. 57. Uniform provisions concerning the approval of headlamps for motor cycles and vehicles treated as such. 15 June 1983		15/06/1983
Trade, Commerce, and Communication	United Nations Regulation No. 58. Uniform provisions concerning the approval of: I. Rear underrun protective devices (RUPDs); II. Vehicles with regard to the installation of an RUPD of an approved type; III. Vehicles with regard to their rear underrun protection (RUP). Geneva, 1 July 1983	Geneva	01/07/1983
Trade, Commerce, and Communication	Statutes of the International Centre for Genetic Engineering and Biotechnology. Madrid, 13 September 1983	Madrid	13/09/1983
Trade, Commerce, and Communication	United Nations Regulation No. 59. Uniform provisions concerning the approval of replacement silencing systems. 1 October 1983		01/10/1983
Trade, Commerce, and Communication	Protocol of the Reconvened Plenipotentiary Meeting on the Establishment of the International Centre for Genetic Engineering and Biotechnology. Vienna, 4 April 1984	Vienna	04/04/1984
Trade, Commerce, and Communication	United Nations Regulation No. 60. Uniform provisions concerning the approval of two-wheeled motor cycles and mopeds with regard to driver-operated controls including the identification of controls, tell-tales and indicators. 1 July 1984		01/07/1984
Trade, Commerce, and Communication	United Nations Regulation No. 61. Uniform provisions concerning the approval of commercial vehicles with regard to their external projections forward of the cab's rear panel. Geneva, 15 July 1984	Geneva	15/07/1984

(continued)

(continued)

Domain	Treaty name	Place of conclusion	Date of conclusion
Trade, Commerce, and Communication	United Nations Regulation No. 62. Uniform provisions concerning the approval of power-driven vehicles with handlebars with regard to their protection against unauthorized use. 1 September 1984		01/09/1984
Trade, Commerce, and Communication	European Agreement on Main International Railway Lines (AGC). Geneva, 31 May 1985	Geneva	31/05/1985
Trade, Commerce, and Communication	United Nations Regulation No. 63. Uniform provisions concerning the approval of L1 category vehicles with regard to sound emission. 15 August 1985		15/08/1985
Trade, Commerce, and Communication	United Nations Regulation No. 64. Uniform provisions concerning the approval of vehicles with regard to their equipment which may include: a temporary-use spare unit, run-flat tyres. Geneva, 1 October 1985	Geneva	01/10/1985
Trade, Commerce, and Communication	United Nations Convention on Conditions for Registration of Ships. Geneva, 7 February 1986	Geneva	07/02/1986
Trade, Commerce, and Communication	United Nations Regulation No. 65. Uniform provisions concerning the approval of special warning lamps for power-driven vehicles and their trailers. 15 June 1986		15/06/1986
Trade, Commerce, and Communication	United Nations Regulation No. 66. Uniform provisions concerning the approval of large passenger vehicles with regard to the strength of their superstructure. Geneva, 2 December 1986	Geneva	02/12/1986
Trade, Commerce, and Communication	United Nations Regulation No. 68. Uniform provisions concerning the approval of power-driven vehicles including pure electric vehicles with regard to the measurement of the maximum speed. 1 May 1987		01/05/1987
Trade, Commerce, and Communication	United Nations Regulation No. 69. Uniform provisions concerning the approval of rear marking plates for slow-moving vehicles (by construction) and their trailers. 15 May 1987		15/05/1987

(continued)

(continued)

Domain	Treaty name	Place of conclusion	Date of conclusion
Trade, Commerce, and Communication	United Nations Regulation No. 70. Uniform provisions concerning the approval of rear marking plates for heavy and long vehicles. 15 May 1987		15/05/1987
Trade, Commerce, and Communication	United Nations Regulation No. 67. Uniform provisions concerning the approval of: I. Specific equipment of motor vehicles using liquefied petroleum gases in their propulsion system; II. A vehicle fitted with specific equipment for the use of liquefied petroleum gases in its propulsion system with regard to the installation of such equipment. Geneva, 1 June 1987	Geneva	01/06/1987
Trade, Commerce, and Communication	United Nations Regulation No. 71. Uniform provisions concerning the approval of agricultural tractors with regard to the driver's field of vision. 1 August 1987		01/08/1987
Trade, Commerce, and Communication	United Nations Regulation No. 73. Uniform provisions concerning the approval of: I. Vehicles with regard to their lateral protection devices (LPD); II. Lateral protection devices (LPD); III. Vehicles with regard to the installation of LPD of an approved type according to Part II of this Regulation. 1 January 1988		01/01/1988
Trade, Commerce, and Communication	United Nations Regulation No. 72. Uniform provisions concerning the approval of motor cycle headlamps emitting an asymmetrical passing beam and a driving beam and equipped with halogen lamps (HS1 lamps). Geneva, 15 February 1988	Geneva	15/02/1988
Trade, Commerce, and Communication	United Nations Regulation No. 75. Uniform provisions concerning the approval of pneumatic tyres for L-category vehicles. Geneva, 1 April 1988	Geneva	01/04/1988

(continued)

(continued)

Domain	Treaty name	Place of conclusion	Date of conclusion
Trade, Commerce, and Communication	United Nations Regulation No. 74. Uniform provisions concerning the approval of category L1 vehicles with regard to the installation of lighting and light-signalling devices. 15 June 1988		15/06/1988
Trade, Commerce, and Communication	United Nations Regulation No. 76. Uniform provisions concerning the approval of headlamps for mopeds emitting a driving beam and a passing beam. Geneva, 1 July 1988	Geneva	01/07/1988
Trade, Commerce, and Communication	United Nations Regulation No. 77. Uniform provisions concerning the approval of parking lamps for power-driven vehicles. 30 September 1988		30/09/1988
Trade, Commerce, and Communication	United Nations Regulation No. 78. Uniform provisions concerning the approval of vehicles of categories L1, L2, L3, L4 and L5 with regard to braking. 15 October 1988		15/10/1988
Trade, Commerce, and Communication	United Nations Regulation No. 79. Uniform provisions concerning the approval of vehicles with regard to steering equipment. 1 December 1988		01/12/1988
Trade, Commerce, and Communication	United Nations Convention on International Bills of Exchange and International Promissory Notes. New York, 9 December 1988	New York	09/12/1988
Trade, Commerce, and Communication	United Nations Regulation No. 80. Uniform provisions concerning the approval of seats of large passenger vehicles and of these vehicles with regard to the strength of the seats and their anchorages. 23 February 1989		23/02/1989
Trade, Commerce, and Communication	United Nations Regulation No. 81. Uniform provisions concerning the approval of rear-view mirrors of two-wheeled power-driven vehicles with or without side car, with regard to the mounting of rear-view mirrors on handlebars. 1 March 1989		01/03/1989

(continued)

(continued)

Domain	Treaty name	Place of conclusion	Date of conclusion
Trade, Commerce, and Communication	United Nations Regulation No. 82. Uniform provisions concerning the approval of moped headlamps equipped with filament halogen lamps (HS2). 17 March 1989		17/03/1989
Trade, Commerce, and Communication	Convention on Civil Liability for Damage caused during Carriage of Dangerous Goods by Road, Rail and Inland Navigation Vessels (CRTD). Geneva, 10 October 1989	Geneva	10/10/1989
Trade, Commerce, and Communication	United Nations Regulation No. 83. Uniform provisions concerning the approval of vehicles with regard to the emission of pollutants according to engine fuel requirements. Geneva, 5 November 1989	Geneva	05/11/1989
Trade, Commerce, and Communication	United Nations Regulation No. 84. Uniform provisions concerning the approval of power-driven vehicles equipped with internal combustion engines with regard to the measurement of fuel consumption. 15 July 1990		15/07/1990
Trade, Commerce, and Communication	United Nations Regulation No. 86. Uniform provisions concerning the approval of agricultural or forestry vehicles with regard to the installation of lighting and light-signalling devices. 1 August 1990		01/08/1990
Trade, Commerce, and Communication	United Nations Regulation No. 85. Uniform provisions concerning the approval of internal combustion engines or electric drive trains intended for the propulsion of motor vehicles of categories M and N with regard to the measurement of the net power and the maximum 30 minutes power of electric drive trains. 15 September 1990		15/09/1990
Trade, Commerce, and Communication	United Nations Regulation No. 87. Uniform provisions concerning the approval of daytime running lamps for power-driven vehicles. Geneva, 1 November 1990	Geneva	01/11/1990

(continued)

(continued)

Domain	Treaty name	Place of conclusion	Date of conclusion
Trade, Commerce, and Communication	European Agreement on Important International Combined Transport Lines and Related Installations (AGTC). Geneva, 1 February 1991	Geneva	01/02/1991
Trade, Commerce, and Communication	United Nations Regulation No. 88. Uniform provisions concerning the approval of retroreflective tyres for two-wheeled vehicles. Geneva, 10 April 1991	Geneva	10/04/1991
Trade, Commerce, and Communication	United Nations Convention on the Liability of Operators of Transport Terminals in International Trade. Vienna, 19 April 1991	Vienna	19/04/1991
Trade, Commerce, and Communication	Amendments to the Convention on the International Maritime Organization (institutionalization of the Facilitation Committee). London, 7 November 1991	London	07/11/1991
Trade, Commerce, and Communication	Amendments to articles 3 (5) and 9 (8) of the Constitution of the Asia-Pacific Telecommunity. Colombo, 29 November 1991	Colombo	29/11/1991
Trade, Commerce, and Communication	International Sugar Agreement, 1992. Geneva, 20 March 1992	Geneva	20/03/1992
Trade, Commerce, and Communication	United Nations Regulation No. 89. Uniform provisions concerning the approval of: I. Vehicles with regard to limitation of their maximum speed or their adjustable speed limitation unction; II. Vehicles with regard to the installation of a speed limiting device (SLD) or adjustable speed limitation device (ASLD) of an approved type; III. Speed limitation devices (SLD) and adjustable speed l…. 1 October 1992		01/10/1992
Trade, Commerce, and Communication	United Nations Regulation No. 90. Uniform provisions concerning the approval of replacement brake lining assemblies, drum-brake linings and discs and drums for power-driven vehicles and their trailers. 1 November 1992		01/11/1992

(continued)

(continued)

Domain	Treaty name	Place of conclusion	Date of conclusion
Trade, Commerce, and Communication	International Convention on Maritime Liens and Mortgages, 1993. Geneva, 6 May 1993	Geneva	06/05/1993
Trade, Commerce, and Communication	United Nations Regulation No. 91. Uniform provisions concerning the approval of side-marker lamps for motor vehicles and their trailers. 15 October 1993		15/10/1993
Trade, Commerce, and Communication	Protocol amending article 1 (a), article 14 (1) and article 14 (3) (b) of the European Agreement of 30 September 1957 concerning the International Carriage of Dangerous Goods by Road (ADR). Geneva, 28 October 1993	Geneva	28/10/1993
Trade, Commerce, and Communication	United Nations Regulation No. 92. Uniform provisions concerning the approval of non-original replacement exhaust silencing systems (NORESS) for vehicles of categories L1, L2, L3 L4 and L5 with regard to sound emission. 1 November 1993		01/11/1993
Trade, Commerce, and Communication	Amendments to the Convention on the International Maritime Organization. London, 4 November 1993	London	04/11/1993
Trade, Commerce, and Communication	Convention on Customs Treatment of Pool Containers used in International Transport. Geneva, 21 January 1994	Geneva	21/01/1994
Trade, Commerce, and Communication	United Nations Regulation No. 93. Uniform provisions concerning the approval of: I. Front underrun protective devices (FUPDs); II. Vehicles with regard to the installation of an FUPD of an approved type; III. Vehicles with regard to their front underrun protection (FUP). 27 February 1994		27/02/1994
Trade, Commerce, and Communication	Agreement to establish the South Centre. Geneva, 1 September 1994	Geneva	01/09/1994
Trade, Commerce, and Communication	Grains Trade Convention, 1995. London, 7 December 1994	London	07/12/1994

(continued)

(continued)

Domain	Treaty name	Place of conclusion	Date of conclusion
Trade, Commerce, and Communication	United Nations Regulation No. 95. Uniform provisions concerning the approval of vehicles with regard to the protection of the occupants in the event of a lateral collision. Geneva, 6 July 1995	Geneva	06/07/1995
Trade, Commerce, and Communication	United Nations Regulation No. 94. Uniform provisions concerning the approval of vehicles with regard to the protection of the occupants in the event of a frontal collision. Geneva, 1 October 1995	Geneva	01/10/1995
Trade, Commerce, and Communication	United Nations Convention on Independent Guarantees and Stand-by Letters of Credit. New York, 11 December 1995	New York	11/12/1995
Trade, Commerce, and Communication	United Nations Regulation No. 96. Uniform provisions concerning the approval of engines to be installed in agricultural and forestry tractors and in non-road mobile machinery with regard to the emissions of pollutants by the engine. 15 December 1995		15/12/1995
Trade, Commerce, and Communication	United Nations Regulation No. 97. Uniform provisions concerning the approval of vehicle alarm systems (VAS) and of motor vehicles with regard to their alarm systems (AS). 1 January 1996		01/01/1996
Trade, Commerce, and Communication	European Agreement on Main Inland Waterways of International Importance (AGN). Geneva, 19 January 1996	Geneva	19/01/1996
Trade, Commerce, and Communication	United Nations Regulation No. 98. Uniform provisions concerning the approval of motor vehicle headlamps equipped with gas-discharge light sources. Geneva, 15 April 1996	Geneva	15/04/1996
Trade, Commerce, and Communication	United Nations Regulation No. 99. Uniform provisions concerning the approval of gas-discharge light sources for use in approved lamps of power-driven vehicles. Geneva, 15 April 1996	Geneva	15/04/1996

(continued)

(continued)

Domain	Treaty name	Place of conclusion	Date of conclusion
Trade, Commerce, and Communication	United Nations Regulation No. 100. Uniform provisions concerning the approval of vehicles with regard to specific requirements for the electric power train. 23 August 1996		23/08/1996
Trade, Commerce, and Communication	Agreement Establishing the Bank for Economic Cooperation and Development in the Middle East and North Africa. Cairo, 28 August 1996	Cairo	28/08/1996
Trade, Commerce, and Communication	Amendments to Articles 6 (6) and 7(1) of the Statutes of the International Centre for Genetic Engineering and Biotechnology. Trieste, Italy, 3 December 1996	Trieste	03/12/1996
Trade, Commerce, and Communication	United Nations Regulation No. 102. Uniform provisions concerning the approval of: I.A close-coupling device (CCD);II. Vehicles with regard to the fitting of an approved type of CCD. 13 December 1996		13/12/1996
Trade, Commerce, and Communication	United Nations Regulation No. 101. Uniform provisions concerning the approval of passenger cars powered by an internal combustion engine only, or powered by a hybrid electric power train with regard to the measurement of the emission of carbon dioxide and fuel consumption and/or the measurement of electric energy consumption and electric range, and of categories M1 and N1 vehicles powere…. 1 January 1997		01/01/1997
Trade, Commerce, and Communication	Protocol on Combined Transport on Inland Waterways to the European Agreement on Important International Combined Transport Lines and Related Installations (AGTC) of 1991. Geneva, 17 January 1997	Geneva	17/01/1997
Trade, Commerce, and Communication	United Nations Regulation No. 103. Uniform provisions concerning the approval of replacement pollution control devices for power-driven vehicles contents. 23 February 1997		23/02/1997

(continued)

(continued)

Domain	Treaty name	Place of conclusion	Date of conclusion
Trade, Commerce, and Communication	Agreement concerning the Adoption of Uniform Conditions for Periodical Technical Inspections of Wheeled Vehicles and the Reciprocal Recognition of such Inspections. Vienna, 13 November 1997	Vienna	13/11/1997
Trade, Commerce, and Communication	United Nations Regulation No. 104. Uniform provisions concerning the approval of retro-reflective markings for vehicles of category M, N and O. 15 January 1998		15/01/1998
Trade, Commerce, and Communication	United Nations Regulation No. 105. Uniform provisions concerning the approval of vehicles intended for the carriage of dangerous goods with regard to their specific construction features. 7 May 1998		07/05/1998
Trade, Commerce, and Communication	United Nations Regulation No. 106. Uniform provisions concerning the approval of pneumatic tyres for agricultural vehicles and their trailers. Geneva, 7 May 1998	Geneva	07/05/1998
Trade, Commerce, and Communication	United Nations Regulation No. 13-H. Uniform provisions concerning the approval of passenger cars with regard to braking. 11 May 1998		11/05/1998
Trade, Commerce, and Communication	Tampere Convention on the Provision of Telecommunication Resources for Disaster Mitigation and Relief Operations. Tampere, 18 June 1998	Tampere	18/06/1998
Trade, Commerce, and Communication	United Nations Regulation No. 107. Uniform provisions concerning the approval of category M2 or M3 vehicles with regard to their general construction. Geneva, 18 June 1998	Geneva	18/06/1998
Trade, Commerce, and Communication	United Nations Regulation No. 108. Uniform provisions concerning the approval for the production of retreaded pneumatic tyres for motor vehicles and their trailers. Geneva, 23 June 1998	Geneva	23/06/1998

(continued)

(continued)

Domain	Treaty name	Place of conclusion	Date of conclusion
Trade, Commerce, and Communication	United Nations Regulation No. 109. Uniform provisions concerning the approval for the production of retreaded pneumatic tyres for commercial vehicles and their trailers. Geneva, 23 June 1998	Geneva	23/06/1998
Trade, Commerce, and Communication	Agreement concerning the Establishing of Global Technical Regulations for Wheeled Vehicles, Equipment and Parts which can be fitted and/or be used on Wheeled Vehicles. Geneva, 25 June 1998	Geneva	25/06/1998
Trade, Commerce, and Communication	Amendments to the Charter of the Asian and Pacific Development Centre. Kuala Lumpur, 16 July 1998	Kuala Lumpur	16/07/1998
Trade, Commerce, and Communication	International Convention on Arrest of Ships, 1999. Geneva, 12 March 1999	Geneva	12/03/1999
Trade, Commerce, and Communication	Amendments to the Agreement establishing the Asia-Pacific Institute for Broadcasting Development. Islamabad, 21 July 1999	Islamabad	21/07/1999
Trade, Commerce, and Communication	European Agreement concerning the International Carriage of Dangerous Goods by Inland Waterways (ADN). Geneva, 26 May 2000	Geneva	26/05/2000
Trade, Commerce, and Communication	United Nations Regulation No. 110. Uniform provisions concerning the approval of: I. Specific components of motor vehicles using compressed natural gas (CNG) and/or liquefied natural gas (LNG) in their propulsion system; II. Vehicles with regard to the installation of specific components of an approved type for the use of compressed natural gas (CNG) and/or liquefied natural gas (LNG) in…. Geneva, 28 December 2000	Geneva	28/12/2000
Trade, Commerce, and Communication	United Nations Regulation No. 111. Uniform provisions concerning the approval of tank vehicles of categories N and O with regard to rollover stability. Geneva, 28 December 2000	Geneva	28/12/2000

(continued)

(continued)

Domain	Treaty name	Place of conclusion	Date of conclusion
Trade, Commerce, and Communication	International Cocoa Agreement, 2001. Geneva, 2 March 2001	Geneva	02/03/2001
Trade, Commerce, and Communication	Agreement on International Roads between Arab Countries. Beirut, 10 May 2001	Beirut	10/05/2001
Trade, Commerce, and Communication	United Nations Regulation No. 112. Uniform provisions concerning the approval of motor vehicle headlamps emitting an asymmetrical passing beam or a driving beam or both and equipped with filament lamps and/or LED modules. Geneva, 21 September 2001	Geneva	21/09/2001
Trade, Commerce, and Communication	United Nations Regulation No. 113. Uniform provisions concerning the approval of motor vehicle headlamps emitting a symmetrical passing beam or a driving beam or both and equipped with filament lamps, gas-discharge light sources or LED modules. Geneva, 21 September 2001	Geneva	21/09/2001
Trade, Commerce, and Communication	United Nations Convention on the Assignment of Receivables in International Trade. New York, 12 December 2001	New York	12/12/2001
Trade, Commerce, and Communication	Amendments to the Constitution of the Asia-Pacific Telecommunity. New Delhi, 23 October 2002	New Delhi	23/10/2002
Trade, Commerce, and Communication	United Nations Regulation No. 114. Uniform provisions concerning the approval of: I. An airbag module for a replacement airbag system; II. A replacement steering wheel equipped with an airbag module of an approved type; III. A replacement airbag system other than that installed in a steering wheel. Geneva, 1 February 2003	Geneva	01/02/2003
Trade, Commerce, and Communication	Agreement on International Railways between Arab Countries. Beirut, 14 April 2003	Beirut	14/04/2003

(continued)

(continued)

Domain	Treaty name	Place of conclusion	Date of conclusion
Trade, Commerce, and Communication	Regulation No. 115. Uniform provisions concerning the approval of: I. Specific LPG (Liquefied Petroleum Gases) retrofit systems to be installed in motor vehicles for the use of LPG in their propulsion systems; II. Specific CNG (Compressed Natural Gas) retrofit systems to be installed in motor vehicles for the use of CNG in their propulsion systems. 30 October 2003		30/10/2003
Trade, Commerce, and Communication	Intergovernmental Agreement on the Asian Highway Network. Bangkok, 18 November 2003	Bangkok	18/11/2003
Trade, Commerce, and Communication	United Nations Regulation No. 116. Uniform provisions concerning the protection of motor vehicles against unauthorized use. Geneva, 6 April 2005	Geneva	06/04/2005
Trade, Commerce, and Communication	United Nations Regulation No. 117. Uniform provisions concerning the approval of tyres with regard to rolling sound emissions and/or to adhesion on wet surfaces and/or to rolling resistance. Geneva, 6 April 2005	Geneva	06/04/2005
Trade, Commerce, and Communication	United Nations Regulation No. 118. Uniform technical prescriptions concerning the burning behaviour and/or the capability to repel fuel or lubricant of materials used in the construction of certain categories of motor vehicles. Geneva, 6 April 2005	Geneva	06/04/2005
Trade, Commerce, and Communication	United Nations Regulation No. 119. Uniform provisions concerning the approval of cornering lamps for power-driven vehicles. Geneva, 6 April 2005	Geneva	06/04/2005

(continued)

(continued)

Domain	Treaty name	Place of conclusion	Date of conclusion
Trade, Commerce, and Communication	United Nations Regulation No. 120. Uniform provisions concerning the approval of internal combustion engines to be installed in agricultural and forestry tractors and in non-road mobile machinery, with regard to the measurement of the net power, net torque and specific fuel consumption. Geneva, 6 April 2005	Geneva	06/04/2005
Trade, Commerce, and Communication	Memorandum of Understanding on Maritime Transport Cooperation between Arab Countries. Damascus, 9 May 2005	Damascus	09/05/2005
Trade, Commerce, and Communication	United Nations Convention on the Use of Electronic Communications in International Contracts. New York, 23 November 2005	New York	23/11/2005
Trade, Commerce, and Communication	United Nations Regulation No. 121. Uniform provisions concerning the approval of vehicles with regard to the location and identification of hand controls, tell-tales and indicators. Geneva, 18 January 2006	Geneva	18/01/2006
Trade, Commerce, and Communication	United Nations Regulation No. 122. Uniform provisions concerning the approval of vehicles of categories M, N and O with regard to their heating systems. Geneva, 18 January 2006	Geneva	18/01/2006
Trade, Commerce, and Communication	International Tropical Timber Agreement, 2006. Geneva, 27 January 2006	Geneva	27/01/2006
Trade, Commerce, and Communication	Intergovernmental Agreement on the Trans-Asian Railway Network (with annexes). Jakarta, 12 April 2006	Jakarta	12/04/2006
Trade, Commerce, and Communication	United Nations Regulation No. 123. Uniform provisions concerning the approval of adaptive front-lighting systems (AFS) for motor vehicles. Geneva, 2 February 2007	Geneva	02/02/2007

(continued)

(continued)

Domain	Treaty name	Place of conclusion	Date of conclusion
Trade, Commerce, and Communication	United Nations Regulation No. 125. Uniform provisions concerning the approval of motor vehicles with regard to the forward field of vision of the driver. Geneva, 9 November 2007	Geneva	09/11/2007
Trade, Commerce, and Communication	Additional Protocol to the Convention on the Contract for the International Carriage of Goods by Road (CMR) concerning the Electronic Consignment Note. Geneva, 20 February 2008	Geneva	20/02/2008
Trade, Commerce, and Communication	United Nations Convention on Contracts for the International Carriage of Goods Wholly or Partly by Sea. New York, 11 December 2008	New York	11/12/2008
Trade, Commerce, and Communication	International Cocoa Agreement, 2010. Geneva, 25 June 2010	Geneva	25/06/2010
Trade, Commerce, and Communication	Multilateral Agreement for the Establishment of an International Think Tank for Landlocked Developing Countries. New York, 24 September 2010	New York	24/09/2010
Trade, Commerce, and Communication	Food Assistance Convention. London, 25 April 2012	London	25/04/2012
Trade, Commerce, and Communication	United Nations Regulation No. 128. Uniform provisions concerning the approval of Light Emitting Diode (LED) light sources for use in approved lamps on power-driven vehicles and their trailers. Geneva, 17 November 2012	Geneva	17/11/2012
Trade, Commerce, and Communication	United Nations Regulation No. 129. Uniform provisions concerning the approval of enhanced Child Restraint Systems used on board of motor vehicles. Geneva, 13 December 2012	Geneva	13/12/2012
Trade, Commerce, and Communication	United Nations Regulation No. 130. Uniform provisions concerning the approval of motor vehicles with regard to the Lane Departure Warning System. Geneva, 13 December 2012	Geneva	13/12/2012

(continued)

(continued)

Domain	Treaty name	Place of conclusion	Date of conclusion
Trade, Commerce, and Communication	United Nations Regulation No. 131. Uniform provisions concerning the approval of motor vehicles with regard to the Advanced Emergency Braking Systems (AEBS). Geneva, 13 December 2012	Geneva	13/12/2012
Trade, Commerce, and Communication	Intergovernmental Agreement on Dry Ports. Bangkok, 1 May 2013	Bangkok	01/05/2013
Trade, Commerce, and Communication	United Nations Regulation No. 134. Uniform provisions concerning the approval of motor vehicles and their components with regard to the safety-related performance of hydrogen-fuelled vehicles. Geneva, 5 December 2014	Geneva	05/12/2014
Trade, Commerce, and Communication	United Nations Convention on Transparency in Treaty-based Investor-State Arbitration. New York, 10 December 2014	New York	10/12/2014
Trade, Commerce, and Communication	International Agreement on Olive Oil and Table Olives, 2015. Geneva, 9 October 2015	Geneva	09/10/2015
Trade, Commerce, and Communication	United Nations Regulation No. 138. Uniform provisions concerning the approval of Quiet Road Transport Vehicles with regard to their reduced audibility. Geneva, 29 March 2016	Geneva	29/03/2016
Trade, Commerce, and Communication	Framework Agreement on Facilitation of Cross-border Paperless Trade in Asia and the Pacific. Bangkok, 19 May 2016	Bangkok	19/05/2016

Appendix B
Categorization of 193 UN Member States in Ten Groups of Geo-Historico-Cultural Regions

#	Country code	Country name	Geo-historico-cultural region
1	AFG	Afghanistan	Islamic East
2	ALB	Albania	Orthodox East
3	DZA	Algeria	Islamic East
4	ADO	Andorra	Old West
5	AGO	Angola	Sub-Saharan Africa
6	ATG	Antigua and Barbuda	Latin America
7	ARG	Argentina	Latin America
8	ARM	Armenia	Orthodox East
9	AUS	Australia	New West
10	AUT	Austria	Old West
11	AZE	Azerbaijan	Orthodox East
12	BHS	Bahamas	Latin America
13	BHR	Bahrain	Islamic East
14	BGD	Bangladesh	Indic East
15	BRB	Barbados	Latin America
16	BLR	Belarus	Orthodox East
17	BEL	Belgium	Old West
18	BLZ	Belize	Latin America
19	BEN	Benin	Sub-Saharan Africa
20	BTN	Bhutan	Indic East
21	BOL	Bolivia	Latin America
22	BIH	Bosnia and Herzegovina	Orthodox East
23	BWA	Botswana	Sub-Saharan Africa

(continued)

T. Inoguchi and L. T. Q. Le, *Digitized Statecraft in Multilateral Treaty Participation*, Evidence-Based Approaches to Peace and Conflict Studies 1,
https://doi.org/10.1007/978-981-33-4485-3

(continued)

#	Country code	Country name	Geo-historico-cultural region
24	BRA	Brazil	Latin America
25	BRN	Brunei Darussalam	Indic East
26	BGR	Bulgaria	Orthodox East
27	BFA	Burkina Faso	Sub-Saharan Africa
28	BDI	Burundi	Sub-Saharan Africa
29	CPV	Cabo Verde	Sub-Saharan Africa
30	KHM	Cambodia	Indic East
31	CMR	Cameroon	Sub-Saharan Africa
32	CAN	Canada	New West
33	CAF	Central African Republic	Sub-Saharan Africa
34	TCD	Chad	Sub-Saharan Africa
35	CHL	Chile	Latin America
36	CHN	China	Sinic East
37	COL	Colombia	Latin America
38	COM	Comoros	Sub-Saharan Africa
39	COG	Congo	Sub-Saharan Africa
40	CRI	Costa Rica	Latin America
41	CIV	Côte d'Ivoire	Sub-Saharan Africa
42	HRV	Croatia	Returned West
43	CUB	Cuba	Latin America
44	CYP	Cyprus	Old West
45	CZE	Czech Republic	Returned West
46	ZAR	Democratic Republic of the Congo	Sub-Saharan Africa
47	DNK	Denmark	Reformed West
48	DJI	Djibouti	Sub-Saharan Africa
49	DMA	Dominica	Latin America
50	DOM	Dominican Republic	Latin America
51	PRK	DPR Korea	Sinic East
52	ECU	Ecuador	Latin America
53	EGY	Egypt	Islamic East
54	SLV	El Salvador	Latin America
55	GNQ	Equatorial Guinea	Sub-Saharan Africa
56	ERI	Eritrea	Sub-Saharan Africa
57	EST	Estonia	Returned West
58	SWZ	Eswatini	Sub-Saharan Africa
59	ETH	Ethiopia	Sub-Saharan Africa
60	FJI	Fiji	New West

(continued)

(continued)

#	Country code	Country name	Geo-historico-cultural region
61	FIN	Finland	Reformed West
62	FRA	France	Old West
63	GAB	Gabon	Sub-Saharan Africa
64	GMB	Gambia	Sub-Saharan Africa
65	GEO	Georgia	Orthodox East
66	DEU	Germany	Reformed West
67	GHA	Ghana	Sub-Saharan Africa
68	GRC	Greece	Old West
69	GRD	Grenada	Latin America
70	GTM	Guatemala	Latin America
71	GIN	Guinea	Sub-Saharan Africa
72	GNB	Guinea-Bissau	Sub-Saharan Africa
73	GUY	Guyana	Latin America
74	HTI	Haiti	Latin America
75	HND	Honduras	Latin America
76	HUN	Hungary	Returned West
77	ISL	Iceland	Reformed West
78	IND	India	Indic East
79	IDN	Indonesia	Indic East
80	IRN	Iran	Islamic East
81	IRQ	Iraq	Islamic East
82	IRL	Ireland	Reformed West
83	ISR	Israel	Old West
84	ITA	Italy	Old West
85	JAM	Jamaica	Latin America
86	JPN	Japan	Sinic East
87	JOR	Jordan	Islamic East
88	KAZ	Kazakhstan	Orthodox East
89	KEN	Kenya	Sub-Saharan Africa
90	KIR	Kiribati	New West
91	KWT	Kuwait	Islamic East
92	KGZ	Kyrgyzstan	Orthodox East
93	LAO	Lao People's Democratic Republic	Indic East
94	LVA	Latvia	Returned West
95	LBN	Lebanon	Islamic East
96	LSO	Lesotho	Sub-Saharan Africa
97	LBR	Liberia	Sub-Saharan Africa

(continued)

(continued)

#	Country code	Country name	Geo-historico-cultural region
98	LBY	Libya	Islamic East
99	LIE	Liechtenstein	Old West
100	LTU	Lithuania	Returned West
101	LUX	Luxembourg	Old West
102	MDG	Madagascar	Sub-Saharan Africa
103	MWI	Malawi	Sub-Saharan Africa
104	MYS	Malaysia	Indic East
105	MDV	Maldives	Indic East
106	MLI	Mali	Sub-Saharan Africa
107	MLT	Malta	Old West
108	MHL	Marshall Islands	New West
109	MRT	Mauritania	Sub-Saharan Africa
110	MUS	Mauritius	Sub-Saharan Africa
111	MEX	Mexico	Latin America
112	FSM	Micronesia (Federated States of)	New West
113	MCO	Monaco	Old West
114	MNG	Mongolia	Orthodox East
115	MNE	Montenegro	Orthodox East
116	MAR	Morocco	Islamic East
117	MOZ	Mozambique	Sub-Saharan Africa
118	MMR	Myanmar	Indic East
119	NAM	Namibia	Sub-Saharan Africa
120	NRU	Nauru	New West
121	NPL	Nepal	Indic East
122	NLD	Netherlands	Reformed West
123	NZL	New Zealand	New West
124	NIC	Nicaragua	Latin America
125	NER	Niger	Sub-Saharan Africa
126	NGA	Nigeria	Sub-Saharan Africa
127	MKD	North Macedonia	Orthodox East
128	NOR	Norway	Reformed West
129	OMN	Oman	Islamic East
130	PAK	Pakistan	Indic East
131	PLW	Palau	New West
132	PAN	Panama	Latin America
133	PNG	Papua New Guinea	New West
134	PRY	Paraguay	Latin America

(continued)

(continued)

#	Country code	Country name	Geo-historico-cultural region
135	PER	Peru	Latin America
136	PHL	Philippines	Indic East
137	POL	Poland	Returned West
138	PRT	Portugal	Old West
139	QAT	Qatar	Islamic East
140	KOR	Republic of Korea	Sinic East
141	MDA	Republic of Moldova	Orthodox East
142	ROM	Romania	Orthodox East
143	RUS	Russian Federation	Orthodox East
144	RWA	Rwanda	Sub-Saharan Africa
145	WSM	Samoa	New West
146	SMR	San Marino	Old West
147	STP	Sao Tome and Principe	Sub-Saharan Africa
148	SAU	Saudi Arabia	Islamic East
149	SEN	Senegal	Sub-Saharan Africa
150	SRB	Serbia	Orthodox East
151	SYC	Seychelles	Sub-Saharan Africa
152	SLE	Sierra Leone	Sub-Saharan Africa
153	SGP	Singapore	Indic East
154	SVK	Slovakia	Returned West
155	SVN	Slovenia	Returned West
156	SLB	Solomon Islands	New West
157	SOM	Somalia	Sub-Saharan Africa
158	ZAF	South Africa	Sub-Saharan Africa
159	SSD	South Sudan	Sub-Saharan Africa
160	ESP	Spain	Old West
161	LKA	Sri Lanka	Indic East
162	KNA	St. Kitts and Nevis	Latin America
163	LCA	St. Lucia	Latin America
164	VCT	St. Vincent and the Grenadines	Latin America
165	SDN	Sudan	Sub-Saharan Africa
166	SUR	Suriname	Latin America
167	SWE	Sweden	Reformed West
168	CHE	Switzerland	Reformed West
169	SYR	Syrian Arab Republic	Islamic East
170	TJK	Tajikistan	Orthodox East
171	THA	Thailand	Indic East

(continued)

(continued)

#	Country code	Country name	Geo-historico-cultural region
172	TMP	Timor-Leste	Indic East
173	TGO	Togo	Sub-Saharan Africa
174	TON	Tonga	New West
175	TTO	Trinidad and Tobago	Latin America
176	TUN	Tunisia	Islamic East
177	TUR	Turkey	Islamic East
178	TKM	Turkmenistan	Orthodox East
179	TUV	Tuvalu	New West
180	UGA	Uganda	Sub-Saharan Africa
181	UKR	Ukraine	Orthodox East
182	ARE	United Arab Emirates	Islamic East
183	GBR	United Kingdom	Reformed West
184	TZA	United Republic of Tanzania	Sub-Saharan Africa
185	USA	United States of America	New West
186	URY	Uruguay	Latin America
187	UZB	Uzbekistan	Orthodox East
188	VUT	Vanuatu	New West
189	VEN	Venezuela	Latin America
190	VNM	Viet Nam	Sinic East
191	YEM	Yemen	Islamic East
192	ZMB	Zambia	Sub-Saharan Africa
193	ZWE	Zimbabwe	Sub-Saharan Africa

Appendix C
Hexagonal Profiles of 193 UN Member States

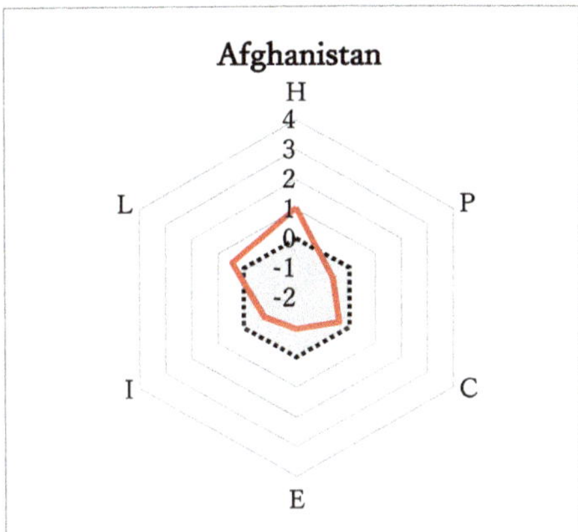

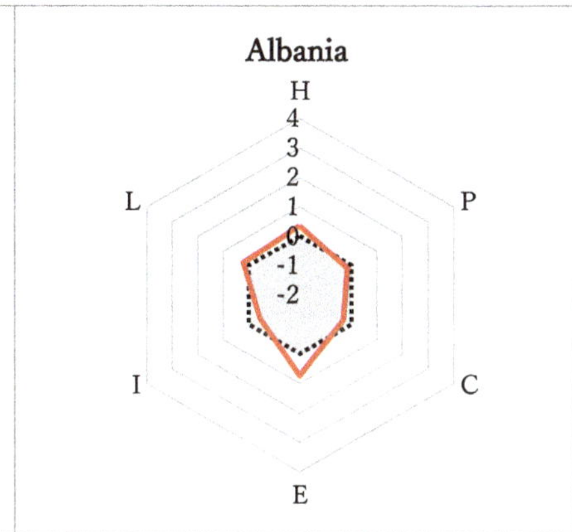

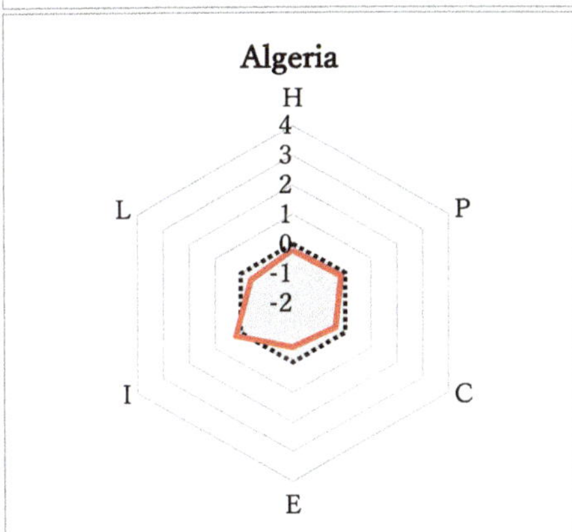

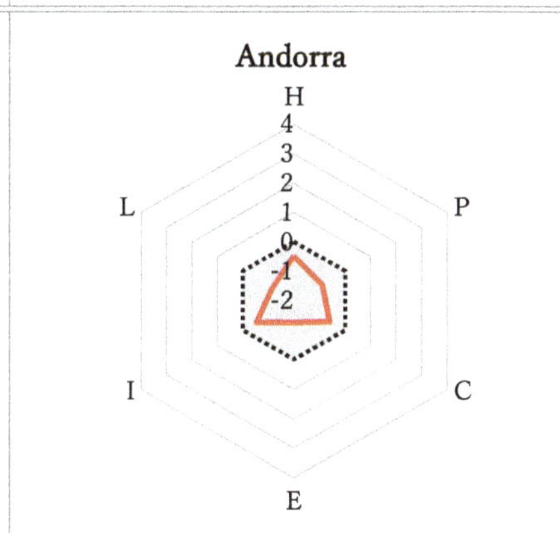

T. Inoguchi and L. T. Q. Le, *Digitized Statecraft in Multilateral Treaty Participation*, Evidence-Based Approaches to Peace and Conflict Studies 1,
https://doi.org/10.1007/978-981-33-4485-3

Angola

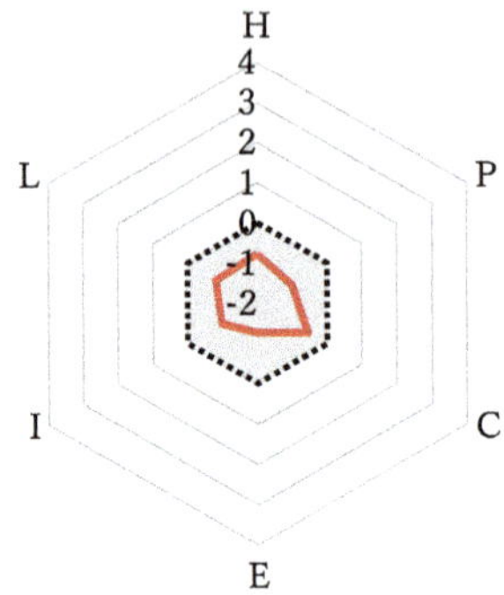

Antigua and Barbuda

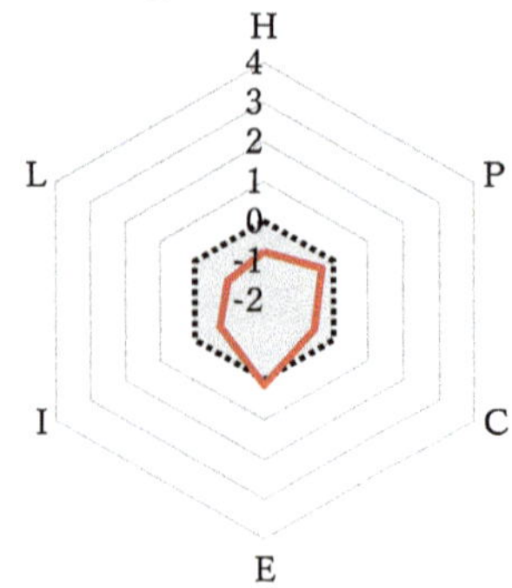

Argentina

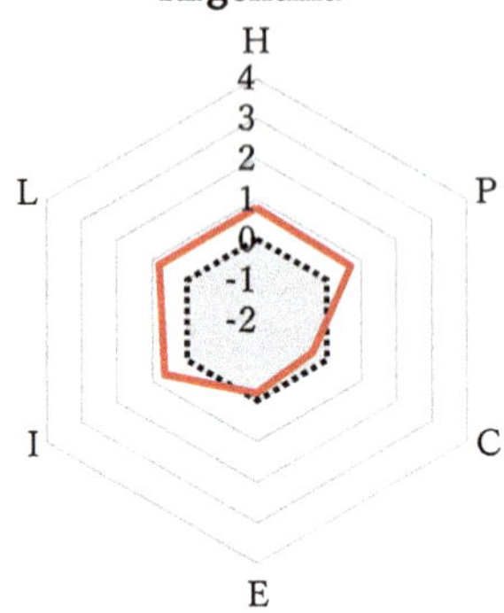

Armenia

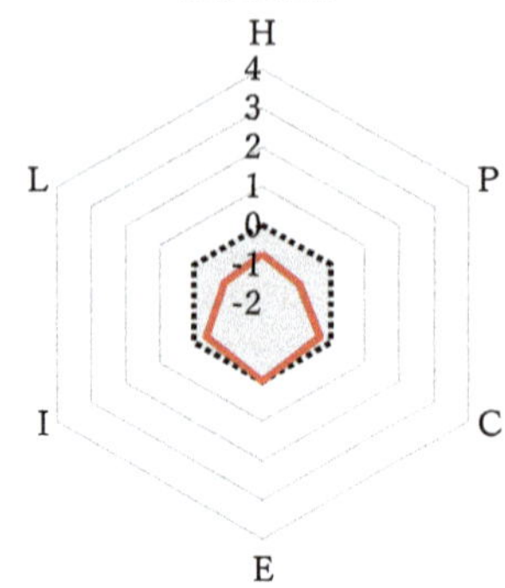

Australia

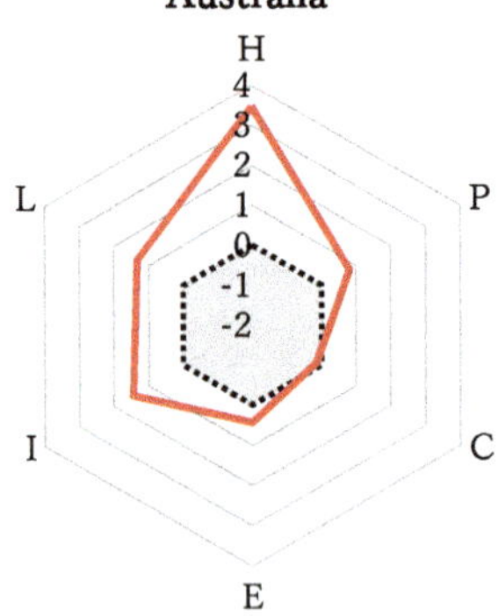

Austria

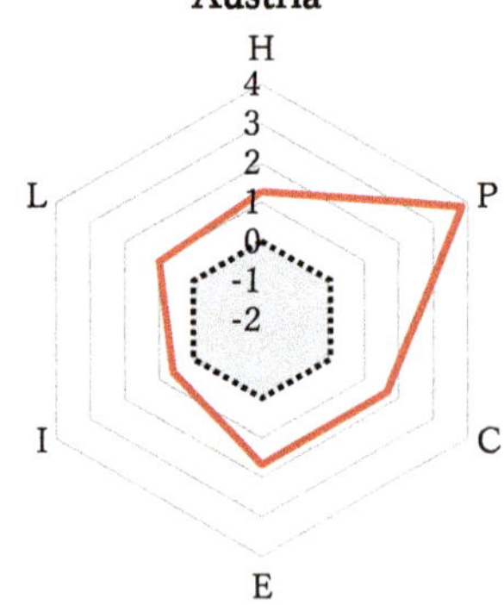

Azerbaijan

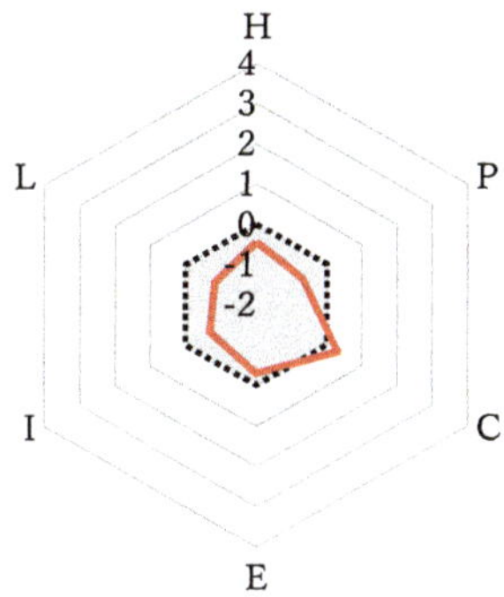

Bahamas

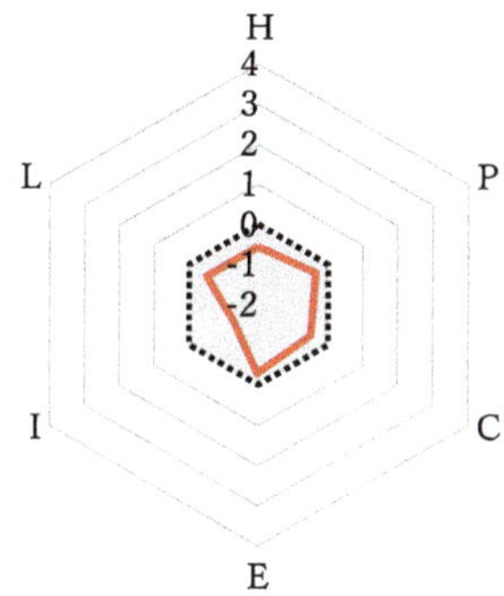

Bahrain

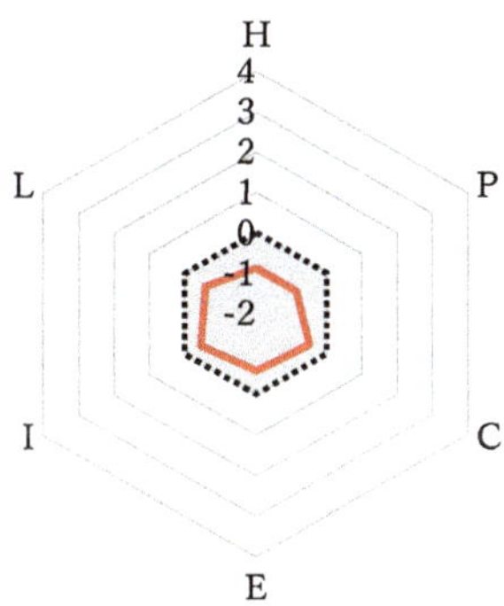

Bangladesh

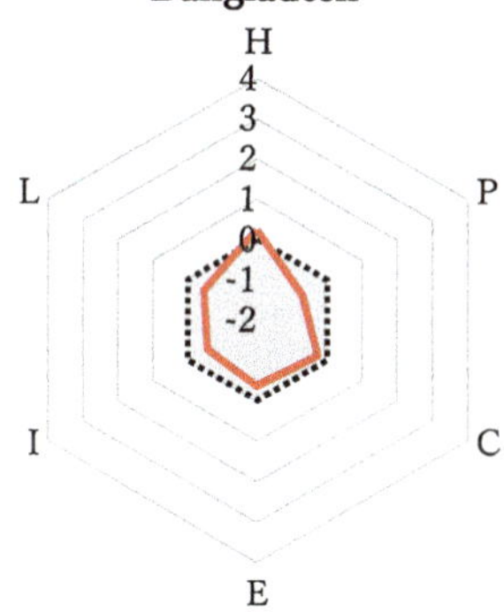

Barbados

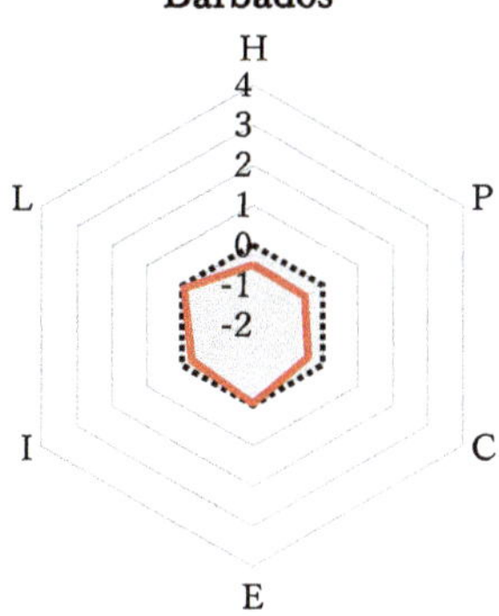

Belarus

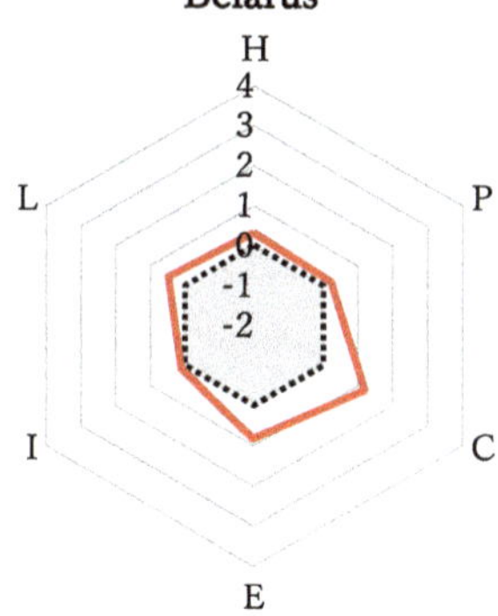

Belgium

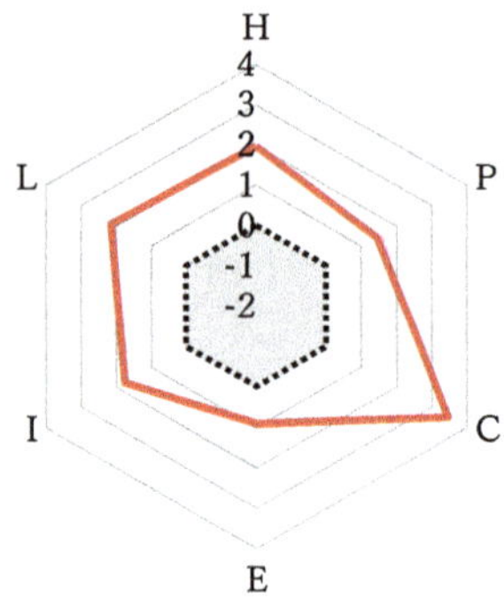

Belize

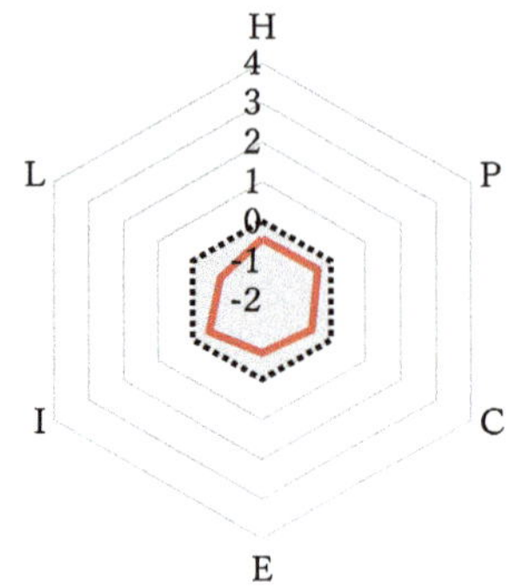

Benin

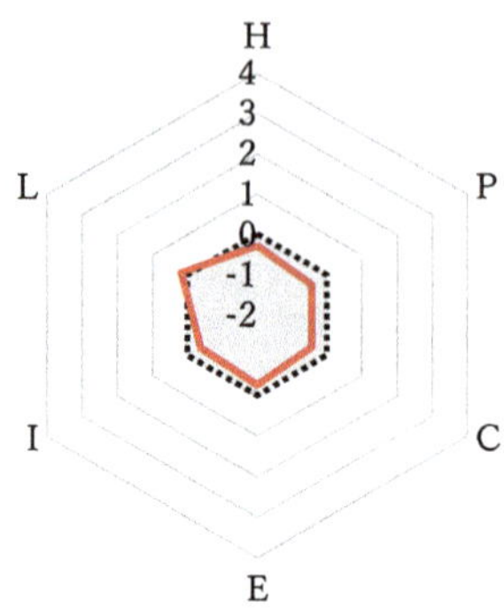

Bhutan

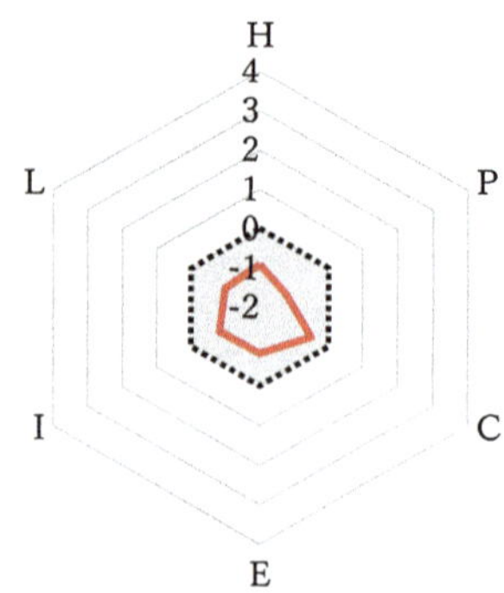

Bolivia (Plurinational State of)

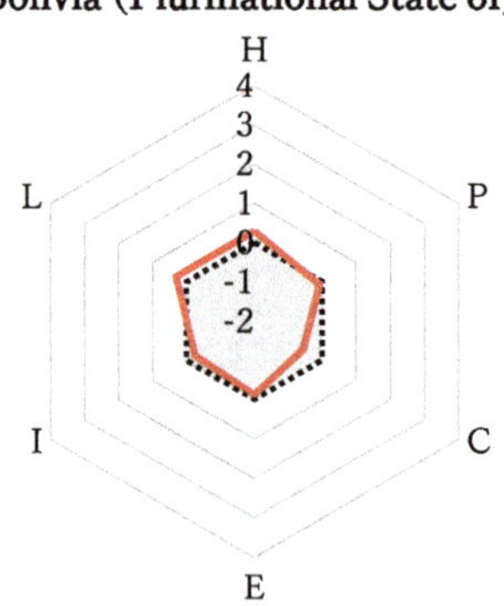

Bosnia and Herzegovina

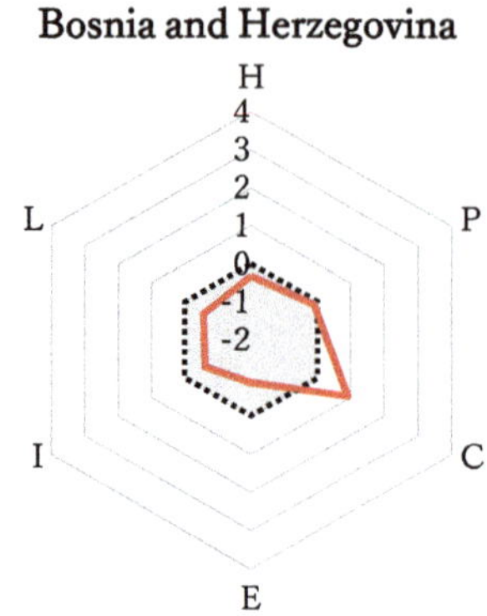

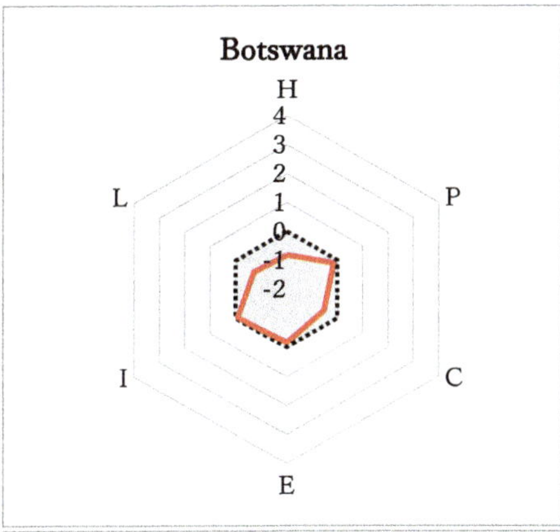
Botswana
H
4
3
2
1
0
-1
-2
P
C
E
I
L

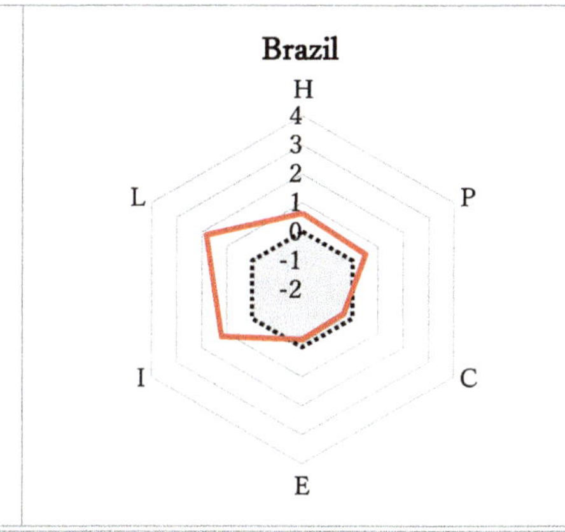
Brazil
H
4
3
2
1
0
-1
-2
P
C
E
I
L

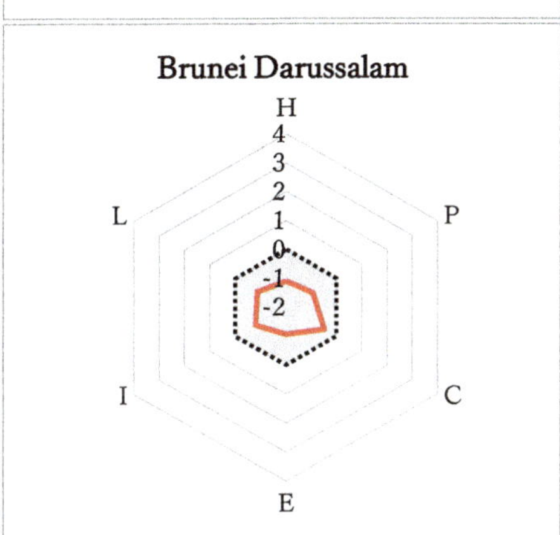
Brunei Darussalam
H
4
3
2
1
0
-1
-2
P
C
E
I
L

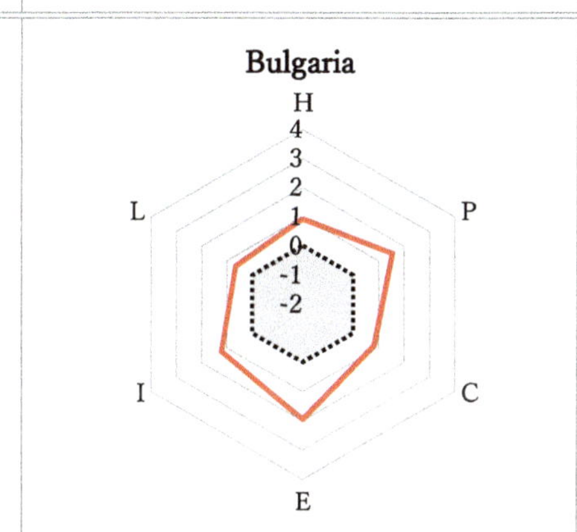
Bulgaria
H
4
3
2
1
0
-1
-2
P
C
E
I
L

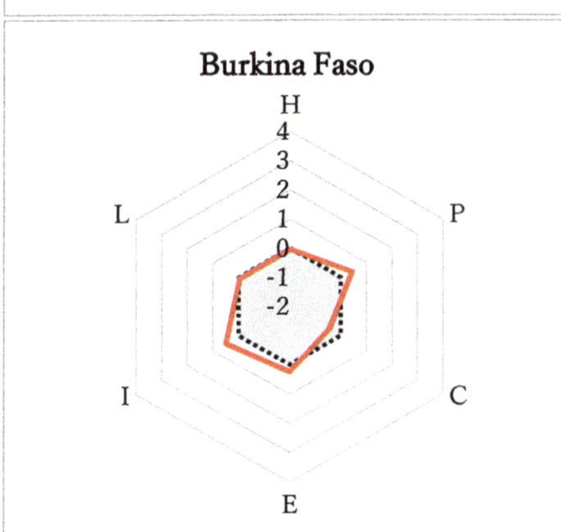
Burkina Faso
H
4
3
2
1
0
-1
-2
P
C
E
I
L

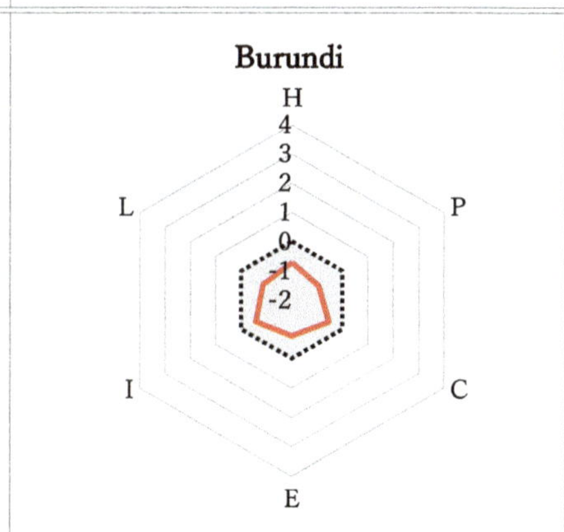
Burundi
H
4
3
2
1
0
-1
-2
P
C
E
I
L

Cabo Verde

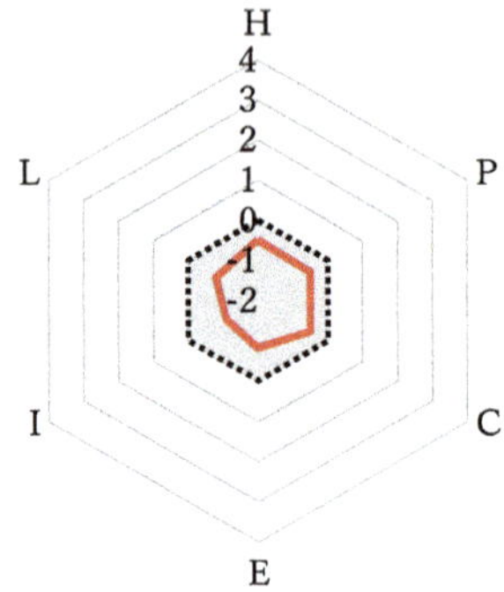

Cambodia

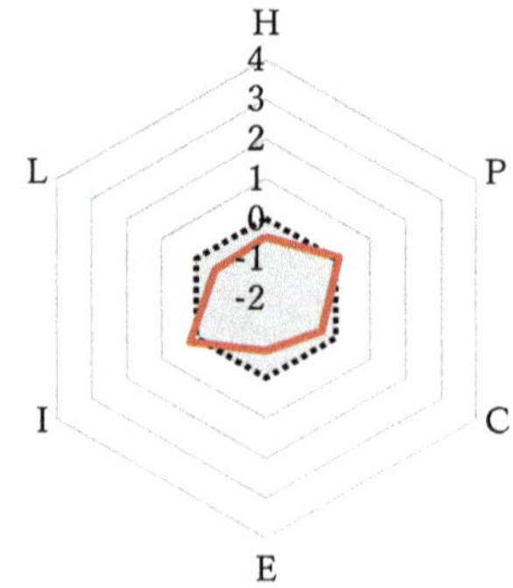

Cameroon

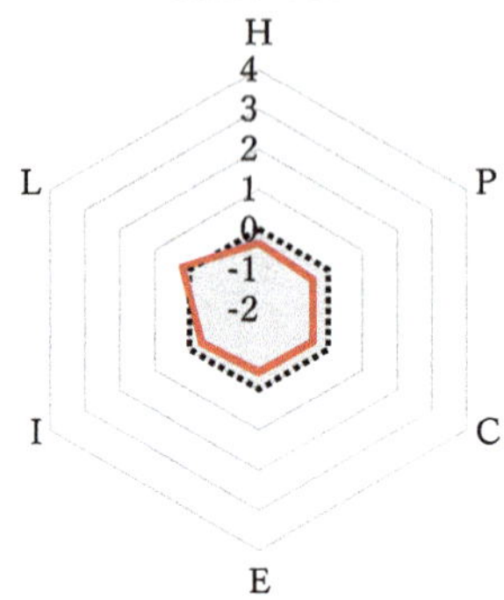

Canada

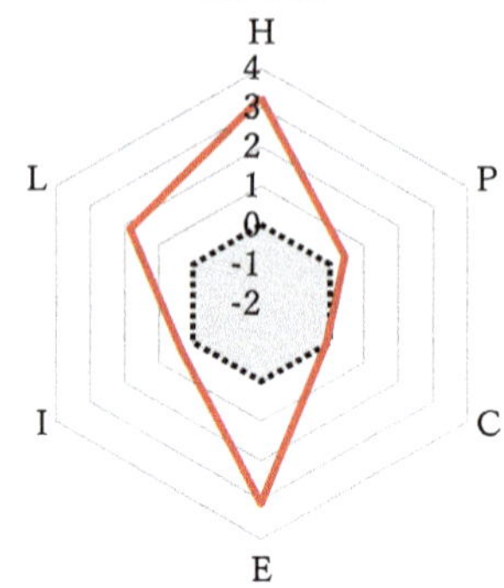

Central African Republic

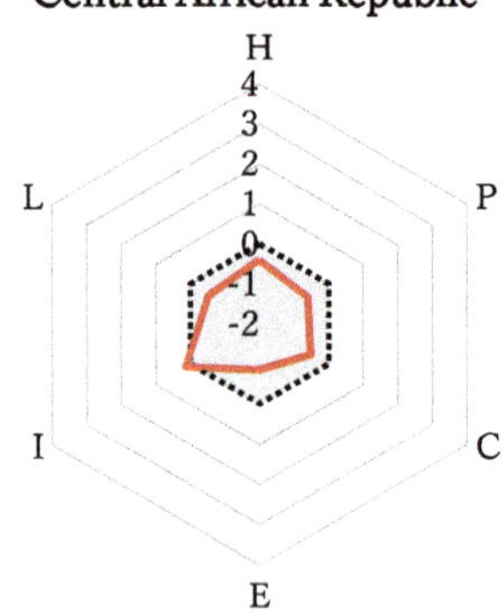

Chad

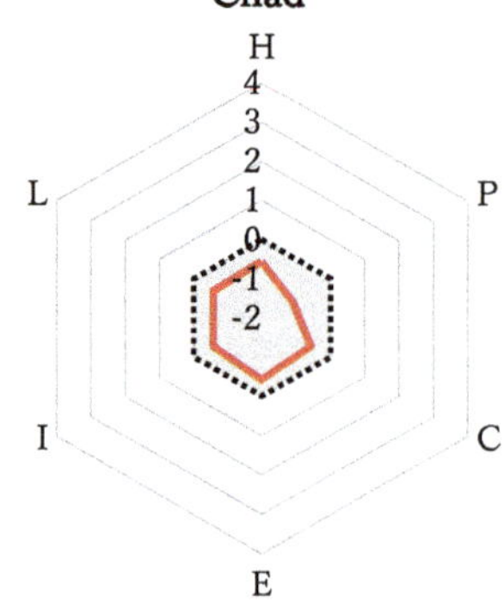

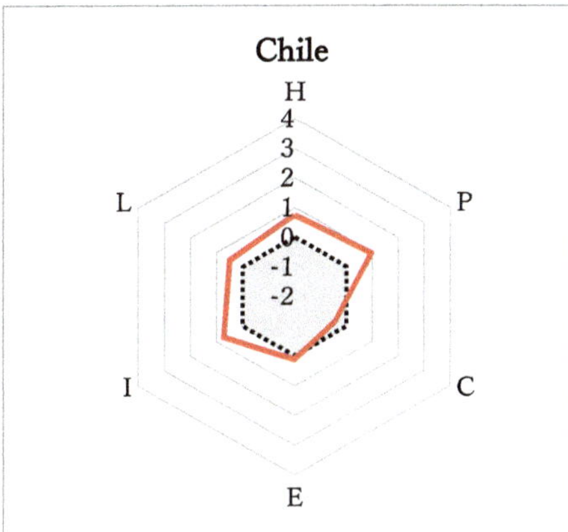
Chile
H
4
3
2
1
0
-1
-2
P
C
E
I
L

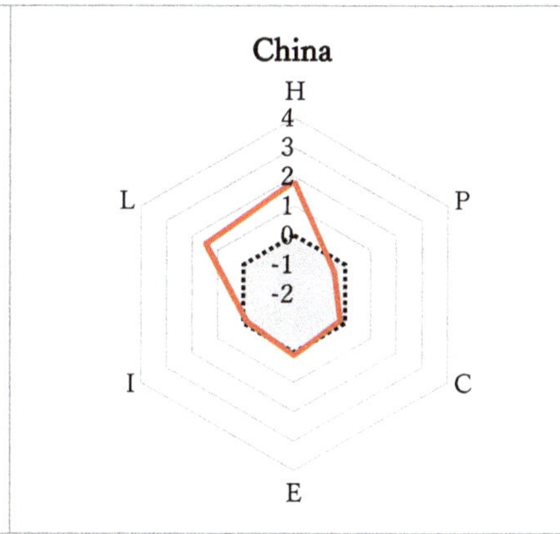
China
H
4
3
2
1
0
-1
-2
P
C
E
I
L

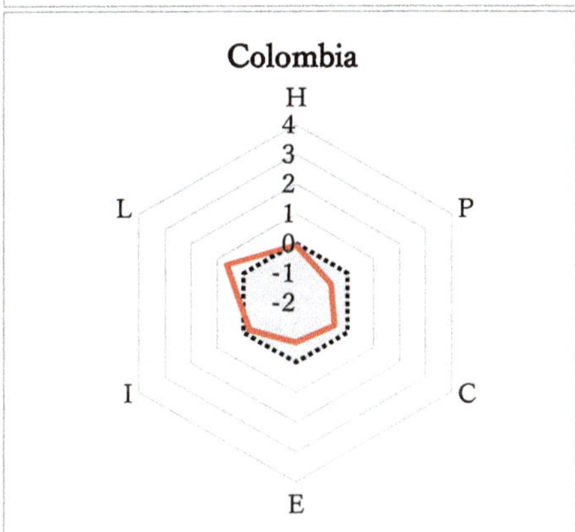
Colombia
H
4
3
2
1
0
-1
-2
P
C
E
I
L

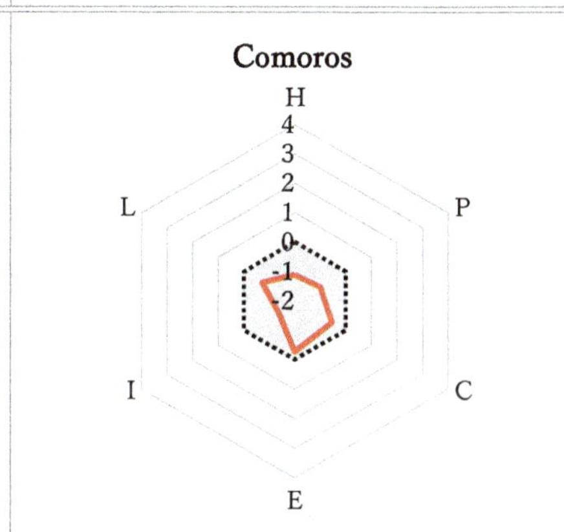
Comoros
H
4
3
2
1
0
-1
-2
P
C
E
I
L

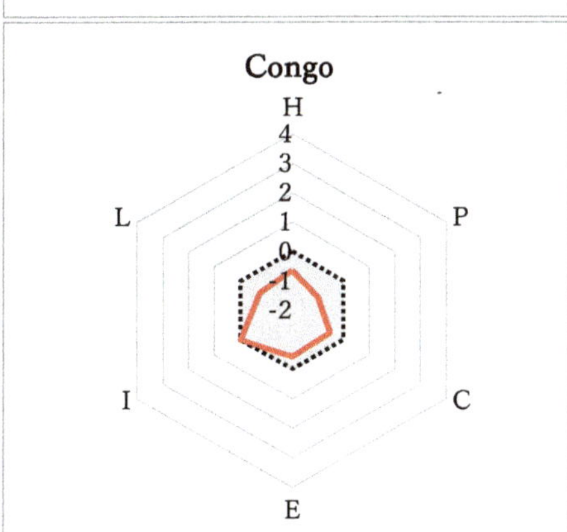
Congo
H
4
3
2
1
0
-1
-2
P
C
E
I
L

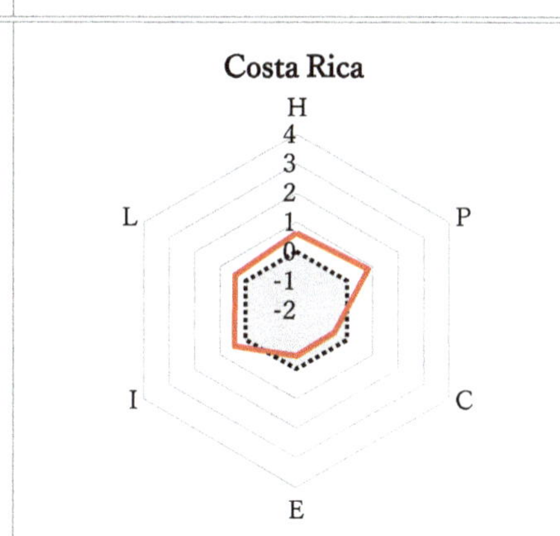
Costa Rica
H
4
3
2
1
0
-1
-2
P
C
E
I
L

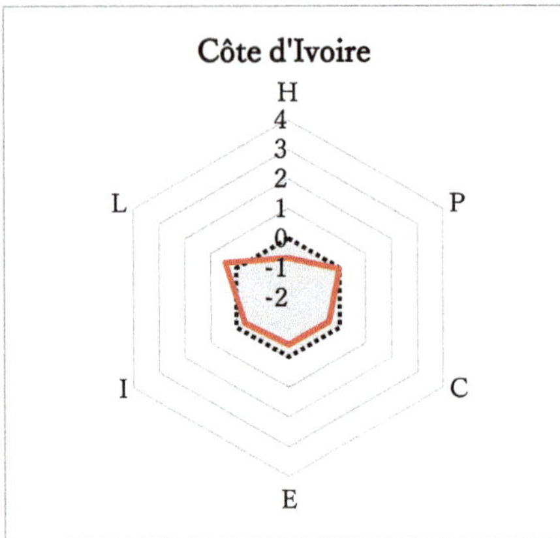
Côte d'Ivoire
H
4
3
2
1
0
-1
-2
L
P
I
C
E

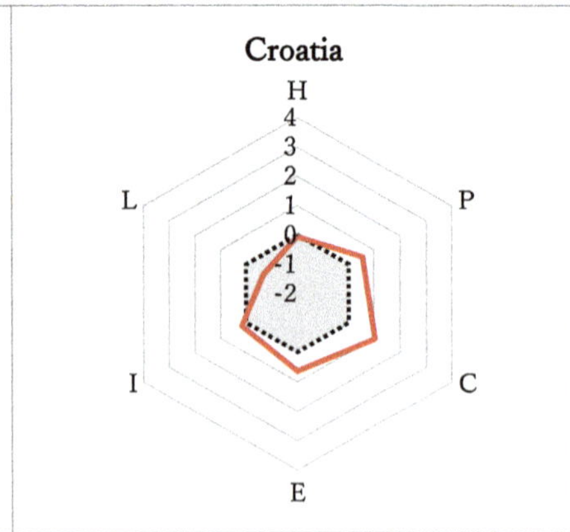
Croatia
H
4
3
2
1
0
-1
-2
L
P
I
C
E

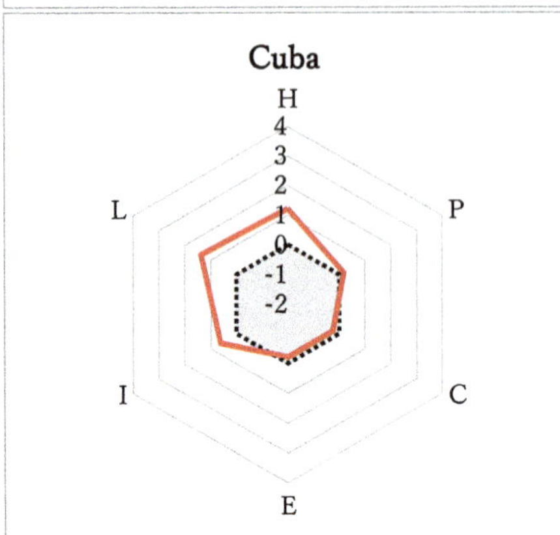
Cuba
H
4
3
2
1
0
-1
-2
L
P
I
C
E

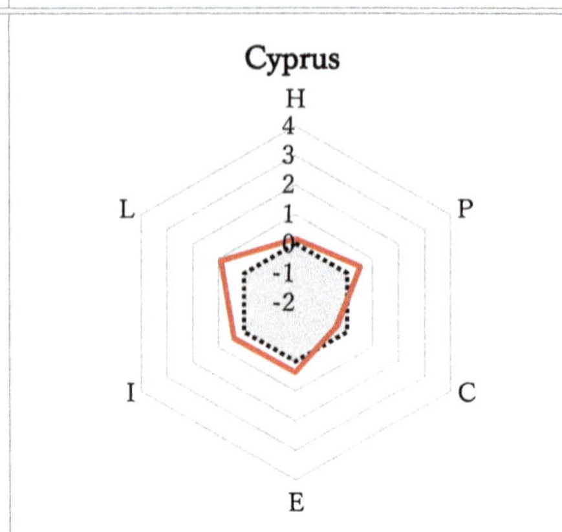
Cyprus
H
4
3
2
1
0
-1
-2
L
P
I
C
E

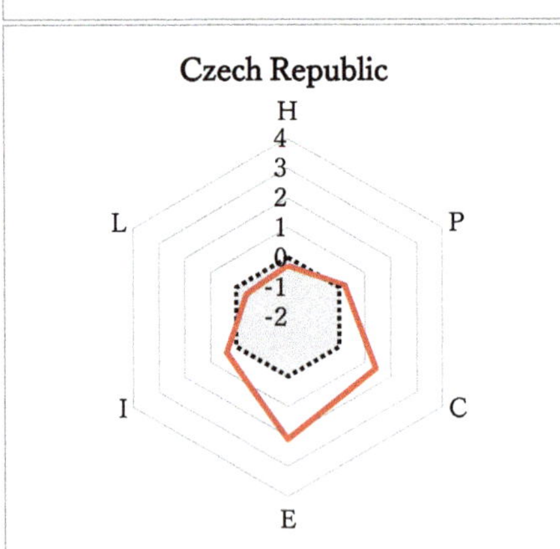
Czech Republic
H
4
3
2
1
0
-1
-2
L
P
I
C
E

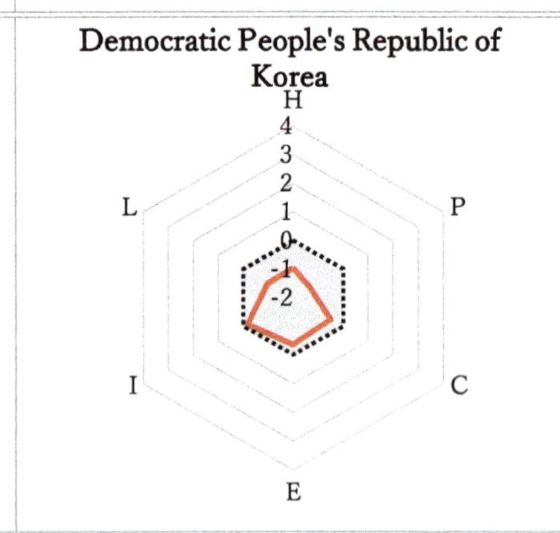
Democratic People's Republic of Korea
H
4
3
2
1
0
-1
-2
L
P
I
C
E

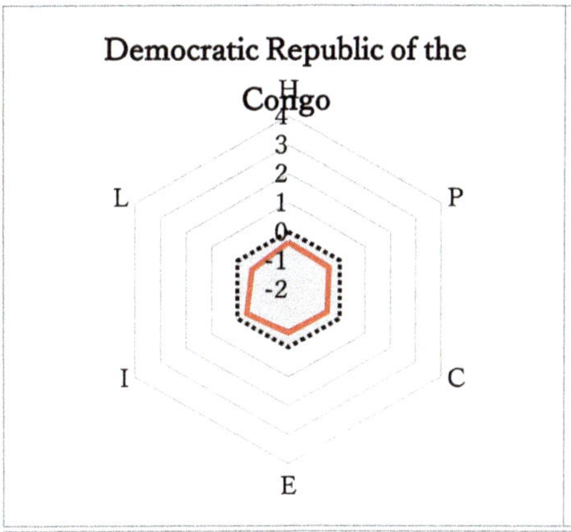
Democratic Republic of the Congo
H
4
3
2
1
0
-1
-2
L
P
I
C
E

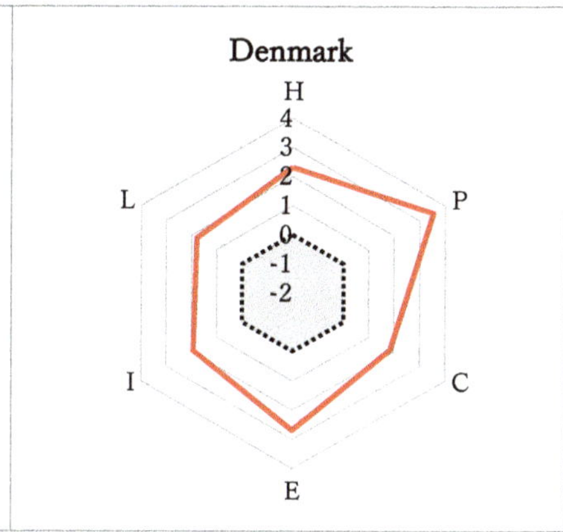
Denmark
H
4
3
2
1
0
-1
-2
L
P
I
C
E

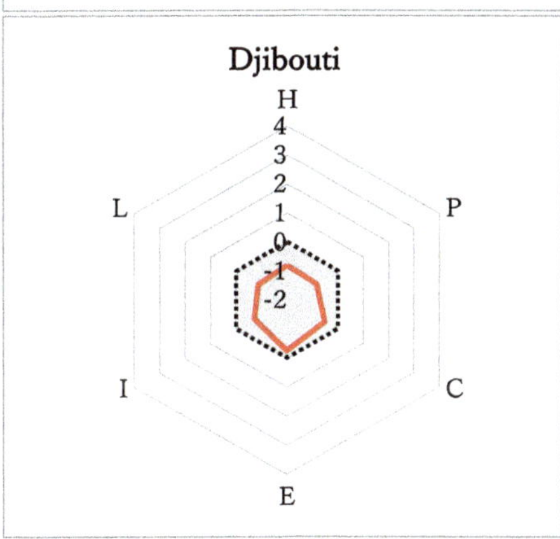
Djibouti
H
4
3
2
1
0
-1
-2
L
P
I
C
E

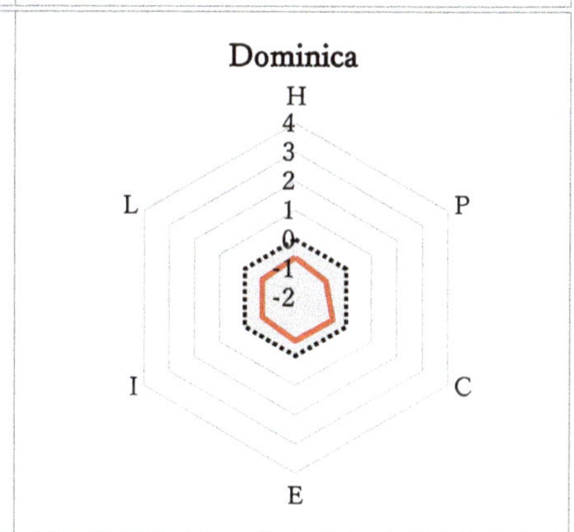
Dominica
H
4
3
2
1
0
-1
-2
L
P
I
C
E

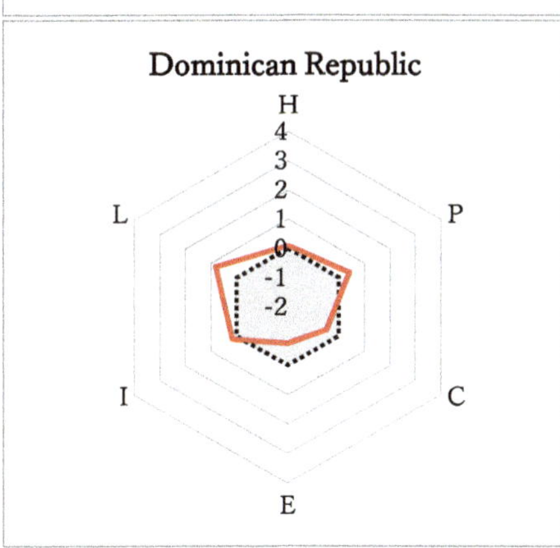
Dominican Republic
H
4
3
2
1
0
-1
-2
L
P
I
C
E

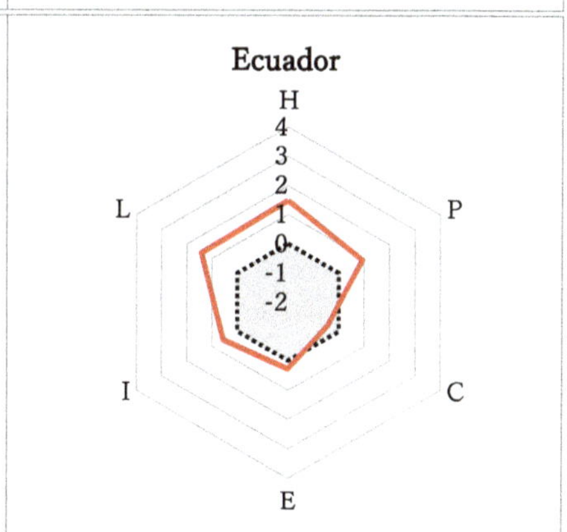
Ecuador
H
4
3
2
1
0
-1
-2
L
P
I
C
E

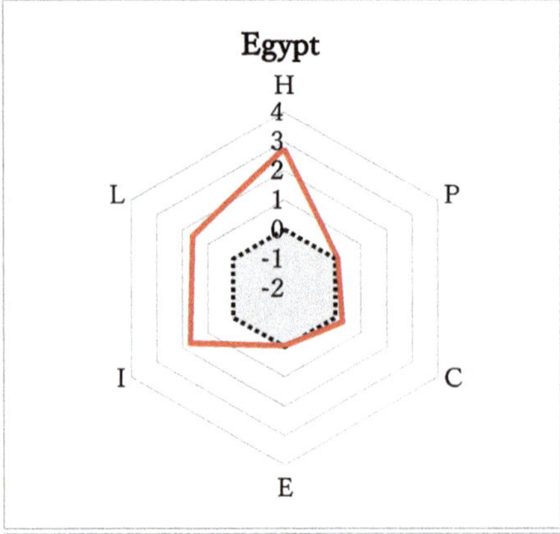
Egypt
H
4
3
2
1
0
-1
-2
P
C
E
I
L

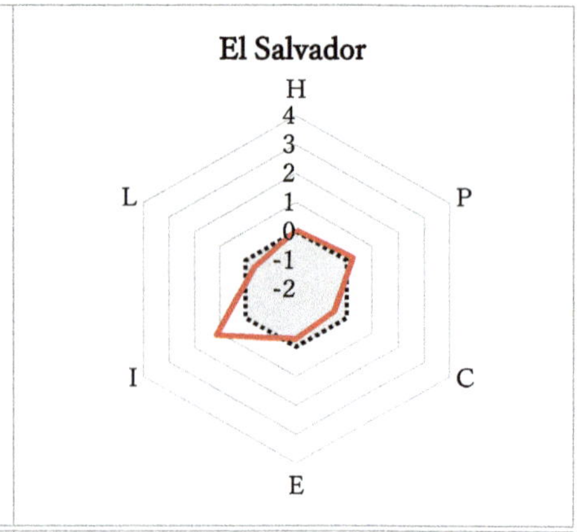
El Salvador
H
4
3
2
1
0
-1
-2
P
C
E
I
L

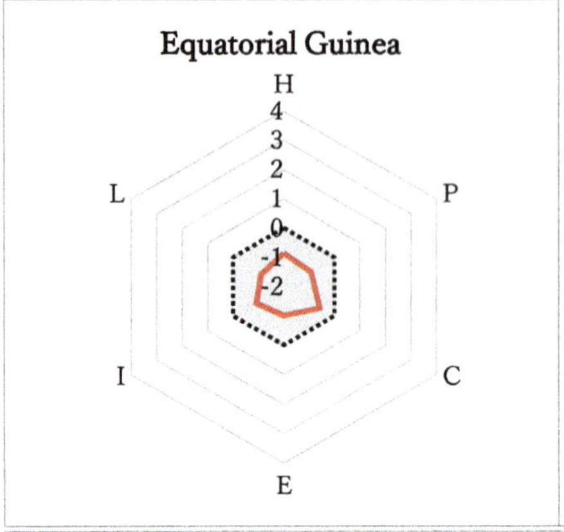
Equatorial Guinea
H
4
3
2
1
0
-1
-2
P
C
E
I
L

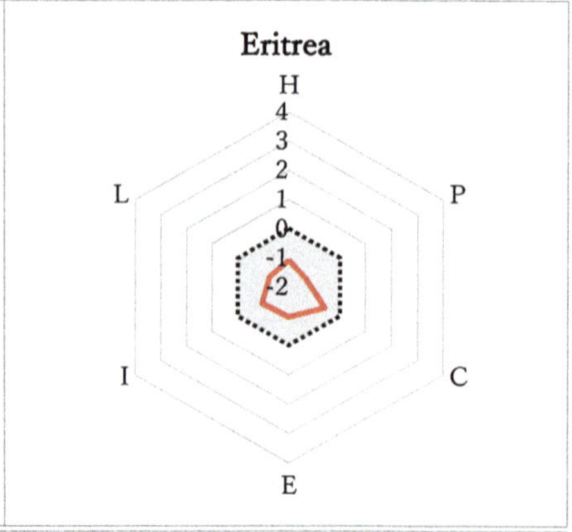
Eritrea
H
4
3
2
1
0
-1
-2
P
C
E
I
L

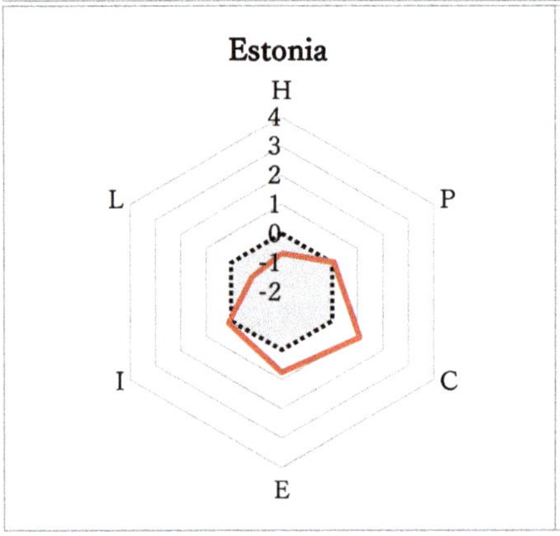
Estonia
H
4
3
2
1
0
-1
-2
P
C
E
I
L

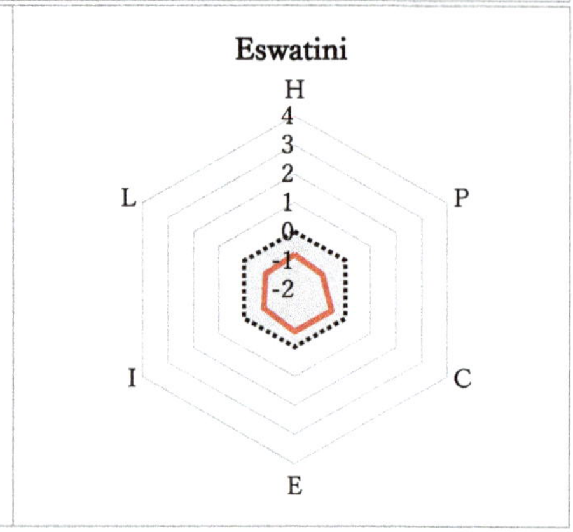
Eswatini
H
4
3
2
1
0
-1
-2
P
C
E
I
L

Ethiopia

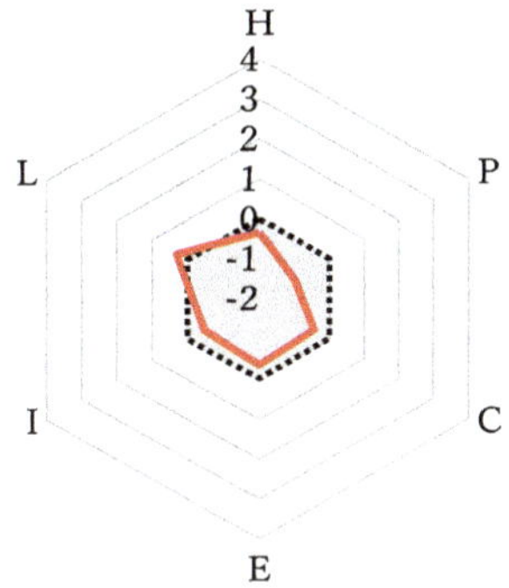

Fiji

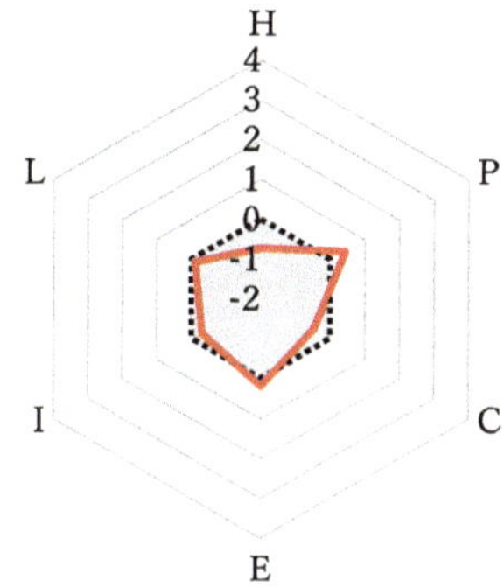

Finland

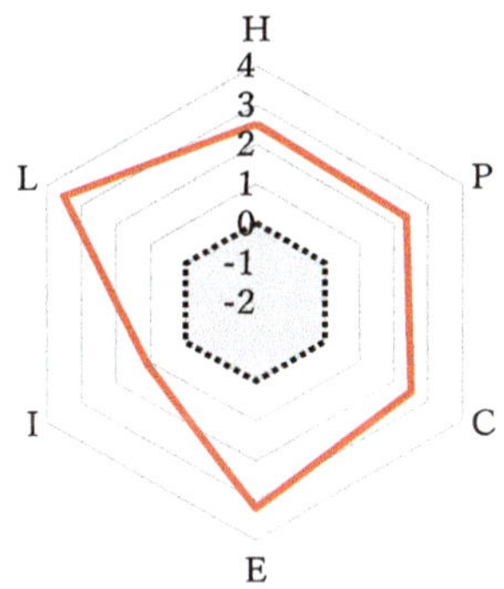

France

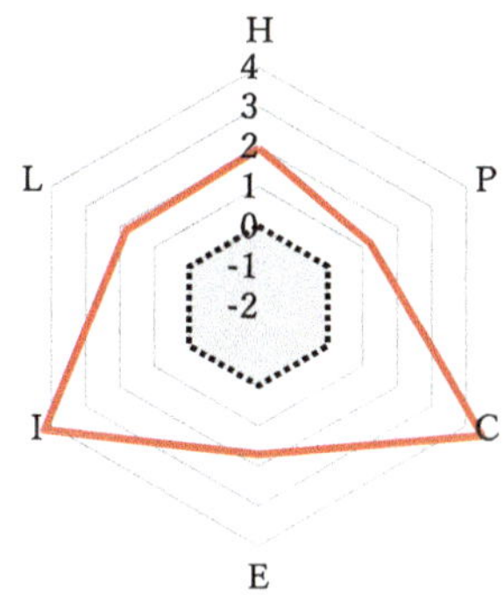

Gabon

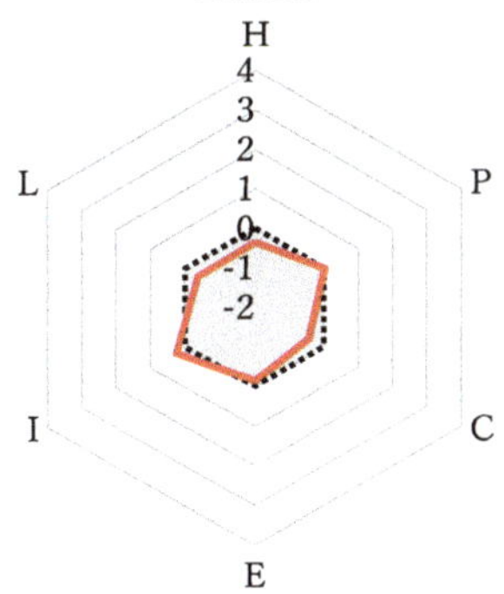

Gambia

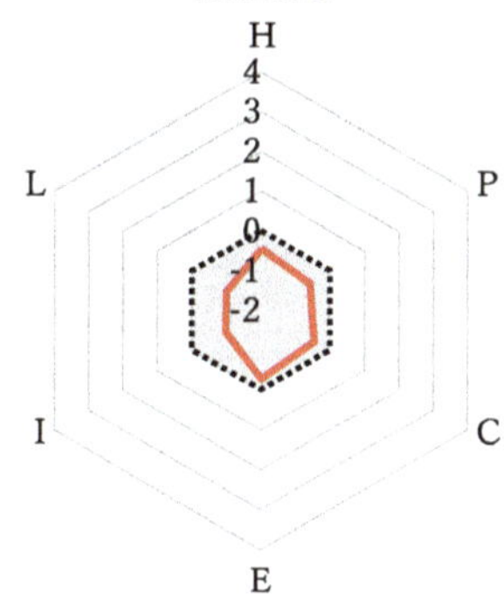

Georgia

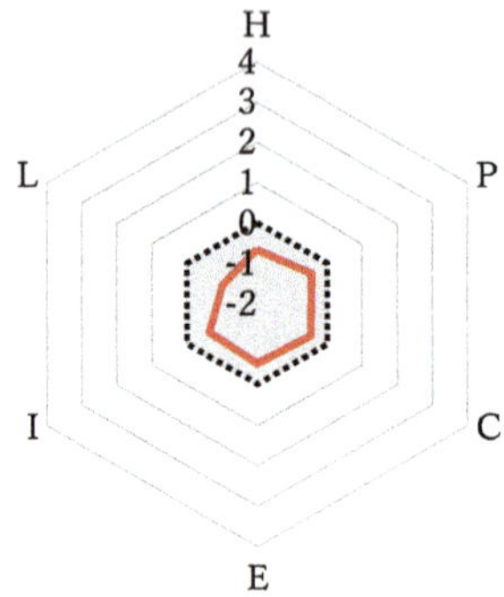

Germany

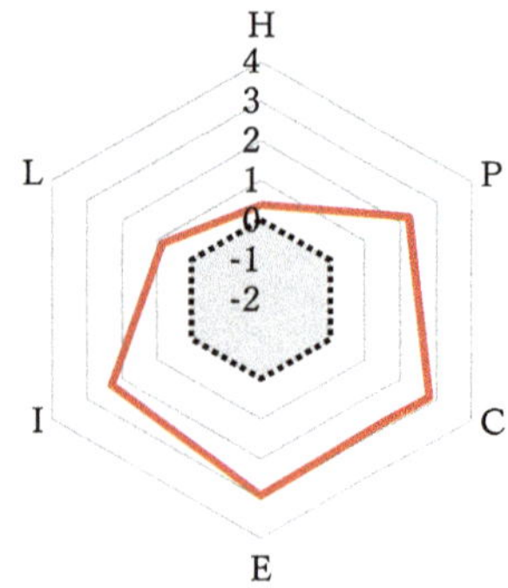

Ghana

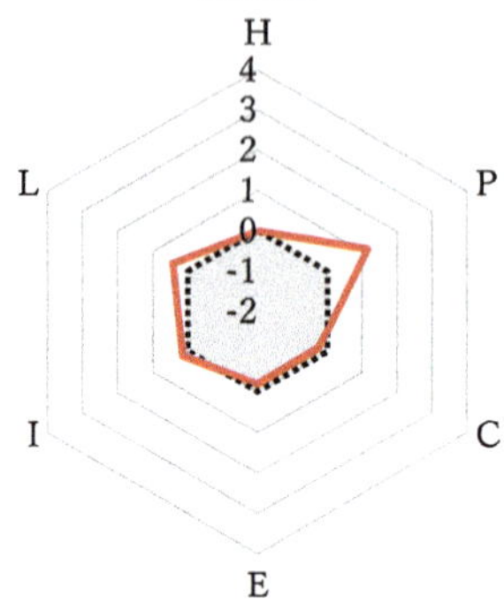

Greece

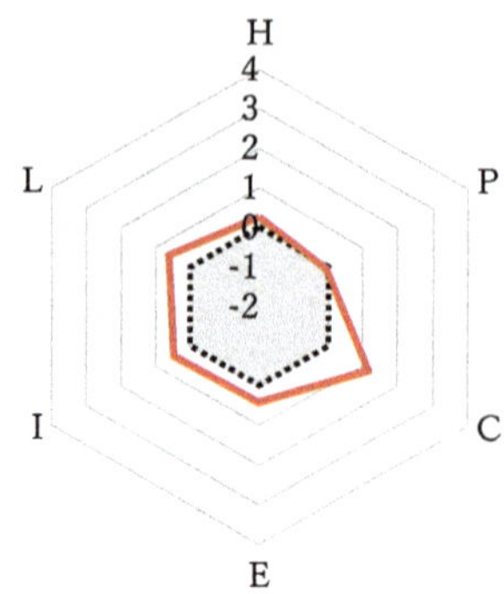

Grenada

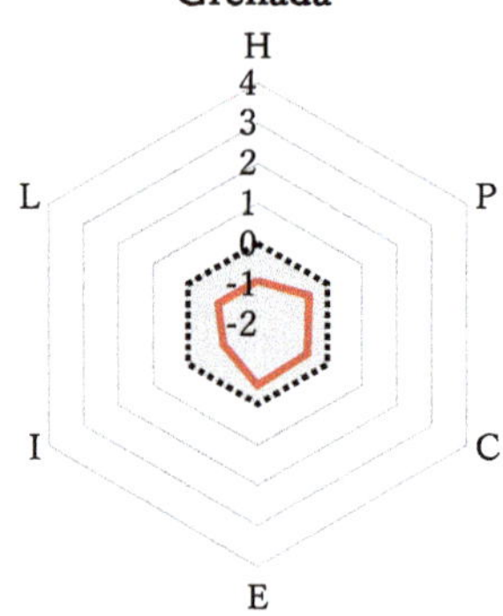

Guatemala

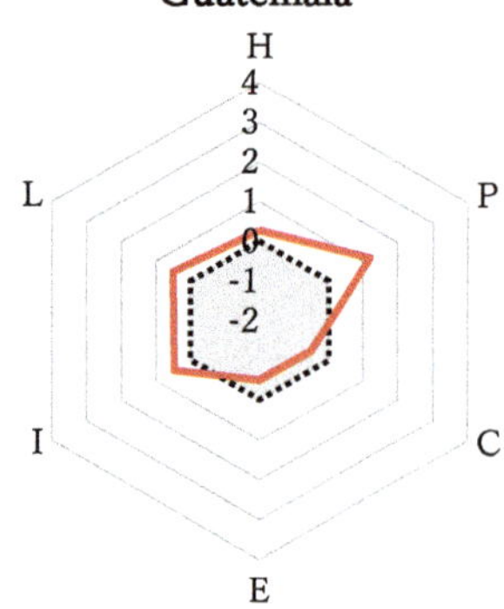

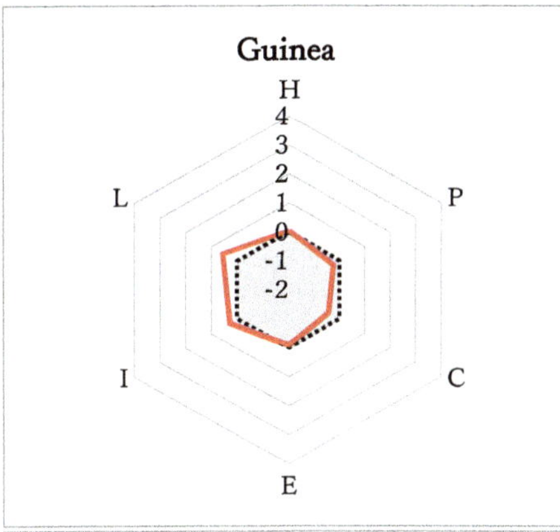

Guinea
H
4
3
2
1
0
-1
-2
P
C
E
I
L

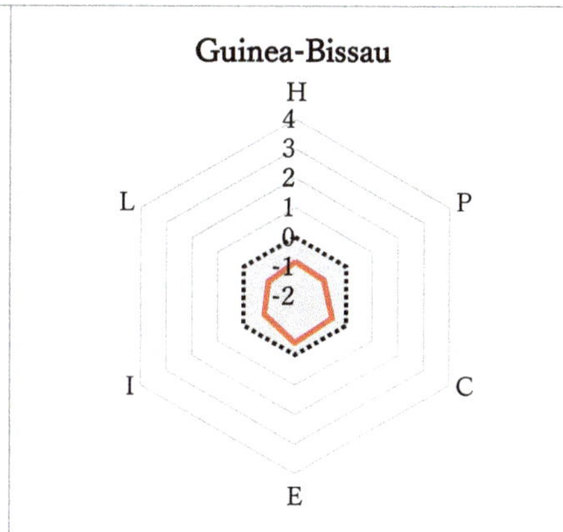

Guinea-Bissau
H
4
3
2
1
0
-1
-2
P
C
E
I
L

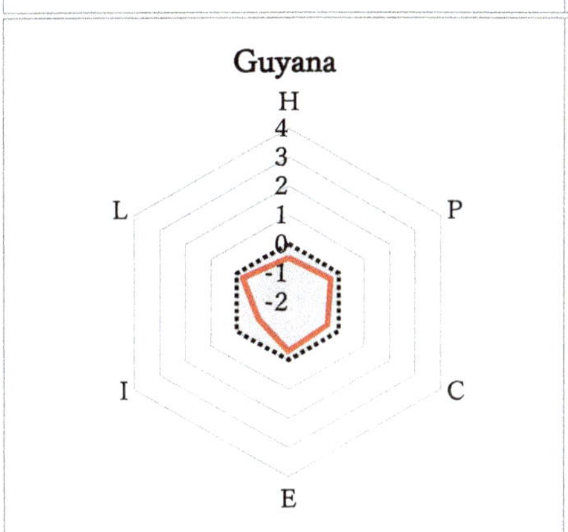

Guyana
H
4
3
2
1
0
-1
-2
P
C
E
I
L

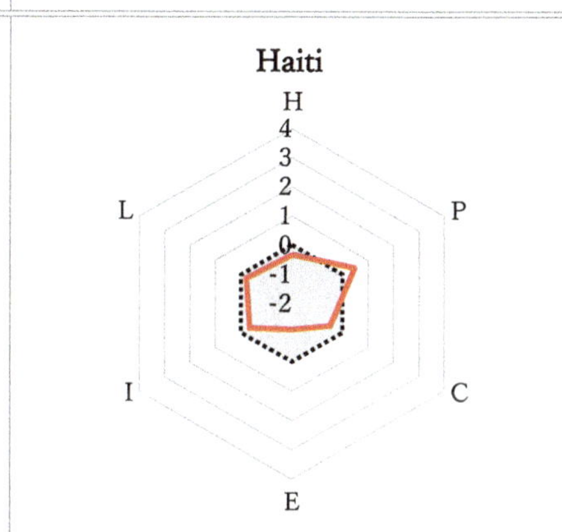

Haiti
H
4
3
2
1
0
-1
-2
P
C
E
I
L

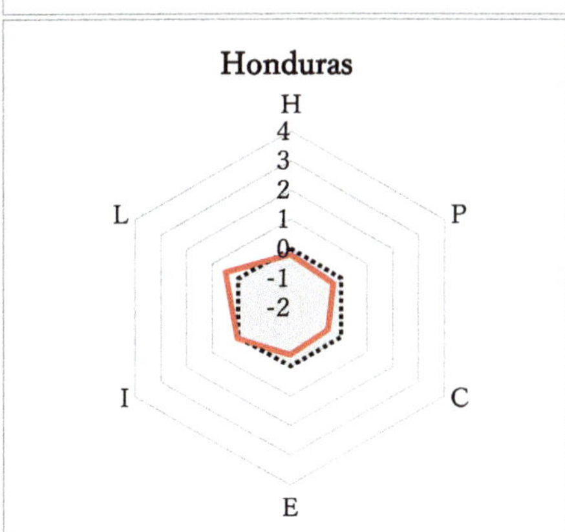

Honduras
H
4
3
2
1
0
-1
-2
P
C
E
I
L

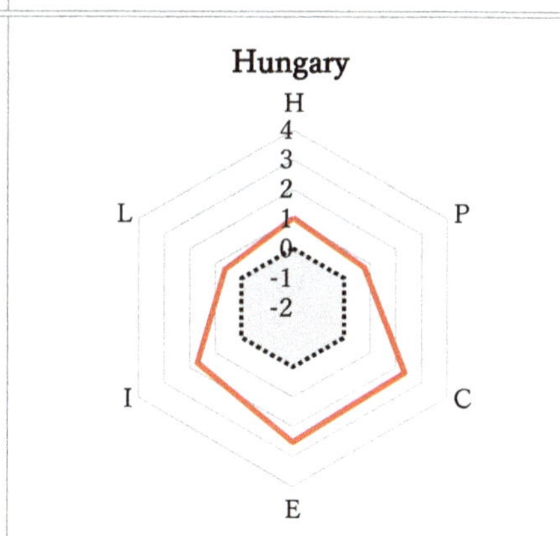

Hungary
H
4
3
2
1
0
-1
-2
P
C
E
I
L

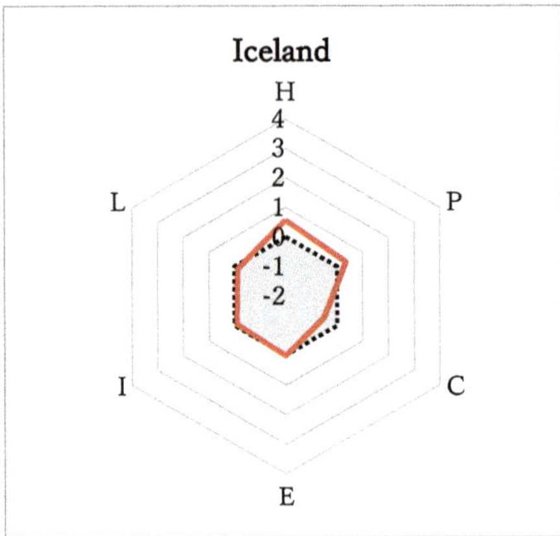
Iceland
H
4
3
2
1
0
-1
-2
P
C
E
I
L

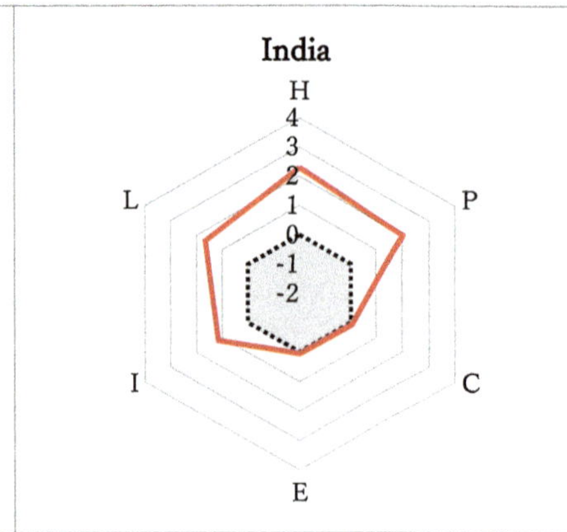
India
H
4
3
2
1
0
-1
-2
P
C
E
I
L

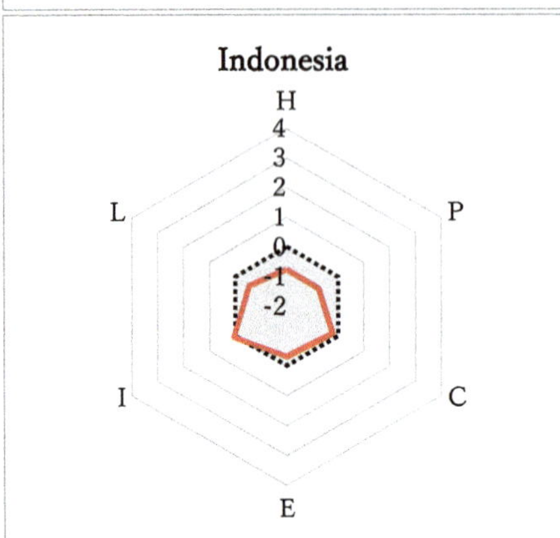
Indonesia
H
4
3
2
1
0
-1
-2
P
C
E
I
L

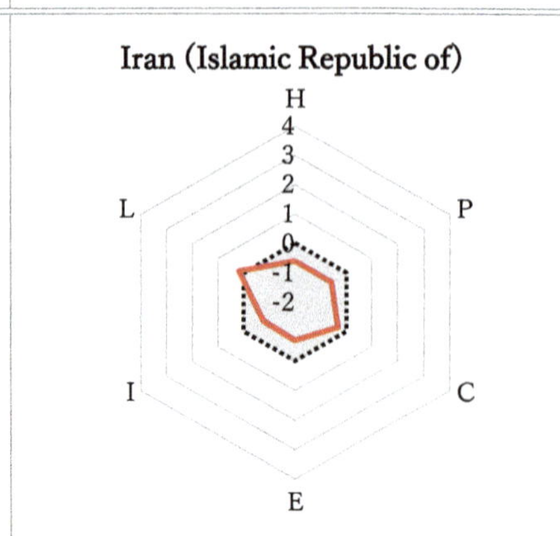
Iran (Islamic Republic of)
H
4
3
2
1
0
-1
-2
P
C
E
I
L

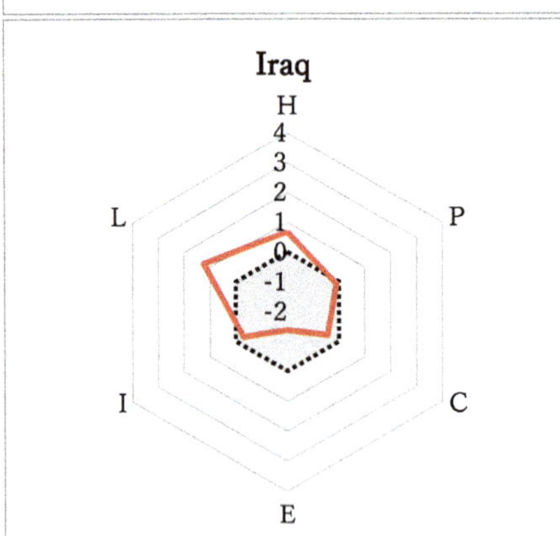
Iraq
H
4
3
2
1
0
-1
-2
P
C
E
I
L

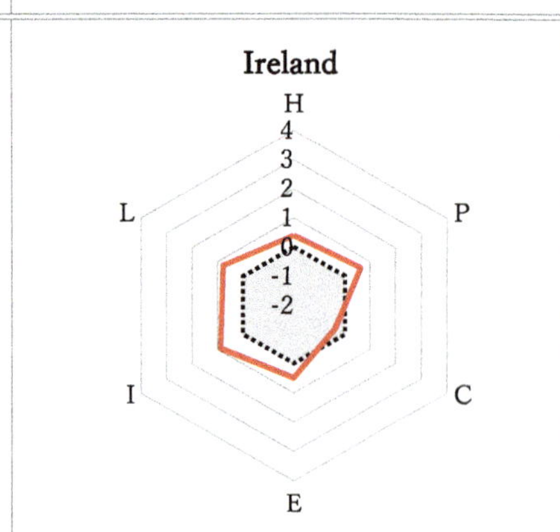
Ireland
H
4
3
2
1
0
-1
-2
P
C
E
I
L

Israel

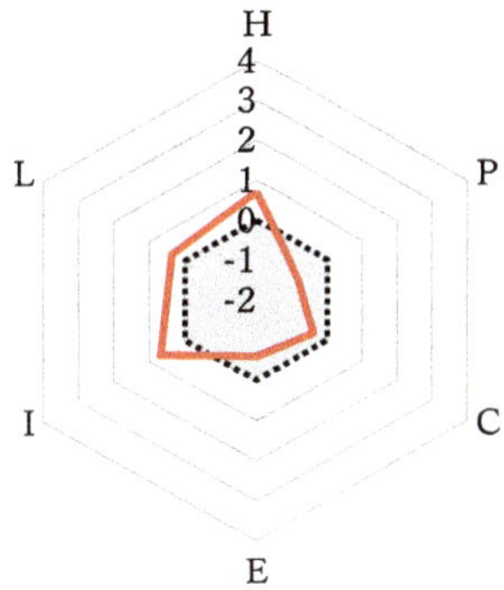

Italy

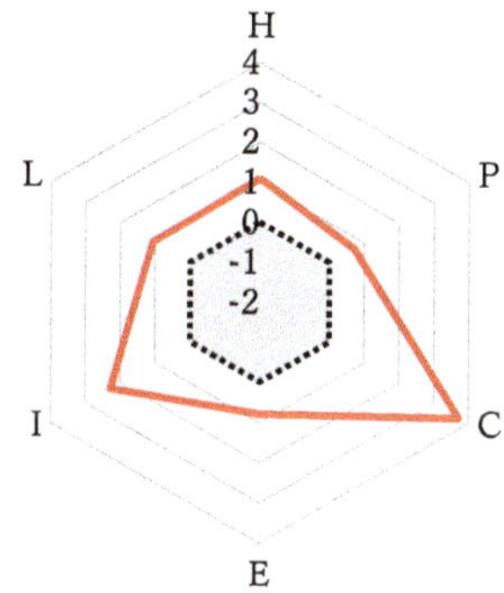

Jamaica

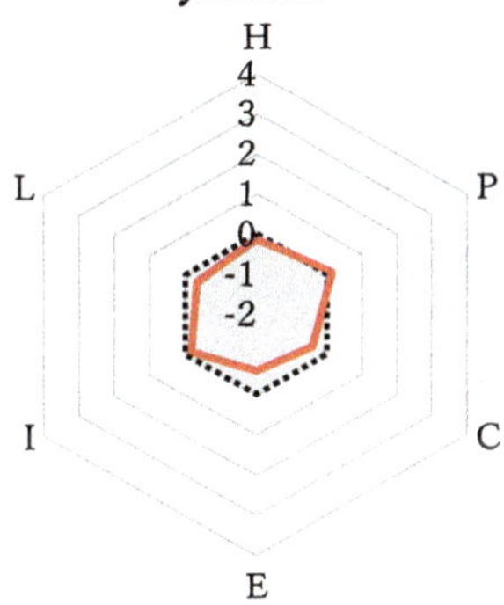

Japan

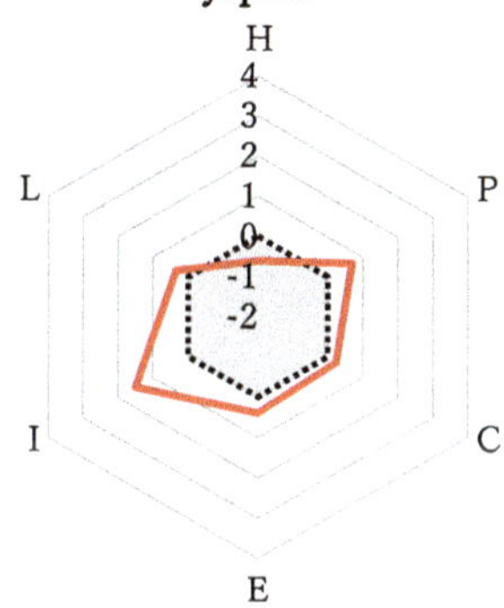

Jordan

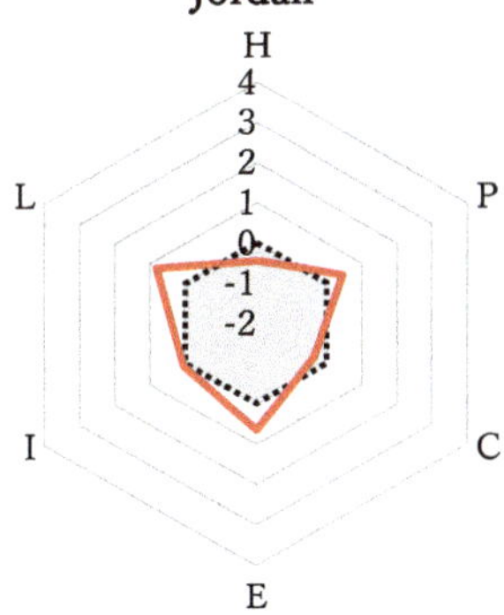

Kazakhstan

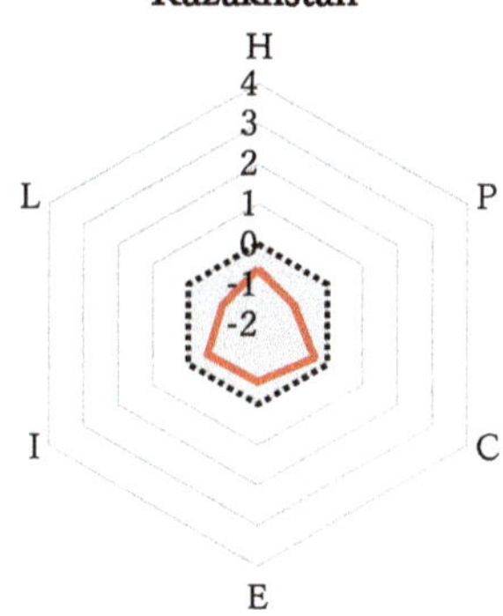

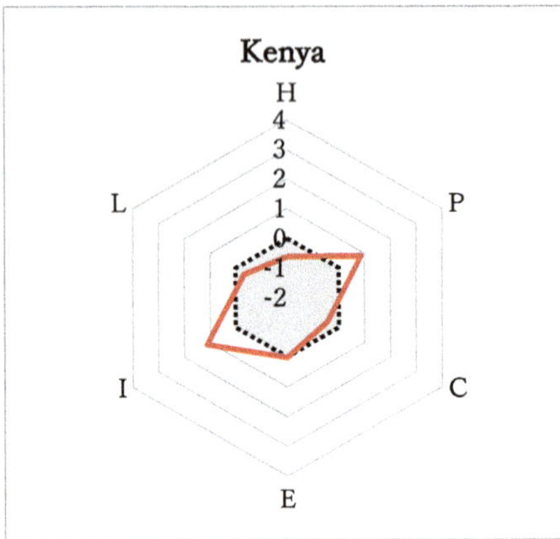
Kenya
H
4
3
2
1
0
-1
-2
P
C
E
I
L

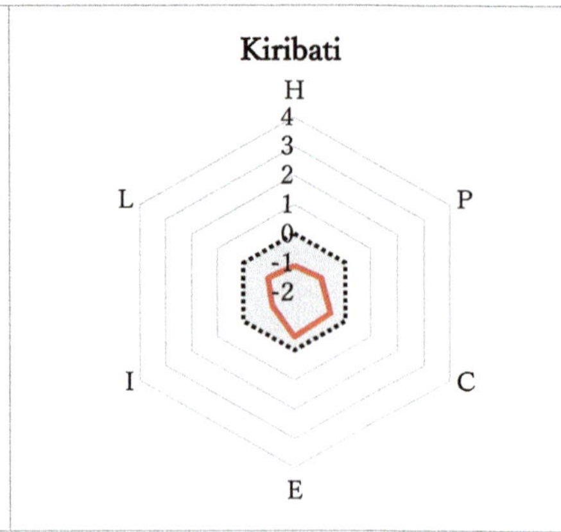
Kiribati
H
4
3
2
1
0
-1
-2
P
C
E
I
L

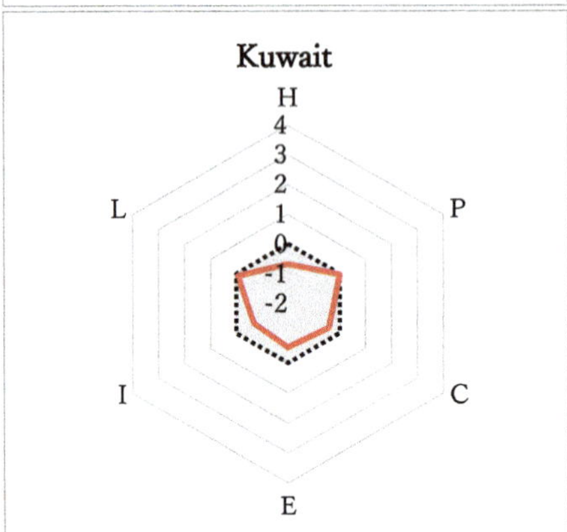
Kuwait
H
4
3
2
1
0
-1
-2
P
C
E
I
L

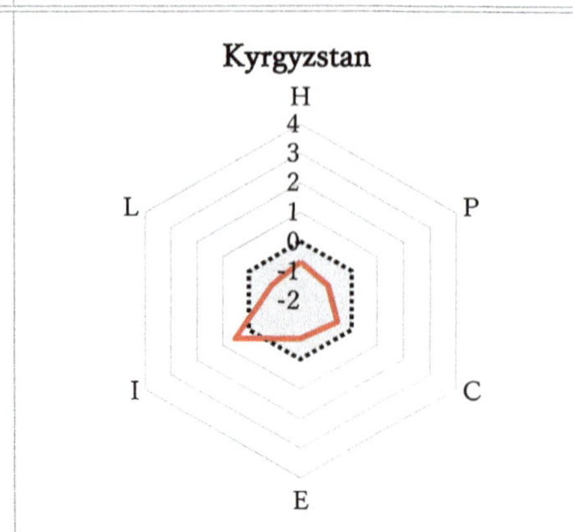
Kyrgyzstan
H
4
3
2
1
0
-1
-2
P
C
E
I
L

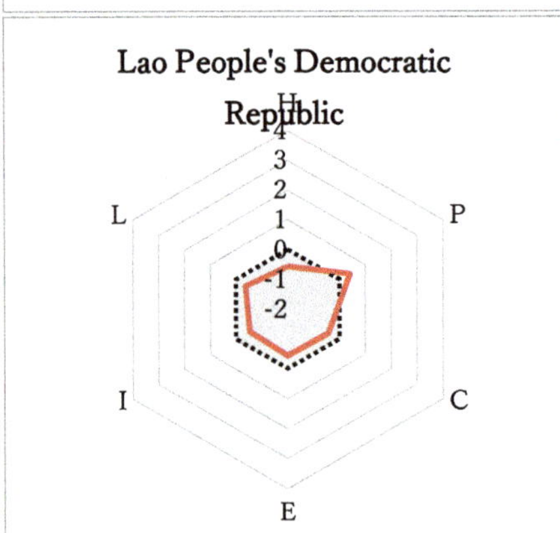
Lao People's Democratic Republic
H
4
3
2
1
0
-1
-2
P
C
E
I
L

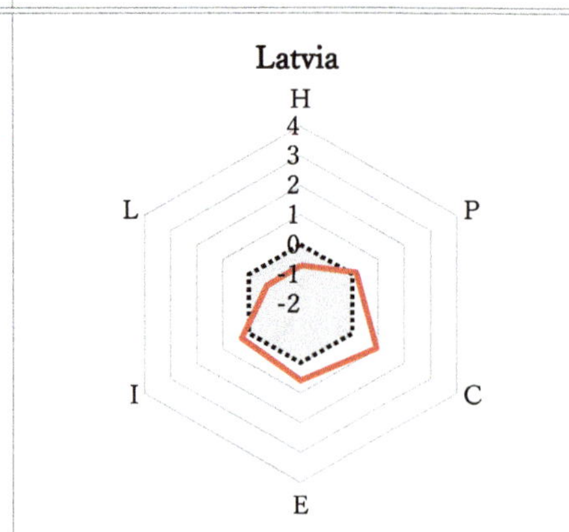
Latvia
H
4
3
2
1
0
-1
-2
P
C
E
I
L

Lebanon

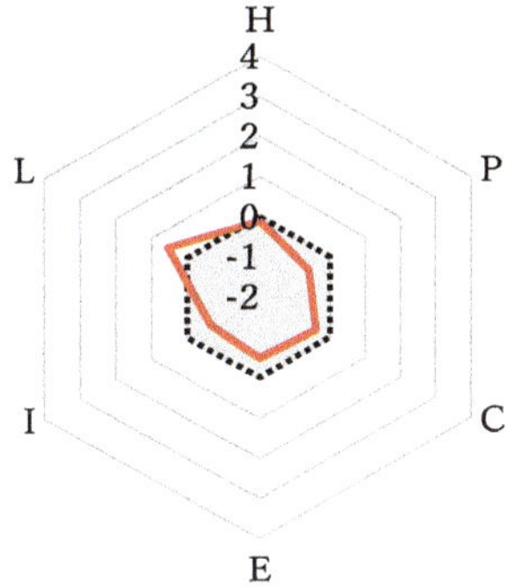

Lesotho

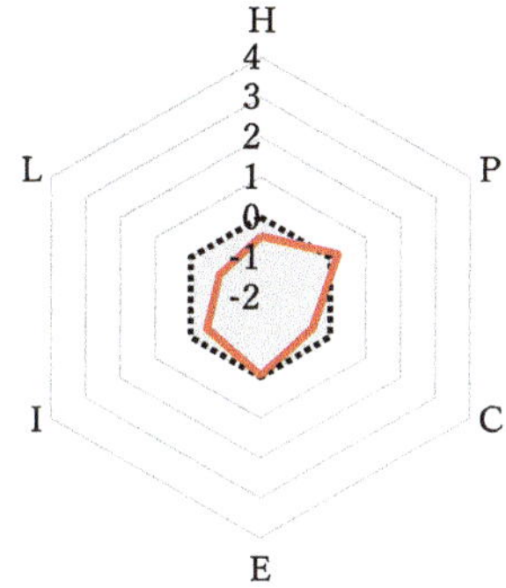

Liberia

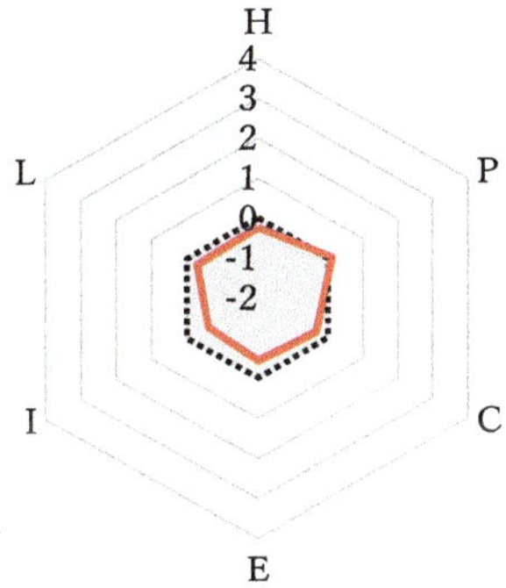

Libya

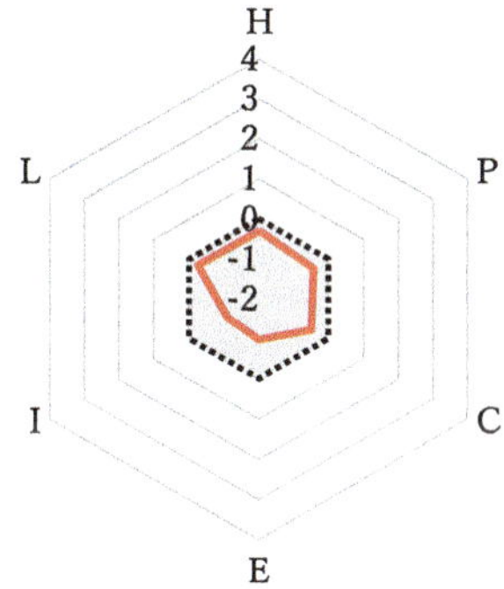

Liechtenstein

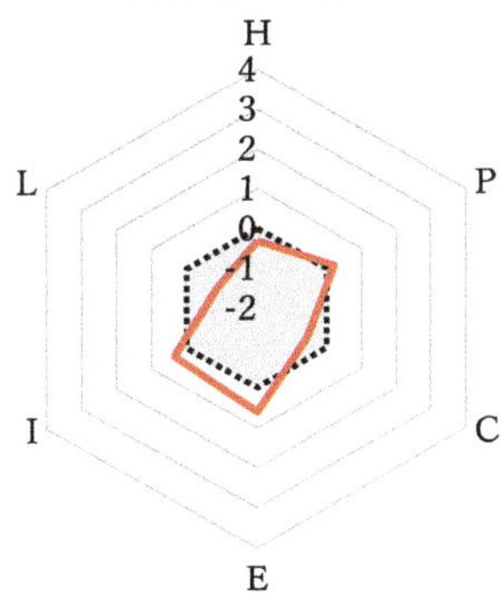

Lithuania

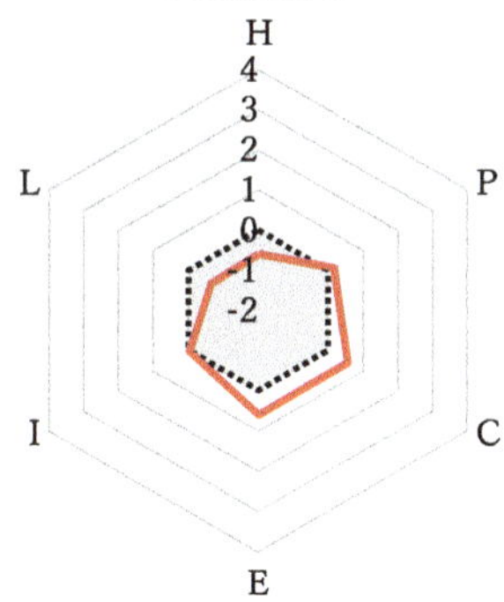

Luxembourg

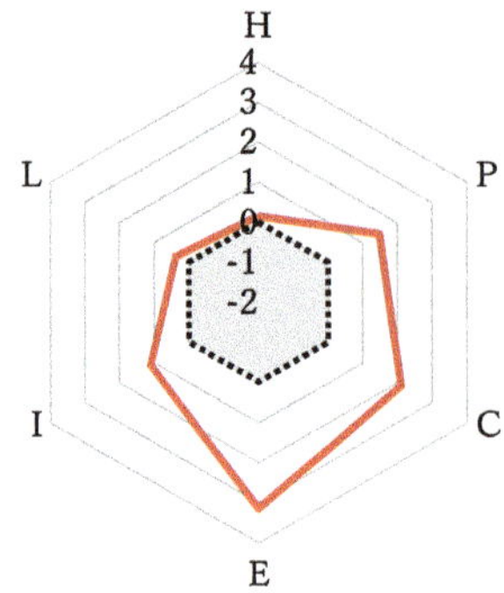

Madagascar

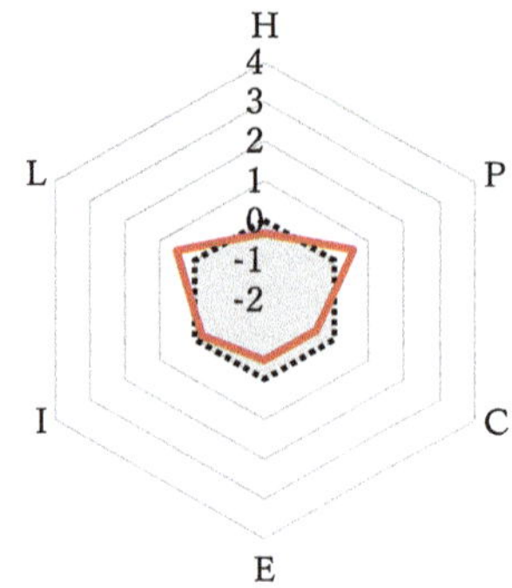

Malawi

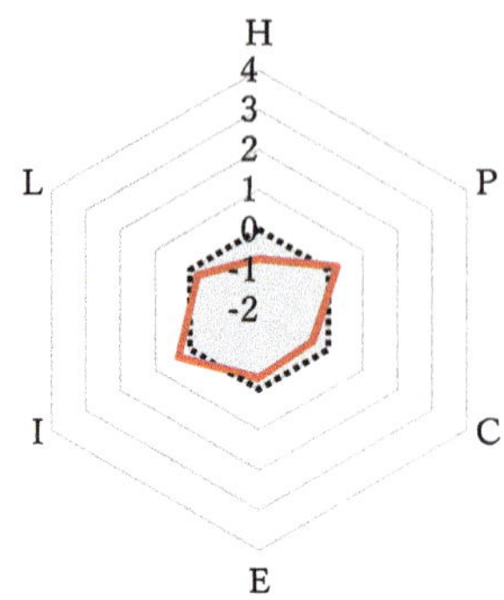

Malaysia

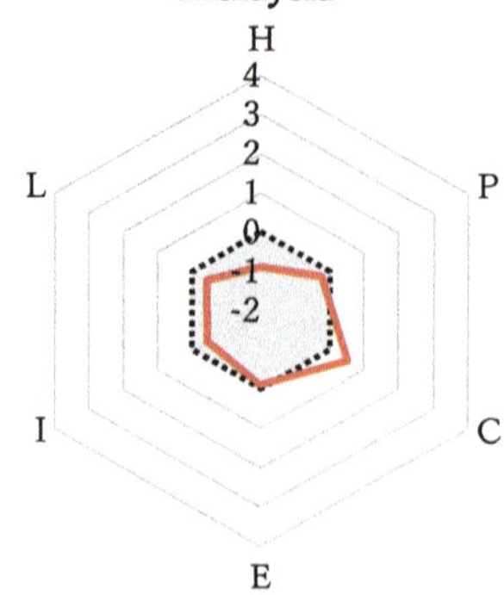

Maldives

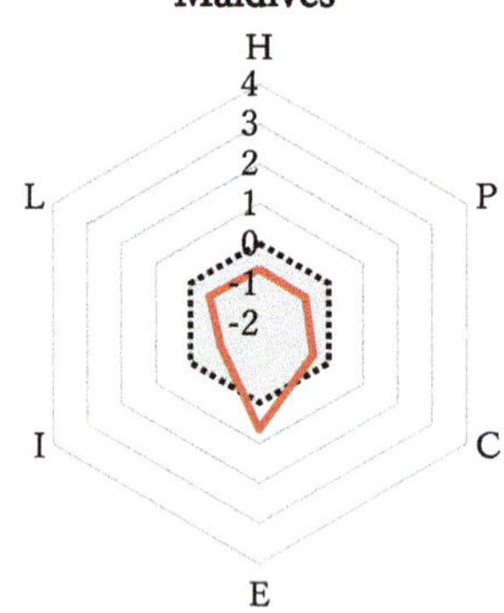

Mali

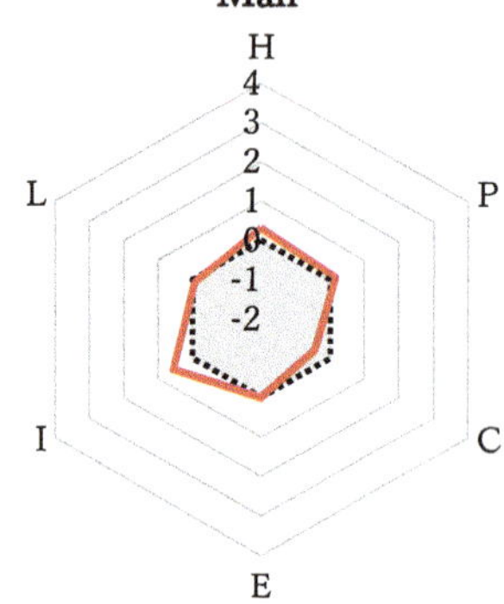

Malta

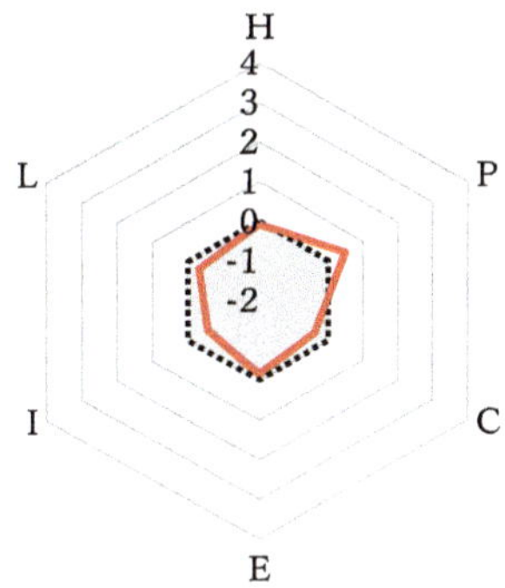

Marshall Islands

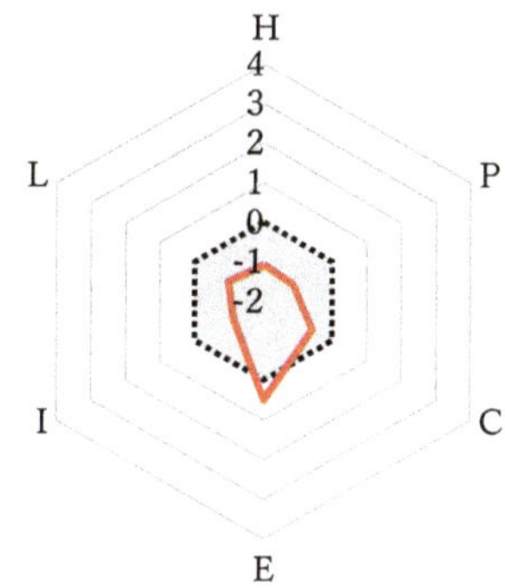

Mauritania

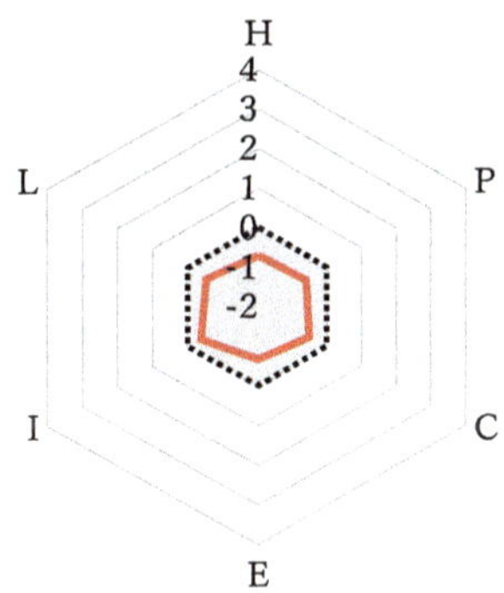

Mauritius

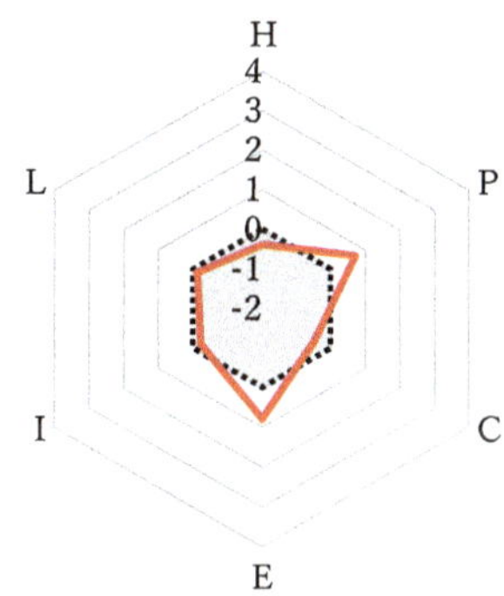

Mexico

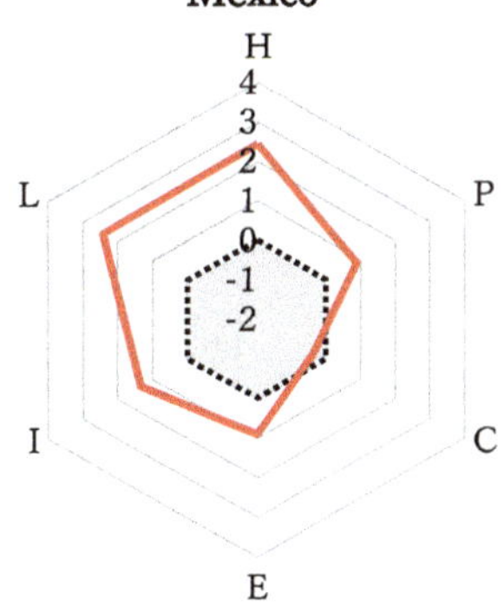

Micronesia (Federated States of)

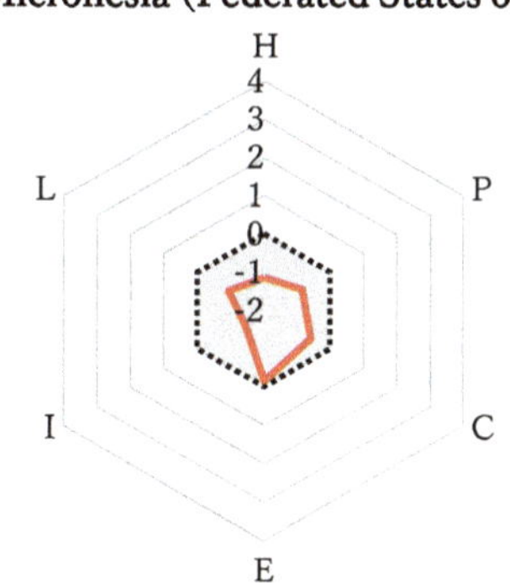

Monaco

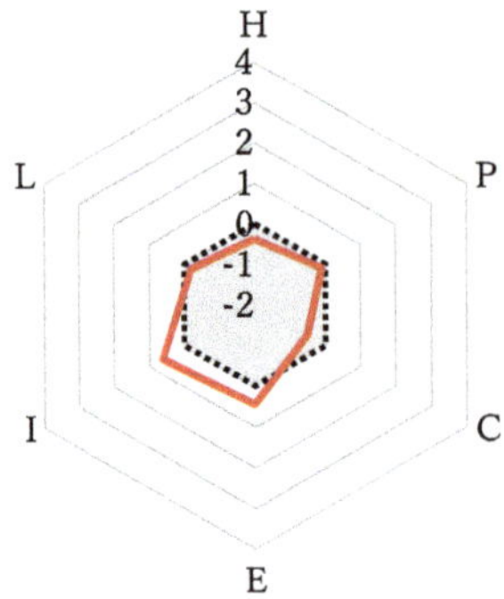

Mongolia

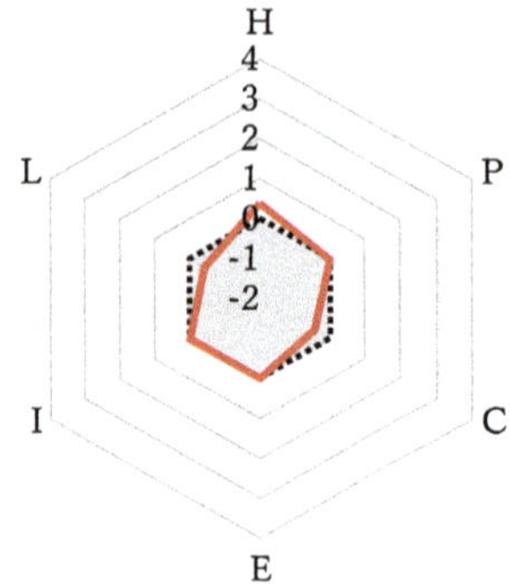

Montenegro

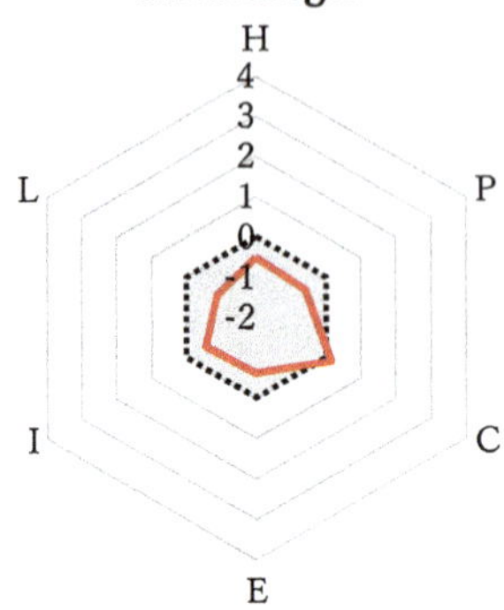

Morocco

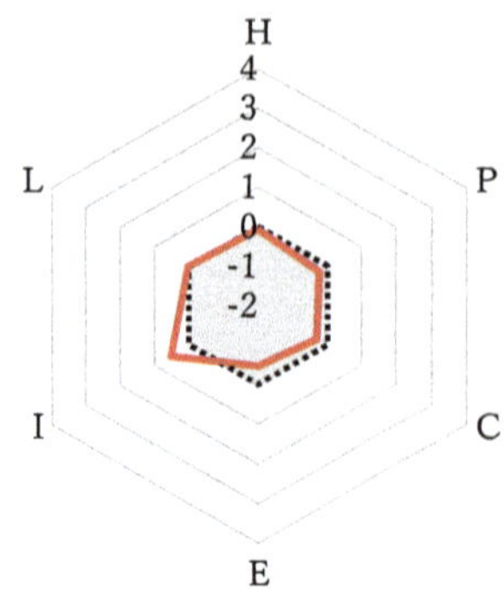

Mozambique

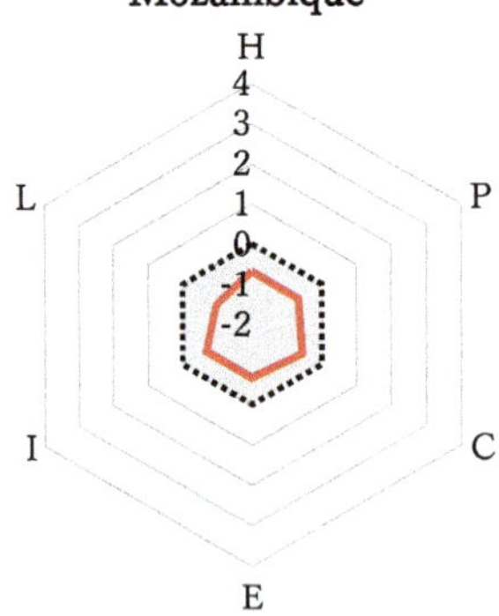

Myanmar

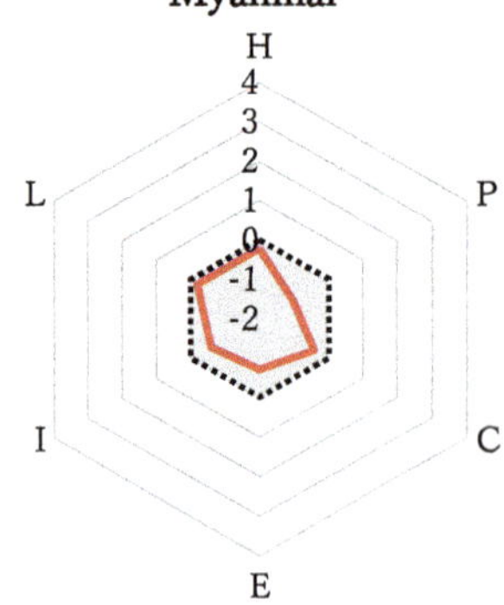

Namibia

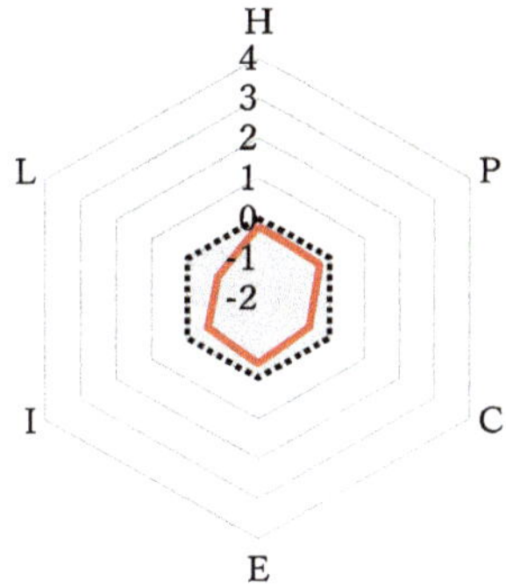

Nauru

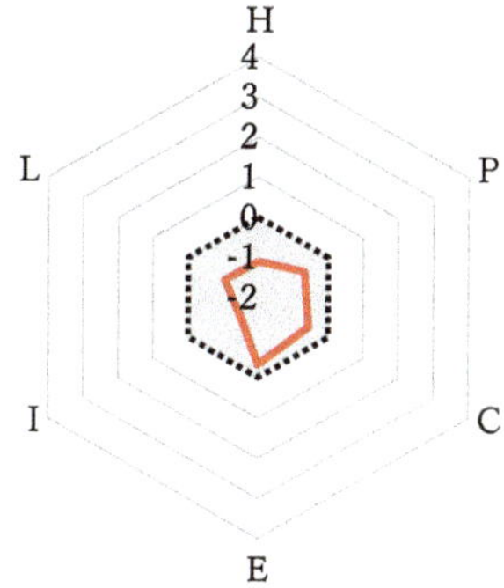

Nepal

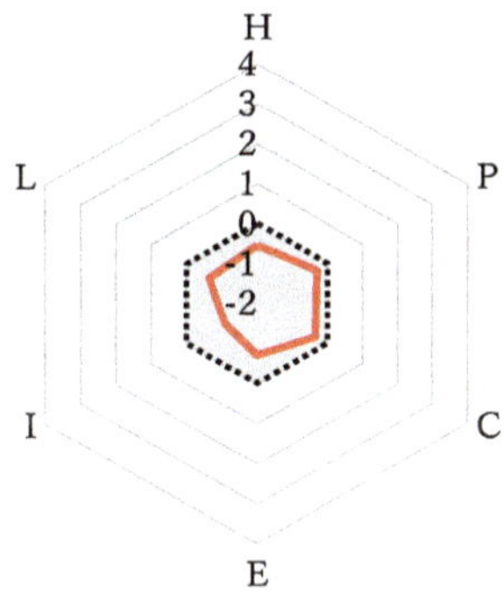

Netherlands

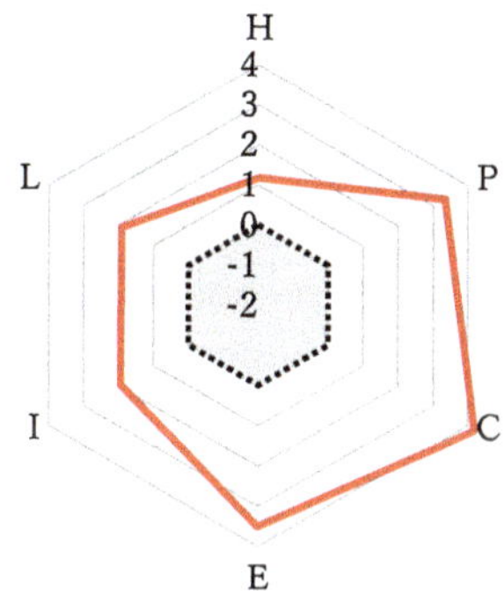

New Zealand

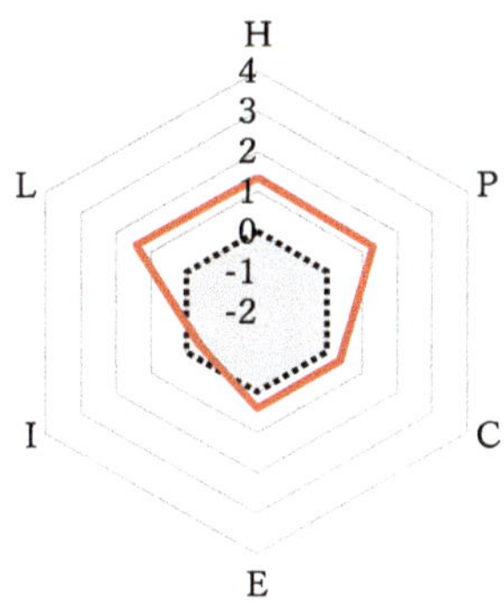

Nicaragua

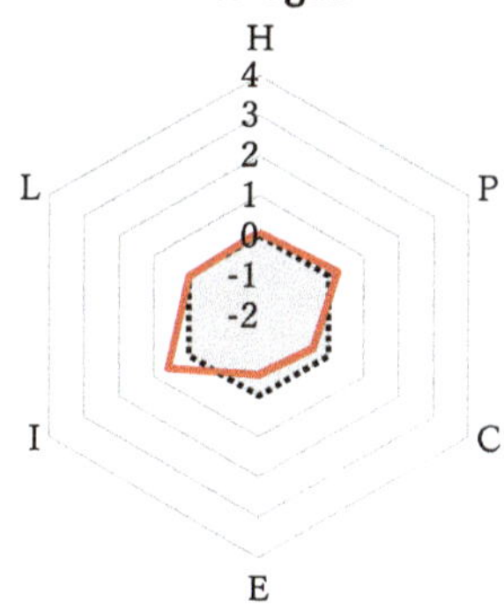

Niger

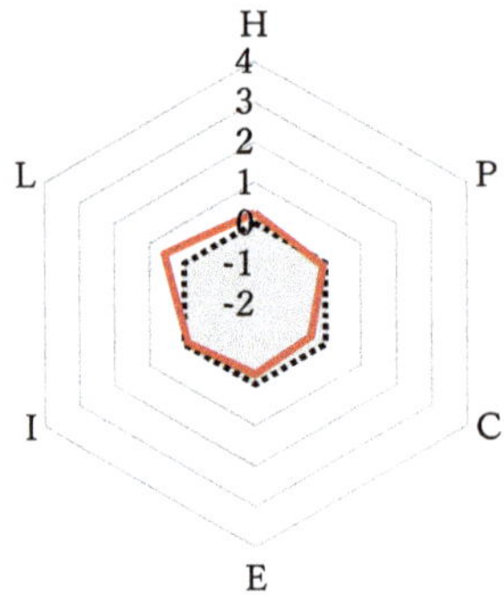

Nigeria

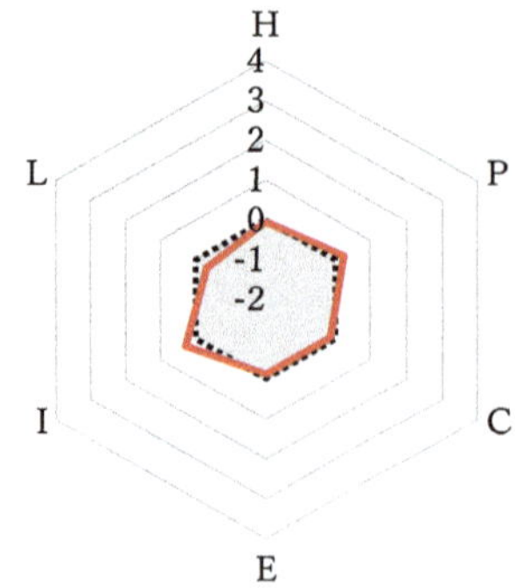

North Macedonia

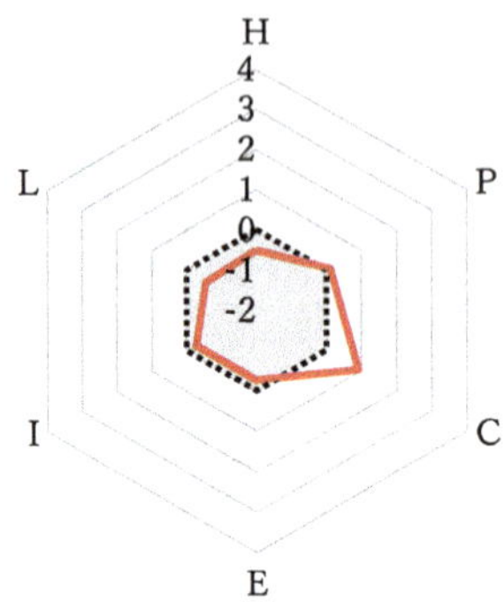

Norway

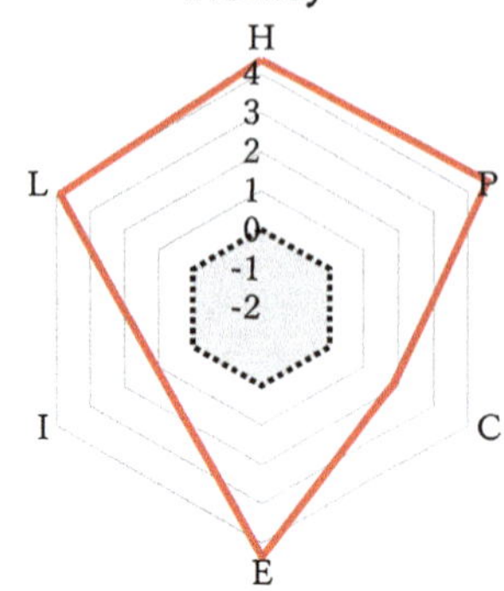

Oman

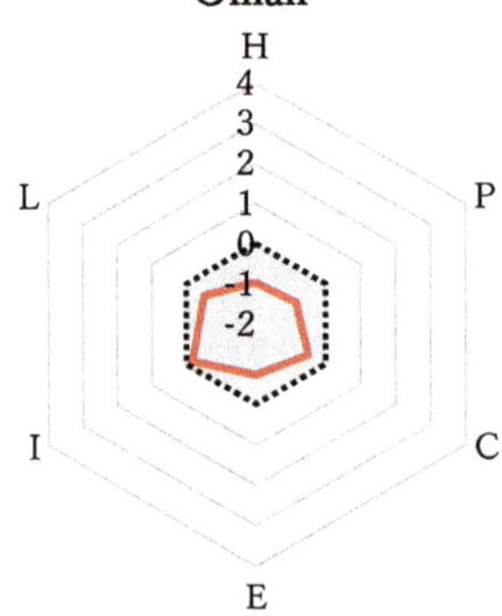

Pakistan

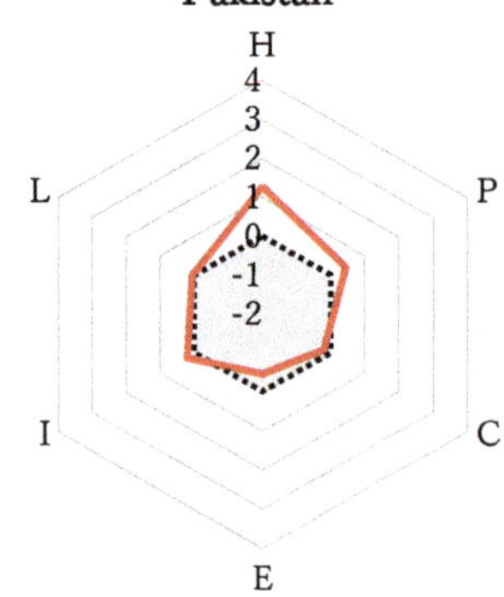

Palau

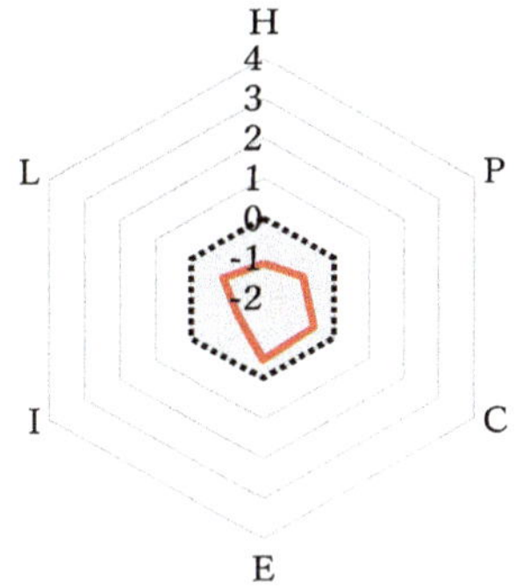

Panama

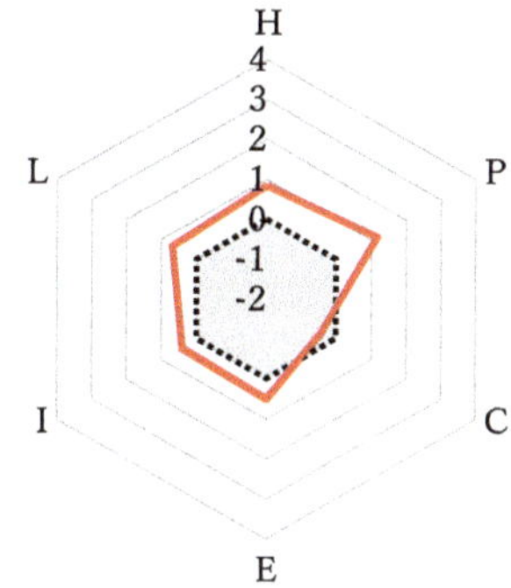

Papua New Guinea

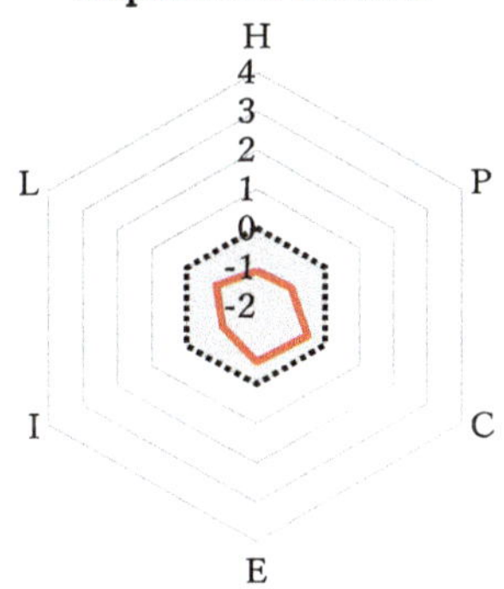

Paraguay

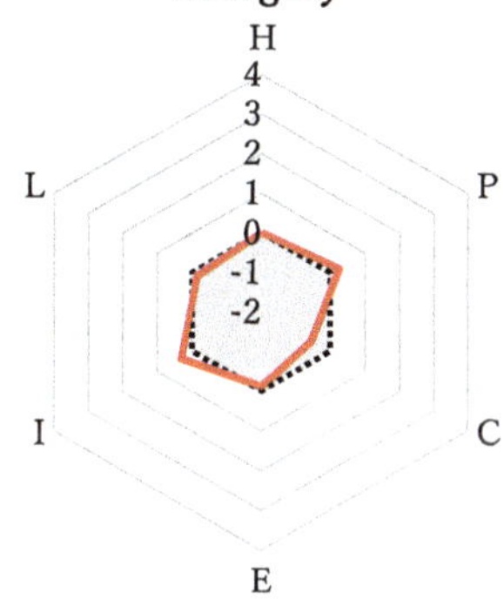

Peru

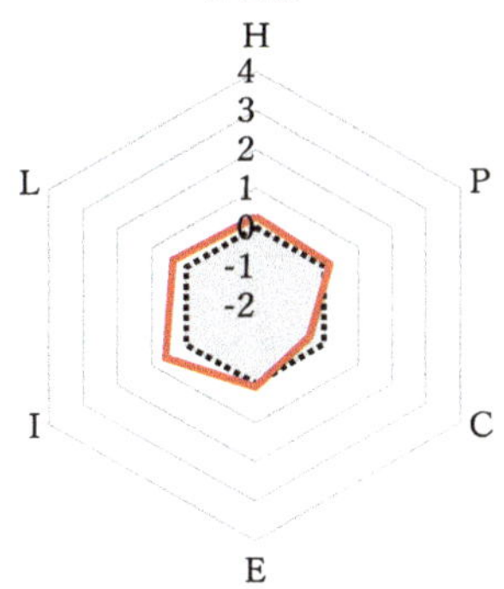

Philippines

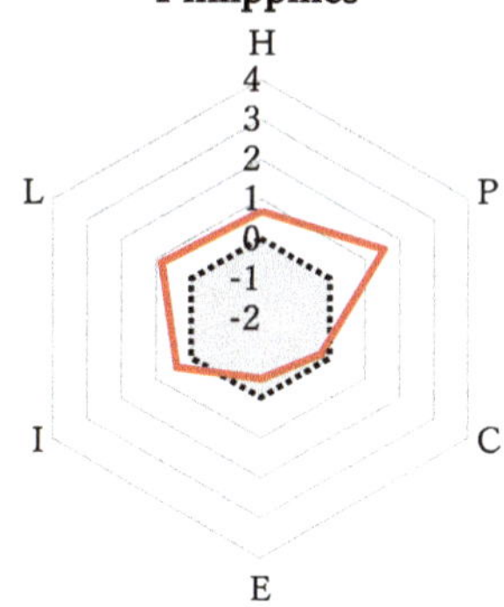

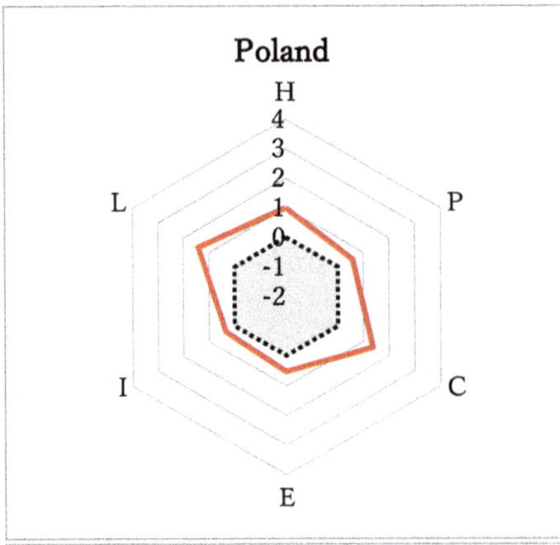
Poland
H
4
3
2
1
0
-1
-2
P
C
E
I
L

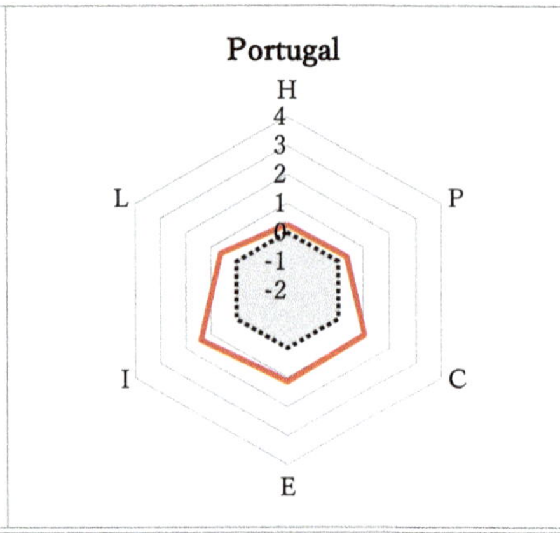
Portugal
H
4
3
2
1
0
-1
-2
P
C
E
I
L

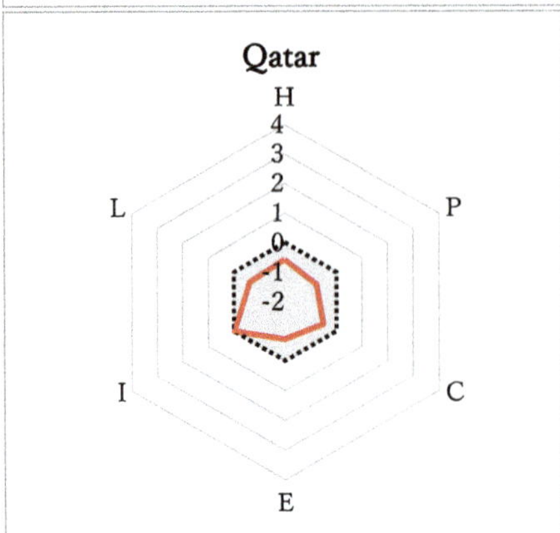
Qatar
H
4
3
2
1
0
-1
-2
P
C
E
I
L

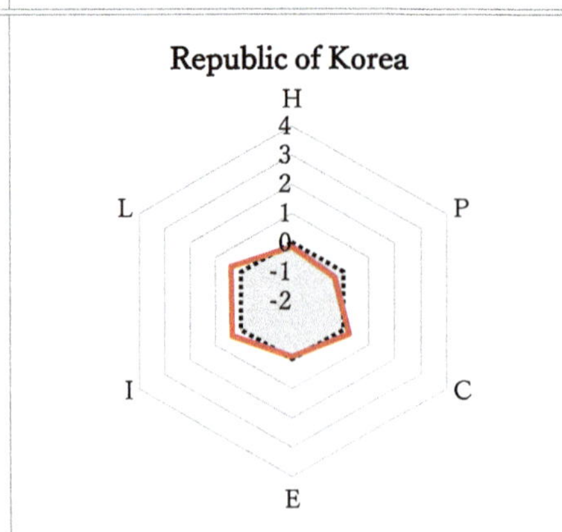
Republic of Korea
H
4
3
2
1
0
-1
-2
P
C
E
I
L

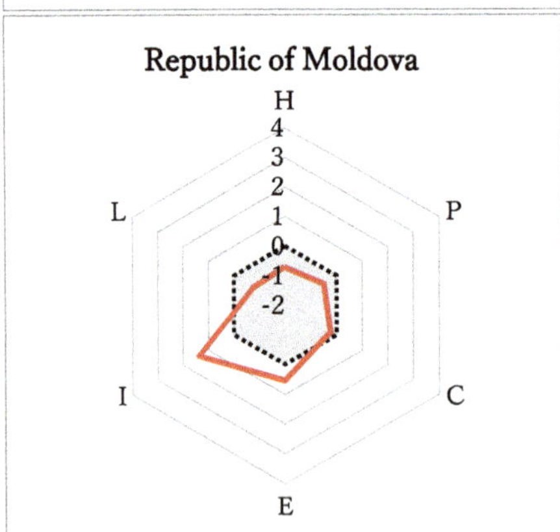
Republic of Moldova
H
4
3
2
1
0
-1
-2
P
C
E
I
L

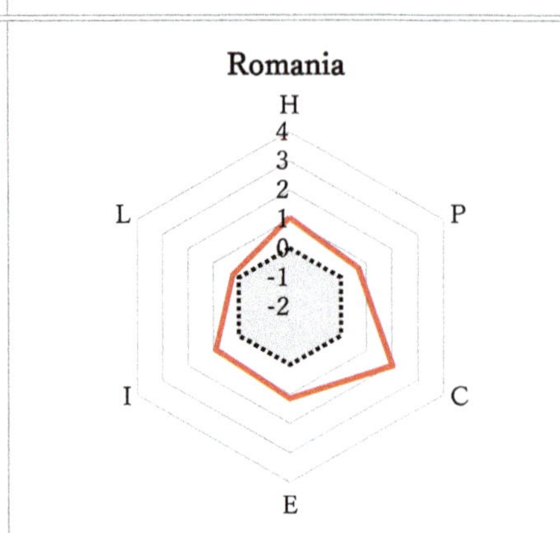
Romania
H
4
3
2
1
0
-1
-2
P
C
E
I
L

Russian Federation

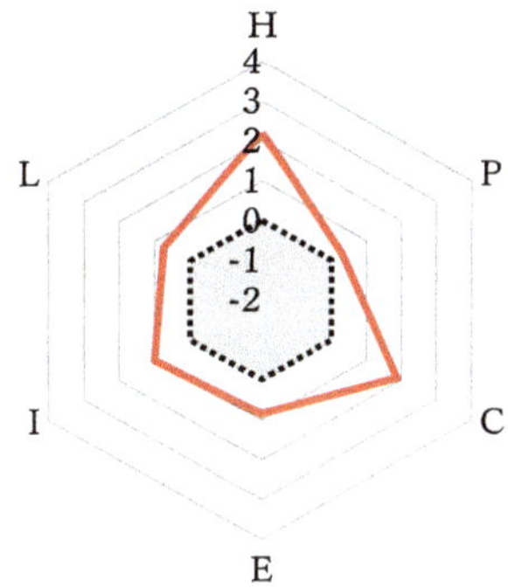

Rwanda

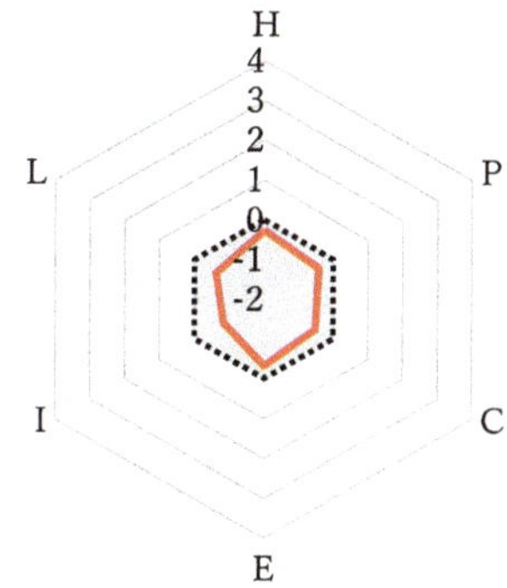

Samoa

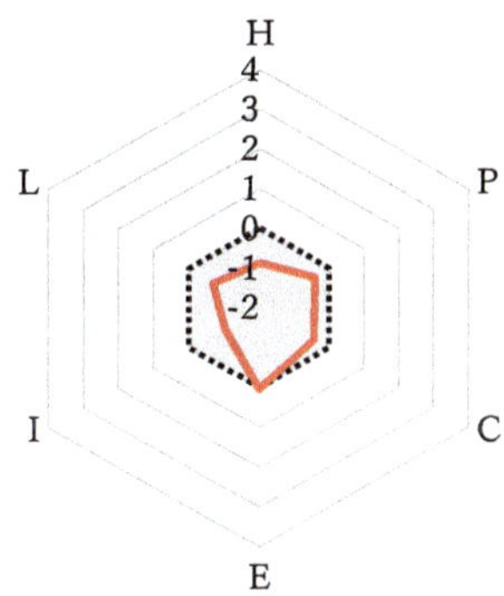

San Marino

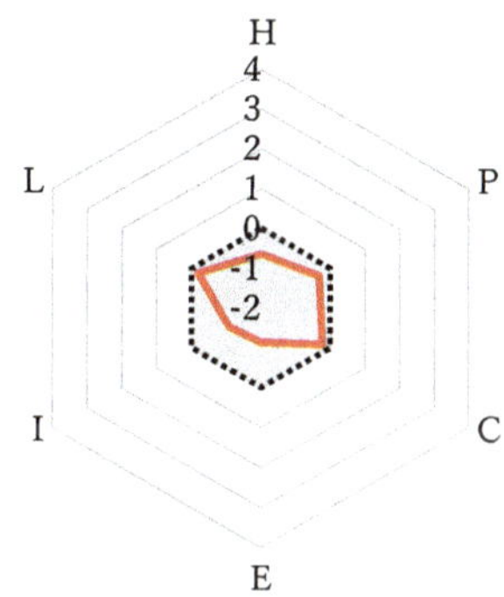

Sao Tome and Principe

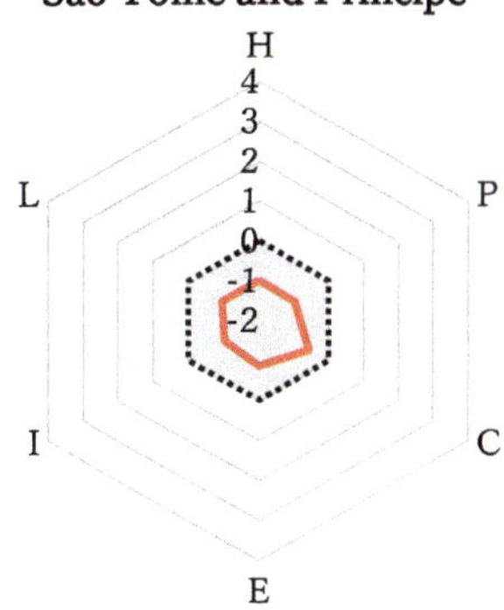

Saudi Arabia

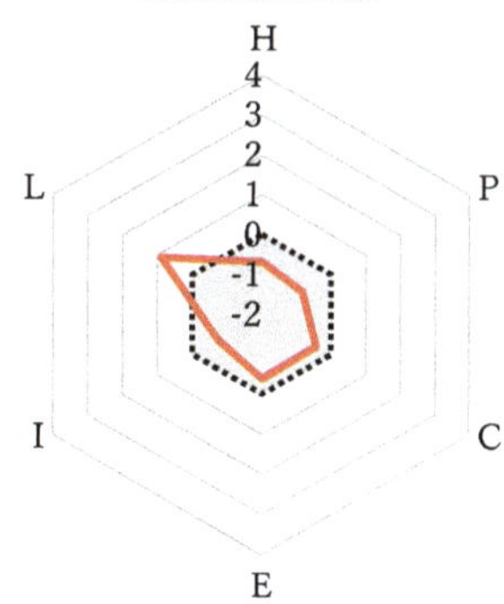

Senegal

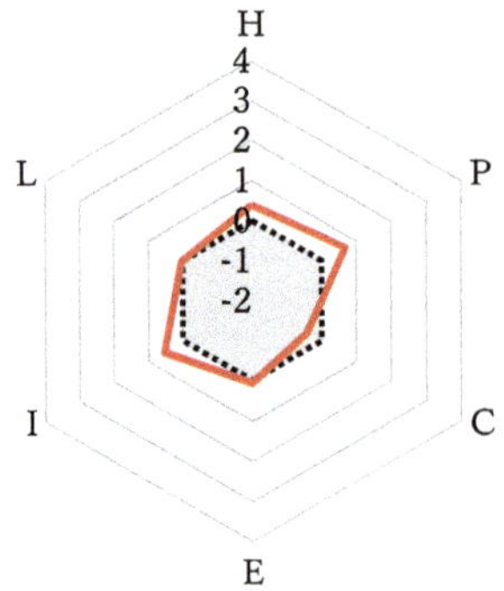

Serbia

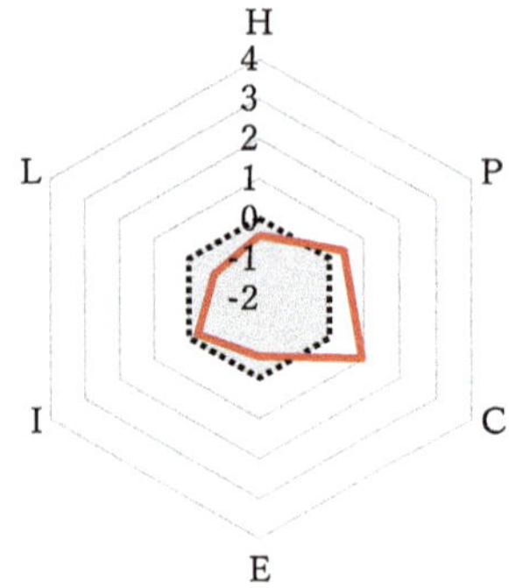

Seychelles

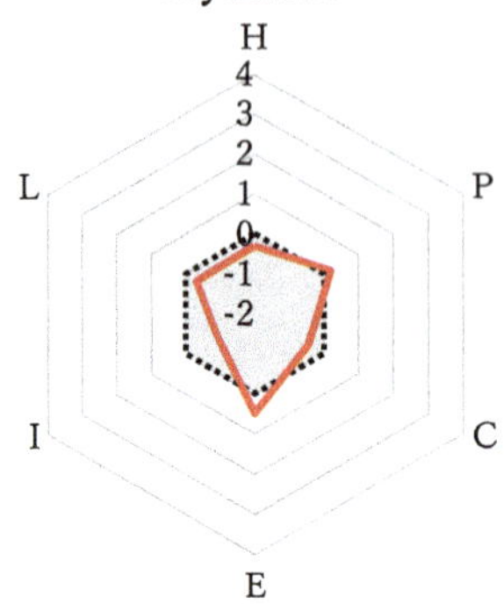

Sierra Leone

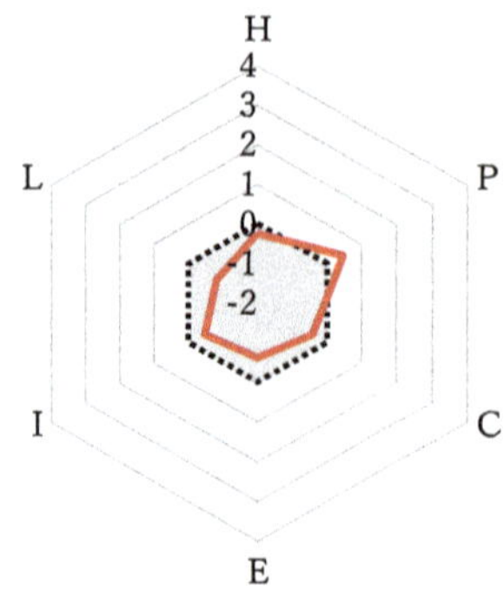

Singapore

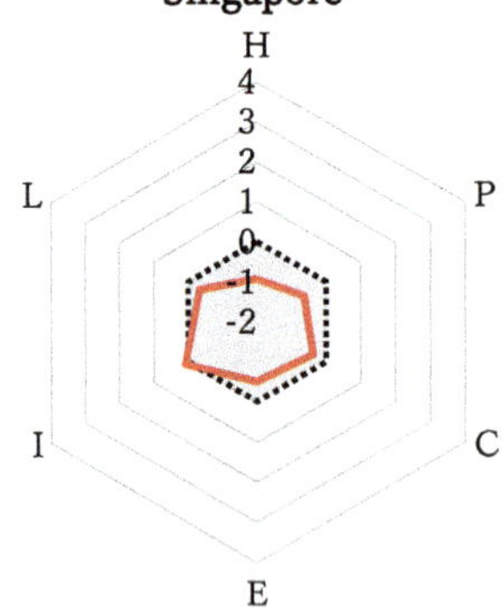

Slovakia

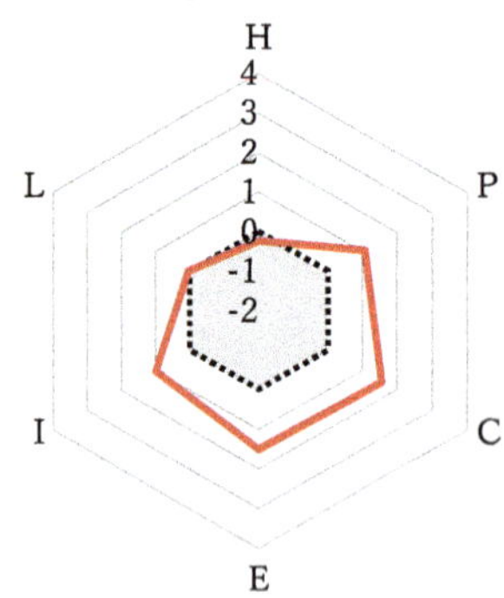

Slovenia

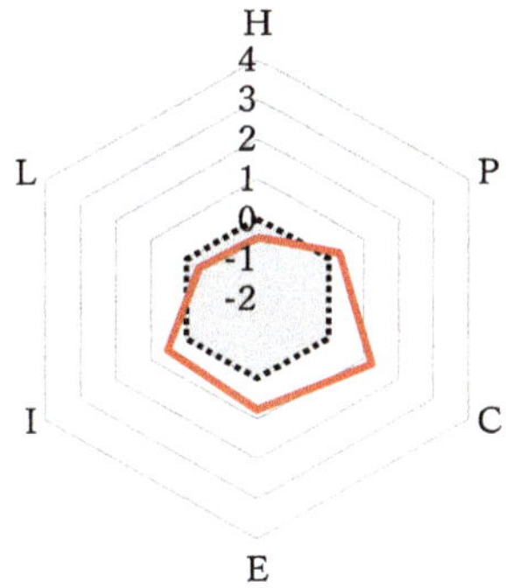

Solomon Islands

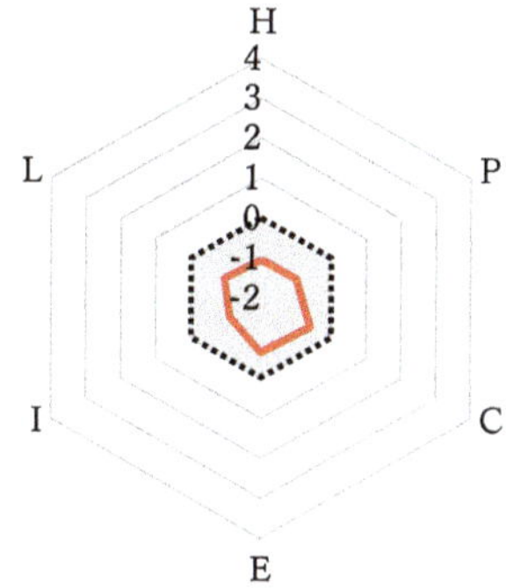

Somalia

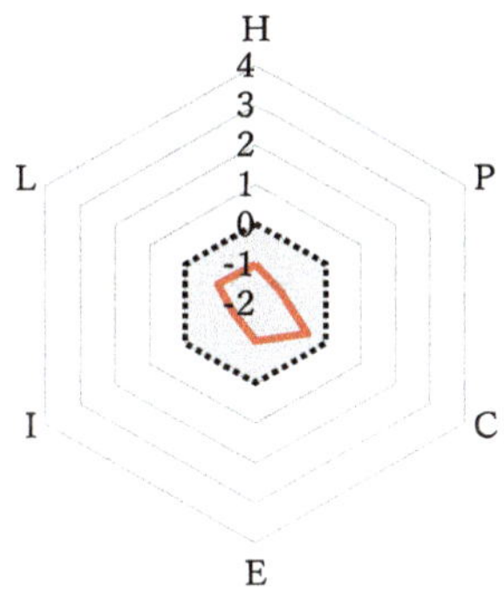

South Africa

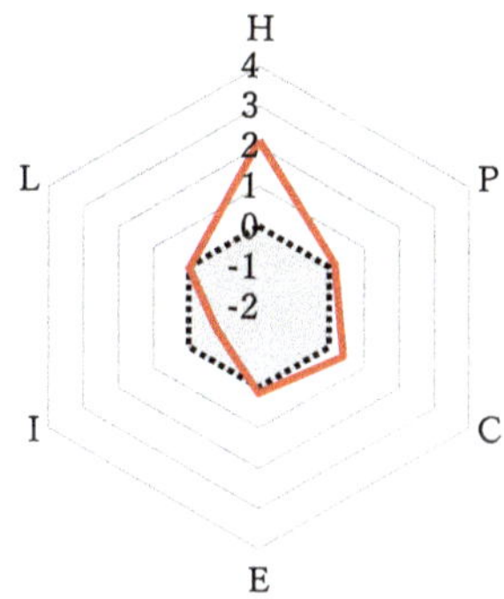

South Sudan

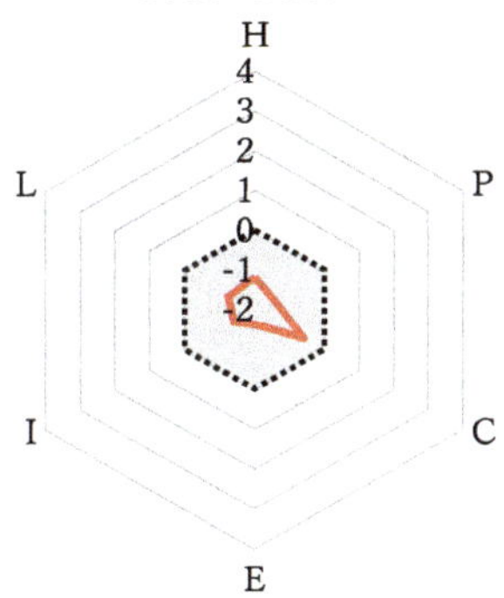

Spain

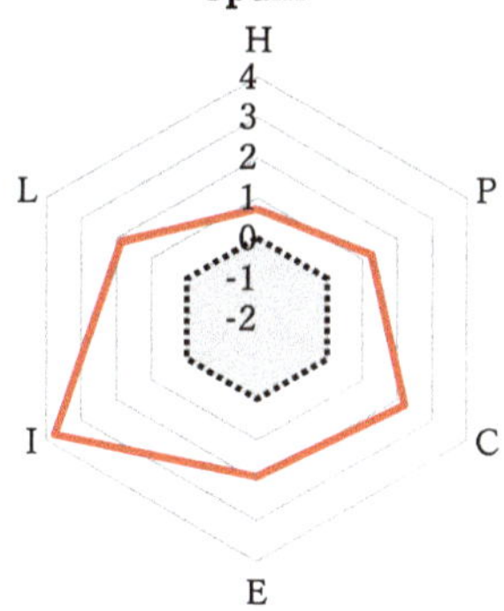

Sri Lanka

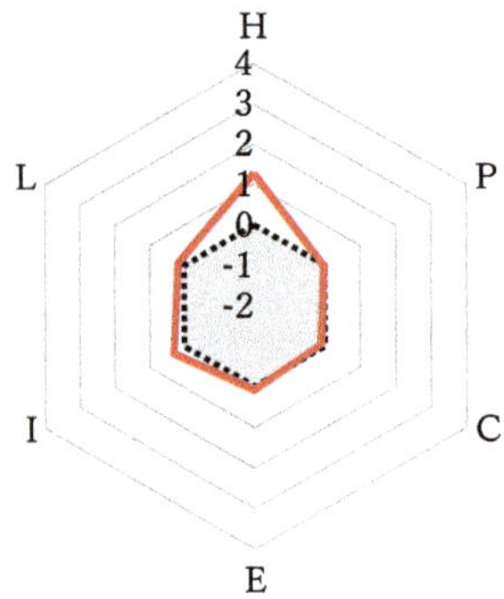

St. Kitts and Nevis

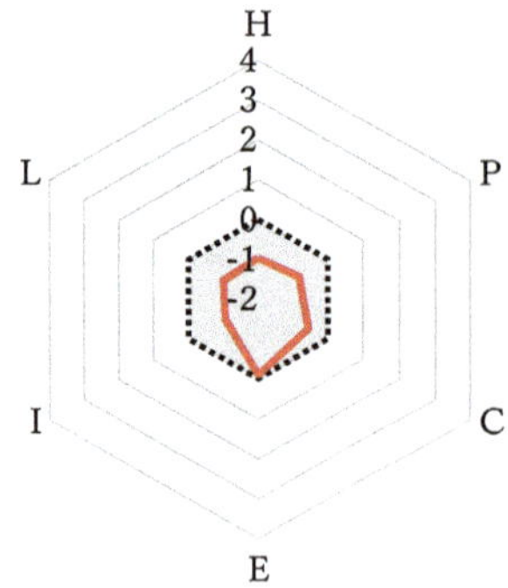

St. Lucia

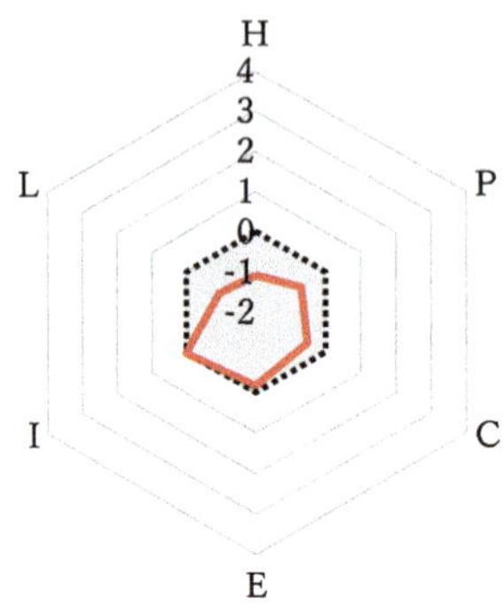

St. Vincent and the Grenadines

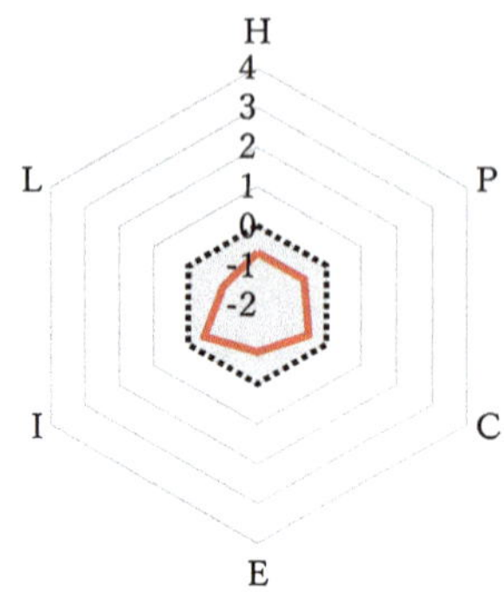

Sudan

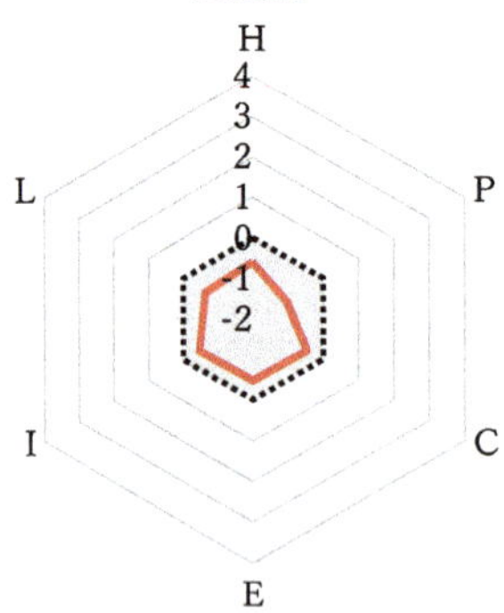

Suriname

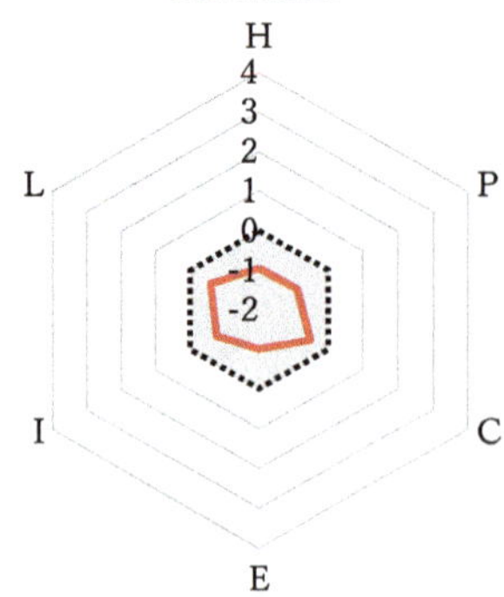

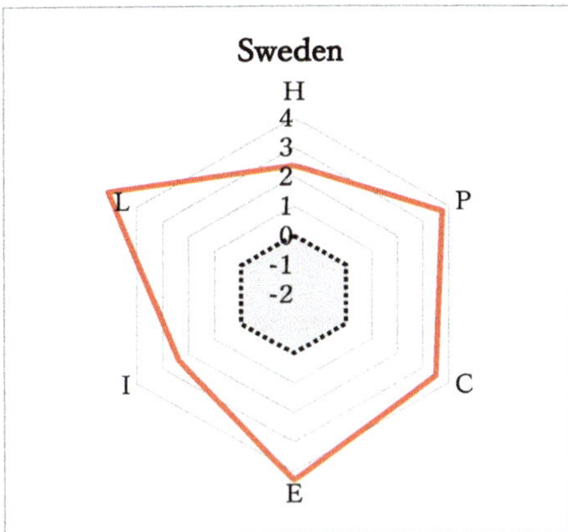
Sweden
H
4
3
2
1
0
-1
-2
L
P
I
C
E

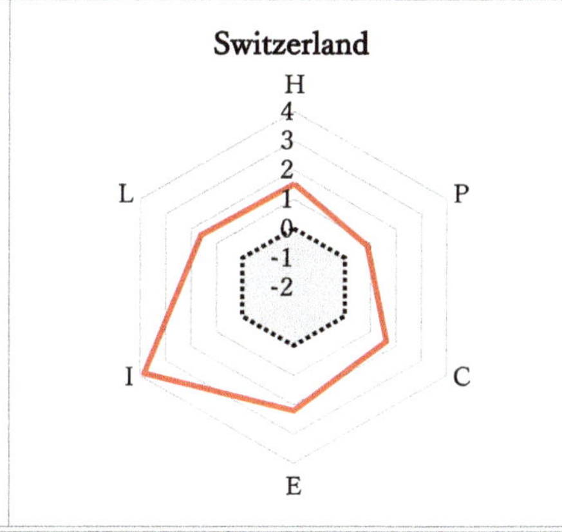
Switzerland
H
4
3
2
1
0
-1
-2
L
P
I
C
E

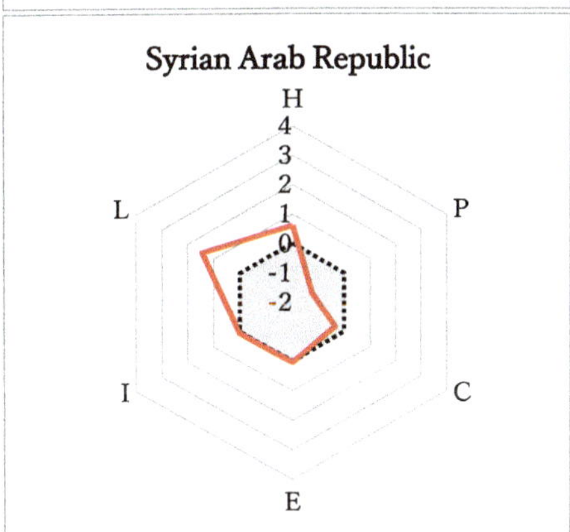
Syrian Arab Republic
H
4
3
2
1
0
-1
-2
L
P
I
C
E

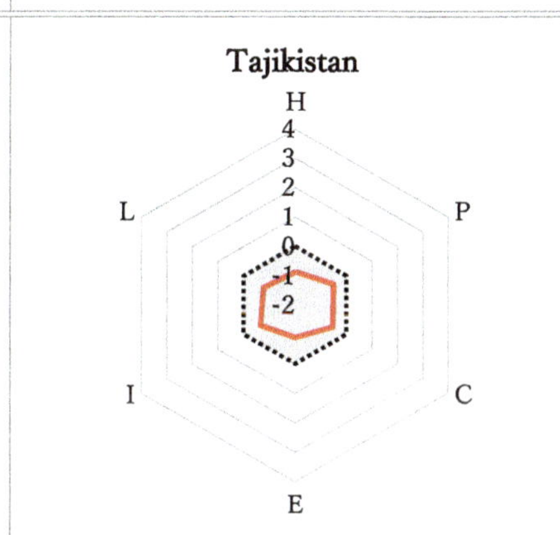
Tajikistan
H
4
3
2
1
0
-1
-2
L
P
I
C
E

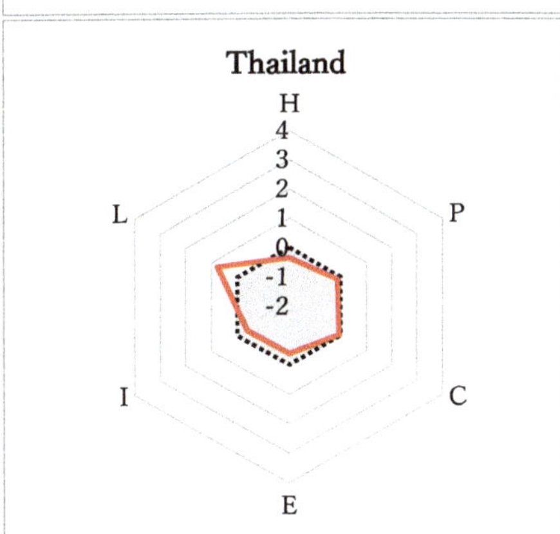
Thailand
H
4
3
2
1
0
-1
-2
L
P
I
C
E

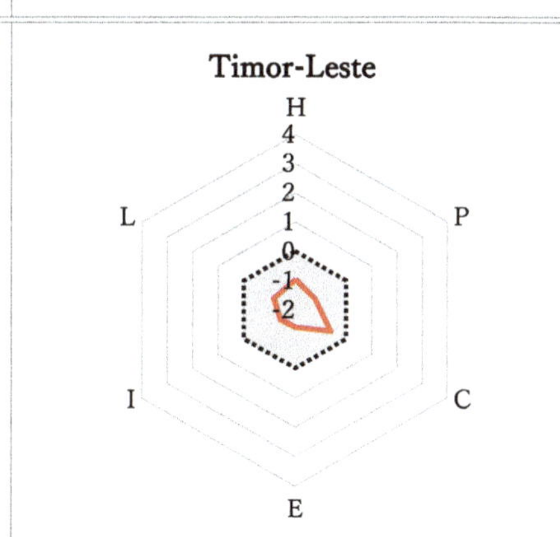
Timor-Leste
H
4
3
2
1
0
-1
-2
L
P
I
C
E

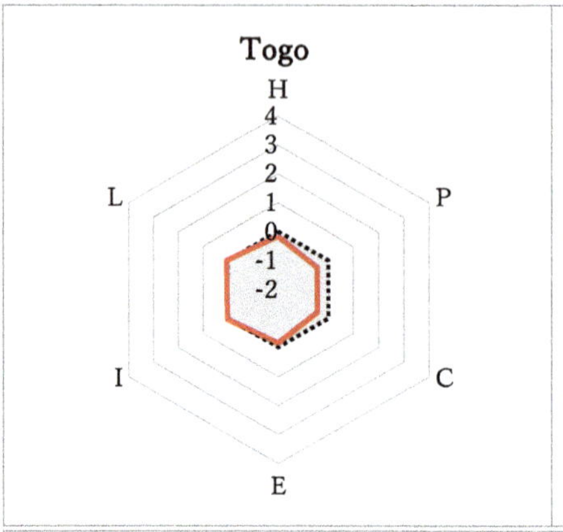
Togo
H
4
3
2
1
0
-1
-2
P
C
E
I
L

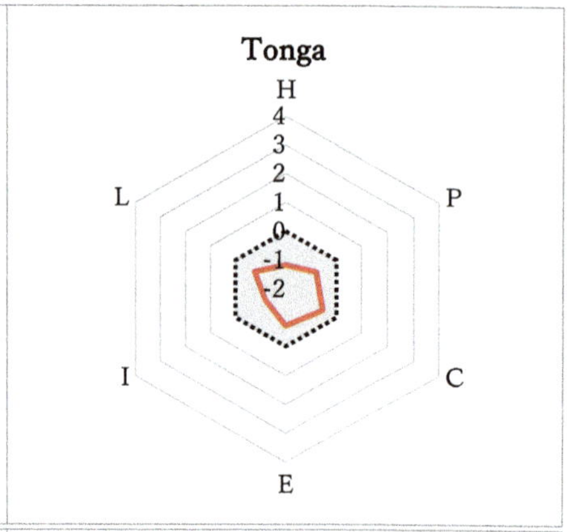
Tonga
H
4
3
2
1
0
-1
-2
P
C
E
I
L

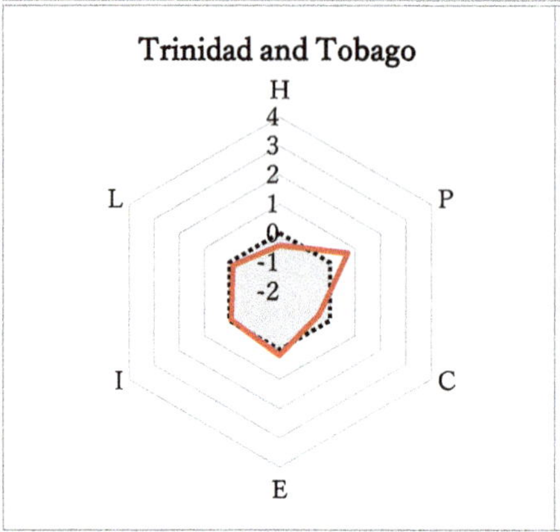
Trinidad and Tobago
H
4
3
2
1
0
-1
-2
P
C
E
I
L

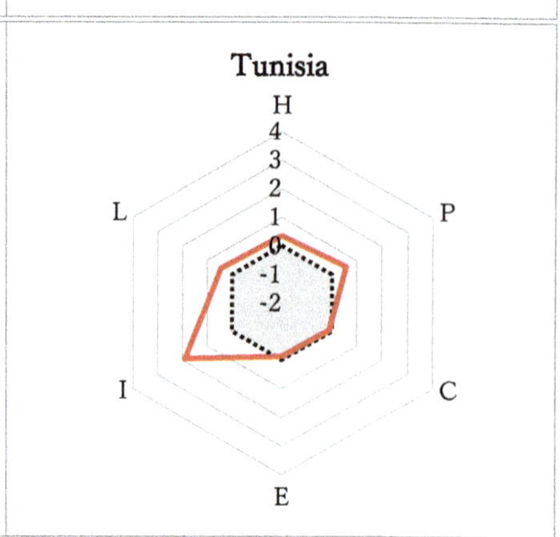
Tunisia
H
4
3
2
1
0
-1
-2
P
C
E
I
L

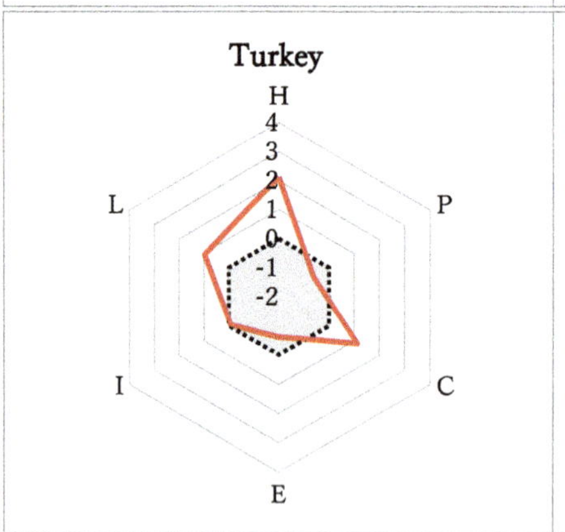
Turkey
H
4
3
2
1
0
-1
-2
P
C
E
I
L

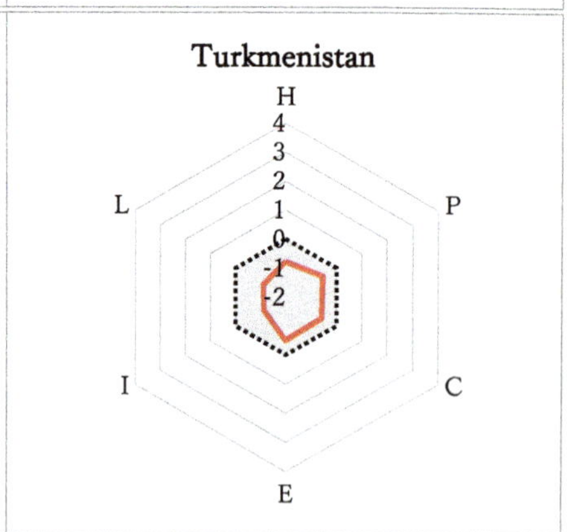
Turkmenistan
H
4
3
2
1
0
-1
-2
P
C
E
I
L

Tuvalu

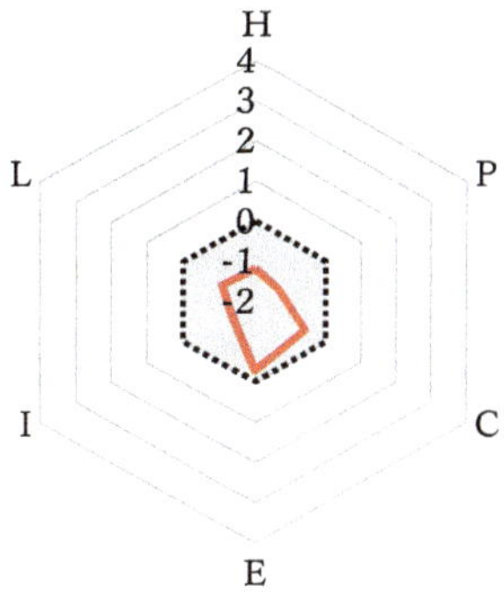

Uganda

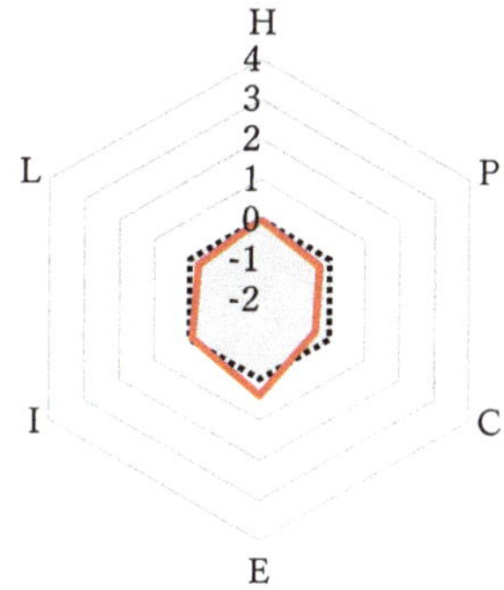

Ukraine

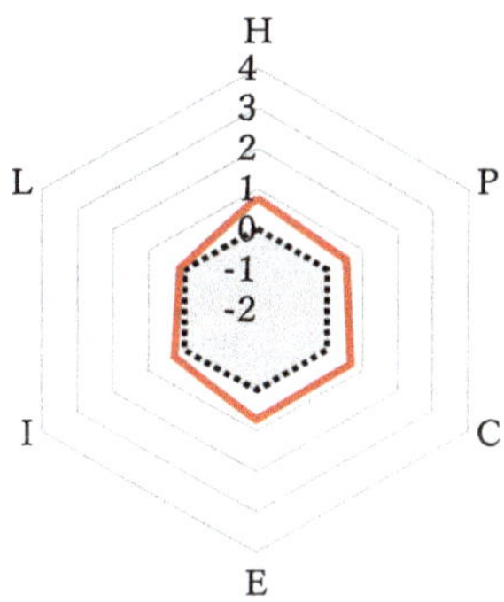

United Arab Emirates

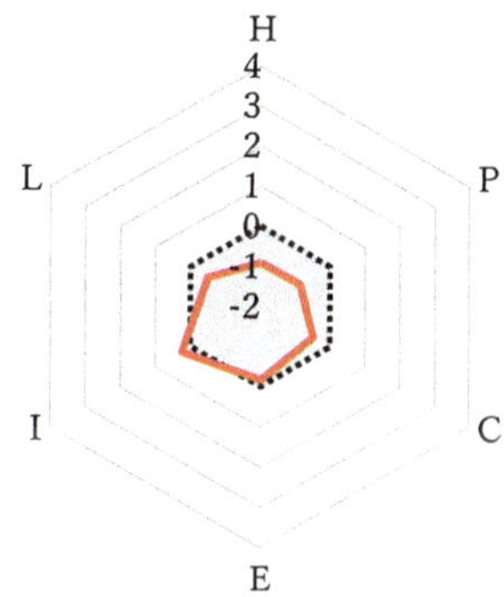

United Kingdom of Great Britain and Northern Ireland

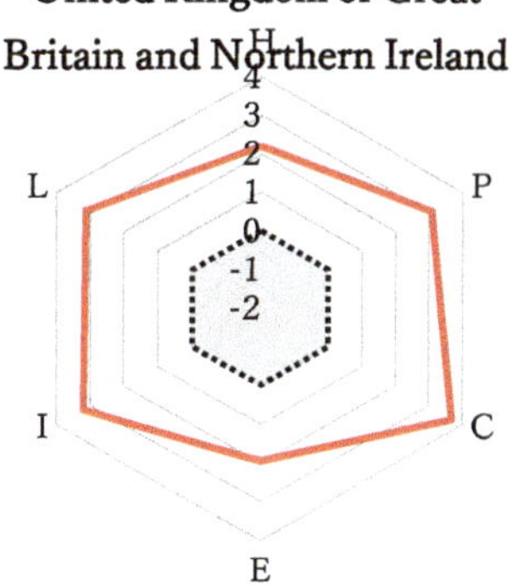

United Republic of Tanzania

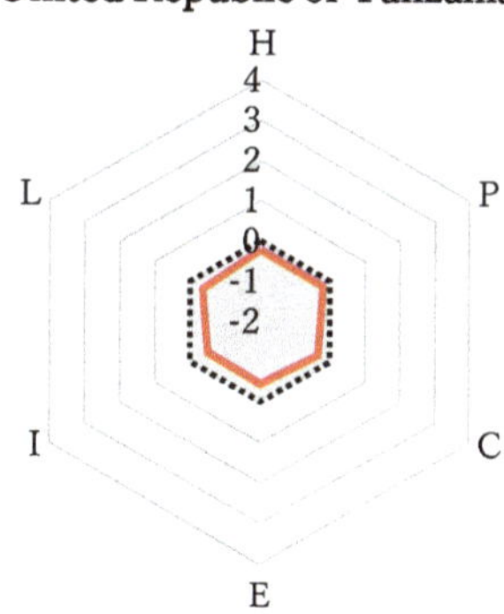

United States of America

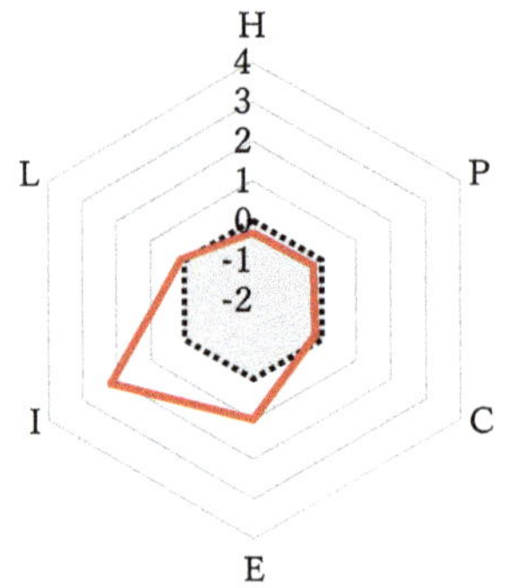

Uruguay

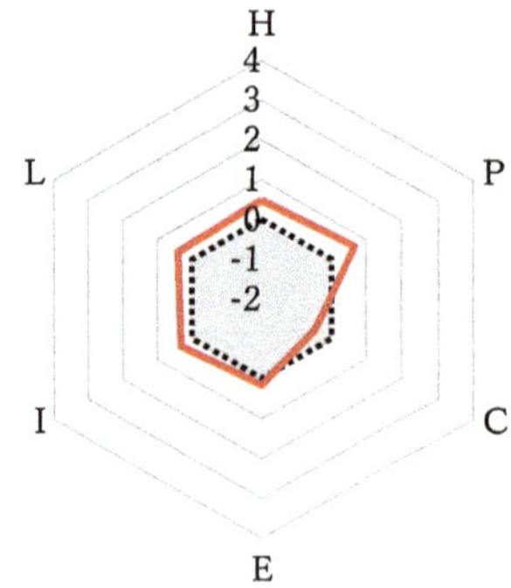

Uzbekistan

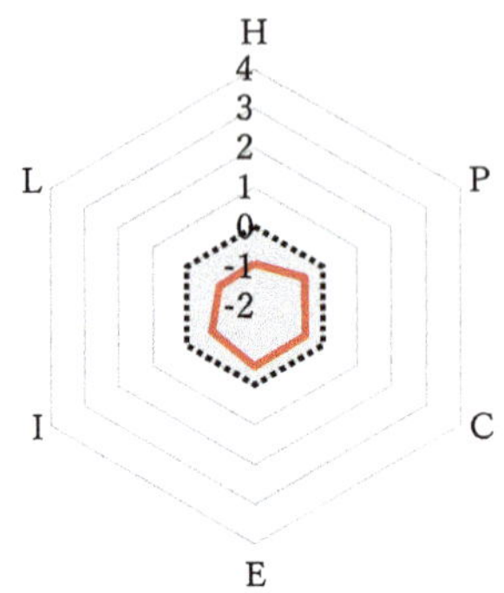

Vanuatu

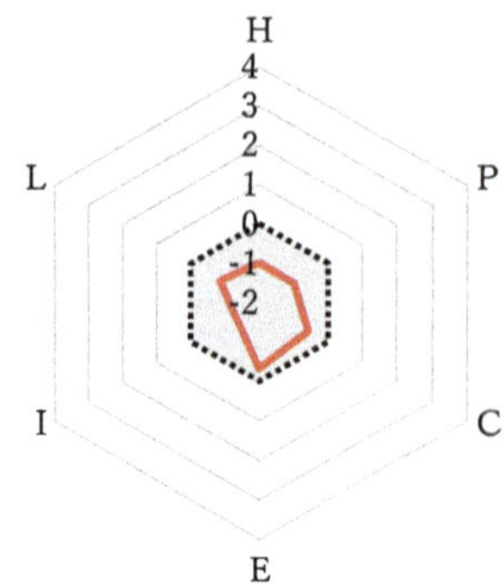

Venezuela (Bolivarian Republic of)

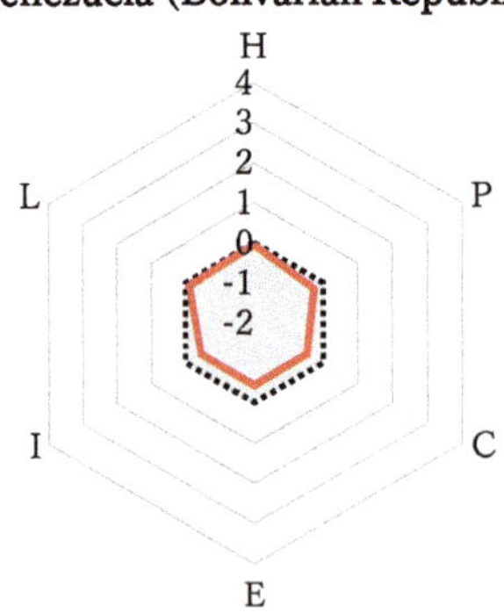

Viet Nam

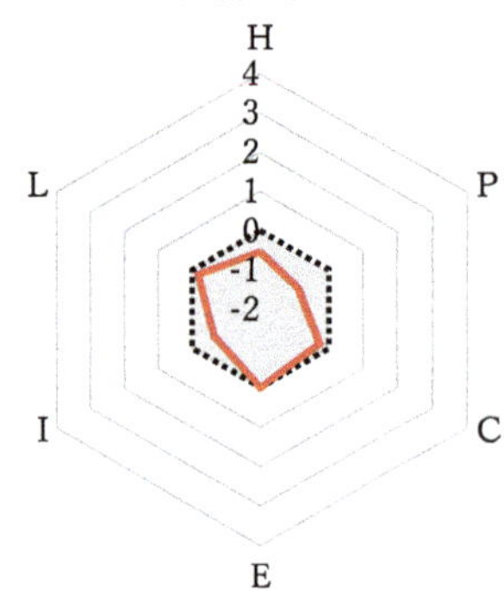

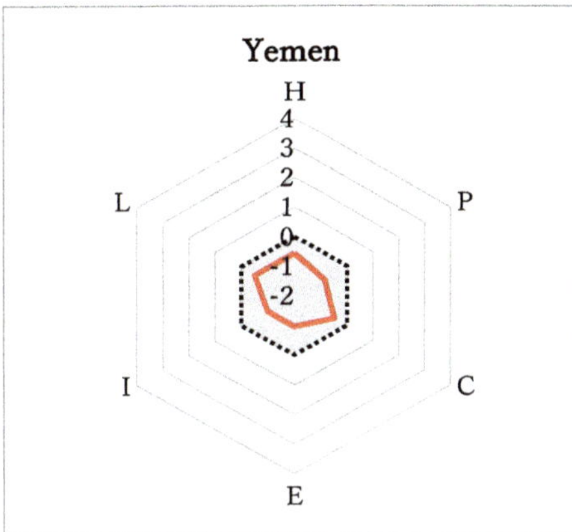
Yemen
H
4
3
2
1
0
-1
-2
P
C
E
I
L

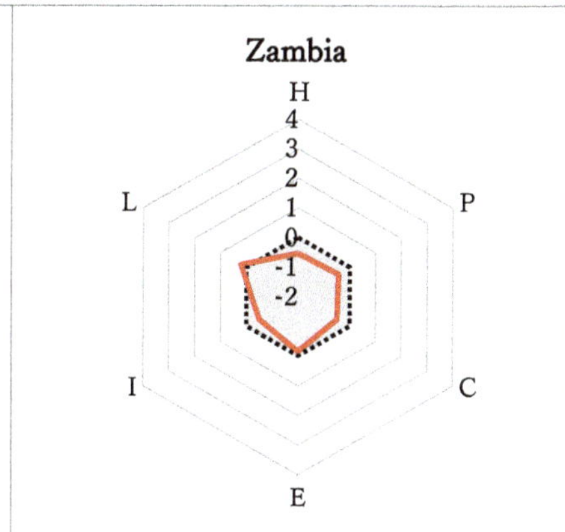
Zambia
H
4
3
2
1
0
-1
-2
P
C
E
I
L

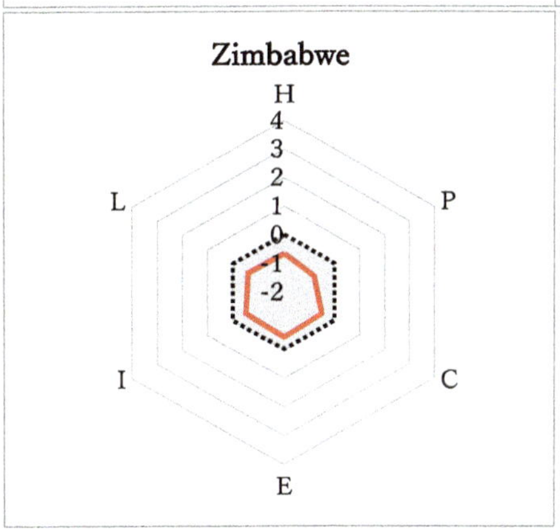
Zimbabwe
H
4
3
2
1
0
-1
-2
P
C
E
I
L

Appendix D
Typology of Global Quasi-Legislative Behavior of 193 UN Member States

Code	Country name	Geo-historico-cultural region	Type
AFG	Afghanistan	Islamic East	ABc
ALB	Albania	Orthodox East	Abc
DZA	Algeria	Islamic East	aBc
ADO	Andorra	Old West	AbC
AGO	Angola	Sub-Saharan Africa	ABc
ATG	Antigua and Barbuda	Latin America	ABc
ARG	Argentina	Latin America	aBc
ARM	Armenia	Orthodox East	Abc
AUS	Australia	New West	abC
AUT	Austria	Old West	abC
AZE	Azerbaijan	Orthodox East	AbC
BHS	Bahamas	Latin America	aBc
BHR	Bahrain	Islamic East	ABc
BGD	Bangladesh	Indic East	ABC
BRB	Barbados	Latin America	aBc
BLR	Belarus	Orthodox East	AbC
BEL	Belgium	Old West	abC
BLZ	Belize	Latin America	ABc
BEN	Benin	Sub-Saharan Africa	ABc
BTN	Bhutan	Indic East	ABC
BOL	Bolivia	Latin America	aBc
BIH	Bosnia and Herzegovina	Orthodox East	Abc
BWA	Botswana	Sub-Saharan Africa	ABc

(continued)

T. Inoguchi and L. T. Q. Le, *Digitized Statecraft in Multilateral Treaty Participation*, Evidence-Based Approaches to Peace and Conflict Studies 1,
https://doi.org/10.1007/978-981-33-4485-3

(continued)

Code	Country name	Geo-historico-cultural region	Type
BRA	Brazil	Latin America	aBc
BRN	Brunei Darussalam	Indic East	ABc
BGR	Bulgaria	Orthodox East	abC
BFA	Burkina Faso	Sub-Saharan Africa	aBc
BDI	Burundi	Sub-Saharan Africa	ABc
CPV	Cabo Verde	Sub-Saharan Africa	ABc
KHM	Cambodia	Indic East	abC
CMR	Cameroon	Sub-Saharan Africa	aBc
CAN	Canada	New West	abC
CAF	Central African Republic	Sub-Saharan Africa	aBc
TCD	Chad	Sub-Saharan Africa	ABc
CHL	Chile	Latin America	aBc
CHN	China	Sinic East	abC
COL	Colombia	Latin America	aBc
COM	Comoros	Sub-Saharan Africa	ABc
COG	Congo	Sub-Saharan Africa	aBc
CRI	Costa Rica	Latin America	aBc
CIV	Côte d'Ivoire	Sub-Saharan Africa	aBc
HRV	Croatia	Returned West	AbC
CUB	Cuba	Latin America	aBc
CYP	Cyprus	Old West	abC
CZE	Czech Republic	Returned West	AbC
PRK	DPR Korea	Sinic East	ABc
ZAR	DR of the Congo	Sub-Saharan Africa	aBc
DNK	Denmark	Reformed West	abC
DJI	Djibouti	Sub-Saharan Africa	ABc
DMA	Dominica	Latin America	aBc
DOM	Dominican Republic	Latin America	aBc
ECU	Ecuador	Latin America	aBC
EGY	Egypt	Islamic East	abC
SLV	El Salvador	Latin America	ABc
GNQ	Equatorial Guinea	Sub-Saharan Africa	ABc
ERI	Eritrea	Sub-Saharan Africa	ABc
EST	Estonia	Returned West	AbC
SWZ	Eswatini	Sub-Saharan Africa	ABc
ETH	Ethiopia	Sub-Saharan Africa	aBc
FJI	Fiji	New West	abC

(continued)

(continued)

Code	Country name	Geo-historico-cultural region	Type
FIN	Finland	Reformed West	abC
FRA	France	Old West	abC
GAB	Gabon	Sub-Saharan Africa	aBc
GMB	Gambia	Sub-Saharan Africa	aBc
GEO	Georgia	Orthodox East	Abc
DEU	Germany	Reformed West	abC
GHA	Ghana	Sub-Saharan Africa	aBc
GRC	Greece	Old West	abC
GRD	Grenada	Latin America	ABc
GTM	Guatemala	Latin America	aBc
GIN	Guinea	Sub-Saharan Africa	aBc
GNB	Guinea-Bissau	Sub-Saharan Africa	ABc
GUY	Guyana	Latin America	aBc
HTI	Haiti	Latin America	aBc
HND	Honduras	Latin America	ABc
HUN	Hungary	Returned West	abC
ISL	Iceland	Reformed West	abC
IND	India	Indic East	abC
IDN	Indonesia	Indic East	abc
IRN	Iran	Islamic East	abc
IRQ	Iraq	Islamic East	aBc
IRL	Ireland	Reformed West	abC
ISR	Israel	Old West	abC
ITA	Italy	Old West	abC
JAM	Jamaica	Latin America	aBc
JPN	Japan	Sinic East	abc
JOR	Jordan	Islamic East	aBC
KAZ	Kazakhstan	Orthodox East	Abc
KEN	Kenya	Sub-Saharan Africa	aBc
KIR	Kiribati	New West	AbC
KWT	Kuwait	Islamic East	aBc
KGZ	Kyrgyzstan	Orthodox East	Abc
LAO	Laos	Indic East	aBC
LVA	Latvia	Returned West	AbC
LBN	Lebanon	Islamic East	aBc
LSO	Lesotho	Sub-Saharan Africa	aBc
LBR	Liberia	Sub-Saharan Africa	ABc

(continued)

(continued)

Code	Country name	Geo-historico-cultural region	Type
LBY	Libya	Islamic East	aBc
LIE	Liechtenstein	Old West	AbC
LTU	Lithuania	Returned West	AbC
LUX	Luxembourg	Old West	abC
MDG	Madagascar	Sub-Saharan Africa	aBc
MWI	Malawi	Sub-Saharan Africa	aBc
MYS	Malaysia	Indic East	AbC
MDV	Maldives	Indic East	ABC
MLI	Mali	Sub-Saharan Africa	aBc
MLT	Malta	Old West	abC
MHL	Marshall Islands	New West	AbC
MRT	Mauritania	Sub-Saharan Africa	aBc
MUS	Mauritius	Sub-Saharan Africa	aBc
MEX	Mexico	Latin America	aBC
FSM	Micronesia	New West	AbC
MCO	Monaco	Old West	abC
MNG	Mongolia	Orthodox East	ABc
MNE	Montenegro	Orthodox East	Abc
MAR	Morocco	Islamic East	abc
MOZ	Mozambique	Sub-Saharan Africa	ABc
MMR	Myanmar	Indic East	ABC
NAM	Namibia	Sub-Saharan Africa	ABc
NRU	Nauru	New West	AbC
NPL	Nepal	Indic East	aBc
NLD	Netherlands	Reformed West	abC
NZL	New Zealand	New West	abC
NIC	Nicaragua	Latin America	aBc
NER	Niger	Sub-Saharan Africa	aBc
NGA	Nigeria	Sub-Saharan Africa	aBc
MKD	North Macedonia	Orthodox East	AbC
NOR	Norway	Reformed West	abC
OMN	Oman	Islamic East	ABc
PAK	Pakistan	Indic East	abC
PLW	Palau	New West	AbC
PAN	Panama	Latin America	ABC
PNG	Papua New Guinea	New West	abC
PRY	Paraguay	Latin America	ABc

(continued)

(continued)

Code	Country name	Geo-historico-cultural region	Type
PER	Peru	Latin America	aBc
PHL	Philippines	Indic East	abC
POL	Poland	Returned West	abC
PRT	Portugal	Old West	AbC
QAT	Qatar	Islamic East	ABc
KOR	Republic of Korea	Sinic East	AbC
MDA	Republic of Moldova	Orthodox East	Abc
ROM	Romania	Orthodox East	abC
RUS	Russian Federation	Orthodox East	AbC
RWA	Rwanda	Sub-Saharan Africa	aBc
WSM	Samoa	New West	AbC
SMR	San Marino	Old West	AbC
STP	Sao Tome and Principe	Sub-Saharan Africa	ABc
SAU	Saudi Arabia	Islamic East	ABc
SEN	Senegal	Sub-Saharan Africa	aBc
SRB	Serbia	Orthodox East	AbC
SYC	Seychelles	Sub-Saharan Africa	ABc
SLE	Sierra Leone	Sub-Saharan Africa	aBc
SGP	Singapore	Indic East	abc
SVK	Slovakia	Returned West	AbC
SVN	Slovenia	Returned West	AbC
SLB	Solomon Islands	New West	abC
SOM	Somalia	Sub-Saharan Africa	aBc
ZAF	South Africa	Sub-Saharan Africa	ABc
SSD	South Sudan	Sub-Saharan Africa	ABc
ESP	Spain	Old West	abC
LKA	Sri Lanka	Indic East	AbC
KNA	St. Kitts and Nevis	Latin America	ABc
LCA	St. Lucia	Latin America	ABc
VCT	St. Vincent and the Grenadines	Latin America	ABc
SDN	Sudan	Sub-Saharan Africa	aBc
SUR	Suriname	Latin America	aBc
SWE	Sweden	Reformed West	abC
CHE	Switzerland	Reformed West	abC
SYR	Syrian Arab Republic	Islamic East	aBC
TJK	Tajikistan	Orthodox East	Abc
THA	Thailand	Indic East	abC

(continued)

(continued)

Code	Country name	Geo-historico-cultural region	Type
TMP	Timor-Leste	Indic East	ABc
TGO	Togo	Sub-Saharan Africa	ABc
TON	Tonga	New West	abC
TTO	Trinidad and Tobago	Latin America	aBc
TUN	Tunisia	Islamic East	abC
TUR	Turkey	Islamic East	Abc
TKM	Turkmenistan	Orthodox East	ABc
TUV	Tuvalu	New West	AbC
UGA	Uganda	Sub-Saharan Africa	aBc
UKR	Ukraine	Orthodox East	AbC
ARE	United Arab Emirates	Islamic East	ABc
GBR	United Kingdom	Reformed West	abC
TZA	Tanzania	Sub-Saharan Africa	aBc
USA	United States of America	New West	abC
URY	Uruguay	Latin America	aBc
UZB	Uzbekistan	Orthodox East	Abc
VUT	Vanuatu	New West	AbC
VEN	Venezuela	Latin America	aBc
VNM	Viet Nam	Sinic East	ABc
YEM	Yemen	Islamic East	aBc
ZMB	Zambia	Sub-Saharan Africa	aBc
ZWE	Zimbabwe	Sub-Saharan Africa	aBc

Appendix E
Methodological Notes of Social Surveys Used for the Book: The AsiaBarometer Quality of Life Survey; The Asia-Europe Democracy Survey; The Sinic East Survey (The Asia Poll)

1. The AsiaBarometer Quality of Life Survey was carried out in 2003–2008 in 31 Asian societies and its vicinities with focus placed on quality of life. It was a nation-wide face to face survey with the average sample size ranging from 1,000 (for example, Brunei, the Maldives, and Bhutan) and 3,000 (for example, India, China, and Japan). The question asked is:

   > Please tell me how satisfied or dissatisfied you are with the following aspects of your life (SA for each). Choose one for each of the 16 daily life aspects: very satisfied, somewhat satisfied, neither satisfied nor dissatisfied, somewhat dissatisfied, very dissatisfied or don't know. Aspects of daily life satisfaction: housing, friendships, marriage (if married), standard of living, household income, health, education, job, neighbors, public safety, the condition of the environment, social welfare system, the democratic system, family life, leisure and spiritual life.

2. The Asia-Europe Democracy Survey was carried out in 2000 in nine Asian and nine European societies each with a nation-wide sampling. The face-to-face interviewing was carried out. The sample size of each of 18 countries is 800. The key question asked is:

   > Here is the same list of issues. Would you please tell me whether each of these problems should be dealt with by each country deciding for itself what should be done or by all countries together deciding what should be done. There may be one or two items on the list that you haven't thought much about. If so, just tell me and we'll go to the next item (Circle one answer for each statement). Choose one for each of the items: problems of human rights, environmental problems, the problem of women's rights, the problem of unemployment, the problems of developing countries, the problem of refugees and asylum seekers, the danger of military conflict in Asia, the danger of military conflict in Europe, the danger of military conflict elsewhere in the world.

3. The Sinic East Opinion Poll (2019 Asia Poll) was carried out in 2019 in the following Sinic East societies: Japan, Vietnam, China, Taiwan, Hong Kong, and South Korea. The sample size was 1,200 in Japan, 400 each of the rest (Vietnam,

T. Inoguchi and L. T. Q. Le, *Digitized Statecraft in Multilateral Treaty Participation*, Evidence-Based Approaches to Peace and Conflict Studies 1,
https://doi.org/10.1007/978-981-33-4485-3

China, Taiwan, Hong Kong, and South Korea). It was carried out by nationwide sampling in Japan and South Korea whereas major cities were selected in China (Beijing, Shanghai, Xi'an, Chengdu), Taiwan (Taipei, Taizhong, Gaoxiong), Hong Kong (Hong Kong, Kowloon, New Territory). In Japan it was carried out as an omnibus survey (poste restante); in South Korea it was carried out as an omnibus survey (visiting and face to face interviewing); in Vietnam and China it was carried out by visiting and face-to-face interviewing: in Hong Kong and Taiwan, it was carried out on streets and face-to-face interviewing). Two questions are asked:

(1) Here is the list of issues. Would you please tell me whether each of these problems should be dealt with by each country deciding for itself what should be done or by all countries together deciding what should be done. There may be one or two items on the list that you haven't thought much about. If so, just tell me and we'll go to the next item. (one answer for each statement). Choose one of the following items: Should be dealt with by each country deciding for itself what should be done. Should be dealt with by all countries together deciding what should be done. Don't know. Haven't thought much about it. Items are as follows: problems of human rights, environmental problems, the problem of women's rights, the problem of unemployment, the problem of developing countries, the problem of refugees and asylum seekers, the danger of military conflict in Asia, the danger of military conflict elsewhere in the world.
(2) Please tell me how satisfied you are with the following aspects of your life (One answer for each statement). Choose one of the following: very satisfied, somewhat satisfied, neither satisfied nor dissatisfied, somewhat dissatisfied, very dissatisfied, don't know, not applicable. Answer the following statements: housing, friendship, marriage (if married), standard of living, household income, health, education, job, neighbors, public safety, the condition of the environment, social welfare system, democratic system, family life, leisure, spiritual life. Lastly, I would like to ask some questions about yourself. Using the scale below, how would you describe yourself? (Single answer only): very optimistic, somewhat optimistic, neither optimistic nor pessimistic, somewhat pessimistic, very pessimistic, don't know (volunteered)

References

1. AsiaBarometer Quality of Life Survey (2003–2008)
Inoguchi, Takashi, and Seiji Fujii. 2013. *The Quality of Life in Asia: A Comparison of Quality of Life in Asia.* Dordrecht: Springer.
Inoguchi, Takashi. 2007. "The AsiaBarometer Questionnaire of 2006." *Japanese Journal of Political Science* 8 (3): 427–453.

2. Asia-Europe Democracy Survey (ASES) (2000)
   Inoguchi, Takashi, and Ian Marsh (eds.). 2008. *Globalization, Public Opinion and the State: Western Europe and East and Southeast Asia.* London: Routledge. ASES Survey Questionnaire in Appendix.
3. Sinic East Survey (2019)
   Japan Research Center. 2019. *2019 Asia Poll Questionnaire.* Tokyo: Japan Research Center.

Index

A
Acharya, Amitav, vi
Adaptation to multilateral treaties, 77
Agency of liberal world order, vi
Angle-global commons vs individual, 35, 48, 49, 51, 54, 57, 58, 60, 61, 66, 99, 136, 146
Anglo-American tradition, vi
Annan, Kofi, 4, 28, 69, 80, 89, 146
Aphorism, 4, 7, 145
Argentine, 39
Artificial intelligence, 26, 146
Australia, 17, 38, 39, 58, 85, 87, 91, 106, 137, 213, 253

B
Belgium, 14, 38, 57, 213, 253
Bodin, Jean, 3
Brazil, 17, 38, 39, 54, 91, 214, 254
Brunei, 39, 48, 133, 134, 140, 141, 259

C
Calculus of state, x
Cambodia, 38, 39, 48, 49, 128, 140, 141, 214, 254
Canada, 28, 38, 39, 58, 80, 85, 87, 214, 254
China, 10–12, 25, 26, 29, 38–40, 45–49, 68, 70, 71, 75–91, 93, 97–99, 101–111, 120–124, 128, 133–138, 140, 141, 146, 214, 254, 259, 260
China, People's Republic of, 45, 75–78, 81, 118, 120, 124
China, Republic of, 46, 75, 76, 78, 110, 118–120
Clinton, Bill, 108
Communication messages, 41
Communication modes, 41
Comparative statecraft, 97
Conditions of the environment, 87, 134
Cumings, Bruce, 76, 81
Czech Republic, 14, 29, 38, 61, 68, 214, 254

D
Daily life satisfaction, 84, 85, 133–136, 138, 140, 141, 259
Danger and military conflicts (Asia), 89
Danger and military conflicts (the world), 89
Data-driven empirical modeling, 9
Democratic system, 84, 88, 134, 259, 260
Deng Xiaoping, 78, 97, 105, 120, 128, 137
The developed North, 29, 36, 37, 47, 68, 70, 71, 77, 80, 88, 91, 98, 101, 120, 136
Developing countries, 10, 12, 87, 89, 91, 259, 260
The developing South, 11, 27, 29, 36, 37, 42, 47, 68–71, 77, 78, 80, 91, 98, 99, 106, 109, 116, 120, 121, 136, 146
Digitized globalization, 7, 10, 26, 42, 67, 103, 116, 145–147
Digitized statecraft, 4, 35, 146

E
Education, 84, 86, 97, 107, 134, 259, 260
Eisenhower, Dwight, 40

T. Inoguchi and L. T. Q. Le, *Digitized Statecraft in Multilateral Treaty Participation*, Evidence-Based Approaches to Peace and Conflict Studies 1,
https://doi.org/10.1007/978-981-33-4485-3

The environment, 5, 9, 10, 13, 18, 28, 37, 67, 69, 82–84, 87–90, 101, 103, 106–108, 112, 116, 121, 124, 128, 138, 259, 260

F

Factor analysis, 4, 29, 43, 66, 67
Family life, 84, 88, 134, 259, 260
Finland, 14, 38, 60, 215, 255
France, 14, 29, 38–40, 57, 68, 70, 76, 77, 79, 80, 83, 127, 140, 215, 255
Friendship, 84, 85, 120, 133, 259, 260

G

Geo-historico-cultural regions of the world, 92
Germany, 10, 11, 14, 29, 38–40, 60, 61, 68, 71, 75, 79, 80, 92, 110, 140, 215, 255
Gilpin, Robert, 26
Global citizens, 3, 37
Global citizens' preference, 135
Global democracy, viii
Globalization, 13, 71, 88, 103, 112, 137, 145
Global legislative politics, 29
Global politics, 36, 37, 45
Global quasi-legislative behavior, 36, 37, 41, 45, 67, 97, 98, 134, 135, 139–141, 253
Global solution, 4, 69, 89–93
Global statecraft, 45

H

Health, 5, 9, 12, 18, 22, 28, 36, 37, 42, 69, 78, 79, 81–84, 86, 103, 108, 112, 115, 119–121, 124, 127, 128, 131, 134, 259, 260
Hidalgo, César, 10, 25, 145, 146
Hiroshima, 80, 111, 146
Hobbes, Thomas, 3
Ho Chi Minh, 87, 111
Hong Kong, 40, 75, 83–93, 101, 103, 116, 134–136, 140, 141, 259, 260
Household income, 84, 86, 133, 259, 260
Housing, 84, 85, 133, 259, 260
Human rights, 5, 9, 11, 13, 18, 22, 28, 37, 67, 69, 78, 79, 81–83, 89, 91–93, 103, 105–108, 112, 113, 116, 117, 120–122, 125, 128, 129, 155–160, 259, 260

I

Ikenberry, G. John, 17, 26, 27
India, 5, 28, 38, 39, 48, 49, 68, 71, 106, 121, 133, 134, 140, 141, 145, 146, 215, 255, 259
Indic East, 28, 45, 48, 49, 65, 80, 213–218, 253–257
Indonesia, 29, 38–40, 46–49, 68, 70, 71, 106, 134, 140, 141, 215, 255
Inglehart, Ronald, 37, 136
Inoguchi, Takashi, 3, 4, 26, 27, 35, 37, 41, 66, 76, 79, 80, 82, 85, 86, 91–93, 102, 133, 135, 136, 145–147
Inoue, Kaoru, 79
Instrumental variables, 27, 28, 41, 65, 66, 146
Intellectual property, 5, 9, 11, 18, 22, 28, 36, 37, 40, 48, 67, 69, 70, 79, 82, 83, 85, 101, 103, 106–108, 112, 114, 116, 118, 121, 122, 124, 126, 128, 130, 160–162
International Bank of Reconstruction and Development, 79
International Civil Aviation Organization, 80, 81, 171
International Energy Agency, 98, 116
International Fund for Agricultural Development, 175, 191
International Labor Organization, 9, 12, 36, 37, 65, 67, 80, 101
International Maritime Organization, 80, 81, 173, 174, 178, 180, 189, 191, 192, 201, 202
International Monetary Fund, 80, 82, 98, 101, 106, 116, 171
International Telecommunication Union, 80, 172
Islamic East, 28, 45, 50, 51, 65, 213–218, 253–258
Italy, 14, 38, 39, 57, 80, 215, 255

J

Japan, 13, 17, 29, 38–40, 45–47, 68, 70, 71, 75, 76, 79–81, 83, 85–93, 97–99, 101–106, 108, 110–112, 116, 117, 120, 124, 128, 134–136, 138, 140, 141, 215, 255, 259, 260
Job, 84, 86, 134, 259, 260

K

Kai-shek, Chiang, 110, 111, 120
Kautilya, Chanakya, 3, 5, 6, 145

Keohane, Robert, 6
Kim Il Sung, 77, 82, 83, 99, 105, 108, 112
Kissinger, Henry A., 22, 25, 78
Korea, Democratic People's Republic of, 45–47, 75, 76, 78, 81–83, 105
Korea, Republic of, 36, 38, 39, 45–47, 75, 76, 80–82, 105, 217, 257
Koremenos, Barbara, 70

L
Labor and health, 5, 9, 12, 18, 22, 28, 36, 37, 69, 78, 79, 81–83, 103, 108, 112, 115, 119–121, 124, 127, 128, 131, 163–170
Laos, 29, 38–40, 48, 49, 68, 71, 140, 141, 255
Latin America, 28, 45, 54–56, 65, 70, 78, 79, 159, 213–218, 253–258
Leisure, 84, 88, 134, 259, 260
Liberal world order, 26, 27, 68, 116
Locke, John, 3, 36
Luxemburg, 38

M
Machiavelli, Niccolò, 3–7, 145
Mao Zedong, 77, 110
Marriage, 84, 85, 133, 259, 260
Meritocratic society, 76
Mexico, 17, 29, 38, 39, 54, 68, 71, 106, 140, 216, 256
Migrants and refugees, 89, 90
Milanovic, Branko, 46, 68, 76, 83, 88, 99, 105, 120, 136, 137
Modified Welzel regional group, 35
Mongolia, 29, 134–136, 140, 141, 216, 256
Multilateral treaties, 4, 5, 9–14, 16–18, 22, 26–30, 36–42, 65–70, 75, 76, 78–84, 89, 98, 99, 101–104, 106–110, 112–131, 134, 135, 138, 146, 149
Multilateral treaty participation, 14, 35, 40, 66, 97, 102, 106, 107, 135, 141, 145, 146
Myanmar, 38, 39, 48, 49, 140, 141, 216, 256

N
Nagasaki, 80, 111
National and/or global solutions, 89, 91
National citizens' preference, 135
National solution, 4, 69, 75, 89, 91, 92
Neighbors, 42, 49, 84, 87, 121, 134, 136, 137, 259, 260
New West, 28, 45, 58, 59, 65, 213–218, 253–258
Norway, 14, 29, 38, 60, 216, 256
Number of current members, 29, 35, 41, 42, 66, 67
Nye, Joseph S., 26

O
Obama, Barak, 120
Old West, 28, 45, 57, 58, 65, 213–217, 253–257
Orthodox East, 28, 45, 51, 52, 65, 139–141, 213–218, 253–258

P
Park, Chung Hee, 81, 82, 99
Peace and disarmament, 5, 9, 12, 13, 18, 22, 28, 37, 67, 69, 82, 83, 103, 115, 117, 121, 125, 128, 170–179
The Philippines, 38, 46–49, 105, 134, 137, 140
Pinker, Steven, vii
Policy domain, 9, 10, 12, 14, 28, 29, 35, 37, 41, 42, 66, 67, 70, 78, 79, 81, 83, 84, 101, 109, 128, 146
Problems without passports, 4, 5, 28, 75, 80, 89, 146
Promulgation, 9, 22, 27, 35, 41, 66, 71, 146
Public safety, 84, 87, 134, 259, 260
Putnam, Robert, 26, 80, 112

R
Ratification, 9, 22, 27, 28, 35, 41, 66, 146
Rebalancing between the East and the West, 76, 80, 83, 120
Reformation, 4, 7, 15, 28, 60, 75
Reformed West, 15, 28, 45, 47, 60, 61, 65, 75, 92, 214–218, 254–258
Renaissance, 3–7
Republic of Korea, 36, 38, 39, 45–47, 75, 76, 81, 82, 105, 217, 257
Returned West, 14, 28, 45, 61, 62, 65, 214–217, 254–257
Rhee, Syngnang, 81, 105, 112
Rousseau, Jean-Jacques, 3, 6, 36
Roy, Arundhati, 134

S
Secular society, 76

Singapore, 29, 38–40, 46, 48, 49, 68, 70, 83, 84, 101, 103, 111, 116, 134–136, 140, 141, 217, 257
Sinic East, 28, 45–48, 65, 75, 76, 80, 83–93, 101, 102, 109–112, 135, 214, 215, 217, 218, 254, 255, 257–259
Slovakia, 14, 38, 61, 217, 257
Social contract among nations, v
Social contract writ global, 4
Social welfare system, 84, 88, 134, 259, 260
Sources of power, 26
South Africa, 17, 29, 38, 39, 53, 68, 106, 140, 217, 257
South Sudan, 29, 38, 53, 217, 257
Sovereign states' physical actions, 9, 35, 146
Speed–agile vs cautious, 29, 35, 50, 53, 54, 57, 58, 60, 61, 66, 146
Speed, angle and strategy, 45, 67
Spiritual life, 84, 88, 134, 259, 260
Stalin, Joseph, 77, 110, 112
Standard of living, 84, 85, 133, 259, 260
St Exupéry, Antoine de, 9
Strategy–aspirational bonding vs mutual binding, 35, 49, 50, 53, 54, 57, 58, 60, 61, 146
Sub-Saharan Africa, 11, 28, 45, 53, 54, 65, 213–218, 253–258
Suzuki, Shogo, 27, 75, 79
Sweden, 14, 29, 38, 60, 68, 75, 140, 152, 217, 257

T

Taiwan, 40, 75, 76, 78, 83–93, 101, 103, 110, 111, 116, 120, 119, 134, 136, 140, 141, 259, 260
Thailand, 29, 38, 39, 46–49, 68, 134, 137, 140, 141, 217, 257
Theory of hegemonic change, vi
Theory of shared norms by governing elites, vi
Trade, commerce and communications, 18, 28, 36
Transformative nature of multilateral treaties, vi
Treaty participation index (TPI), 22, 27, 29, 35, 41, 42, 66, 67
Trump, Donald, 17, 40, 70, 91, 108, 116, 120, 121, 138
Turkey, 15, 29, 38–40, 50, 68, 71, 106, 140, 218, 258
Typology of societies, 133

U

UN depository, 67
Unemployment, 89, 90, 93, 259, 260
The United Kingdom, 15, 38–40, 60, 77, 79, 80
United Nations Convention on the Law of the Sea, 175, 176
United Nations Economic and Social Council, 80, 83, 92
United Nations Educational, Scientific and Cultural Organization, 80, 81, 171
United Nations Food and Agricultural Organization, 11, 80, 81
United Nations General Assembly, 11
United Nations Human Rights Council, 77, 80, 83, 92
United Nations Industrial Development Organization, 11
United Nations Organization, 68, 105
United Nations Secretary General, 4, 9, 11, 13, 18
United Nations Security Council, 38, 70, 77, 80, 120
United Nations World Tourism Organization, 179
The United States, 10, 12, 17, 18, 25–28, 37–40, 45–47, 53, 54, 58, 76–81, 83–87, 91, 98, 99, 101, 103, 105, 111, 116, 120, 121, 124–126, 128
Universal Postal Union, 80, 172
UN Special Commissioner's Office for Refugees, 11

V

Values and norms, 4, 37, 133, 135, 136
Vehicle of liberal world order, 26, 27
Vietnam, 38–40, 46, 49, 68, 75, 76, 83–93, 97–99, 101, 108–111, 124, 126, 127, 128, 134–137, 140, 141, 259
Vietnam, Socialist Republic of, 45–47, 75, 76, 83, 84, 99, 128, 137
Vogel, Ezra, 78, 81, 105, 112, 120

W

Washington, George, 40
Wei, Yuan, 105, 121
Welzel, Christian, 4, 15, 28, 35, 37, 65, 66, 92, 133, 136
Women's rights, 89, 92, 259, 260
Woodside, Alexander, 76
World Health Organization, 12, 78, 80–82, 84, 112, 120

World Intellectual Property Organization, 9, 11, 36, 37, 65, 67, 82
World Meteorological Organization, 80, 81

Y
Year of deposit, 29, 35, 41, 42, 65–67
Year of membership, 29, 35, 41, 42, 66, 67

GPSR Compliance
The European Union's (EU) General Product Safety Regulation (GPSR) is a set of rules that requires consumer products to be safe and our obligations to ensure this.

If you have any concerns about our products, you can contact us on

ProductSafety@springernature.com

In case Publisher is established outside the EU, the EU authorized representative is:

Springer Nature Customer Service Center GmbH
Europaplatz 3
69115 Heidelberg, Germany

www.ingramcontent.com/pod-product-compliance
Ingram Content Group UK Ltd.
Pitfield, Milton Keynes, MK11 3LW, UK
UKHW022213051026
15624UKWH00001B/138
9789813344846